Hedda Hopper's Hollywood

AMERICAN HISTORY AND CULTURE

General Editors: Neil Foley, Kevin Gaines, Martha Hodes, and Scott Sandage

Guess Who's Coming to Dinner Now? Multicultural Conservatism in America
Angela D. Dillard

One Nation Underground: A History of the Fallout Shelter
Kenneth D. Rose

The Body Electric: How Strange Machines Built the Modern America
Carolyn Thomas de la Peña

Black and Brown: African Americans and the Mexican Revolution, 1910–1920
Gerald Horne

Impossible to Hold: Women and Culture in the 1960s
Edited by Avital H. Bloch and Lauri Umansky

Provincetown: From Pilgrim Landing to Gay Resort
Karen Christel Krahulik

A Feeling of Belonging: Asian American Women's Public Culture, 1930–1960
Shirley Jennifer Lim

Newark: A History of Race, Rights, and Riots in America
Kevin Mumford

Children's Nature: The Rise of the American Summer Camp
Leslie Paris

Raising Freedom's Child: Black Children and Visions of the Future after Slavery
Mary Niall Mitchell

America's Forgotten Holiday: May Day and Nationalism, 1867–1960
Donna T. Haverty-Stacke

On the Make: Clerks and the Quest for Capital in Nineteenth-Century America
Brian P. Luskey

Hedda Hopper's Hollywood: Celebrity Gossip and American Conservatism
Jennifer Frost

Hedda Hopper at her office, 702 Guaranty Building, Hollywood Boulevard, 1954.
(Courtesy of the Academy of Motion Picture Arts and Sciences.)

Hedda Hopper's Hollywood

Celebrity Gossip and
American Conservatism

Jennifer Frost

NEW YORK UNIVERSITY PRESS
New York and London

NEW YORK UNIVERSITY PRESS
New York and London
www.nyupress.org

Portions of this book were previously published as "Hedda Hopper,
Hollywood Gossip, and the Politics of Racial Representation in Film,
1946–1948," *Journal of African American History* 93 (Winter 2008), 36–63.

Library of Congress Cataloging-in-Publication Data
Frost, Jennifer, 1961–
 Hedda Hopper's Hollywood : celebrity gossip and American conservatism /
Jennifer Frost.
p. cm. — (American history and culture)
Includes bibliographical references and index.
ISBN 978–0–8147–2823–9 (cl : alk. paper) — ISBN 978–0–8147–2824–6
(e-book : alk. paper)
1. Hopper, Hedda, 1890–1966. 2. Hopper, Hedda, 1890–1966—Political and social views.
3. Gossip columnists—United States—Biography. 4. Press and politics—United States—
History—20th century. 5. Motion pictures—Political aspects—United States.
6. Motion picture industry—California—Los Angeles—History—20th century.
7. Conservatism—United States—History—20th century. I. Title.
PN4874.H64F76   2010
070.4'49'9143092—dc22
[B]   2010028042

For my mother,
Ann B. Frost,
who—thank goodness—was nothing like Hedda Hopper,
either personally or politically

Contents

List of Abbreviations   xi

Acknowledgments   xiii

Introduction: "Malice in Wonderland"   1
    Escape from Altoona   8

1 The Making of a Celebrity Gossip   17
    A Columnist Is Born   18
    Gilding Hollywood's "Golden Age"   27
    Publicity and Right-Wing Politics   33

2 Readers, Respondents, and Fans   45
    Crafting Columns, Creating Community   47
    Reading Hopper, Writing Hedda   54
    Hollywood Gossip as Public Sphere   61

3 Hopper's Wars   67
    Prewar Isolationist to Cold Warrior   68
    Civil Liberties in Times of War   77
    Chasing Charlie Chaplin   82

4 Cold War Americanism, Hopper Style   91
    Selling Americanism   93
    Fighting the "Un-Americans"   103

5 Blacklisting Hollywood "Reds"   113
    Establishing the Hollywood Blacklist   114
    Hedda's Black (and Gray) List   126
    Enforcement Efforts   134

6   Representing Race in the Face of Civil Rights   139
     An Oscar for Uncle Remus   141
     In Defense of Mammy   149
     Presenting Poitier   160

7   "Family Togetherness" in Fifties Hollywood   165
     Hopper's "Home Life and Good Citizenship"   168
     The Sinatra Situation   175
     The Liz-Debbie-Eddie Incident   180

8   Taking on "Hollywood Babylon"   191
     A Career's End   193
     Reporting on a Fading Hollywood System   200
     From Old to New Right   210

Conclusion: Movies, Politics, and Narratives of Nostalgia   219

Notes   225

Index   273

About the Author   281

Abbreviations

CBS   Columbia Broadcasting System
CFA   Committee for the First Amendment
CPUSA Communist Party USA
CO   conscientious objector
CSU   Conference of Studio Unions
FBI   Federal Bureau of Investigation
HH   Hedda Hopper
HUAC   House Committee on Un-American Activities
IATSE International Alliance of Theatrical Stage Employees
INS   Immigration and Naturalization Service
LAT *Los Angeles Times*
MGM   Metro-Goldwyn-Mayer
MPA   Motion Picture Alliance for the Preservation of American Ideals
MPAA   Motion Picture Association of America
NAACP National Association for the Advancement of Colored People
NBC   National Broadcasting Company
PCA   Production Code Administration
SAG   Screen Actors Guild
SDG   Screen Directors Guild
UN   United Nations

Acknowledgments

There are many people and institutions to thank, as this book has evolved over a long time, and colleagues, friends, and family members have contributed to my thinking and provided support along the way.

The project began at the University of Wisconsin–Madison, and so I need to thank the Department of History for a Special Travel Grant, which allowed me to undertake an initial research trip to explore available primary sources in Los Angeles. Jeanne Boydston, Paul Boyer, Nancy Isenberg, Earl Mulderink, and John Pettegrew in History provided guidance early on, and courses I took with Jackie Byars, John Fiske, and Stephen Vaughn in Communication Arts proved influential. Over the years, I also have benefited from presenting conference papers on this topic as part of panels organized with fellow Wisconsin graduate colleagues, including Ellen Baker, Andrea Friedman, Leisa Meyer, Laura McEnaney, and Kevin Smith. Most recently, Janet Davis offered helpful and timely advice.

I returned to this project while teaching in the Department of History at the University of Northern Colorado. With the strong support of my Department chair, Barry Rothaus, encouragement from colleagues Marshall Clough and Ron Edgerton in History and David Caldwell and Elena del Rio in English and Film Studies, and funding from a Faculty Research and Publications Board Grant, I completed much of the research. The staff and setting at the Margaret Herrick Library, Academy of Motion Picture Arts and Sciences, fostered my work in the Hedda Hopper papers, especially archivist Barbara Hall, who provided expert and generous guidance. The hospitality of friends Eftihia Danellis and Kathy Tatar and my sister, Millicent Frost, made this part of the process much easier and more enjoyable.

My move to the University of Auckland in New Zealand yielded a New Staff Research Grant, a University Research Fellowship, and Research and Study Leave to finish my research and write the manuscript. My Department heads—Barry Reay, Jamie Belich, and Malcolm Campbell—not only endorsed this project but also the importance of balancing its completion with family life. The history subject librarian Philip Abela facilitated my access to crucial primary and secondary sources at just the right time, and graduate students Charlotte Burgess and Sam Finnemore, as well as my mom, Ann Frost, my sister, Millicent, and father-in-law, Denis Taillon, provided research support. My participation in a National Endowment for the Humanities summer institute on "African American Civil Rights Struggles in the Twentieth Century," with Waldo Martin and Patricia Sullivan at the W. E. B. Du Bois Institute at Harvard University, furthered my thinking on racial representation and activism around film, and a Blaom Family Scholar-in-Residence Fellowship spurred my writing later on.

Friends and colleagues James Bennett, Sara Buttsworth, Kathy Feeley, Dolores Janiewski, Alison Kibler, and Joe Zizek have read and critiqued sections of the book. History and film scholars John Bodner, Mike Budd, Douglas Gomery, Larry Levine, Lary May, and Steven Ross offered critical guidance at different points in this process, and Jeffrey Kovac helped with key primary sources. Presentations on my research at the University of Auckland and the University of Texas–Austin yielded comments from colleagues that shaped my thinking at the beginning and end of this project.

Parts of this book have appeared in various publications: "Conscientious Objection and Popular Culture: The Lew Ayres Case," in Peter Brock and Thomas Socknat, eds., *Challenge to Mars: Essays in the History of Pacifism, 1914–1945* (Toronto: University of Toronto Press, 1998), 360–369; "'Good Riddance to Bad Company': Hedda Hopper, Hollywood Gossip, and the Campaign Against Charlie Chaplin, 1940–1952," *Australasian Journal of American Studies* 26 (December 2007), 74–88; "Hedda Hopper, Hollywood Gossip, and the Politics of Racial Representation in Film, 1946–1948," *Journal of African American History* 93 (Winter 2008), 36–65; "Dissent and Consent in the 'Good War': Hedda Hopper, Hollywood Gossip, and World War II Isolationism," *Film History: An International Journal*, vol. 22, no. 2 (2010): 170–181; and "Hollywood Gossip as Public Sphere: Hedda Hopper, Reader-Respondents, and the Red Scare, 1947–1965," *Cinema Journal* 50 (Winter 2011). I appreciate the comments of readers and editors for these publications and New York University Press, all of which have been very helpful in clarifying my ideas and correcting my facts.

While family and friends offered all kinds of concrete help along the way, they also provided encouragement and enthusiasm. My father, Jim Frost, long ago sparked my dual interests in Hollywood and politics. Friends Eftihia Danellis and Kathy Tatar have been there from the beginning, and family, especially Ann, Millicent, and Jamie Frost, Lynne, Joe, Steve, and Felicia Baca, Denis and Joyce Taillon, Ellen Anderson, Kay Williams, and Hattie and

Norm Goodman, have all played a part. My husband and fellow historian, Paul Taillon, has been a true partner throughout the entire life of this project, not least in sharing in the parenthood of our children, Cealagh and Luc Taillon, and in the joy and wonder of it all. Notes of sadness during the creation of this book have been the loss of Jeanne Boydston, Larry Levine, Kay Williams, and my mother. I always had intended to acknowledge their contributions here and in the dedication; I only wish they were here to share it.

Hedda Hopper in a studio photograph when under contract as a Hollywood motion picture actress, photographed by Clarence Sinclair Bull, 1920s. (Courtesy of the Academy of Motion Picture Arts and Sciences.)

Introduction

"Malice in Wonderland"

In 1944, just six years into her career as a nationally syndicated Hollywood gossip columnist, Hedda Hopper quipped that her future memoirs would be titled "Malice in Wonderland." Witty and catty, Hopper's title perfectly captured her reputation in Hollywood. Malicious was the least of it: "unpredictable and ruthless," "cold-blooded," "a vicious witch," and, due to her right-wing politics, "fascist."[1] Hopper herself did not shy away from such descriptions. When actress Merle Oberon asked why she wrote such cruel things in her column, Hopper replied, "Bitchery, dear. Sheer bitchery."[2] Hopper was fifty-two years old and an underemployed, struggling supporting actress when the *Los Angeles Times* picked up her fledgling movie gossip column, "Hedda Hopper's Hollywood," in 1938. She soon became a powerful figure in the film industry during its "golden age," when the movies were the dominant form of mass entertainment in the United States. Syndicated in eighty-five metropolitan newspapers as well as small-town dailies and weeklies during the 1940s, Hopper had an estimated daily readership of 32 million (out of a national population of 160 million) in the mid-1950s and remained influential into the next decade.[3]

Hopper in her famous hats became a Hollywood icon, yet her nasty reputation dominated her career, persists today, and overshadows her historical significance. Industry participants attributed Hopper's malicious gossip to her jealousy as a failed actress toward others' success, to her strident conservatism that propelled her on political witch hunts, and to her bitter rivalry with Louella Parsons, who preceded and competed with her in the movie gossip business. The rival columnists were "guardian Furies," the renowned playwright Arthur Miller noted in his memoirs, "the police matrons planted at the portals to keep out the sinful, the unpatriotic, and the rebels against propriety."[4] But this image of Hedda Hopper, while not without substance, owes much to her style and self-fashioning and has obscured her cultural and political importance. Hopper's distinctive contribution to U.S. popular and political culture between 1938 and 1966 lay with how she combined and wielded gossip about the worlds of both entertainment and politics in her column. Her aims were threefold: to distinguish and propel her career, to push her agenda of moral and political conservatism, and—furthering both—to connect with and mobilize her vast readership.

Letters from readers demonstrate Hopper's success with motivating them to join in conversations and campaigns around the typical topics of movies and stars, as well as the social and political issues of great concern to the conservative Hopper. In an industry that routinely disposed of letters from fans and readers, Hopper saved many of hers and published some of them in her column, revealing her respect for, and dependence on, her audience.[5] These letters provide a unique source base for understanding "the lost audience" of Hopper's gossip and Hollywood's past.[6] Like all historical collections of both public and private letters, however, they also are limited as historical evidence in terms of representativeness.[7] Not every filmgoer read Hopper's column, not every reader wrote to Hopper, not every letter was collected and preserved, and not every letter was published or published intact. Moreover, the topics these letters addressed were generated by Hopper herself through the content of her daily column, frequent radio programs, and later television appearances, and often came in response to direct requests from Hopper.

Recognizing these limitations, and that all primary historical sources are partial and incomplete, this reader response allows for a close examination of Hopper, her respondents, and their practice of Hollywood gossip over the middle decades of the twentieth century. Such an approach differentiates this study from the popular and scholarly biographies that exist of Hopper as well as of her powerful contemporaries in the gossip field, Walter Winchell and Louella Parsons.[8] While traditional biography aims to explore and explain a person's entire life story, historians—whether microhistorians or "biographers not"—are reimagining the biographical form "to see through the life" to larger historical contexts and processes.[9] Similarly, the focus here is on the story of Hopper's gossip career and her relationship with her audience. Indeed, extant mail from Hopper's readers shaped the content of this book more than events from Hopper's own life, although the two together can tell us much about American popular and political culture.

As practiced by Hopper and her respondents, Hollywood gossip intersected with and illuminates key developments in mass media gossip, American movies and movie culture, newspaper journalism, and conservative politics during the 1940s, 1950s, and 1960s. In these years, these four areas of American life underwent significant change. Celebrity gossip increasingly permeated the mass media, the motion picture industry enjoyed and then declined from its golden age, print journalism dedicated even more column inches to "soft" news (items about entertainment and celebrity) as opposed to "hard" news (information about politics and foreign policy), and a political conservatism dominated by an "Old Right" gave way to an emerging "New Right." As a purveyor of and participants in mass media gossip, as a movie industry insider and moviegoers, as a celebrity journalist and newspaper readers, and as a political figure and citizens, Hopper and her respondents reflected and affected these changes through their practice of Hollywood gossip.

The mass media gossip of Hopper and her readers shared many of the characteristics of traditional gossip that make it an important and influential means of communication. Although formerly overlooked or trivialized, gossip is increasingly recognized as a significant aspect of the human condition. The evolutionary biologist Robin Dunbar even has suggested "that language evolved to allow us to gossip."[10] Gossip is "private talk"—true or false talk about private life—voiced, often illegitimately, in the public realm. Gossip also is and historically has been seen as the private talk of women. With the assumption that women were situated primarily in the private sphere and greatly interested in private lives and personal issues, this gendering of gossip contributed to negative evaluations of gossip as trivial, inaccurate, or damaging. Cultural aphorisms—such as the Danish "The North Sea will sooner be found wanting in water than a woman at a loss for a word" and the Chinese "The tongue is the sword of a woman, and she never lets it become rusty"— confirm this view.[11] As a woman, Hopper, as well as Parsons, fit the stereotype of the gossip as female, and neither woman won the recognition of the New York–based male columnist Walter Winchell. Hopper and Parsons were "like two biddy schoolmistresses," Winchell's biographer Neal Gabler argues, "until the world passed them by."[12] Furthering the association of women and gossip, most of the extant letters from Hopper's respondents—about eighty percent—are from women.

Hopper's columns and readers' letters reveal the private pleasures and personal benefits they received from what was dismissed as women's "trivial" or "idle" talk, but their Hollywood gossip had a crucial public function. As in traditional societies, it resulted in shared information and knowledge, allowed for discussion and exchange, and contributed to relationships and a sense of community among participants. Gossip also could be wielded, as Hopper and her readers surely did, as "a weapon of the weak" to assail the powerful in society and to reinforce dominant norms by stigmatizing those celebrities who stepped outside the boundaries of what the community deemed appropriate behavior.[13] For all these reasons, celebrity gossip was a powerful discourse in Hopper's time that has proliferated across and permeated mass media outlets in our own time as well.

Hopper and her readers' Hollywood gossip contributed in important ways to the functioning of the U.S. motion picture industry during and just after its golden age. As film historians expand their scholarly inquiry to "people and processes outside the immediate circles of filmmaking," the functions fulfilled by movie gossip, its purveyors, and participants emerge not as ancillary but as central to the film industry.[14] As a gossip columnist during the era of the old studio system, when a few major studios controlled the production, distribution, and exhibition of most films, Hopper was dependent on and dedicated to the industry. Yet she was not just an extension of it. Instead, she occupied a position "in-between" the movie industry and its audience. Given the industry assumption that women constituted the majority—seventy to eighty percent—of filmgoers, Hopper's readers and her relationship to them were viewed as important for Hollywood.[15] In turn, confirming recent theories of cinema spectatorship, Hopper's respondents were active, conscious, selective filmgoers who produced, circulated, and acted on their own meanings of film.[16] Their letters conveyed the experiences and opinions of actual consumers of Hollywood film, especially women, revealing the significance of movies and movie culture in their personal and political lives, as well as their public efforts, together with Hopper, to influence the direction and output of the motion picture industry.

One of Hopper and her readers' most vital industry functions involved the shaping of "star personas" through private talk. What differentiated a star from an actor was that audiences were interested in, and thought they knew something about, the star's "real life" in addition to their "reel life" on film. Gossip played a key role in the mix of film roles and off-screen personalities, of public images and personal information that created the star persona.[17] As they lived their public-private lives, stars sparked interest, discussion, and often controversy. When Hopper publicized actual—and manufactured—details about the private lives of film stars, and her respondents sought out and made sense of those details, they both confronted changing social and sexual mores and contributed to a Hollywood star system in which studios sold the stars and stars sold the movies. When the studio system declined in the transition to "New Hollywood" by the 1960s, so too did the place of Hopper, her readers, and their practice of Hollywood gossip.

Yet movie stardom still depended on the publicity provided by celebrity journalism, and Hopper and her readers confirmed and challenged long-term trends in the news coverage of celebrities. When Hopper became a celebrity journalist in the late 1930s, she entered a well-established field. As historian Charles L. Ponce de Leon demonstrates, celebrity gossip, news items, and feature stories already were a "staple of the metropolitan press" by the 1880s, as "entertainment values became increasingly emphasized" in print journalism.[18] In most ways, Hopper was an imitator of those who had come before her, not an innovator. She adopted the conventions—both in form and content—of the genre of celebrity journalism, conventions that in the 1920s Walter Winchell had taken in new directions in New York and Louella Parsons had perfected for Hollywood. Like her predecessors, she believed that "a person's real self could only be viewed in private," therefore private talk revealed the truth, and she considered invasions of privacy in the interests of democracy; her readership had a "public's right to know" about prominent figures.[19] Also like her predecessors, Hopper became a celebrity in her own right, a "star" journalist generating her own publicity and public interest in her private life, particularly among her readers and fans.

The celebrity journalism written, or rather dictated, by Hopper and read by her readers fell into the category of what has come to be called "soft" or entertainment news, as opposed to "hard" or political news, but, like earlier women journalists or "front page girls," Hopper actually created a hybrid.[20] She included gossip and news about the film industry, local and national politics, and particularly the politics of films and filmmakers in her column and radio shows. In the process, she gave celebrity status to both entertainers and politicians. While Winchell already had accomplished this for New York and the nation, Parsons had not done quite the same for Hollywood. Hopper's hybrid of soft news and hard news could be seen as an unwelcome insertion of celebrity and entertainment into politics, but it is more accurate to say she departed from journalism's twentieth-century trajectory toward depoliticized "infotainment" by inserting politics into her coverage of celebrities. Moreover, she understood and addressed her audience as citizens, not just readers, spectators, or consumers, and her mostly female respondents reciprocated in kind.[21]

Hopper saw her readers as citizens because she saw herself as a political figure and activist, and together they helped shape popular conservative politics in the mid-twentieth century. A new, revisionist literature has transformed historical understandings of conservatism during this period, placing it within the mainstream of American political life, rather than at the margins.[22] The conservative Hopper also should be taken seriously, rather than dismissed as "rabid" or "a crank" who engaged in "pinko purges," and so too should her readers.[23] Revealing an important popular culture dimension to political conservatism, Hopper used her journalistic platform throughout her career to promote traditional morals and conservative politics, to admire and attack members of the film industry for their moral behavior and political views, and to mobilize her readers around related issues and campaigns. Always a proud and highly partisan member of the conservative wing of the Republican Party, she expressed and sought to build opposition to the New Deal in the 1930s, U.S. intervention in World War II, Communism at home and abroad during the Cold War, the Civil Rights Movement, and modern manners and morals. Her respondents joined her in these efforts and were characteristic of the women and men who built the grassroots base of the era's conservative movement.[24]

Hopper was a popularizer of conservatism, not an intellectual or a theorist, but she conveyed a unifying set of ideas and values at a time when the libertarian and traditionalist strains of American conservatism were in "uneasy and sometimes volatile contradiction to one another," according to historian Donald T. Critchlow.[25] Hopper was what came to be called a "libertarian," strongly committed to the separation of a private realm of activity— the economy and personal life—from a public realm of activity—the state and politics. As a member of the Old Right, she advocated the free market and antistatism, condemning the welfare state and government regulation of the economy. She also supported the traditional moral values central to the emerging New Right agenda, although as a libertarian she was reluctant to use the state to intervene in private matters. Instead, she sought to use gossip to enforce community norms. Her consistent anti-Communism also bridged the libertarian-traditionalist divide, as it did for all conservatives.[26] Hopper's integration of political ideas and values associated with the Old Right, the New Right, and what they shared allowed her to address and mobilize all her conservative respondents and demonstrates a crucial continuity in twentieth-century conservatism.

Taken together, Hedda Hopper and her respondents' practice of Hollywood gossip made her column part of the public sphere. The idea of the public sphere is associated with theorist Jürgen Habermas and "designates a theatre in modern societies"—distinct from civil society and the state—"in which political participation is enacted through the medium of talk."[27] While Habermas posited one public sphere with newspapers as a central institution, scholars since have proposed multiple and alternative public spheres, as film historian Miriam Hansen did with the cinema.[28] Appearing in newspapers and covering the cinema, Hopper's column fulfilled many public sphere functions, becoming an arena for sharing information, conveying values and ideas, engaging in discussion and debate, forming and advocating opinions, and taking political action about significant issues of public and private life. The conversations of Hopper and her respondents through columns and letters demonstrate how participation in Hollywood gossip created new modes of citizenship, particularly for women, in the mid-twentieth-century United States.

Yet Hopper's movie gossip column was a distinctive and limited site within the public sphere. While Habermas considered the public sphere a place where distinctions were made between the public and private worlds of participants, Hopper's column privileged gossip, a form of talk that collapsed boundaries between the public and the private, the political and the personal.[29] While public sphere participants in Habermas's formulation sought reasoned discussion and debate, Hopper's writings modeled and encouraged emotional statements and exchanges based on fear, anxiety, hate, and, yes, malice. And while Habermas's ideal public sphere guaranteed access to all citizens, freedom of expression, and open-ended deliberations, Hopper through her column both excluded and censored letters from respondents who disagreed with her and sought confirmation and support for her predetermined moral and political views.[30] Hopper's commitment to the ideals of citizen participation in the public sphere, or reader participation in her column, only extended as far as the promotion and protection of her career necessitated and her campaigns for moral and political conservatism warranted.

Although Hopper's gossip career and conservative campaigns were mutually reinforcing, bringing her visibility and power inside and outside Hollywood, they also could be seen as contradictory. She sought to restore what she saw as the values and verities of an earlier age, but she made her career at the intersection of the film industry and celebrity journalism and endorsed free market capitalism—three forces in modern America credited with propelling the social and cultural changes she lamented.[31] There was another apparent contradiction. Hopper presented herself as the voice of small-town America and nostalgically harked back to the era of scattered, small "island communities," but in her youth she could not wait to leave the town where she had been raised, Altoona, Pennsylvania.[32]

Escape from Altoona

"From the time she was very young, she was determined to escape from the big family," Hedda Hopper's youngest sister, Margaret, recalled. "To leave Altoona. To find a place in the world she knew in her imagination." Such determination and dreams also appeared in Hopper's two books of memoirs, published in 1952 and 1963 when she was in her sixties and seventies, and in her columns and interviews.[33] In all her autobiographical musings—as is true of most autobiography, biography, and even celebrity profiles—Hopper reconstructed as well as fictionalized past events and experiences to link past and present and to give a purpose and shape to her life. In "writing a woman's life," Hopper created a narrative that explained and justified the persona she later adopted and projected as Hedda Hopper, gossip columnist.[34] Her published remembrances asserted a continuity of identity and intention from her youth through adulthood, and drew more on the form and content of the celebrity profiles Hopper often wrote than on the genre of women's autobiography. In contrast to the passivity found in most women's self-writings, Hopper's memoirs emphasized her "industry, perseverance, and will power," an emphasis found in celebrity journalism.[35] Hopper was born Elda Furry in 1885 (she later claimed 1890) to strict Quaker and Republican parents, David and Margaret Furry. She hated her name. "Elda Furry has always sounded to me like a small blonde animal with soft skin that people like to stroke," she later noted. "Being stroked makes my hair rise on my head." Other commentators thought the name appropriate; "I think it should have been pronounced Fury," stated Hopper's editor at the *Los Angeles Times*. Born in "peaceful, pretty" Hollidaysburg, Elda and her family soon moved to Altoona, where David Furry owned a butcher shop.[36]

Hopper's stories of life in Altoona emphasized her strong and independent spirit, politically conservative and patriotic upbringing, fascination with fashion, performance, and the theatrical world, and rejection of family and gender expectations. Seeing the celebrated actress Ethel Barrymore on stage changed her life: she decided to become an actress. Inspired as much by Barrymore's costumes as her acting technique, Elda soon acquired her first store-bought hat. "Of bright green straw trimmed with red velvet geraniums," her hat sparked great interest at church on Easter Sunday. "I said if a hat can get the attention of this many people, I'll never go bareheaded," and it was a lesson she never forgot. Her favorite holiday was Fourth of July. "Orators weren't ashamed to stand up and say what America meant to them," the patriotic Hopper recalled, "and as kids we were pretty proud."[37]

But she also told stories of hard work, sibling rivalries, and family resent-
ments. As the middle child of seven surviving children in a family with an
ill mother—"an angel on earth"—and a father who "thought women should
be the workers," Elda cooked meals, "did the washing, ironing, cleaning,
and helped Dad in his butcher shop," while her brothers shirked. She also
blamed her mother's infirmity on the "raft of children" her father's "selfish-
ness" had created.[38] "I spent most of my early life fighting," she recalled in
the 1920s. "I hated men, because I thought them all selfish, grasping, and
overbearing." Meanwhile, she dreamt of Broadway stardom and saw herself
as a "rebel." Although her father discouraged her dreams of a career in the
theater, "it only made me the more determined to find out if I could do it,"
and when "life became intolerable at home, I ran away to New York and
went on the stage."[39]

In later describing her theatrical career, Hopper adopted the self-mocking
tone typical of women who recognized their challenge to traditional gender
expectations, but her frank acknowledgment of her ambitions and struggles
again fit more with celebrity coverage than women's self-writing.[40] Without
her parents' prior knowledge or approval, Elda first joined a theatrical troupe
in Pittsburgh, then arrived in New York in 1908 at age twenty-two, signed
on and toured with various opera companies as a chorus girl, and eventually
worked her way up to larger roles in plays and musical comedies. "Things
were different in those days," Hopper later remembered. "There weren't a
hundred stage-struck girls for every job." Her attributes were many. "I was
young and pretty. My figure wasn't bad. I had a peaches-and-cream complexion." Others agreed on her good looks. "She was very beautiful, had
this wonderful complexion and great poise and bearing," remembered her
friend, screenwriter Frances Marion. Charles Brackett, also a screenwriter,
claimed, "Elda had the most beautiful legs in the New York theater."[41] She
also benefited from entering the theater at a time of expanding popular culture, burgeoning consumer culture, and growing emphasis on "personality"
and appearances.[42] But she was not known for her singing, dancing, or even
acting ability, and she knew it. "I was working under one handicap," Hopper
recalled. "No talent." Still, "just to be behind the footlights was wonderful,"
and she was ambitious and worked hard, because if she failed she faced "a
fate worse than death—go home to Altoona."[43] Moreover, it was through the
theater that she met her future husband, De Wolf Hopper.

In recounting the sad, often humiliating story of her marriage, Hopper's
remembrances departed from both women's writing and celebrity journalism, revealing a woman willing to admit to unhappiness in her private life

and finding fulfillment in her public life.[44] Calling herself Elda Curry, she met De Wolf Hopper while appearing in her first New York production. "Never was there an unlikelier physical candidate for a ladies' man," Hopper's biographer George Eells argued. A famed stage actor, singer, and comic opera star, De Wolf Hopper was tall, with bold features, no hair, and a bluish tint to his skin from gargling silver nitrate for his throat, but he was very charming and popular with women. "I remember my first glimpse of him," Hopper later recalled, "a tall, striking-looking man with a marvelous voice. Every woman within earshot was leaning toward him worshipfully."[45] He was four years older than her own father and already had four failed marriages behind him. When they married in 1913, she had just turned twenty-eight; De Wolf was fifty-five. In 1915 their son, William De Wolf Hopper, Jr., was born, and by 1918 Elda had changed her name. She sought to distinguish herself, or so she always said, from her husband's four previous wives—Ella, Ida, Edna, and Nella—and consulted a numerologist, who came up with "Hedda." Her new name hardly got away from the "two-syllable names ending in 'a'" she had desired, but the alliteration with her husband's last name worked.[46] Still, Hedda's status as De Wolf's fifth wife did not last long. His insults and infidelities proved to be too much, and she filed for divorce in 1922. Marriage convinced Hopper that a "man must be worth marrying before a woman will give up her independence," and she never married again.[47]

Hopper's energetic, engaging descriptions of her theatrical and early motion picture work during her marriage further acknowledged her challenge to traditional gender expectations, and they were consistent with the self-promotion of celebrity journalism and not the "narrative flatness" of women's autobiography.[48] Hopper's discussions of her acting revealed her pride in and commitment to her career, as well as her resentment of her husband's opposition to a wage-earning wife. Because De Wolf Hopper wanted a "wife who'd stay home while he did the acting for the family," she retired for a brief period of time until her "lord and master changed his mind." But in many ways Hopper was a "new woman," spirited, competent, and self-reliant.[49] She felt frustrated with her dependence on her profligate and unreliable husband and soon returned to work. She described being "excited" about a part, how she "loved" a play, and having a "delightful time" during a film shoot. While both she and her husband tried movie acting, illustrating how "theater people were at last forced to take the cinema seriously," only she liked and succeeded at it. Hopper found that "motion-picture work is the most fascinating form of acting. It develops all one's resources and every day's work means a new adventure."[50] By the time she divorced, her film career was flourishing, she was earning $1,000 per week—as much or more than her husband did in the theater—and her success was causing marital conflict. From this experience, Hopper concluded that "women should work" and not see marriage as "the end and aim of all women." She believed "most women can support themselves, most jobs are open to women these days, and even the hardest job is easier than pleasing a man."[51]

Despite her evident success, the self-mockery Hopper used to discuss her theatrical talents appeared again in her stories about film acting, as did her tributes—characteristic of celebrity journalism—to hard work and making the most of opportunities.[52] She first appeared in the motion picture *Battle of Hearts* (1916), and during the next fifty years she made over 140 films, mostly playing fictional characters but also appearing as "herself," her Hollywood gossip columnist persona. Her "nonexistent acting technique," according to her biographer Eells, "proved more compatible to the camera" than to the stage.[53] She appeared in *Virtuous Wives* (1918), the first film of the future production head at Metro-Goldwyn-Mayer (MGM), Louis B. Mayer. Hers was a supporting role, but she made the most of it. At this time actresses wore their own clothes for film shoots, so Hopper spent her entire salary of $5,000 on an expensive wardrobe and outshone the leading lady. "The picture made a solid reputation for me as a clotheshorse and upped my salary," Hopper recollected. "Producers who didn't know my name began to say, 'Get what's-her-name who played the rich woman in *Virtuous Wives*—she'll dress this.'" By embracing fashion and the latest styles, she drew on a popular means of constructing and expressing personal identity and "new beginnings" to create and make her reputation as an actress.[54]

Over the years and with a coveted MGM contract in the 1920s, Hopper perfected the role of the well-dressed society matron, often "brittle and worldly," and was rarely cast as anything else. Such typecasting was crucial to the Hollywood star system, aided the factorylike efficiency of movie production in the studio era, and was a powerful box office tool.[55] Hopper's typecasting enabled her to secure roles in the "society films" that were very popular during the 1920s and, according to historian Steven J. Ross, projected harmonious class relations, the benefits of individualism, and the myth of upward mobility—all conservative political messages with which Hopper agreed.[56] Again and again, she played wealthy wives and aristocratic ladies such as Mrs. Collingswood Stratton, Lady Wildering, the Countess of Rochester, and Madame Zoe in films with titles like *High Society Blues*, *The Snob*, *Her Market Value*, *Such Men Are Dangerous*, *Adam and Evil*, *The Cruel Truth*, *Sinners in Silk*, and *Another Scandal*. Hopper credited her highly "affected" accent, which "nauseated myself and my friends," with getting her "all those phony society-female roles that I played on the screen."[57]

Hopper's discussions and critics' reception of her film roles and typecasting foreshadowed her style and self-fashioning as a gossip columnist. While she received good notices in the 1920s for "lending charm, distinction, and élan" to various films, having no colleague "who can better play the lady," and creating mothers that are "smart, up-to-date and the rival of the flappers," most commentaries focused on her ability to play the "jealous woman" and "the matron on the make."[58] Early in her career, she was happy with such roles. "I like to play bad women, frankly," she said during the making of *Virtuous Wives*. "Good women are so deadly dull." But later in her career and in her memoirs, Hopper expressed frustration with her typecasting. "I was the mean woman who made the stars look good," she recalled. "I never played a good woman on the screen till my contract with Metro was finished."[59] Even so, Hopper's typecast screen persona as the classy, flamboyant, and bitchy older woman translated into her later gossip career. She partly constructed her persona as a gossip columnist out of her film roles, just as Ronald Reagan did later as a politician. Moreover, members of the industry and newspaper audience familiar with Hopper's acting "read" her gossip columnist persona through those roles. As historian Michael Rogin found for Reagan, the merging of "on- and off-screen identities" revealed a powerful "conflation of movies and reality" for Hopper as well.[60]

In reflecting back on her ability to change careers in the late 1930s from acting to gossip, Hopper credited her perseverance, with having "guts enough to stick it out" and "wear down Hollywood's resistance," another theme of celebrity profiles.[61] Her decades-long experience in the industry gave her an extensive knowledge of movies, moviemaking, and movie culture and a wide circle of friends and acquaintances. Beginning in 1915, she had lived in Hollywood on and off before making the move west permanent following her divorce in the 1920s, "a remarkable era of growth" in Los Angeles when the population rose 140 percent.[62] Originating in Altoona, middle-class, Protestant, and conservative, Hopper fit the profile of many westward migrants, and she too brought from the country's heartland to southern California "nostalgia," as journalist Carey McWilliams understood it at the time, "for an America that no longer exists."[63] Over her lifetime, the continuous flow of her fellow migrants contributed to the region's booming economic growth as well as its conservative political culture. Hopper made her home in Hollywood in the "golden twenties," when filmmaking became California's top industry, but stayed through the Great Depression, and her movie career mirrored the economic times.[64]

She was struggling even before she lost her savings in the stock market crash and her MGM contract in 1932—Louella Parsons, movie gossip columnist for the newspaper empire of William Randolph Hearst, had deemed her "Queen of the Quickies" for trying to make a living out of many minor roles—and work was scarce in hard times. "I had been around too long," she later concluded. "Producers were tired of my face. Of course, I was tired of it, too, but I couldn't do anything about it."[65] She had only five small parts in 1933, and when she appeared in her typical role as a snobbish "society leader" in *Alice Adams* (1935), starring Katharine Hepburn as an ambitious small-town girl, studio publicity noted her return "to the screen after an absence of two years." Moreover, her pay had dropped to $1,000 per film in 1935 from $1,000 a week in 1917.[66] To make ends meet, she wrote a play, ran for a political position and lost—"thank goodness the citizens had a better idea!"—worked as a talent agent, promoted Elizabeth Arden cosmetics, acted in theater, and returned to selling real estate, an activity she had pursued during the previous decade when a housing boom made the real estate salesperson the "archetypal Los Angeleno of the 1920s." Her friends, such as Frances Marion, did what they could to help the struggling Hopper.[67]

In fact, Hopper's memoirs showed how her women friends contributed to the beginning of her gossip career by providing her with lucky "breaks," another theme in celebrity journalism. "Writing a column is the only job ever handed to me on a silver platter," she wrote. "I'd worked so hard finding picture parts that many times I pushed my luck away from me."[68] Marion Davies, an actress and longtime mistress to William Randolph Hearst, and Ida Koverman, who served as executive assistant to Louis B. Mayer at MGM, were particularly helpful. Hopper met Mrs. Eleanor (Cissy) Patterson, the publisher of the *Washington Herald*, through Davies, and Patterson, "captivated by Hedda's brittle and spicy observations about Hollywood," hired her in 1935 to write a "letter from Hollywood," Hopper's first published gossip.[69] Although this job did not last long, and Hopper tried and failed at radio gossip in 1936, in 1937 she signed with Esquire Feature Syndicate for a gossip column with the crucial behind-the-scenes support of MGM, or so the story goes. Reportedly, an MGM publicist told Esquire, "We don't know if Hedda Hopper can write, but when we want the lowdown on the stars, we get it from her." Meanwhile, Mayer, who wanted a rival columnist "strong enough to curb Louella's power," followed Koverman's suggestion and secretly backed Hopper in the newspaper business.[70] In the end, when the *Los Angeles Times* picked up "Hedda Hopper's Hollywood" in 1938, Louella Parsons had a real rival, and Hopper had a new career at the age of fifty-two. With a little help from her friends, she had finally "found, at the end of her rainbow, the pot of gold into which she now dips her pen."[71]

Hopper also had found an outlet for her private talk and, once she gained the necessary clout and confidence, her moral and political views. She had long delighted in gossip. "Sundays were always exciting for me," she wrote of her life in Altoona. "I devoured every scrap of scandal and fashion news in the Sunday supplement."[72] When she moved to Hollywood in 1923, she became known as a seeker and source of good gossip. She sought out the "inside story on everyone in order to spice up her conversation" and sent "long, gossipy letters" to Parsons. The two were contemporaries—Hopper joked she was "one year younger than the age Louella claims to be"—and on friendly terms. Parsons, then still writing her column from New York, appreciated hearing from the Hollywood-based Hopper, "the lady who knows it all." In return, Parsons promoted Hopper and her career in her successful syndicated movie gossip column, as when she noted the actress had off-screen "experience as a troubled wife" before she played one on-screen as Mrs. Crombie in *Conceit* (1921).[73] Parsons had begun writing a newspaper gossip column in 1915 and by the 1930s was known as "the first lady of Hollywood." While she had a reputation for gushing, promotional prose about the film industry and its employees—"Marion Davies has never looked lovelier" became a famous phrase—Parsons was powerful, and Hopper knew it.[74] Their shared devotion to gossip first underpinned, and then undermined, their mutually beneficial relationship.

Similarly, Hopper's "juicy gossip about film stars" was one reason Ida Koverman gravitated to her and formed a friendship with her; another reason was Hopper's political conservatism, rooted in her small-town Pennsylvania childhood during the long period of Republican Party electoral dominance. Before she became Mayer's assistant, Koverman had been a secretary for the future Republican president Herbert Hoover, and both women worked at MGM, one of Hollywood's most conservative studios.[75] For Hopper, enfranchised by the women's suffrage amendment in 1920 at age thirty-five, politics mattered. When she acted on her political convictions—propelled by financial desperation—and ran for a seat on the Republican County Central Committee in 1932, Koverman supported her, as did Parsons. "Even if we differ with her in politics," noted Parsons, at the time a Democrat, "we can't help but hope that Hedda will be elected." Losing the election, despite swamping the voters with fifteen thousand handbills, did not stop her political activism. Two years later she represented Mayer, then chairman of the California

Republican Party, at a campaign gathering for Hoover's reelection bid. She energetically campaigned for Hoover, who shared her conservative Quaker upbringing, values, and qualities, including commitments to individual enterprise, social responsibility, and "ruthless righteousness." "It will be an everlasting disgrace to the women of California if Hoover is not re-elected. The country will backslide a century," she warned, if the Democratic challenger, Franklin Delano Roosevelt, won.[76] Hopper maintained her interest in political conservatism and involvement in the Republican Party throughout her gossip career.

Hopper also remained committed to moral conservatism. Despite her own divorce, single motherhood, and living over forty years in "Hollywood Babylon," seen as a site of sin and scandal, Hopper believed in and upheld the moral respectability of the Quaker girl from Altoona. Hopper was rumored to have ruined her career at MGM by refusing to recline on Mayer's casting couch, and her friends and family reported she had "no lovers, no love affairs," only "platonic relationships." Hopper did have one significant romance in her early forties, however. "I'm in love for the first time in my life," she reported to Frances Marion. But she broke off the relationship when the married man could not secure a divorce from his Catholic wife. Marion considered this heartbreaking decision "the root of Hedda's virulent self-righteousness," according to her biographer Cari Beauchamp. "She had suffered, she had vigilantly held to her moral ideals; those who did not must also pay a price."[77] With her deeply held moral values, long-standing conservative views, and a column to call her own, Hedda Hopper was set to pursue and practice the politics of Hollywood gossip.

Hedda Hopper at her desk, engaged in her work as a gossip columnist, 1944. (Courtesy of the Academy of Motion Picture Arts and Sciences.)

The Making of a Celebrity Gossip

On October 22, 1939, Hedda Hopper broke a story that made the front page of the *Los Angeles Times* and her career as a gossip columnist. In an "exclusive" interview with James Roosevelt, eldest son of the sitting president, Franklin Delano Roosevelt, and a producer and executive vice president at Samuel Goldwyn Studios, Hopper confronted "Jimmy" about the state of his marriage. "Is it true," she asked, "that you and your wife are going to be divorced?" Roosevelt "refused to deny or affirm" the truth of Hopper's question, giving her the answer, or rather non-answer, she wanted, and her story went on to detail his geographic separation from his wife, his public appearances with another woman, and his moves toward divorce.[1] Hopper's "first big scoop" was picked up by news media throughout the country. When it turned out that Hopper's interview had occurred at 11:15 p.m. on a Saturday night outside Roosevelt's Beverly Hills home, as a "disheveled . . . Jimmy came out in bare feet and bathrobe," *Time* magazine noted the up-and-coming celebrity gossip had "set a new record for keyhole journalism."[2]

The James Roosevelt divorce story not only proved Hopper an aggressive player in the competitive world of celebrity journalism and triggered her decades-long feud with Louella Parsons, but also demonstrated Hopper's dual interest in entertainment and politics.[3] Roosevelt operated in both the capitals of "power and glitter," Washington and Hollywood, and the bulk of Hopper's article detailed his public life and work, including campaigning for his father in the 1932 and 1936 elections and assisting in the White House. Although on friendly terms with him, Hopper delighted in facing "the young scion of the No. 1 political family in America," as she put it, and tarnishing the moral reputation of her political opponents, the Roosevelts of the Democratic Party.[4] From the very start of her career, Hopper publicized private talk to ends both political and partisan.

A Columnist Is Born

Following her Roosevelt divorce scoop, Hedda Hopper's gossip career took off. Crucial to her career were syndication services, which provided newspapers with articles, stories, and columns, and by the 1890s had laid the foundation for national celebrity by carrying entertainment news and features.[5] In 1940, Hopper moved her column, "Hedda Hopper's Hollywood," from the Esquire Features Syndicate to the Des Moines Register–Tribune Syndicate, and then in 1942 she signed with the much larger and more prominent Chicago Tribune–New York News Syndicate, nearly tripling the number of her readers. "THE QUEEN IS DEAD, LONG LIVE THE QUEEN!" headlined *Variety*, but "Queen" Louella Parsons was far from dead. With the power of the Hearst press behind her, she still had 17 million readers through hundreds of newspapers, while Hopper's column, appearing in less than one hundred papers and reaching 5.75 million daily readers and 7.5 million on Sunday, had about a third of Parsons's circulation.[6] Even so, Hopper's numbers grew quickly. Within five years, her column reportedly appeared in 110 newspapers with a total circulation of 22.8 million.[7] Newspapers carrying her column included most prominently the *Los Angeles Times* and the papers heading her syndicate, the *New York Daily News* and the *Chicago Tribune*, but also major metropolitan newspapers across the country and overseas. Within a few years of launching her column, Hopper had mastered the long-standing conventions of celebrity journalism, marketed her attention-getting gossip columnist persona, and risen "to the top of this ink-stained pile of professional reporters" who covered Hollywood.[8]

Hopper's accomplishment did not go unnoticed, particularly by her rivals. In changing careers from acting to gossip, Hopper had left one crowded and competitive field for another. When she began her gossip career, an estimated 325 columnists, fan magazine writers, and reporters for American, foreign, and trade newspapers worked the "Hollywood beat," more than in any other U.S. city except New York and Washington, D.C.[9] The number of Hollywood columnists alone was great, and prominent figures—beyond Louella Parsons—included Sheilah Graham, Jimmie Fidler, Sidney Skolsky, and Edith Gwynne. Moreover, New York–based columnists such as Walter Winchell and Ed Sullivan published movie news and gossip. Newspapers and syndication services often carried more than one Hollywood columnist. In the *Los Angeles Times*, for example, "Hedda Hopper's Hollywood" appeared early on with Edwin Schallert's "Town Called Hollywood" and Reed Kendall's "Around and About Hollywood." With so many columnists in town, rivalries were fierce for personal relationships with, and press releases from, Hollywood moviemakers. As a result, Hopper often had testy if not hostile interactions with her fellow columnists, most famously Parsons. The Hopper-Parsons feud marked a change from their earlier relationship, when Hopper sent missives to Parsons in return for mentions in Parsons's column. Parsons also had supported Hopper's initial foray into column writing for the *Washington Herald* in 1935, but all that ended with Hopper's Roosevelt scoop.

Although Parsons was the much more experienced and established writer, she felt threatened by the middle-aged upstart, and Hopper did not mind posing a threat. Parsons, a college graduate who began newspaper writing in 1902, was the professional; Hopper, who had an eighth-grade education and lacked basic typing skills, was the amateur. Yet Hopper had a place at the *Los Angeles Times*. "Simply because of this, Hedda became important," observed a longtime Hollywood insider. "You don't make it in this town to the same degree unless you have a local outlet. Hedda had the best." "She's trying to do in two years what took me thirty," Parsons was quoted as saying, "and I resent some of the things she says about me."[10] Commentators credited Hopper's competition with "breaking Parsons' stranglehold on the studios," largely through ending her exclusive right to stories forty-eight hours in advance of other columnists, but they also recognized Parsons's continued power. In fact, a decade into their rivalry, Parsons still received the majority of scoops from the studios, "about 60%, and that is probably the clearest measure of her edge on Hedda."[11] Samantha Barbas, Parsons's most recent biographer, perceptively analyzes media coverage and construction of the "war of words" between the two gossips as "exaggerated," "antifeminist," and "playing on the stereotype of aggressive females as catty." Pretend, playful feuds were commonplace in show business, and Hopper later presented hers with Parsons as "good for both of us. It was a good gag."[12]

But the Hopper-Parsons feud was real. They refused to attend parties together, at premieres they demanded seats in the same row but at opposite ends, and they competed over who would be photographed first with a star. Their feud was also in print. When Parsons carped in her column that "Hollywood was raising its eyebrows" over actress Agnes Moorehead winning a New York Film Critics Award, Hopper in hers "cracked that she had looked carefully and failed to see a single elevated eyebrow." And when Hopper barged in on Bette Davis to get the story of the actress's new baby, Parsons had a story of her own. "Since Bette Davis has had so many unwelcome visitors, she has had to have her gate padlocked." Yet the "rival scoopsters, gargoyles of gossip" did attempt to reconcile once.[13] What sparked the brief détente was Hopper's praise for a new film produced by Parsons's daughter, Harriet, *I Remember Mama* (1948). As it turned out, both women were always kind to the other's offspring, a fact one observer explained as each woman feeling "with a mother like that, I'm not going to add to *that* child's troubles!" Their reconciliation lunch made the *Hollywood Reporter, Time,* and *Collier's* magazine, as well as Hopper's column. "Louella Parsons and I lunched together at Romanoff's the other day and the town still is agog."[14] The armistice in the gossip war did not last long, however, and by 1949 the two women were back to fighting.

Despite their rivalry, Hopper, Parsons, Winchell, and other gossip columnists understood what they shared: the power of private information. "Darling, if you and I ever get together and compare notes, we'll rock this town on its heels," Hopper told Parsons before their famous lunch.[15] Exposure of the private was the point and purpose of a gossip column, and gossip delivered through mass-circulation newspapers beginning in the early nineteenth century was the primary means of shifting the line between the private and the public. In publicizing private talk, newspaper gossip made more aspects— and increasingly more intimate aspects—of private life open to public knowledge and scrutiny over time. Yet where to draw the line between the private and the public remained controversial. In the 1890s, jurists proposed the "right to be let alone" as a legal right, and concerned citizens with a "sense of the sacred and the shameful" advocated for "reticence" on sexual matters in public, but they lost the legal and cultural battles.[16] By the 1920s and 1930s, when journalists defined a code of ethics that allowed privacy invasions only with "sure warrant of public right as distinguished from public curiosity," Winchell, more than any other celebrity journalist, sensationally and controversially revealed more of the private in public, raising the question of whether such revelations were justified as "the public's right to know."[17]

For Hopper, the answer was a resounding "yes!" In 1913, when she had been the target of celebrity journalists pressing about her marriage to De Wolf Hopper, however, she had a different answer. "Domestic affairs are private property," she insisted. Now that she was on the other end of the question and in Hollywood, where the denizens "have as much privacy in their work or lives as a Broadway traffic policeman," she believed in exposure.[18] On a trip to Chicago, she toured an apartment house set on Lake Michigan and built of glass set in steel. "What a boon it would be . . . if we had a couple of these glass apartment houses," she commented. "We could look right through the walls and see what the dwellers inside were doing." Columnists would have a "field day."[19] Her and her readership's right to know justified such invasions of privacy. In most cases, such as engagements, marriages, births, family, home life, and travel, the content of Hopper's private talk was favorable, benign, and often given to her by the subjects, their studios, or press agents. She rarely had to defend herself against invasions of privacy in these cases. But with negative or damaging gossip about sexual affairs, adultery, divorce, or unlawful activities, Hopper publicized and "narrativized" transgressions of social and legal norms, thereby creating scandals.[20] In these cases, she received and deflected criticism by arguing that the subjects of her gossip should not have committed the scandalous acts she made public. "The only way to prevent adverse yarns from getting into print," she contended, "is not to let them happen in the first place."[21] Hopper believed that calls for privacy always covered up wrongdoing; those who did nothing wrong had nothing to fear from publicity. One of the virtues of gossip, in her eyes, was it hurt only those who deserved it.

While Hopper deployed and defended private talk, her column covered industry and political news as well. According to a writer for *Life* magazine in 1944, Hollywood hosted a large group of "professional journalists, who report soberly on production plans and the affairs of the studios generally, and the gossipists," a smaller but more influential group.[22] At the time and since, commentators placed Hopper squarely with the gossipists. Indeed, her early Sunday columns had headlines such as "Hedda Hopper Reviews Hollywood Styles," while her fellow columnist Schallert wrote about taxation in the movie industry with "Major Organizations Face Heavy Imposts." "Miss Hopper reported very little hard news of the industry, preferring to concentrate on its personalities and what they told her," stated the *New York Times*.[23] Hopper's newspaper editors and fan magazine colleagues knew better, however. Several times during her career the political content of her column prompted editors to complain, but she simply ignored them, with no loss of business until near the end of her career in the 1960s. "Unlike other Hollywood columnists who simply covered gossip," *Photoplay* also noted, "Hedda took an interest in working conditions and often battled in her column for better standards in movies."[24]

With her coverage of recent events and developments in both entertainment and politics, Hopper declared herself a journalist. "I put gossip in the same category as news," she maintained.[25] Not everyone agreed. She called different newspaper editions "issues," one writer noted, and when she had late-breaking news she yelled, "Stop the presses, whatever that means!" Agnes DeMille, the choreographer and niece of the famous film director Cecil B. DeMille, observed that Hopper "was a failed actress before she turned to journalism, if you want to call it that." Editors at the *Los Angeles Times* saw her more as an entertainer than a journalist, calling her a "newspaper personality." In fact, journalism historians have put celebrity gossip into the "soft news" category or even "the non-news field."[26] The distinction between hard news and soft news emerged as journalism professionalized and moved away from the political partisanship that characterized American newspapers in the eighteenth and nineteenth centuries and toward the neutrality and objectivity sought in the twentieth century, and it was often understood in gendered terms. Hard and soft reportage differed by topic—politics and foreign policy as opposed to entertainment and opinion—and tone—rational, objective, and "masculine" instead of emotional, subjective, and "feminine."[27] As a column of movie gossip and personal commentary written by a woman, "Hedda Hopper's Hollywood" departed from accepted journalistic codes, but that did not deter Hopper. "With each advance, Hedda assumed additional mannerisms of the stereotype news hen," her biographer George Eells contended. "Her vocabulary grew rougher, and she developed a 'hardboiled' exterior." She also refused to associate herself with the pejorative image of women journalists as "sob sisters" who reported the news with sympathy and sentimentality. "I suppose all the sob sisters in the world will now go to work," Hopper commented after one tragic Hollywood event.[28]

Hopper's efforts to claim the status of a journalist covering hard news were part of an attempt to make a name for herself in the gossip business. Given that most of what she was doing as a gossip columnist fit within the conventions of celebrity journalism and imitated her predecessors in the field, she needed to differentiate herself. To this end, she fashioned a gossip columnist persona that got her the attention she wanted. It helped that she was an actress. Not only was Hopper still trim and attractive, "the handsome, headlong gossip," according to *Time* magazine; she also was comfortable with role playing and self-promotion.[29] Moreover, being a movie actress meant Hopper easily adopted one of the strategies of celebrity journalists: appearing as an insider and an intimate of their subjects. Reporting on the industry she knew so well lent Hopper legitimacy and authenticity. "Hedda is well fitted to write," commented one writer, "for she's more than a reporter, setting down gossip. She knows the business."[30] In her column Hopper continually referred to her acting career and asserted her expertise with regard to movies, stars, and the industry. She could judge acting talent, because "I've known them all." In discussions of certain films, she would add, "I know—I was in it." And when a film needed casting, she would comment, "Don't contact me."[31]

Hopper's acting career and roles provided another aspect of her gossip columnist persona: her nastiness. When she began her column, her friend

Frances Marion advised, "Don't bite the hand that feeds you caviar," and Hopper took her advice. "I shall not set myself up as a judge or critic," she wrote in her first column. As one reporter told it, "Hedda was too nice to people." As Hopper told it, "sweetness and light" was not selling, so she "put salt on its tail." This development was seen as more consistent with her actual personality. "Wake up. Be yourself," urged her business manager, Dema Harshbarger.[32] It also was in keeping with her film typecasting as the classy and catty society woman. "Miss Hopper's candid and sometimes acid wit came as no surprise to those familiar with the smartly knowing society women she had played in more than a hundred films," wrote two film writers.[33] At the time, celebrity writer Florabel Muir saw it differently. Hopper's film persona as a "screen vixen was too much for Hedda," Muir argued. "Her manner was too brittle, her voice too sharp, her comments too catty." But it worked. "The minute I started to trot out the juicy stuff," Hopper recalled, "my phone started to ring."[34]

As an actress, Hopper also was comfortable with public display and attention getting, and nowhere were these characteristics more apparent than with her trademark: her famous hats. She became wholly identified with hats and earned titles such as the "Hollywood Hatter," "Mad-Hatter Hopper," and "Queen of Hats." According to legend, "an effective test of Hollywood sobriety was the ability to recite: 'Hedda Hopper has a horde of hooted hats; a horde of hooted hats has Hedda Hopper.'"[35] While Winchell with his ever-present fedora made hat wearing part of the image of the gossip columnist, Hopper claimed her love of hats, and the attention they garnered, originated in her Altoona youth. "I learned early what every smart woman knows," she wrote for a women's magazine. "A becoming hat is a worth-while investment."[36] For Hopper, as for most of her contemporaries, hat wearing fostered both fitting in, when everyone in the United States wore hats, and standing out, when hats could express "flamboyance and whimsy." Hopper often stood out, wearing "some of the most startling headgear in the annals of millinery." She wore hats with "zany hat ornaments," including toy horns, large Easter eggs, and the Eiffel Tower.[37] One hat labeled "Salad Chapeau" and made of fresh endive, carrots, cabbage, and grapes looked "pretty darn good," she said. "I created a sensation at the Beverly Club last night in your black feathered hat," she wrote one designer. "Of course, I couldn't see, but everybody saw me and came over and commented."[38]

As part of an industry that used movies to present "spectacles for consumption" at a time of expanding consumer culture, Hopper's hat wearing and hat buying appealed "to the acquisitive fantasies" of her readers.[39] She bought an estimated 150 hats per year from designers such as Lily Daché, Sally Victor, and Rex. The $5,000 she annually spent on hats at the beginning of her career had doubled to $10,000 by the end. At times even she had to admit this expense was too much, as when she bought a new hat and confessed to a friend, "I need it like I need a hole in the head."[40] The news media covered her visits to designers' studios, attendance at fashion shows, choice of styles, and purchases. "Hedda Hopper conservatively chose a flying saucer," *Time* magazine reported in 1956, "with tuliplike cosmic-ray receptors on top."[41] The Rochester Museum of Arts and Sciences requested her hats for an exhibit in 1947, and apparel companies, individuals, and even the military made hats for her. In 1963, the Air Force Association created one for her out of a hard hat "used by personnel on the launch crews" as "a symbol of the missile and space business." "We have had it painted a 'rose pink,' and on the front of it your name appears in military fashion: 'H. Hopper.'" Cecil B. DeMille summed up Hopper's relationship to hats best: "If the pen is her rapier, the hat is her flag."[42]

Hopper's hats were only part of her style as a gossip columnist. Despite the craziness of many of her hats, she was known for her fashion sense and often made the list of "best-dressed women in the movie colony." The actress Debbie Reynolds recalled Hopper as "always well groomed and well dressed" and "always [in] pinks and lavenders."[43] Hopper saw herself as an arbiter of fashion and commented on changing styles. Yet her personal style encompassed more than how she dressed. She had an energetic, vibrant personality and "a sharp sense of humor," filled her language with profanities, worked twelve-to-fifteen hour days "without visible fatigue," and did everything quickly. She moved fast, talked fast with "her rat-a-tat-tat delivery," and drove fast. "Hell-on-the-Highway Hopper, they call me," she quipped and with good reason. She not only frequently received speeding tickets, she once was driving forty-eight miles per hour in a twenty-mile-per-hour zone, and she also failed to keep dates in traffic court.[44] She never took a vacation away from her column, because "I'm too much of a ham not to want to pick up the paper tomorrow morning and find out what Hedda Hopper has to say." To some observers Hopper appeared "high-strung and hyperemotional, [with] a tendency to get rattled," while for others "she just had amazing vitality and endurance." "At least a dozen Hollywood columnists have bigger circulations than Hedda," *Time* noted in 1940, "but none of them makes so much of a splash as she does."[45]

And Hopper was making a splash. By 1942, she had her column, articles appearing in movie fan and mainstream magazines, a radio gossip show, and more movie work; in 1944 she earned an income of about $100,000 (the equivalent of about $800,000 today).[46] Indicating Hopper's increasing cultural authority, her column commentaries were picked up and used by other celebrity journalists in their writings. In an item on Lena Horne and her role in MGM's *Cabin in the Sky* (1943), Billy Rowe of the *Pittsburgh Courier* wrote, "Hedda Hopper raves [she] is the greatest performer to come along in decades." Hopper had a presence on radio as well, during a period when "Hollywood contributions played a major role" in radio programming.[47] Although the title, network, format, and sponsor of her radio gossip show changed over time, Hopper broadcast on radio nearly continuously from 1939 to 1947. "Good afternoon to some of you, good evening to more of you, and good luck to all of you" was her famous radio signoff. She also had acting roles on dramatic radio shows. "Radio I love! It's almost a vacation," she wrote in 1944. "It gives me a chance to act and that I'd rather do than eat."[48]

As with radio, Hopper's film work included performances as an actress playing fictional characters and as "herself," her gossip columnist persona. She even played fictional gossip columnists such as Dolly Dupuyster in *The Women* (1939), whose few lines included, "Oh, hello girls. My, but you look lovely. Got any dirt for the column?" and "Oh boy, dirt!" According to George Eells, "She fought to be cast in *The Women* because it was a Broadway success [and] it reeked of prestige."[49] Based on a play by Clare Boothe Luce, produced by Hopper's old studio MGM, with an all-female cast "headed by a galaxy of stars, notably Norma Shearer, Joan Crawford, Rosalind Russell, and Paulette Goddard," the film follows a group of New York society women— "that feminine kennel," described Hopper—as they engage in mean-spirited gossiping and destroy reputations and lives in the process. The film was a major hit, considered one of the best of the year, and a formative one for Hopper's emerging malicious gossip persona.[50] Between 1941 and 1942, Hopper also made six one-reel short films titled "Hedda Hopper's Hollywood" for Paramount Studios to be shown in movie theaters. A sign of her growing success, her movie salary rose to up to $5,000 a week. She no longer needed the kinds of roles she had taken earlier, such as Lady Hammond in *Dracula's Daughter* (1936) and Penny Reed in *Tarzan's Revenge* (1938); she was now in demand.[51]

Moreover, Hopper was now a celebrity. Like Winchell and Parsons, Hopper joined the ranks of celebrity journalists who became celebrities themselves. She was celebrated for her accomplishments as a mass media gossip, but she also soon became known for her "well-knownness," to quote Daniel J. Boorstin's famous formulation of celebrity.[52] The media covered her public activities and private life, and she became the subject of celebrity profiles.

Magazines publicized her 1941 move into her new house on Tropical Drive in Beverly Hills—"*Life* Goes to a House Moving"—and six years later a ceremony for her new granddaughter, Joan Hopper—"*Modern Screen* Goes to a Christening." An article in *American Home* detailed her "fabulous collection of Bristol glass" as well as the presence in her garden of the hybrid "opalescent pink" tea roses named after her in 1952.[53] Sought after for lectures and charity events, Hopper earned $1,500 a lecture, drew crowds of ten thousand and more in cities such as St. Paul and Pittsburgh, donated hats for charity auctions, and devoted much time and energy to campaigns for the Salvation Army and the Easter Seal Fund, for which she served as national chairwoman in 1960. She also became a point of reference in American popular culture. "Headache Hoopla" and her rival "Polly Parsnips" showed up in a cartoon, and songwriter Cole Porter worked Hopper into a song lyric. "When people talk about those columnists, such as Walter Winchell, Ed Sullivan, Westbrook Pegler, Hedda Hopper, Dorothy Thompson, Dorothy Kilgallen, and that frightfully vulgar girl they all call ELSA, I take a BROMO-SELTZA."[54]

Perhaps most indicative of Hopper's celebrity was the marketing of her column and the visibility given her by her Chicago Tribune–New York News syndicate. Advertisements for the syndicate touted her column as a way to build circulation and readership, particularly among women, and increase advertising revenue for newspapers subscribing to the service. "Hedda Hopper the number-one reporter of a fabulous industry. An actress turned newspaperwoman, her HOLLYWOOD column reflects her own vibrant, dynamic, charming personality. She says what's on her mind." Hopper's column was at the top of the list in advertisements designed "To Help You Sell Women," and her flamboyant persona and celebrity status made her a regular speaker at annual meetings of publishers and editors.[55] "These are the men who buy film columns from the syndicates," an invitation from the president of an editorial association stated. "It dawns on me that you could show the boys one helluva good time by talking to them for an hour or so about Hollywood." "At the same time," he added, "you might be giving them the idea that your column would be a damn good one to have in their own papers."[56] "When she went to the Newspaper Publishers Convention every year in New York," one of her employees, Spec McClure, recalled, "Hopper had a radiant vitality. She bowled over those editors. A lot of the job of doing a damn column is selling it." As a celebrity, Hopper's "attention-getting capacity" not only made her a commodity but also aided her success in marketing multiple commodities: her column, her reading public, and, most important for the industry she loved, Hollywood, movies, and the stars.[57]

Gilding Hollywood's "Golden Age"

As a new celebrity purveyor of movie gossip, Hedda Hopper crucially contributed to the functioning of the industry that at the time produced the
most popular form of American entertainment. "Gossip," argued *Time* magazine in 1947, "is big business, and it has become as indispensably bound up
in the making of U.S. movies as cameras." What Hopper's column provided
was considered the "lifeblood" of the film industry: publicity.[58] Hollywood
both needed good publicity and feared bad publicity. In publicizing industry
news and gossip, Hopper shaped the meanings of the industry and its products, the movies and the stars. She added another "text" to the "intertextual"
or "extratextual" flow and context within which cinema spectators saw and
made sense of film.[59] Hopper's gossip column influenced this process for her
vast readership, and the film industry had a stake in this as well. In contrast
to her nasty reputation, much of Hopper's column presented the industry
in a positive light, unsurprisingly given that her career depended on its success and access to its information, and, in return, studios kept her informed
and gave her interview subjects. Yet Hopper, like Parsons and other columnists, was never simply an extension of the studios; in fact, Hopper's credibility with her audience required her to demonstrate a critical independence
from the industry. As a consequence, constant negotiation and give-and-take
characterized the relationship between Hopper and Hollywood, access and
publicity.

When Hopper joined the ranks of successful movie gossip columnists, the
movie industry was "a study in paradox," according to film scholar Thomas
Schatz, "with Hollywood in the full flowering of its 'golden age' while the
industry foundered economically." Eight big companies—an oligopoly—
dominated the industry: five "majors," which owned theaters (Loews/MGM,
Warner Brothers, Paramount, 20th Century-Fox, and RKO) and three
"minors," which did not own theaters (Universal, Columbia, and United Artists).[60] With film production in Hollywood and distribution and exhibition
controlled by corporate management in New York, the companies created
the studio system, a factorylike arrangement of mass production designed to
generate a consistent product, and a consistent supply of product, to appeal
to a wide audience and to supply and fill the theaters. The Great Depression hit the industry hard, as indicated by Hopper's loss of her MGM contract in 1932. Although box office revenues rose during the mid-1930s, and
the industry ranked fourteenth in business volume in the United States in
1937, earning over $400 million, that year's recession reversed the promising

trend.[61] The precarious economic situation pervaded the content of Hopper's early columns and lent them a nostalgic tone, as she longed for "the good old days" when she had a studio contract and moviegoers had the money to "go to see anything." "Let's face it," she lamented, "those days are gone forever." Within this context, Hollywood insiders viewed Hopper's publicity, along with Parsons's, as a necessity. As David Niven remembered, "At every Hollywood breakfast table or office desk, the day started with an avid perusal of the columns of Louella Parsons and Hedda Hopper." "Their columns were the first thing we looked at every morning," Bob Hope recalled, "to see what was going on."[62]

What Niven, Hope, and others read in Hopper's column combined information culled by her and her staff from a variety of sources. Publicists for the studios and press agents for individuals provided Hopper with material and sought to "plant" items in her column. "There appeared every morning in Hedda Hopper's office," one of her staff noted, "an envelope stamped 'rush'" containing press releases. Niven called these "bundles of gibberish," and their utility varied greatly. One useless item quoted a "famous San Francisco scalp specialist" saying "Victor Mature has Hollywood's 'most magnificent head of hair (male).'"[63] In addition to offering such information, studio publicists and hired press agents worked to manage or control what Hopper published. "Press agents are good for tips," she once said, because "they get around," but she also called them "suppress agents" for trying to keep information away from her and out of the news.[64] Other sources were informants at the studios, such as stagehands and technicians, and informants in town, including "dentists, beauticians, nurses, furniture salesmen, servants, laboratory technicians, and morticians." A dentist, for example, informed her that Clark Gable intended to enlist in the Air Force during World War II; the dentist had fixed Gable's teeth, allowing him to pass the physical examination. Hopper's "legmen" were especially important, as they were her "legs" out gathering the news at the studios and press conferences while she remained in her office. Her legmen included Hy Gardner, Spec McClure, King Kennedy, Jaik Rosenstein, Joe Ledla, Rod Volt, and Robert Shaw, but her column hid their role, giving the impression that she often visited the movie studios and sets herself.[65]

Hopper's contribution to news gathering—or as she put it, "snooping and scooping"—for her column included talking on the phone for many hours, attending social events, and having lunch at the Brown Derby restaurant, which also functioned as Parsons's "unofficial office." As Hopper wrote in 1944, "Luncheon at the Brown Derby can last anywhere from three to four hours, and during that time I might have talked to fifty different people and gotten a snip of news from each."[66] She often acted like she knew more than she did, and she always took a refusal to deny a story as a confirmation of its truth, as she did in her 1939 interview with James Roosevelt. Hopper also called on friends and colleagues, as photographer George Hurrell recalled. "My God, George, help me out. Got any dirt? I've got to get this damned column out every day—and it ain't easy!" At times, she sent a letter in advance. "One of these days I'm coming over to see you and get a story," she wrote Louis B. Mayer. "And when you see me coming, don't shut up like a clam, but give."[67]

In her interactions, Hopper had a "brisk staccato way of demanding replies rather than asking questions," David Niven noted. The actress Susan Hayward emerged from an interview feeling cross-examined: "She's acting like a district attorney."[68] A one-sided telephone conversation between Hopper and Joan Crawford about rumors of a serious romance demonstrated her interview technique:

> Hello. This is Hedda Hopper. Put Joan on . . . Hello, Joan? . . . All right, dear, tell me all about it . . . Well, he says it's pretty serious . . . Oh, come on, you can't fool me. Are you in love with him? . . . Now look, dear, I always ask personal questions . . . Well, how do you get a man to hang that much mink around your neck if you're not serious about him? . . . I know you're hedging. You can't fool Hopper . . . Well, you can answer whether you're in love with the guy and intend to marry him . . . All right, dear, you've given me your answer by indirection.[69]

To be on the receiving end of the Hopper treatment was not easy. Moreover, if a movie star refused to grant an interview or to give her the information she wanted, Hopper insulted or ignored them. "She had two weapons," Simone Signoret observed, "words that wound or the silence that kills." Some performers, such as Greta Garbo, did not submit to Hopper and survived unscathed, but many did not. One less prominent actress did her best to avoid Hopper until the columnist publicly announced that she had gained "twelve extra, unflattering pounds."[70] Ingrid Bergman remembered sitting at a party next to Gene Tierney, who had not told Hopper she was expecting a baby. "Wait till your next picture comes out," Hopper threatened. "Don't think you can expect anything good about it from me."[71]

Hopper expended even more effort to "hurt and humiliate" those who instead provided information to Louella Parsons; indeed, her rivalry with Parsons most revealed her capacity for vindictiveness and retribution. "Hedda," gossip columnist Sheilah Graham contended, "tried to ruin people who gave their stories to Louella."[72] As a consequence, "Hedda's devils became Louella's angels and vice versa." "There were two factions," Marion Davies commented. "If you talked to one, you were no friend to the other." For those who wished to remain neutral, it was a "nightmare to be invited to Hedda's and Louella's on the same night."[73] It also was a mistake to "double-plant," giving the same scoop to two columnists. During one such incident, Hopper blew up at the actress involved. "That sneaky little bitch! I'm on to her," she yelled. "She's a bitch! And I'll never use her name again!" Even Hopper's friends had to admit that "she could be a wonderful friend and a bitter enemy."[74]

Hopper's victims reacted differently. Some stars retaliated. Joseph Cotten famously "planted a kick to her posterior" at a Hollywood party, after she refused to stop printing items linking him with Deanna Durbin and upsetting his wife. Cotton later offered Cary Grant a shoe to use against the columnist when she offended him in print. In another well-known episode, Joan Bennett sent Hopper a skunk with the note, "I stink, but so do you." Hopper wrote about her "present" in her column: "It's the cutest thing! . . . I christened it Joan."[75] For other Hollywood denizens who suffered from Hopper's attacks and insults, however, negotiation was the best way forward. The studio executive and liberal Democrat Dore Schary insisted her attacks "don't concern me." "Believe me, she has no power," he wrote a friend. Even so, he kept a careful record of his appearances in her column, corresponded with and about her over the years, and sought retractions of damaging items in her column in exchange for leads on new information. "Dear Hedda," he wrote, "This telegram carries an exclusive and a plea for a retraction."[76]

Shaping such interactions was the power of Hopper's "agenda-setting" function in the industry. The content of Hopper's column told her readers "what to think *about*," and in this way she helped to establish the terms of discussion and debate about Hollywood, films, and stars. She fulfilled this function most with regard to Hollywood stars, as she provided the publicity that celebrity stardom required. Hopper's gossip was seen as "crucial to star arrival—and survival."[77] In her star coverage, she commented on their film performances and professional careers and gossiped about their personal lives. When Ingrid Bergman appeared in *Intermezzo* (1939), the film that made the actress a star in the United States, Hopper praised her performance as revealing "a unique charm" and "ease." "In other words," Hopper concluded, "she's got it!" The film's producer, David O. Selznick, thanked Hopper, adding, "I think you will be able to point back on these comments as indicating that you are something of a prophet." As an actress herself, Hopper carried confidence and credibility in her assessments of the "star-as-per-former."[78] Actors saw her as "one of them." Hattie McDaniel believed Hopper's column showed "the deep understanding that comes from years previously spent in the acting profession." "I think Hedda, having been an actress," Joan Crawford agreed, "has a right to criticize us and take us to task."[79]

Hopper's acting career, as well as her dependence as a columnist on studio cooperation and her political conservatism, also informed her judgments of the "star-as-professional."[80] Although Hopper worried about working conditions in Hollywood, she nearly always sided with studio management or followed their line. Her annual selection of "New Faces" among film actors during the last decade of her career reinforced the studios' emphasis on actors as photogenic personalities rather than workers with skills and abilities, and she joined the studios in presenting "legitimate worker complaints" as the "outbursts" of spoiled actors. When performers misbehaved on the job, studio executives would call on Hopper, as well as Parsons, to punish them in print. When Tab Hunter refused a role because "he didn't think the part was good enough," Hopper asked "how a fellow as young as Tab gets that way."[81]

As a gossip columnist, Hopper followed the stars in public and private. Whether actual or manufactured, the content of her private talk about stars was more often positive than negative and followed the conventions of celebrity journalism. She portrayed movie stars as achieving the American Dream, rising from "rags to riches" with fortitude and gratitude. "Hollywood performers on the whole are a pretty thankful lot," she declared. "Most of them came from humble beginnings."[82] She never acknowledged any barriers to upward mobility. Of Crawford, Hopper believed that "with her determination, ambition and showmanship it's a fairly foregone conclusion that she'll make a success of anything she takes up." In the case of McDaniel, she contended that "Hattie, like most people who are willing to work and sacrifice to achieve their ambition, believes that America is still full of opportunity."[83] In her private talk, Hopper repeated the "master plot of celebrity journalism," ascertained and analyzed by Charles L. Ponce de Leon as "the struggle of celebrities to achieve 'true success'"—that is, happiness in their private lives.[84] To demonstrate "true success," Hopper dedicated entire columns to the topics of happy marriages, "successful wives," and the importance of "parenthood among our screen people." In 1942, she presented the married stars Lucille Ball and Desi Arnaz as "happy as larks and just as good at the box office"—until their separation in 1944. "Doubtless they have their spats, as which couple doesn't," she wrote after their reconciliation in 1946, "but it's nothing serious."[85]

In the case of Ball and Arnaz, Hopper's claims of "true success" were false, and she knew it, revealing that she—knowingly or not—could publish fact or fiction. As a publicist of private talk, Hopper's work was fraught with complications. At times, her column included items intentionally designed to sustain a fiction, a situation not uncommon in Hollywood gossip. "My parents' whole relationship was basically a press release," Carrie Fisher admitted of the 1950s marriage of her mother, Debbie Reynolds, and her father, singer Eddie Fisher. Similarly, when the gay actor Rock Hudson was "forced" to marry a secretary named Phyllis Gates in 1955, "the first thing they did was call Hollywood gossip columnists Hedda Hopper and Louella Parsons."[86] As with Hudson's homosexuality, Hopper at times chose not to publish items that she knew to be true. The "weapon" of the gossip columnist was that of "truth," according to historian Garry Wills, but "it was a weapon in the sense that theorists of [nuclear] deterrence advocate: it was powerful so long as she never had to use it." Hopper knew more about the private lives of Hollywood denizens than she told, and individuals and the industry relied on this arrangement and feared exposure. "That's the house that fear built," Hopper said of her Beverly Hills home.[87] Sometimes she hinted at a hidden truth, as when she wrote about the "interesting trio" of Peter Lawford, Keenan Wynn, and Dorothy Dandridge at a restaurant. Although this dinner occurred during an adulterous affair between Dandridge and Lawford, Hopper raised the possibility of a homosexual affair between Lawford and Wynn. There also were times when Hopper published private information she thought true but turned out to be false. "You can't fool this old bag," she used to say, but she could be fooled and, when she was, she was furious.[88]

By publishing private talk, Hopper contributed to the construction of what film scholars have called star personas, a concept that integrated what was known—or what the studios wanted known—about stars both on-screen and off-screen. A product of the "star-making machinery" and successful typecasting of the studio system, star personas emerged from a powerful star system, which interlinked specific stars, studios, and film genres, and produced and sold the movies as star vehicles.[89] Many stars resented the exposure of true or manufactured private lives that stardom entailed. "The bad part of Hollywood is that you have to live your life in a goldfish bowl," Ronald Reagan told Hopper when his marriage to Jane Wyman failed. "I like to keep my private life private," Ingrid Bergman informed Hopper, but the columnist believed stars could not have "their popularity and their privacy too." Other stars agreed. "It *is* a necessary part of the trappings of Hollywood," Joan Crawford said of gossip.[90] Star personas needed private talk, and by publicizing it Hopper fulfilled her most important industry function.

Early in her career, Hopper presented stars' on- and off-screen lives as consistent, with their fictional characters and actual personalities similar in values, attitudes, behavior, and background. In 1940, she wanted her fellow Republican Irene Dunne to play the role of the Progressive-era reformer Jane Addams in a biographical film. "You see, Jane Addams, having been one of our greatest philanthropists and devoted her life to service, must be played by a woman without any taint or suspicion of scandal."[91] In seeking consistency, Hopper shared the studios' aims rather than that of fan magazines, which explored the "gap between a star's public persona and her or his 'real' self," according to film scholar Sarah Barry, "in ways that emphasized the existence rather than the closure of that gap." Hopper sought closure with regard to both morality and politics. Yet the existence of that gap between "reel" and "real" lives—the "clash of codes" in film scholar Richard Dyer's terms—provided the best material for her column: star scandals.[92] Even better, in Hopper's eyes, were political scandals involving the opposition party, the Democrats.

Publicity and Right-Wing Politics

Hedda Hopper never provided publicity for Hollywood alone. "I'm very much interested in politics," she declared in 1944.[93] From the beginning of her career as a gossip columnist, she covered the developments in domestic politics and foreign policy—the hard news—that concerned her, advocated for her agenda of political and moral conservatism, and publicized her Republican Party affiliation and activities. Due to such political content, editors and publishers often reminded her that she was hired to write about entertainment, not politics. "A word of warning to you," wrote one before Hopper attended a Republican Party convention, "you are a Hollywood, not a political correspondent." She was "frequently warned" to focus on cinema and celebrities and "not try to settle international affairs."[94] But admonitions did not stop her; instead she proudly promoted herself as a political figure. In 1944, when announcing a new play "about a Hollywood columnist who aspires to be a political columnist," she added, "I couldn't be more flattered!" And at President Dwight D. Eisenhower's inauguration in 1953, she reported commiserating with Irene Dunne about "our nonexistent political careers" and wishing it otherwise.[95]

During her gossip career, the Democratic Party dominated national politics, with only one Republican president—and, to Hopper, an insufficiently conservative one—Eisenhower in the 1950s. Moreover, at the beginning and end of her career, Hollywood appeared to be dominated by liberal-left politics. In the 1930s, the movie capital vote for Franklin D. Roosevelt was well over eighty percent, "making Hollywood solid New Deal territory," and in the 1960s Democrats could count on a "parade of big names" for their events, while Republicans "had to rely on a rather small coterie of old-time stars who had long decorated conservative banquets."[96] Consequently, Hopper felt on the defensive politically. "I was almost thrown out of the industry," she believed, due to her conservative politics. "I was almost thrown out of Hollywood."[97] While the era of liberal consensus no longer looks so monolithic to historians of the mid-twentieth-century United States—a view reinforced by the political aspects of Hopper's gossip career—it felt monolithic to Hopper, shaped her strident political tone and perspective, and put her on the lookout for ways to bring public disgrace on the Democratic opposition. In her political commentary, as in her industry news and gossip, she eschewed any semblance of journalistic neutrality or objectivity and instead acted the bully, asserted opinions, appealed to emotions, and argued in what now would be called "sound bites."[98]

Hopper often presented herself as a lone voice on the political Right, but she was far from alone. There always were powerful conservatives in the movie capital, in Los Angeles, and in the newspaper business. Studio executives were generally politically conservative and definitely antiunion. An early example of studio-driven political campaigning occurred against the Socialist writer Upton Sinclair's bid to be governor of California in 1934, and by the 1950s "the Hollywood conservatives' victory over the reviled left seemed total and irreversible." Even *Motion Picture Magazine* touted itself to Hopper as "this Republican stronghold" when trying to keep her as an author.[99] The city of Los Angeles not only had a reputation for reactionary politics but also, together with neighboring Orange County, gave rise to a New Right that successfully challenged the dominance of the Old Right and began to transform American politics during Hopper's lifetime. Moreover, Hopper's home newspaper and syndicate reinforced her political conservatism. Under the leadership of Harry and then Norman Chandler, the priority at the *Los Angeles Times* was the promotion of local business interests, including those of the Chandler family, while Colonel Robert R. McCormick, owner of the *Chicago Tribune* and the Chicago Tribune–New York News Syndicate, stood for "the ultraconservative right wing in American politics."[100] It was in Hopper's correspondence with McCormick that she most fully and revealingly expressed her right-wing politics.

In offering political commentary, Hopper was not even unique among gossip columnists, although the depth of her political commitment and the continuity in her conservative ideas and beliefs over her long career stood out. Ed Sullivan commented on politics, a fact she resented later in her career when she had been "muzzled" by her editors. "I don't understand why he can write about politics and I can't," she wrote in 1960.[101] Louella Parsons also discussed political issues, particularly anti-Communism. Yet, as an employee of the increasingly right-wing William Randolph Hearst, her anti-Communist stance "was less a matter of personal ideology than company policy," according to Samantha Barbas. George Eells agreed that "her heart was not in politics." Walter Winchell's heart was. In the 1930s, inspired by President Roosevelt, he "made the seemingly improbable leap from gossipmonger to political commentator," Neal Gabler states.[102] Even so, Winchell's politics were personal, very much influenced by relationships rather than ideology, and he shifted from supporting liberal causes in the 1930s to conservatism in the 1950s, where he found common ground with Hopper. In contrast, Hopper's politics, while also personal, were primarily ideological—whereby long-standing conservative ideas and beliefs determined the political positions she took—and she never wavered in her dedication to using her column in the interests of her political agenda.

Hopper was a traditional liberal or "libertarian," although the term was not used until later in her life, and embraced antistatism. Committed to the principle of liberty in economic and civic life, she joined other conservatives in fearing that "big government" undermined individual liberty. "Already we've traveled quite a distance down the highway toward 'statism'—a system of government that sticks its nose into and regulates every form of human endeavor," she asserted.[103] She vociferously criticized the New Deal and the Roosevelts she blamed for it, and she opposed any government intervention in the economy, be it social provision or regulation, particularly of the motion picture industry. As it turned out, the beginning of Hopper's gossip career in 1938 coincided with the beginning of the U.S. government's successful antitrust case, later called the Paramount case, against the big movie companies to end their oligopolistic control of the industry. One trade practice Congress took aim at was block booking of movies, whereby theater owners had to take all the films produced by a studio in a given year, and Hopper strongly opposed the resulting Neely bill. "Each film has to be sold alone and on its merit," she explained, warning in 1940 the bill's passage would mean high ticket prices and poor-quality films. That year a consent decree between the government and the major studios did limit block booking, but without the consequences Hopper predicted.[104]

What most symbolized the state for Hopper, as for other antistatist Americans, was the income tax.[105] She consistently complained about her federal and state taxes, although she was delighted when the Internal Revenue Service allowed her a $5,000 deduction for her famous hats as a business expense. She referred to "the days BT—before taxes" and to one of her relatives, her Uncle Sam, as "not the one who collects taxes."[106] In a 1940 column, Hopper featured a tax protest in Albany, New York, involving eight thousand taxpayers marching under the banner, "Save us from the tax ruin." "Come On, Wake Up," she urged, glad that Americans were "beginning to bestir themselves." Hopper also discussed the "top tax" rates applied to Hollywood filmmakers and provided specific figures for income minus federal and state taxes, as with one actress who earned $150,000 and paid $65,000 in federal taxes and $14,450 in state taxes. After that, Hopper claimed little remained. "You can begin saving pennies for Ginger Rogers," she wrote in 1943. "It's a cinch she'll soon be on the street corner with a tin cup."[107]

Hopper's antistatism and fear of government eroding individual freedom dovetailed with her anti-Communism. In her fight against Communism, she corresponded and cooperated closely with FBI agents and bureau director, J. Edgar Hoover, and worked with other anti-Communist forces, including the American Legion. She was one of the few who welcomed the scrutiny of Congressman Martin P. Dies, a Texas Democrat, dedicated anti-Communist, and chairman of the Special Committee on Un-American Activities, forerunner of the House Committee on Un-American Activities (HUAC). In January 1940, Dies contended that Communist subversives had infiltrated Hollywood, and he launched an investigation of the movie industry the following month. Given that "the line between Marxism and Judaism seemed to be indistinct" for Dies, many Jewish filmmakers feared "a witch-hunt."[108] Hopper, in contrast, welcomed the investigation. Hollywood should be "grateful," she argued, as Dies was not just "talking about the Red activities in Hollywood" but also bringing "the names of the guilty out into the open." "You see, we have so many color-blind people here—perhaps from the glaring sunshine—lots of them don't know the difference between red, pink, and blue."[109] In August 1940, Dies cleared some leading actors but claimed "numerous" others were Communists or sympathizers.[110] According to Hopper, her readers agreed. "Judging by comments coming my way from all directions, it's evident that the public still thinks it sees a bright red tinge in Hollywood," and she urged her readers to take action so that "un-American activity in Hollywood will end."[111]

Although "un-American activities" also included fascism, Hopper's main focus was Communism, and she first looked for Communists in labor unions. Hopper was fiercely antiunion. Well-known as an antiunion company town, Hollywood, "virtually unorganized in 1929," became "fully unionized from top to bottom" by 1945, at the same time union membership in the United States went from eight percent of the national workforce to forty-five percent.[112] During that period, the talent guilds organized, including the Screen Actors Guild (SAG), of which Hopper was a reluctant and unhappy member. She only joined in June 1937, after SAG won recognition as a bargaining unit and a contract for actors, and membership became required for employment.[113] She supported anyone in Hollywood who took an antiunion stance, as she did in 1945 when Cecil B. DeMille refused to pay a required one-dollar union assessment for a political cause he opposed. Hopper dedicated a section of her column, "Stand Wins Praise," to the "thousands of letters C. B. De Mille got praising him for his stand." She also compared the talent guilds unfavorably to what had been the industry's company union, the Academy of Motion Picture Arts and Sciences, under which she claimed employers and employees "worked in harmony and did a magnificent job." "During that time we had no strikes," she added, blaming "radicals" and the guilds, rather than employers, for the existence of labor conflict in Hollywood.[114]

Hopper's libertarian opposition to government stopped at the nation's borders, as national defense was one function she believed the state should provide, yet her position on the use of the U.S. military changed over time. At the beginning of her career, she was a committed isolationist and campaigned in her column against U.S. intervention in World War II. In the postwar period, however, she joined other "old isolationists in the Cold War era" and became an aggressive interventionist.[115] Motivating both positions was her fervent belief in America's national greatness. Despite her Quaker heritage, Hopper was not a pacifist, but rather a militant conservative and nationalist. "Let's make a greater nation by preserving peace and freedom," she exhorted as war began in Europe in 1939.[116] But in the Cold War era, the same aim required intervention to protect the United States and stop the spread of Soviet Communism. In both the World War II and Cold War eras, she endorsed a strong defense as well as America's "informal empire." In contrast to other isolationists who were strongly anti-imperialist, such as Senator Robert A. Taft, Republican of Ohio, Hopper was very comfortable with the United States seeking and holding overseas territories. In 1939, Hopper wrote a glowing review of the American occupation of the Philippines, then a U.S. commonwealth but scheduled for independence in 1946. "Only a few dictator politicians in Manila want an independent government," she inaccurately claimed.[117]

While libertarian principles motivated most of Hopper's political positions, personal prejudices also played a role, including anti-Semitism and nativism. Operating in an industry dominated by Jewish businessmen, Hopper recognized that "the Jews invented Hollywood."[118] She publicly maintained a strong stance against anti-Semitism and privately maintained caring relationships with Jewish Americans. When accused of being anti-Semitic, Hopper offered a defense typical of those accused of prejudice: "I am *not* anti-Semitic. Many of my friends are Jewish!" Of Hopper's private attitudes, close Jewish friends later said "if any prejudice existed, it was unconscious." Yet, when given a chance to help the daughters of Louis B. Mayer enroll in an exclusive private school, she refused. "They will not take Jews," she said. Moreover, in her personal correspondence, she revealed anti-Semitic attitudes. When discussing various "Jewish gentlemen" in a letter to Robert McCormick, she referred to "their race," separating Jews from gentiles and using religion and culture to distance McCormick and herself from Jews, whom she called "those of little faith."[119]

But Hopper's anti-Semitism was not always "off-the-record," and neither was her nativism. Her long-lasting campaign against Charlie Chaplin exposed both prejudices. Hopper assumed the actor and filmmaker was Jewish, as did many other critics on the political Right, and she often drew on anti-Semitic stereotypes to denounce him.[120] She continually referred to his personal wealth, estimated at upwards of $30 million, and accused him of miserliness. Instead of giving to her favorite charities, "Mr. Charlie Chaplin has held onto all his . . . money." "He's had an opportunity to contribute to the Motion Picture Relief Fund Home," she declared. "He didn't." When Chaplin denied the mistaken assumption that he was Jewish, Hopper criticized him. "Jews should be proud of their heritage," she wrote smugly. "Christ was a Jew."[121] As a nativist, Hopper also believed non-Americans living within the borders of the United States posed a threat to the nation, and Chaplin was the immigrant alien she saw as most threatening. The English-born Chaplin infuriated Hopper, as he had lived in the United States for decades, making movies and money, and yet never became an American citizen. She constantly referred to his lack of U.S. citizenship, calling Chaplin "the man who came to dinner and stayed 40 years" and considering him insufficiently appreciative or patriotic toward the United States: "He—who's not an American citizen—continues taking advantage of the tolerance of a country which made him millions and gave him a home."[122]

Hopper also held racial prejudices against African Americans and other groups, although, as with her anti-Semitism, she refrained from expressing these prejudices publicly. In fact, she criticized overt racial discrimination, as when singer Marian Anderson was required to use the freight instead of the passenger elevator at a hotel. Yet, when Jackie Robinson, the legendary baseball player who integrated the major leagues, traveled to Hollywood to consult on his biopic *The Jackie Robinson Story* (1950) and made the requisite stop at Hopper's house for an interview, he heard her yell to her maid, "Maude, if you see a nigger around the house, don't be scared. It's only Jackie Robinson."[123] Hopper's casual and continued use of a pejorative term well-known to be hated by African Americans, subjected to organized protests in Hollywood, and successfully cut from some movie dialogue, indicated the limits of her racial attitudes. So, too, did her paternalism toward members of minority groups whom she saw as inferior and often demeaned, albeit unconsciously. "Our stars have had some mighty tough competition lately from babies and animals," she wrote in a 1940 item on the growing prominence of black performers in film. "Now they'd better look out for the colored race."[124] Hopper's endorsement of Hollywood's racial representations that repeated and reinforced stereotypes, such as the smiling, submissive, happy "darky," further demonstrated her belief in white superiority and became one way she sought to undermine the modern Civil Rights Movement.

Informed by both principles and prejudices, Hopper's political conservatism went together with her moral conservatism. She believed in the importance of family and religion, and while she reflected many of the changes in women's lives that occurred over her lifetime—including the decline of the patriarchal family, the rise of divorce, the expansion in women's wage earning, and the achievement of women's suffrage—she very much stood apart on sexual matters. Despite a dramatic change, even a "revolution," in American women's sexual conduct in the first decades of the twentieth century, Hopper remained true to the Victorian ideals of the century in which she was born. "You see Hedda came from Quaker stock," Frances Marion stated. "While the rest of us were throwing our petticoats over the windmill, she never would."[125] Hopper not only believed vehemently in sexual virtue for herself but for others in Hollywood as well. When she arrived in the movie capital in the 1920s, the industry was amid a "moral makeover" in the wake of several star scandals, most shocking being the comedian Roscoe "Fatty" Arbuckle's arrest and trials for manslaughter due to the death of a young actress in 1921 and 1922. As part of the makeover, the studios inserted "morals clauses" into employee contracts, allowing the studios to fire an employee for social or sexual impropriety or causing a public scandal. For Hopper, the existence of morals clauses sanctioned her media exposure and moral judgment of private beliefs and behavior.[126]

Despite her moral conservatism, Hopper departed from so-called traditional family values with regard to women, gays, and lesbians. She prioritized and promoted marriage and motherhood for women, as did other celebrity journalists, but this stance reflected her sincere belief that marriage and motherhood were keys to women's happiness rather than the only vocations open to women. In keeping with the reality of her own life, she always defended wage-earning women and felt they deserved equality and respect in the family and the workplace. And while she made disparaging private remarks about homosexuality, and Hollywood insiders have described her as "homophobic," the author William J. Mann sees this description as "an oversimplification." She had lesbian and gay friends and colleagues and dutifully kept Hollywood's homosexual secrets from the American public—at least until the end of her career. What raised Hopper's ire, according to Mann, were gay people who "tried to *pass*" with her and the rest of the industry.[127] She wanted and demanded access to everyone's "real" lives. Where Hopper could, however, she did act as a "moral gatekeeper," a role that dovetailed with her conviction that the movie industry had a "mission to instruct and to entertain in good taste" and included her campaigns for "wholesome" film content.[128]

Hopper's campaigns went beyond Hollywood, however, as she dedicated herself and lent her celebrity to Republican Party activism. She was particularly interested in working with and mobilizing women through the party's Women's Division and Republican Women's Clubs. Like other prominent Republican women, Hopper would never have called herself a "feminist," but she advocated strongly for women's rights and advancement in politics. She campaigned for Republican candidates for various offices, most prominently the presidency, beginning in 1932 with Herbert Hoover and ending in 1964 with Barry Goldwater. In 1940, she urged her readers not to vote for President Roosevelt when he ran for an unprecedented third term in office. "The old slogan, 'You can't change horses in mid-stream,' doesn't hold," she argued. "You can change anything any time if it's for the better." November 4 "is our last opportunity to vote for freedom," she proclaimed in 1952, before the election that brought her party back to power, with victories for the presidential ticket of Dwight D. Eisenhower and Richard M. Nixon, as well as a Republican majority in Congress. During their reelection campaign in 1956, she held at her home the kickoff meeting for the "Women's Brigade for Ike and Dick."[129] She took seriously the Republican Party's reputation as the "Party of Lincoln" and extended her racial paternalism to pose for photographs with black Republicans to "show the friendship we have for our colored friends."[130] She spoke at political rallies and in political advertisements. For the 1950 midterm elections, she recorded messages for a radio series called "Republican Women Speak Up," which a Republican Party official deemed "wonderfully effective." Moreover, Hopper contributed funds and conducted fundraising for the Republican Party. "Your spirit and your ability and prestige are tremendous assets to the Republican Party," wrote the executive director of the party's Women's Division. "If we could we would add a halo to every one of your famous hats."[131]

Hopper saw herself as a player in the Republican Party. She attended the Republican National Convention for the first time in 1944—"I go—not as an onlooker, not as an actress—but as a correspondent for the syndicate and radio commentator"—and attended regularly thereafter. At the conventions, like most rank-and-file Republican women in the post–World War II period, she always sought to nominate the most conservative of candidates, as in 1948 and 1952 when she favored Senator Robert Taft, leader of conservatives in Congress and known as "Mr. America." His defeat by moderate Republicans in 1952, despite arriving at the convention with a majority of delegates, "left a lingering bitterness in the mouths of many conservatives," and Hopper was no exception. "All of us who believed Bob Taft and gloried in what he stood for will have a tough time finding another Mr. America," she wrote following his death in 1953.[132] Hopper also attempted to mediate disputes between opposing politicians within her party, as in the 1950s when she took it on herself to write both President Eisenhower and Senator Joseph R. McCarthy. She told Eisenhower she supported McCarthy in his efforts to root out Communists in government—as should "everyone who calls himself a Republican and an American"—and warned McCarthy not to criticize Eisenhower for being insufficiently anti-Communist, because "if you split the Republican party, the Commies and the Democrats are going to have the last laugh." Hopper corresponded with, interviewed, and promoted prominent political figures throughout her career. When Ronald Reagan, a New Deal Democrat in his youth, "finally saw the light" and "joined her list of patriots," Hopper dedicated a column to his political convictions. "Ronnie is opposed to all forces that seek to curb or destroy individual liberty," she reported happily.[133]

While Hopper's participation in the Republican Party was not always welcome or without conflict, her party appreciated her attacks on Democrats. In rare instances, she treated members of the opposing party kindly. She confessed to being charmed when she first met President Roosevelt. "I'm getting out of here quick before you make me into a Democrat." More typical of her interactions with Democrats was her rude refusal to shake President Harry S. Truman's hand, because even if he was the president "I didn't help put him there."[134] Also more typical were her public maneuvers and private machinations to destroy the Democratic opposition. One Democrat Hopper set out to demolish was Helen Gahagan Douglas, a former actress married to actor Melvyn Douglas. Hopper worked against Gahagan Douglas from her first congressional run in 1944, because she "is running from . . . a district filled with communists and negroes." "I feel she'd be a very dangerous woman if she's ever elected to Congress," Hopper wrote.[135] She then strongly supported Richard Nixon in his bitter, no-holds-barred 1950 campaign against Gahagan Douglas for a U.S. Senate seat from California. After Nixon's resounding victory, when Gahagan Douglas was in line for a position at the United Nations, Hopper asked Nixon what she could do "to kill Helen Gahagan's chances at the U.N." Days later on her radio show Hopper announced, "Helen Gahagan wasn't acceptable to the citizens of the state of California as Senator [and] now she's representing the whole United States in the United Nations."[136]

Hopper's Republican Party activism brought together partisan politics and mass media gossip, an intertwining that fell into the long tradition of gossip in American public life documented by writer Gail Collins.[137] For Hopper, her Republican Party activism was a way to advance her political standing and her gossip career and to achieve, as her business manager wrote on the eve of Hopper's participation in the 1952 Republican Convention, "a greater position in the nation, and the admiration of your public." Through her party politics and her newspaper column, Hopper pushed her agenda of political and moral conservatism. This combination of aims made Hopper something of a "fusionist" before conservatives adopted "fusionism" in the 1950s as a way to bridge the libertarians and traditionalists among them.[138] Yet, in promoting the power of gossip—not that of the state—to police personal life, she sided more with the libertarian principles at the core of the Old Right than with the traditionalist convictions of the emerging New Right. Importantly,

Hopper's political efforts occurred during what she considered the dark days of Democratic Party rule, when the electoral future of the Republican Party seemed in doubt. Within this political climate, Republicans decided to pursue "politics by other means," such as scandalmongering and accusing Democrats of being "soft on communism."[139] The public exposure of political and moral corruption, whether true or false, was a pursuit Hedda Hopper felt well suited and well positioned to undertake. After all, she had an audience of millions, and numerous readers eager to read and respond to her movie and political publicity.

Hedda Hopper signs autographs for her fans at a movie premiere, 1941. (Courtesy of the Academy of Motion Picture Arts and Sciences.)

Readers, Respondents, and Fans

"My dear Mrs. Hopper," wrote one of Hedda Hopper's respondents. "Since I am a reader of your column, one of the few I consider worth reading pertaining to Hollywood, I would like to take some of my time and also some of yours to give you some views my friends and I have reached concerning movies, etc." She then went on to describe herself. "I am 25 years old, married 9 years, and the mother of 3 children . . . just an average housewife who used to like to go to the movies." This letter was characteristic of those saved by Hopper. In demographic terms, the letter writer was a woman, married, with children, a homemaker, and from a city, in this case Oklahoma City. Moreover, the letter's content fit with how Hopper's fans represented their experience and understanding of Hollywood gossip.[1] A warm relationship with Hopper, the value assigned to reading Hopper's column, an interest in the movies and the movie industry, a desire to offer opinions, recognition of Hopper's column as a forum for expression, and community connections and conversations appeared in other extant letters to Hopper.

This reader's primary purpose in writing also appeared in her letter. "But lately we would rather stay home," she told Hopper. "Why? I'll tell you it's because of the personal lives of most of the Top Stars. They behave so disgustingly in public that frankly we do not wish to use our money [in] support." "Perhaps if enough people stay away," she advocated, "the men who make the movies will insist on Stars with clean morals. Then I shall be happy to return to the Movies."[2] For this reader, Hollywood gossip offered the public exposure of private acts, a place to express moral condemnation, and a spur to political action, in this case a consumer boycott to bring about change in Hollywood.

Letters such as this one were prompted, published, and prized by Hopper to demonstrate her significance and support among her readers, but they also recounted how some members of her audience read and made meaning out of Hollywood gossip within the context of their own lives and experiences. For historians familiar with limited access to sources from actual, historical consumers of popular culture, the extant letters to Hopper constitute a large collection, perhaps a thousand. Yet this reader response is only a very small number of the letters Hopper likely received during her twenty-eight-year career, given the volume sent to other gossip columnists. In the 1920s, Louella Parsons received over a thousand letters per week, while in the 1940s Jimmie Fidler got seven hundred letters per week when writing his column and three thousand to five thousand when his radio program aired.[3] Given the small proportion of letters saved and safeguarded, this collection cannot be considered representative of Hollywood filmgoers, Hopper's readers, or even her respondents generally. Instead, these are the letters Hopper or her staff selected to keep and archivists managed to preserve. Moreover, the oftentimes substantive and political content of these letters indicates that these qualities must have been emphasized in the initial selection process; certainly, these qualities can be found in the portion Hopper felt worthy of publication.

With awareness of the highly selective, partial, and constructed nature of these published and unpublished letters, they illuminate the practice of Hollywood gossip among Hopper's respondents, particularly women. Together with Hopper, these reader-respondents made her column part of the public sphere where they exchanged information, debated issues, advocated action about both entertainment and politics, and transformed their cinema spectatorship into new forms of citizenship. While Hopper's respondents engaged in public sphere activities, they also were participating openly and explicitly in what scholars define as "fandom," a collectivity of active, enthusiastic cultural consumers or, in the words of theorist John Fiske, "excessive readers" who differ "in degree rather than kind" from ordinary spectators.[4] Many of Hopper's respondents embraced identities as fans, signing their letters "A 'Fan' of Yours" or "A Movie Fan," but a striking number denied they were fans of Hopper or the movies. They included statements such as "I have never written a fan letter," "I am writing my very first 'fan letter,'" and "I have never been a so-called 'fan.'" Both groups often put "fan" in quotation marks. The term "fan" in the context of the movies connoted a young girl and a desire for memorabilia, such as the photographs or autographs of stars. "Never a week goes by without letters in my mail back from movie-struck youngsters," Hopper wrote. One of Hopper's legmen described Hopper's typical reader as "Minnie Schmo, lying in bed and cramming her face with milk chocolates and reading hungrily about Hollywood."[5]

Both male and female letter writers sought to differentiate themselves from these negative connotations. "I've never written to any celebrity," wrote one man to Hopper. "I'm no autograph hound." "Being 'fair and fat and fifty,' I am way out of the fan class," wrote a woman from Georgia.[6] The word "fan" also suggested an element of irrationality, emotionality, even hysteria, from the word "fanatic." One who was a fan by definition could not engage in the rational discourse required for the serious discussion of public issues, which was exactly what they were doing in the forum provided by Hopper's gossip column. For respondents who rejected the fan identity, disassociating themselves from negative, demeaning views of fans allowed them to claim political legitimacy. For other respondents, however, identifying as fans never posed a contradiction as they joined Hopper in the practice and politics of Hollywood gossip.[7]

Crafting Columns, Creating Community

Hedda Hopper recognized the importance of her readers, respondents, and fans to her gossip career and political agenda, and she crafted her columns, as well as other writing and performances, with this importance in mind. She sought to foster a sense of community and participation among her readers and listeners. For some scholars, gossip delivered through the mass media is not truly gossip, because the information flows only one way rather than being exchanged as with face-to-face gossip.[8] But exchanges of information typified Hopper's work, as she asked for and answered letters from members of her audience and encouraged others to participate by writing letters of their own. These efforts paid off, as Hopper used her mail with newspaper editors, radio executives, and movie producers to support her positions and demonstrate her influence. "I have 50 letters expressing the same sentiment," she wrote an editor at the *Los Angeles Times*. "So you see I do have some readers." Louella Parsons also used her fan mail to get back on the air after her radio series was cancelled in the 1950s. In Hollywood, the volume of Hopper's mail allowed her to represent herself as "speaking for the public" in an industry uncertain of "what the public wanted."[9] This situation existed most clearly early in Hopper's career, when her and Hollywood's primary audience—women—appeared to overlap. She also was not beyond manipulating her audience, as when she published an item just to create controversy and generate letters, allowing her to brag about her influence. According to one media commentator, "in the name of the great American public, she fixes an authoritative eye on the industry," and, due to her relationship with her vast readership, "in the outlands Miss Hopper represents a strident voice of authority that Hollywood has learned to heed."[10]

Where Hopper most directly and consistently addressed her readers was in her regular weekday and Saturday columns, which brought the distant world of cinema closer. These columns averaged eight hundred words, while her Sunday stories were about twice as long, and were profiles of a single motion picture personality based on an interview. She also published short news stories that announced late-breaking developments, such as marriages, divorces, and births and often appeared on the front page of the newspaper. In all her writings, Hopper made it clear she was an avid filmgoer. She would exclaim that an actor or actress in a particular movie "broke my heart" and "brought tears to my eyes," or that a film "swept my emotion with it," and she often thanked the movie industry for "giving us all the lifting hours." In this way, Hopper reinforced the idea of movies as primarily entertainment, which fit with the code of "pure entertainment" held by studio executives and with the desires of theater owners. "'If you want to send a message, use Western Union,' snapped Sam Goldwyn, or maybe it was Harry Warner," film historian Thomas Doherty writes.[11] But this contention that Hollywood films were escapist hid the fact that messages—social, cultural, and political—were always sent, and Hopper knew it. She just wanted the messages to be her own.

In her Hollywood reporting, Hopper sent her own messages, and mostly she promoted the industry. Early in her career, she regularly reported to the studios "the number of plugs" she had given their stars and films. "I don't know of anyone in the industry who will praise a good picture or a good performance more than Hedda Hopper," Joan Crawford recalled. "I don't know anyone who will take her whole column and do that."[12] At a time when the Academy Awards were studio-controlled, and "all Oscar voting patterns were subject to change at the drop of a memo," Hopper supported the industry's ceremony of self-congratulation, praised and even created Oscar contenders in her column—"Insiders say that Joan Crawford is delivering such a terrific performance in 'Mildred Pierce' that she's a cinch for the Academy Award"— and campaigned for special Oscars for those she felt deserving. In return, movie advertisements quoted Hopper's compliments of films and filmmakers. "Superb," Hopper said about *For Whom the Bell Tolls* (1943), starring Ingrid Bergman. "After seeing it you're so proud to be connected with an industry that can do a superb job."[13] While she devoted most attention to the work and contributions of the "above the line" employees, such as directors, screenwriters, and starring actors, she did not neglect the less well-known "below the line" workers, such as general cast members and technicians.

Hopper also strongly criticized the industry, earning the respect of her audience but also the wrath of studio executives. "Why do we give her the material," one asked, "and then have her turn around and slug us with it?"[14] "I can only do the job I try to do in Hollywood by being honest," she wrote. "After all, I haven't been brought up in the Hollywood School of Journalism. I've never learned its rules. So, therefore, when I have an opinion, I express it—no matter if I lose face or friends by doing so."[15] In addition to passing concerns, such as the fate of unemployed actors and the push for actresses "to reduce to the point of emaciation," she consistently condemned the industry for its unequal treatment of women and for the decline of glamour. "Hollywood is unfair to women and I'm out to prove it," she argued, and over time she pointed out the lack of women producers, directors, and, later in her career, actresses in the list of "Top Ten Box-Office Stars." She proposed starting a "movement" for more women directors, and exclaimed when a woman rose from script girl to screenwriter to coproducer "Hurray! Another Hollywood woman gets her chance." As for the "cause of glamour," Hopper commented at the end of her career, "I've been fighting a losing battle for years." And she had. "We've deglamourized Hollywood," she stated in 1938. "Good-bye to the romantic age of motion pictures," she said the next year.[16]

A similar mix of praise and criticism typified Hopper's coverage and reviews of specific films. She commented on films at different points in the process: from production, through distribution, to exhibition. She considered herself a "casting arbiter," insisting on certain performers, such as Ingrid Bergman, playing or not playing certain roles. Hopper claimed and received credit for Bergman's casting as a nun in The Bells of St. Mary's (1945). Hopper knew about studio screen tests and referred to them in her column, even after a film was made with different players. "If Ann Richards had played the part, she would have broken your heart."[17] She expressed concern about the industry's system of self-censorship, run since 1934 by the Production Code Administration (PCA). Although Hopper agreed with the conservative "moral vision" of the Production Code and believed it kept the "sin out of cinema," she sought a "more workable system" between the PCA and the studios. In one case due to a PCA "edict, two extra days of shooting were required on the picture." Echoing studio criticisms, she found this time-consuming, costly, and "surprising," because the PCA "okays the script before it goes into production."[18] If Hopper liked a film—and its filmmakers—she reviewed it favorably and promoted it fully. "Socko" was the heading for her discussion of Fort Apache (1948), which "put us back in the picture business." But if she disliked a film and those who made it, particularly because of their leftist or liberal politics, she did not hold back either. She found Orson Welles's controversial masterpiece Citizen Kane (1941) "chopped up" and "lacking any great imagination," and named a Dore Schary film her choice for "1st worst picture of all time."[19]

Hopper issued her judgments from her office, where she worked on her columns, stories, and radio scripts with her staff. Her office suite was located in the Guaranty Building near the corner of Hollywood and Vine, included a lobby and three rooms, one of which was Hopper's. Her legman, Jaik Rosenstein, described it:

> The atmosphere is that of a combination newspaper office, junk shop, wardrobe closet, and theatrical dressing room. There are hats and hatboxes, a dress hanging precariously over the door, a broken lamp, an old period chair lacking one arm, a beat old sofa, shelves disorderly piled with all kinds of books and bric-a-brac. And a great, weatherbeaten old desk, cluttered with hundreds of fan and business letters, paste jars, pencils, scissors, notebooks, magazines, lipsticks, compacts, hairpins, and a silk stocking with a bad run.[20]

Hopper employed a sizable office staff. By 1942, "two leg men, one rewrite woman, two girl clerks to handle fan mail, two secretaries," and a business manager, her "brain" Dema Harshbarger, worked for her.[21] "She'd come sailing into the office in the morning," Patsy Gaile remembered, "calling out, 'Hi, slaves! How's everybody?' And then she'd start: 'Get me Walt Disney and that son of a bitch at Columbia!' We'd ask which one and she'd say, 'The baldheaded one!'" Hopper could not type and so dictated her column in a "frenzied manner," while smoking "incessantly" and pacing the floor. "That was why her column was different from anyone else's," Gaile added. "Hedda never sat down to write."[22]

Hopper's work process contributed to the chatty tone of her gossip, which fit her personality and the conventions of celebrity journalism. As did other gossip columnists, including Louella Parsons, Hopper adopted an intimate and breezy style. "Last week I had one of those days," she noted, or after relating her busy schedule exclaimed, "What a life!"[23] She treated Hollywood stars informally, calling them by their first names and implying intimacy, although she did not do the same for studio heads or producers. Like Walter Winchell, but not quite with his panache, she included slangy phrases, as when she used "do-re-mi" to refer to money for a musician or had "a don't-quote-me chat" with a Hollywood star. She introduced an item with "this came by mule train," and she corrected small errors in her column with "my typewriter slipped." Hopper drew analogies and metaphors from current events, as during the Cold War when an actor she interviewed "exploded like an atomic cocktail" and a couple's marital difficulties meant "an iron curtain of silence has been thrown around the Beverly Hills home."[24] Her eighth-grade education and lack of journalism training showed up in her poor grammar, including split infinitives and dangling participles, which her staff tried to correct. "Let 'er split! Let it dangle," she would holler. According to the *New York Times*, "there was a fey quality to Miss Hopper's columns," owing to dictating, little editing, and no fact-checking.[25]

Hopper's gossip also had a choppy structure. Winchell famously innovated with his placement of ellipses, or "three dots" as he called them, in between items, creating "a fragmentary new journalistic form."[26] Hopper did not use ellipses, but her column similarly jumped from item to item, rarely with a transition. The juxtaposition of some items could be jarring, as when she moved from a rousing attack on "our Red brethren" to "Bette Davis and Bill Sherry are remodeling."[27] She frequently shifted from entertainment to politics and back again in her column and on the air. One of her radio series regularly included two interviews: one with a Hollywood personality, such as Humphrey Bogart, and another with a "public figure," such as the American Legion national commander Erle Cocke. In her personal correspondence, she did the same. "To go from movies to politics for a minute," she wrote one correspondent.[28] Hopper's Sunday stories offered more opportunity to develop a narrative, usually about stars achieving the American Dream or "true success" in their personal life, and these stories worked to foster audience sympathy and identification with the stars.[29] But an uneven structure characterized Hopper's column, allowing it to be easily edited for size and content, particularly political or libelous material, and reordered by local newspapers subscribing to her syndication service. This editorial process meant audiences could be reading very different columns depending on their location.

Hopper's chatty tone and choppy structure mimicked conversation, particularly women's conversation, and she joined other columnists and radio broadcasters in bringing a personal style of communication into the public forum of the newspaper.[30] Her column sounded as if she was chatting over the backyard fence rather than communicating through the mass media, and easily allowed for interruptions and breaks in concentration just as radio serials and television soap operas did. Her direct address to her audience reinforced this conversational quality and shrank the distance between newspaper columnist and readers. Assuming that women constituted her audience, she used phrases such as "you women" and "well, M'lady" to address them.[31]

Brief items at the end of her column came with the comment, "Remind me to do a story about this some day," and she was sure "you'd be horrified to know" about the latest Hollywood scandal. She also could be self-reflexive—"I'm told—this is gossip, mind you"—about practicing her trade. The *New York Times* attributed Hopper's popularity precisely to "her chatty approach in her columns," which "endeared her" to millions of readers.[32]

As in a conversation, Hopper inserted herself in her column by providing information about her life, although she endeavored to keep her son out of the public eye.[33] This content, along with the tone and structure of her column, expressed and sustained a sense—however false and manufactured—of trust and friendship.[34] She reported on her new hairstyles. One "swirls up the back with a bang in front. Looks like a Kansas tornado, but it's becoming." And she described her new hats. One was a "blue lace straw with . . . bits of red, white and blue. I look a little like an army of flags when I wear it." She told of visiting her mother in Altoona, happily anticipating her mother's first visit to Los Angeles, and filled in her readers on how well both visits went. She devoted an entire column to "a day in the life of a Hollywood columnist," in which she discussed her messy desk and poorly appointed office.[35] Just as she did to Hollywood denizens, Hopper freely dispensed advice to her readers and listeners on everything from "must-see" movies and party politics to marriage, divorce, and "what . . . a gal ha[s] to do to be a 'woman's woman.'" "Such ordinariness promoted a greater sense of connection and intimacy between the famous and their admirers," argues sociologist Joshua Gamson. The conversation of Hopper's column revealed and cultivated a relationship between columnist and audience, a relationship—as is the case of gossip participants generally—that often was more important than the information shared.[36]

Building on this relationship, Hopper invited her audience to share and exchange information with her and one another, just as in face-to-face gossip. "Letters are my only means of knowing what interests my readers," she insisted, as she offered and asked for opinions on movies and politics. When she listed what she considered the year's best films, she added, "You, the reader, can name dozens more." After presenting her choices for the Academy Awards, she exclaimed, "Now that my neck is out, chop it off!" She ended a discussion of the growing number of "sexy pictures" with "Sex or no sex—which is to be? What do you want?" Her political commentaries similarly invited reader response, and once she began to receive letters she referred to them.[37] "Like all columnists I have a mailbag," she announced on one of her radio shows. "I'm trying to bring up the points that have been written to me in letters." She also explained how the content of readers' letters shaped the content of her Hollywood gossip. "You asked for it! Hundreds of fan letters tell me there's a crying need all over the country for a good movie digest of the month," she wrote. "So here it is," and she listed a number of films by genre for her readers' information. The next month she added the names of the stars, as "there were so many requests for it," demonstrating studio success with marketing films through their stars.[38]

Hopper also printed in her column or quoted on the air letters or excerpts from letters; a few times letters constituted her entire column. She introduced readers' letters amid her own discussions and then followed them up with her own views, simulating the back-and-forth of conversation. "But here's one of the many letters I've received in protest, and I think she clarifies it much better than I ever could," she interjected into her coverage of the latest Hollywood controversy. Hopper often noted that her respondent "says it better than I," and she always asked for further comment. "And I'm wondering how many of your fellow Americans will agree with you." Hopper's policy of including direct feedback from readers was common among fan and mainstream women's magazines, but it was not a regular feature of most gossip columns.[39]

In this way, Hopper sought to foster both participation and community among members of her audience. Despite the physical distance, respondents joined an ongoing, national conversation, and they could become part of a community of shared interests and mutual understandings—if Hopper permitted. "We feel close to those with whom we converse," concludes one scholar of gossip, and Hopper fostered such feelings among her audience by using "we" and "us."[40] But she did not allow every respondent to be part of her "circle of we." Her censorship, or "editorial gate-keeping," meant letters critical of her or the kind of entertainment and politics she favored rarely appeared in her column. The few times this happened, she deliberately published it to make a point, as with a letter from Wilbur Jerger during the Cold War. She quoted his letter in her column, followed by her pointed anti-Communist commentary. "I'm interested in good pictures and just Government. I feel you are not," Jerger wrote Hopper. Familiar with her practice of censorship, he doubted "whether you'll have the justice or nerve to print this." Hopper responded to Jerger's challenge. "Well, here it is, Mr. Jerger; I'll write you a letter too—if you think there's justice or nerve enough in Moscow to get it printed in a Russian paper."[41] The relative absence in her column of letters such as Jerger's contrasted with the presence of letters enthusiastically endorsing her views, and revealed the limits of her commitment to audience participation. Although Hopper invited her readers and listeners to participate in conversations with her and with one another about the issues she raised, and her respondents accepted that invitation, she only heard and published those with whom she agreed.

Reading Hopper, Writing Hedda

For these respondents, Hedda Hopper's column and the industry she covered constituted an important, regular part of their daily lives, and the existence and content of their letters demonstrated the public and participatory dimensions of their cinema spectatorship. They shared with Hopper their reading practices, which occurred in private but connected them to a public world. "Dear Miss Hopper," a male reader began. "I read your column every day in the New York Daily News as I have been doing for the last 20 years." "Needless to say your column is part of our breakfast routine," reported another man. "I look for your column the very first thing," wrote one woman, and another noted, "Of course I turn to your page first every morning."[42] While letters came from cities all over the country, a sample revealed that about thirty-five percent of letters writers lived in southern California, reflecting the great interest in Hollywood among local residents, a geographical connection with Hopper, and the staunch political conservatism of the region. In addition, while men read, listened, and wrote to Hopper, about eighty percent of letters came from women, the vast majority married homemakers, with children, and apparently middle class (a portion sent letters on engraved stationery). At the time, women were assumed to be, and often disparaged as, Hopper's audience. Of her gossip, her legman Rosenstein believed, "Hens from Hollywood to Huckleberry Corners lap it up by the spoonful." When one of Hopper's broadcasting ventures needed a sponsor, it was promoted as taking "advantage of the well-known fact that the American female has an insatiable appetite for glamour gossip involving celebrities."[43] These images of Hopper's female readers as voracious consumers of Hollywood gossip implied they were uncontrolled and believed everything they read, and mocked their pleasure in the process.

But whether male or female, Hopper's respondents did convey the pleasure they received from Hollywood gossip. As one reader expressed to Hopper, "you've given me some happy reading." Gossiping is a pleasure and, if the private information shared ought not to be made public, often a guilty pleasure. "Gossip answers a wide range of human needs," argues Gail Collins, from exchanging knowledge to building community.[44] While Hopper's column included news and gossip about politics and entertainment, she devoted much space and attention to matters of private life often considered trivial and unimportant but of much concern on the individual, personal level. Readers often told of how they found the information and knowledge in Hopper's column useful and relevant to their everyday lives. Some readers— and their numbers increased over time—worried about gossip as an invasion of privacy. In fact, the first letter Hopper published, under the title "Mr. John Public," asked, "How about a little privacy for the stars on approaching motherhood?" But most respondents agreed with Hopper that invasions of privacy were justified, particularly for those who violated norms of political and sexual behavior. As one reader put it, "Movie stars and players may be entitled to a certain measure of privacy, if they follow accepted standards of behavior."[45] In this view, only the deserving were punished by Hopper's private talk, allowing respondents to appreciate the opportunity to read about the private lives of the rich and famous. "I enjoy your columns," wrote a New York woman, "they are smooth—easy reading and friendly." Moreover, as a leisure activity, reading "the gossips" meant taking time out of a busy day for oneself, a measure of both autonomy and enjoyment. "You're a grand person and 'steadily read-ily' by me (couldn't resist the pun!)."[46]

Part of the pleasure of reading Hopper's column was the relationship respondents felt they had with the columnist, whom most addressed as "Miss Hopper," although a good proportion felt on a first-name basis with "Hedda." Their relationship prompted them to write. "I feel as though I know you personally, having read your column since your first issue," offered a San Diego woman. "I believe you would be glad to know the negro point of view," contended an African American man.[47] Readers eagerly sought and accepted her advice on a range of topics, from which movies to see and cooking black bean soup to her recommendation for a plastic surgeon in Los Angeles "who excels in pretty noses." They provided intimate details about their personal lives and problems, and gave Hopper guidance and encouragement in return. One assured Hopper at age seventy-three that she "still had her good looks," and others complimented her profusely. "You are wonderful Hedda, I always read your column with great pleasure," stated a New York woman. "Three cheers for you." One fan even named her daughter after Hopper. "On March 3 my baby girl was born here, and I've named her Hedda after you," wrote Mrs. T. M. Henderson. "Good luck to you, Hedda Henderson!" chimed Hopper.[48] A number of respondents contrasted Hopper favorably with Louella Parsons. As happened among Hollywood denizens, avid fans of Hopper were not fans of Parsons. "I have read your work for the past five years," noted a

Chicago man, and he rejected the "conceited egotism based on one's monop-oly of Hollywood news as expressed by your female colleague." "I am <u>greatly</u> <u>disappointed</u> in Louella Parsons," wrote a woman about Parsons's stand on a Hollywood scandal.[49]

As with their relationship with Hopper, respondents valued the oppor-tunity to participate in Hollywood gossip through their letters. Just as let-ter writing is a "genre for self-expression," gossiping, even long distance, was a crucial means of articulating thoughts and feelings.[50] "Since you are one of the few columnists in Hollywood who is not afraid to express her mind on the happenings in Hollywood, I wish to let a little steam off my chest," declared a New York woman. A woman from Beverly Hill ended her letter, "I feel 'getting this out of my system' has even helped me," and another offered Hopper "my sincere thanks for listening."[51] Readers felt comfortable with questioning the accuracy of Hopper's column and correcting her grammar. When Hopper used the term "Negress" in her column, she received a quick response from an African American woman. "The correct term for feminine of Negro is Negro woman and not Negress, as our books on grammar tell us."[52] Like Hopper's gossip, respondents' letters could be either negative or positive. One woman denied she was a fan, because the content of her letter was critical. "It is usually those who have something complimentary to say that write fan letters." Another woman thought her negative letter was less a fan letter than a "pan" letter.[53] Often their reason for writing was expressed in how they signed off, as with "A very irate movie goer," "A Puzzled Fan," and "Disgustingly." Respondents also could hope or expect Hopper to acknowl-edge publicly their queries and comments. "Hope to see your comment in our Tribune," a Chicago reader ended her letter. "I shall be reading your col-umn," a San Diego woman concluded, "and who knows, I may read in the Times paper the reply to this letter."[54]

In addition to being enjoyable and relevant, participating in Hollywood gossip contributed to a sense of community among Hopper's respondents, making their letters both private expressions and public acts.[55] Because of Hopper's practice of referring to and publishing letters, readers saw them-selves as participating in a conversation not only with her but also with other readers. "I have wanted to 'sound off' too," an agitated reader wrote, "so allow me to join the others you mentioned in today's column." "I have never writ-ten to a columnist before," admitted a Maryland woman. "But I always read your column and last night when you mentioned letters . . . I decided to express my opinion too."[56] Hopper's column served as a point of connection for them, as did movies and movie stars. They reported discussing the information in her column with friends, family, and the broader community. "We have a business here and I talk to the public a lot, so you can bet I get a lot in," asserted a Virginia woman. Of a controversy, a Los Angeles reader observed, "one still hears about it everywhere one goes."[57] "All the people to whom I have spoken about that front page interview, join me in warmest thanks," conveyed a Chicago woman. Readers even joined together to write to Hopper, as did "Eight Mothers," "5 couples," and "Three Fans." They also went beyond their own local communities and recognized they were one of "thousands (or is it millions?) of people reading your column every day."[58] They began letters with "As just one of your many fans" and signed off as "One of Your Readers," revealing identities as fans and constituencies of readers activated by the gossip column. In this way, Hopper helped to catalyze new, national forms of community out of her readers' experience and engagement with the cinema.

From their sense of community, Hopper and her respondents used their gossip to define who was "in" and who was "out." As with traditional gossip, those on the inside share certain views and moral standards, while those on the outside are assumed to not; gossip can be used to establish and reinforce those boundaries.[59] For Hopper and her respondents, the boundaries were both moral and political. "That terrible woman," one woman wrote of the proximate cause of a Hollywood sex scandal, "should be thrown out of the movie colony and not accepted by decent people." Of immigrants accused of Communist sympathies, a New York man believed they should have to leave the United States. "We have enough worthy and capable native Americans who can be a credit to Hollywood and the country in general." Those condemned for not conforming to moral and political standards "should be promptly erased from public limelight, except for public denunciation," demanded a California reader.[60] In defining who was acceptable and who was not, Hopper and her respondents solidified their sense of community and engaged in what they saw as justified moral and political policing.

Hopper's respondents also used their gossip to extend their pleasures, experiences, and knowledge as moviegoers. They called movies "our favorite entertainment" and expressed feelings about movie stars. "I love them, and have always had my favorites." They always referred to stars by their first names, as did Hopper, offering the "illusion of intimacy" about relationships that were neither close nor reciprocal.[61] Because they saw Hopper as an intermediary, they asked her to provide more news about a favorite star or details about an upcoming movie, and they wrote to her and—assuming she could ensure delivery, and she often did—enclosed letters addressed to movie stars and studio heads. "Dear Miss Hopper," began one. "At first I thought I would send this to Warner Brothers but then I thought better of it," and instead she sent it first to Hopper.[62] Concerned readers urged her to come to the aid of an actor or actress they saw as troubled, professionally or personally. "Help Judy get her twisted ideas straightened out," a Texas couple wrote about Judy Garland, and "somebody ought to put some sense in Lucy's head," proclaimed a Chicago woman about Lucille Ball. "I don't know of anyone but yourself who could possibly put her back on the right track."[63] Readers used their extensive experience with Hollywood movies to express opinions and make suggestions. They reviewed and recommended films, praised or criticized star performances, and condemned Hollywood publicity—even at times Hopper herself—as excessive and deceptive. They also corrected her movie facts. When Hopper mixed up two similarly titled films, *The Desert Fox* and *The Desert Rats*, readers corrected her. "You are so right," she responded, "I certainly got my facts haywire. I have had one hundred letters to tell me of it."[64]

By offering glimpses of Hollywood "behind-the-scenes," Hopper's column fostered and reinforced her readers' sense of participation in the industry and in the lives of its performers.[65] With a strong interest in the production process, they commented on movie remakes, plotlines in movie serials and later television series, and casting decisions. When an actress sought to leave a series, and news leaked out that producers planned a fatal accident for her character, one of Hopper's readers was distraught. "Wouldn't it be nicer to say she became a nun? The thought of her dead just makes me feel so dreadful."[66] Readers often asked to see their favorite stars in more films and recommended actors and actresses for certain roles. "In your column today I read," a San Francisco man wrote Hopper, "Bette Davis [has signed] to play 'Hettie Green.' In my estimation it is excellent casting." He continued, "What about further good casting of Carolyn Jones as the daughter . . . ? Miss Jones' resemblance to Miss Davis makes her almost natural for the role."[67] Readers not only justified casting suggestions in terms of physical resemblance or their admiration for an actor or actress. They also sought, as did Hopper, consistency between the on- and off-screen lives of actors and actresses, whereby performers shared morality, politics, and various traits with the fictional characters they played. One New York respondent felt similar ethnicity should be an important factor in casting. "It is ridiculous having an Italian playing the part of an Irish born Irishman," he argued. "It is just silly and makes a mockery of the intellect of the audience."[68] Such concerns confirmed studio assumptions, as well as scholarly findings, that the presence of a star in a particular movie mattered very much to filmgoers and affected both their anticipation and reception of a film.[69]

Hopper's respondents also conveyed publicly through their letters the personal meanings they made out of Hollywood movies. As cultural theory proposes and audience research confirms across a range of media, reception is shaped by more than the "text" itself. In film studies, spectators do not view or interpret an individual movie or star performance in isolation, but rather with knowledge drawn from their own social experience as well as from other movies, publicity, and media coverage.[70] Hopper's readers indicated their intertextual or extratextual process of meaning making, bringing into their letters information gathered from sources beyond Hopper's column as well as their own lives. When African Americans objected to Hopper's endorsement of black stereotypes in films like *Green Pastures* (1936), an all-black musical about black folk religion, they explained their objections with reference to their own social and historical experience. In arguing against caricatures of "the negro as a shiftless, lazy, laughing, dice-shooting, chicken stealer and Uncle Tom," one reader informed Hopper, "The negro is human, Miss Hopper. His feelings can be hurt as easily as anyone. Perhaps he is more sensitive because he has been hurt more. That is why we die a little every time we see a negro character showing none of the honest characteristics of the race." "All we want is understanding that we are not clowns," he urged. "We know how terrible can be the effect of a bad pictures and I hope and pray that the last of the 'Green Pastures' and 'Uncle Toms' are gone—not only for my race's sake, but for the sake of all America."[71] Although such compelling arguments did not change Hopper's views of racial, and racist, filmic representations, letters revealed the range of factors shaping and complicating "specific acts of reception and making of personal meaning" among her readers and respondents.[72]

In expressing their meanings made of specific film or star texts, respondents exhibited many of the behaviors typical of fans. They were devoted spectators of certain film genres and especially certain stars. "We all love them, and never miss them." They talked about stars being "as much as part of our family, as they can be, and not actually know them." They copied stars, such as Lucille Ball. "Do you know, I wear my hair like Lucy and I never had it so becoming in my life?" They emotionally identified with stars and their problems, and Hopper worked to foster such identification. "About thirty years ago I had the same experience as she did," wrote one woman about revelations of a husband's adultery.[73] Hopper's respondents sought and made connections to other fans. "I am sincere in the opinion expressed in this letter," an Indianapolis reader penned, "and hope others feel the same."[74] They also engaged in evaluation, as they made critical judgments about the personal and professional lives of stars, and in activism. Their two main forms of activism were letter writing—to Hopper, stars, producers, studios, and politicians—to campaign for or protest against various actions in the entertainment industries, and consumer boycotts of films, stars, or the sponsors of radio and television shows. Although Hopper prompted such activism, it also came from readers themselves. A furious reader condemned the mistreatment of the American flag—"rolled and crammed into a saddle bag"—in a western film. "Now what way is that for children, or anyone for that matter, to see our flag so disrespectfully treated?"[75]

Hopper's respondents presented the world of cinema as mattering very much in their lives, and they claimed deep feelings about events and developments in that world, be they personal or political. "Life in Hollywood is undoubtedly hard on marriage," a Connecticut woman observed about a star divorce, "especially when both husband and wife pursue careers." Even so, she continued, "we the public have had another blow to our idealism at this one's failure." "The news . . . in your column was the first I had heard about it and I was just sick," a California reader admitted of a political scandal.[76] "I have a lot of very strong convictions on what goes on in the movie colony," asserted a woman from Wisconsin, "because I feel that movies and the stars and players often influence the morals of young people." "My Dear Miss Hopper," stated another, "I am so disgusted with myself because I have let this scandal upset me."[77] The range of fan behavior revealed in letters to Hopper substantiates film scholarship that questions the notion of spectators, especially female spectators, as "over-identificatory, passive, and mindlessly consumerist," and instead shows them to be "distanced, skeptical, and active."[78]

In these various public forms, participants in Hopper's Hollywood gossip expressed their experience of cinema spectatorship. Most significant of these forms was the political content of their letters, which revealed and established Hollywood gossip as an arena for discussion and debate about contested issues of what was understood to be public and private life, such as war and politics, race relations, gender and sexuality. Given Hopper's agenda of political and sexual conservatism, she addressed her readers as citizens as well as spectators or consumers, and assumed they were concerned about the issues of the day. At the very least, extant letters point to respondents who were concerned, understood themselves as citizens, and adopted a "civic identity" in their correspondence, signing off their letters with "A Plain Citizen" and "A Citizen Who Wants Fairness." Letter writing provided Hopper's readers, just as it does other men and women, "with a space to explore their identity as citizens of a particular nation."[79] The conversation and exchange of Hopper and these respondents emerged from and shaped Hollywood's influential discourses about national and international politics, society, and culture over the middle decades of the twentieth century.[80]

Hollywood Gossip as Public Sphere

Through their practice of Hollywood gossip, Hedda Hopper and her readers made her column part of the public sphere, but in ways that departed from the ideal, Habermasian model by merging activities and attitudes categorized as both public and the private.[81] Gossip exposed ostensibly private matters to public scrutiny. Hopper was a publicist of private talk, she brought a personal tone to her public writings, and she made her personal connections to her audience and her political commitments to the Republican Party equally central to her public persona as a gossip columnist. Her respondents read and wrote from the privacy of their homes yet located themselves in the public world. They constituted a "public," a group "of private people connected through common concerns," sparked in this case by a common text.[82] Finally, the content of her columns and their letters concerned "high" politics—elections, government, foreign policy—and personal politics—interactions and power relations between individuals and within families. In justifying their political discussion and participation, Hopper and her women readers, like American women in the past, invoked both public and private identities. "I am a native born citizen and a mother," Hopper noted before launching into an extended political statement. Her respondents welcomed the opportunity provided by her column for political discussion on a range of issues. "God Bless you for your beliefs, and keep up the good work," a California woman wrote. "I enjoy your column, not for the gossip on celebrities, but for all the good you do in many other ways."[83] They also saw her column as a legitimate arena for political expression. "My dear Miss Hopper—Am not in the habit of writing letters to Senators, Congressmen, or columnists, but I am writing to you about a matter which is shocking to me and a large number of people I know, people who are good citizens and decent human beings."[84]

Hopper and her readers used her column to share and exchange information about both private and public life. Hopper's readers wrote her for information about political events and developments. "I've been swamped with inquiries from readers about the strike," Hopper noted about a Hollywood labor conflict, and she supplied them with an entire column, shaped by her antiunion perspective, on labor relations and trade union issues among actors in the industry. Like Hopper, her readers understood private information as revealing the "truth" of the public person. When Hopper reported a compliment Richard Nixon bestowed on his wife, a reader believed his "diplomatic" relations with his wife translated directly into an "ability to create goodwill among people, both at home and abroad."[85] Readers also passed on their own information and even conducted research, whether about the presumed Communist affiliations of a filmmaker or the drinking habits of an actress. After the former child star Shirley Temple filed for divorce from her first husband, John Agar, Temple testified that one of their marital conflicts concerned drinking alcohol. Agar disliked that she chose not to imbibe and therefore she was not "any fun," while his excessive drinking angered her when he "went out and came back drunk." A New York woman sent Hopper a letter taking Agar's side in the divorce and scoffing at Temple's testimony. To reinforce her points, she attached a newspaper clipping with a photo of Temple and Agar in a nightclub. "She seems to be drinking here," the respondent inscribed on the clipping.[86]

The exchange between Hopper and her readers also conveyed deeply held moral and political values. Many respondents endorsed Hopper's moral conservatism, praising her stands for marriage, family, and, especially, sexual fidelity. "It's a good thing for the American public that we have journalists with your strength of character and fortitude who will speak out against . . . flaunting of accepted moral standards," emphasized a southern California woman. "Long live Hedda and her desire to bring about a decent moral code in Hollywood," cheered another. Respondents similarly supported Hopper's political conservatism, particularly her anti-Communism. "Dear Hedda: Being a fan of yours, and never missing your column," a Chicago woman wrote. "We admire your American stand and criticism of our Washington 'bureaucrats' who seem to be too soft on communism."[87] Yet a few respondents criticized Hopper's values, and advocated moral and political tolerance. An Illinois reader was "bitter" toward parties involved in a sex scandal "until a voice asked me 'Who are you and what right have you to condemn?'" Another reader sent Hopper a passionate and eloquent defense of political freedom at the height of Cold War anti-Communism. Using a pseudonym, "One Voice" believed Americans had the right to join any political party they chose, including the Communist Party. "Thus, if the government permits two, three, or even more parties to list their candidates, it automatically becomes the citizen's privilege to vote for whomever he wishes." "Is it not time that responsible leaders," this respondent asked, "respect an ordinary citizen's rights and privileges?"[88]

In the process of sharing information and values, Hopper and her readers engaged in discussion and debate through columns and letters. At times, the discussion occurred only in the exchange of letters between reader and columnist, but generally a greater number of participants were involved, as Hopper referred to and published readers' letters and other readers saw themselves as joining in the conversation with letters of their own. Such discussions and debates occurred around a range of issues over the course of Hopper's career, demonstrating how respondents used Hollywood gossip as a form of inquiry to interrogate mid-twentieth-century moral and political norms. Hopper so liked the idea of her column as an example of "civic journalism" and her readers engaged in conversation as political participants that at times she simulated debates about important issues.[89] She did this by subtly juxtaposing readers' views with contrary views or facts drawn from other sources, giving the impression that all those involved were respondents concerned about, and dedicated to discussing, various controversies, when, in fact, they were not. When Hopper attempted to translate the political content of her column into a radio show later in her career, she was much criticized. In her defense, she forwarded onto her network letters from readers supporting political discussion within the context of a Hollywood gossip program. "I think you will recognize the fact that the radio listening public wants more than cheap entertainment," Hopper argued.[90]

Hopper and her readers entered these discussions and debates with different perspectives; most were firm in their opinions on the issues, while others were more open-minded. Hopper, of course, knew what she thought and rarely changed her mind, and most of her respondents were similarly opinionated. "These women who wantonly wreck marriages and deprive children of their fathers should be held up to public scorn," urged a Chicago woman. Most respondents held strong opinions regardless of whether they agreed with her morals and politics. "I think you are un-American, Miss Hopper," wrote a Los Angeles man. "I refuse to take it lying down when anyone attempts to impose an iron curtain around my mind."[91] Yet other respondents viewed their participation in Hollywood gossip as an open-ended discussion. "One Voice" approached Hopper believing her "a self-respecting American who will not stoop to 'witch-hunt,'" and, therefore, will discuss the issue of civil liberties for Communists. Naïve and wary, but hoping for sincere engagement with Hopper and others, this respondent noted, "It seems that if one even dares to whisper the world 'communism,' one is immediately branded a Red."[92] The African American man who objected to racist caricatures similarly sought to engage Hopper. "That is why I am writing this too-lengthy letter in the hope that it will induce you to speak my race's feelings in your column. I know that negroes all over the country will be encouraged by this forward leap." Still others showed how taking part in Hollywood gossip had changed their views and opinions. "I had always considered Miss Temple as an example of a fine American girl, a movie star who could lead a respectable life," an Ohio woman imparted. "Now my opinion has been radically altered."[93]

The conversation and exchange that characterized Hopper's gossip column was not just empty or directionless opinion but translated into substantive political action for many respondents, as it did for Hopper. She endorsed a range of actions, from letter writing and boycotts, to organization building and voting, all aimed at moving contemporary society, culture, and politics toward her vision of what the United States should be. "Now, what can we do about it? We can vote," she advocated. "Any American who stays away from the polls this year is a slacker." Hopper called for lobbying—"Help defeat the bill," she urged on various occasions—as well as voting to achieve political aims.[94] Many of her respondents already were politically active and did not need a Hollywood gossip columnist to spur them to action. They reported being members of the Republican Party, League of Women Voters, Daughters of the American Revolution, American Legion Women's Auxiliary, and California Federation of Women's Clubs, as well as mobilizing around various conservative campaigns. They wrote letters directly to movie stars and Supreme Court justices criticizing their liberal politics or judicial decisions. As individuals, families, and communities, they pledged to boycott films with what they saw as politically or sexually objectionable content and, in the wake of political and moral scandals, stars, their star vehicles, and, if on radio or television, their sponsors. "You can be assured I will <u>never</u> patronize any picture she ever appears in." "I shall <u>never, never</u> watch her show again— I am 100% American!!!" "My entire family will never tune in her TV show or attend any of her movies. That means 3 families beside my own."[95]

The letters of Hopper's readers indicated their "activist repertoire" as they transformed their varied experiences as spectators and citizens into new forms of public life in the mid-twentieth-century United States.[96] The largely conservative politics of these active and activist readers further undermines the equation of active participation in popular culture with political resistance that characterized the "naïve kind of populism" of early fan studies.[97] Even so, through their responses they made Hopper's gossip column part of the public sphere. Hopper's efforts alone could not have achieved this; the participation of her readers, respondents, and fans was crucial and necessary. Additionally, while men and women read and responded to Hopper's column, women predominated. Hollywood gossip provided these American women with a discursive arena within the male-dominated public realm during a historical period in which organized feminism in the United States was at an ebb. While neither Hopper nor her women respondents called themselves feminists, they certainly believed women "belonged to the world," held equal citizenship to men, and had a legitimate right to take part in public sphere activities.[98] Their first opportunity to express political views and mobilize around political issues came soon after Hedda Hopper's career as a nationally syndicated columnist took off and just as the world moved toward war.

Hedda Hopper rides in an American Legion convention parade, Milwaukee, Wisconsin, 1941. (Courtesy of the Academy of Motion Picture Arts and Sciences.)

Hopper's Wars

In the late 1930s, as a syndicated gossip columnist with a radio show and a growing and eager audience, Hedda Hopper became a national public figure, allowing her to participate in, and pontificate on, the world of politics beyond Hollywood, particularly the politics of war. In the years before the United States entered what came to be called World War II, Hopper fiercely embraced isolationism at a time when her own Republican Party divided on the issue. "Settle our home problems," she urged in 1939, "and stop trying to run the rest of the world!" Hopper's stance against intervention can be viewed, like that of the vast majority of Americans, as an "intense antiwar spirit," more a "mood than a political position," in historian Michael S. Sherry's words.[1] Yet she articulated clear ideological and political commitments that fit with the right-wing isolationist movement, and used her column to spur her readers to action, as did other isolationists in journalism such as William Randolph Hearst. In her first attempt to mobilize her readers around a political issue, she called for and supported a mothers' movement to keep the United States out of war.[2] After U.S. entry into the war, Hopper officially fell in line. She included reasons for "why we fight" in her column, justifying and giving meaning to the U.S. war effort, and lauded Americans for fulfilling their patriotic duty by entering the military or pursuing war-related activities. But she never "went to war with gusto" or fought "the Good War," as World War II came to be remembered, in quite the same way as the rest of Hollywood.[3] In sharp contrast, she readily committed herself to fighting the Cold War, but then Communism always provoked more opposition from Hopper than did fascism, at home or overseas.

Hopper's conservatism, antistatism, and anti-Communism shaped her transformation from pre–World War II isolationist to a Cold War interventionist. Her transformation occurred as Hollywood moviemakers and movies gained greater cultural authority and political influence. During World War II, movies came to be seen by audiences, moviemakers, and government officials as "critical carriers" of cultural meanings and messages, powerfully influencing politics and guiding Americans through the hardships created by the war. "Moving images became the new alphabet, the hieroglyphics of meaning and memory for American culture," Thomas Doherty argues.[4] In her role as scribe and interpreter, Hopper profited professionally and politically from these developments. As a columnist, she now reported on the country's most powerful form of popular culture, and, as a political figure, she now had greater credibility and standing in public life. Building on her failed isolationist efforts but using her newly gained credibility, Hopper took on two campaigns during World War II. First, she launched a defense of Lew Ayres, star of the antiwar film *All Quiet on the Western Front* (1930), when he decided to become a conscientious objector, demonstrating Hopper's commitment to protecting private conscience in a time of war that did not translate into the Cold War era. Her second campaign involved an attack on Charlie Chaplin's professional, political, and personal life, which culminated in his leaving the United States in the early 1950s. Both campaigns stood precisely at the intersection of public and private life, sparked discussion and garnered support from Hopper's respondents, and demonstrated the power and politics of Hollywood gossip during the World War II and Cold War eras.

Prewar Isolationist to Cold Warrior

Hedda Hopper's isolationism, or anti-interventionism, was motivated by and encompassed many concerns. Scholars criticize "isolationism" as a derogatory term that originated with interventionists and as a "simplistic" and even inaccurate term, because it fails to capture the multiple and even contradictory positions held by those in—or placed by their opponents in—the isolationist camp. Hopper was a good example. She justified her isolationism in antistatist terms, as did the leaders and backers of the isolationist America First Committee. Hopper believed and feared that war mobilization would further centralize and strengthen the federal government and erode individualism.[5] "Are we going to toss the heritage and strength our pioneer forbears gave us into the ashcan?" she asked dramatically. What Hopper sought as an isolationist was to maintain the United States at peace, independent, and free to act unilaterally in the world. To achieve this aim, she believed in building a strong military defense for "Fortress America"—something pacifists opposed—and avoiding "entangling alliances" with a conflict-ridden Europe.[6] "Let's stay home and prepare a defense so strong no one will dare attack us," she argued in September 1939 after war broke out in Europe, "so that when they've made another hash of Europe we can give what's left of civilization a shelter and new hope." This anti-Europe position reflected her strong belief that American participation in World War I had been a mistake, a belief reflected in American public opinion. Hopper's opposition to the Second World War stemmed from her understanding of the First, and she determined "to stay out of the European mess and keep our boys from marching 'over there.'"[7]

Hopper's antipathy toward Europe further revealed her nativism, anti-Semitism, and Anglophobia, prejudices not uncommon among isolationists. As Hollywood became a destination for European filmmaker refugees fleeing Nazi Germany and war in Europe, Hopper joined with other conservatives to express concern about British, Jewish, and other foreigners in the motion picture capital and threatened that the "refugee situation would be looked into." She believed refugees were taking jobs from Americans "who can speak English without an accent."[8] Hopper explicitly expressed a lack of concern for European Jews, unlike pacifists motivated by humanitarian concerns. She opposed, along with anti-Semitic and right-wing groups, a 1939 bill to allow into the United States twenty-thousand refugee children from Germany ("of various faiths," the *New York Times* was careful to note). "Every mother is sympathetic to this idea. But charity begins at home," Hopper argued. "So let's first climb on the bandwagon for our own underprivileged before bringing in more."[9] Moreover, during a much-criticized 1938 visit to Hollywood by Leni Riefenstahl, Adolf Hitler's favorite filmmaker and director of *Triumph of the Will* (1935), Hopper defended her in several columns. "Leni's only here to sell her picture!"[10] Of her anti-British stance, Hopper was similarly outspoken, although she could be friendly to individuals, commenting on "our nicest Britishers." The historian John E. Moser links Anglophobia to the United States' historic wariness toward the British monarchy and imperialism. Hopper certainly feared the power of Great Britain to involve the United States in another unwanted war, as did the head of her Chicago Tribune–New York News syndicate, Robert McCormick, who "warned against the wiles of 'Perfidious Albion.'"[11]

Hopper's Anglophobia, as well as her insistence on consistency between actors and their film characters, showed up most fully in her opposition to the casting of British actors in American films. In January 1939, she devoted her entire column to condemning the fact that Vivien Leigh and Leslie Howard won starring roles in David O. Selznick's production of *Gone with the Wind* (1939). She reported receiving a phone call informing her that "Mr. Selznick had decided upon his Scarlett, Vivien Leigh. And Leslie Howard for Ashley. Now, why call me?" Hopper asked. "Why not the House of Parliament in England, and say: 'Well, you've won again.'" She went on to criticize Selznick's two-year search for "his Scarlett" and considered it an insult to "every girl born here" that "out of millions of American girls couldn't find one to suit him."[12] Other columnists, such as Louella Parsons and Ed Sullivan, and Hopper's readers also objected to the casting. Hopper gave most of a column to "one of the many letters I've received in protest," a passionate letter from a reader who clearly loved the story about a southern family during the Civil War and Reconstruction told in the best-selling 1936 novel by Margaret Mitchell, on which the film would be based. Kay Clement Peddell expressed outrage at the "almost unbelievable news that David Selznick has chosen an (practically) unknown ENGLISH actress to do Scarlett O'Hara, the most AMERICAN role of modern times." Demanding the same nationality for the "real" actress and the "reel" character, Peddell could not imagine Vivien Leigh in the role. "NO! A thousand times NO!" "I'm sure millions of Americans will stay away from the picture in a gesture of protest," Peddell concluded.[13]

Other readers agreed with Hopper and Peddell and understood the casting of Leigh and Howard in *Gone with the Wind* as an unacceptable gap between the personal characteristics of stars and the roles they played, and as indicative of pro-British and pro-interventionist sentiments in Hollywood. Indeed, Selznick did express such feelings when he argued, "These are the days when we should all do everything within our power to help cement British-American relationships and mutual sympathies." One of Hopper's readers demanded that the Jewish Selznick forget "his European forebears and realize America comes first last and always." This reader went on to blame Great Britain for the international crisis the United States now faced. "But how willing England is to draw us in, our gold in Peace and our men in war."[14] Such anti-British feelings among Hopper and her readers indicated "the widespread fears of Anglo-American collaboration" to bring the United States into the war over 1939 and 1940. "Congratulations," wrote one of Hopper's readers in 1940, "on not being overcome by the proximity of so many British in Hollywood, to the extent of losing your sense of values, and being willing to sacrifice our American boys a second time."[15] Hopper's criticism of the British casting for *Gone with the Wind*, however, did not uniformly transfer to other films, nor did it last.

After attending a preview of *Gone with the Wind* in December 1939, Hopper backed off from her criticism of the casting and instead used the film to make an argument against intervention in the European war. After seeing Vivien Leigh's performance in the film, Hopper had to "do something I dislike very much. And that is, chew my own words. In January, I devoted a whole column in a seething, scornful denunciation of David O. Selznick because he couldn't find, in this country, a Scarlett—therefore chose an English girl. And now, by golly, I've got to congratulate him and everyone concerned for picking Vivien Leigh. It's an incredible, unbelievable performance." But Hopper also pointed out that the film "couldn't have been released at a more propitious time than the present when practically the whole world is at war." She felt "Margaret Mitchell wrote a great sermon against war" and singled out a powerful scene depicting the mass bloodshed and brutality of total war: "the one where 2500 men fill the screen—all wounded, all broken, all helpless." Hopper had viewed this same scene of wounded and dying Confederate soldiers at the Atlanta railroad station while the film was in production. "There was nothing inspiring about it," she noted at the time, and hoped "it will be a strong plea for peace."[16]

Hopper's emphasis on the inglorious, personal costs of war for the individual soldier as portrayed in *Gone with the Wind* always appeared in her more extended arguments for isolation and connected to a mother's concern for her son. She feared her son, Bill Hopper, would be drafted into the armed forces should the United States enter World War II, and she knew other women, including those in her newspaper and radio audiences, shared her fears. "Let our sons know we don't believe they're cowards when they refuse to fight another's battle," she told her readers, and they agreed.[17] "I am one of the ordinary sheltered home keepers," wrote a Los Angeles reader, "a mother of four splendid sons and a son-in-law, just as splendid, very much interested and concerned in the terrible possibility we are facing. Any move toward honorable peace has my whole hearted sanction." An Iowa woman concurred. "I don't intend to see my two nephews sent 'over there' to be slaughtered if I can help it."[18] Such private concerns and emotions, Hopper hoped, could be transformed into political action. Her sentiments, rhetoric, and actions dovetailed with that of the mothers' movement, a coalition of mothers' groups that worked to oppose U.S. intervention into World War II and involved about five to six million women. That the first mothers' organization, the National Legion of Mothers of America, was founded in Los Angeles indicated a possible overlap with Hopper's audience.[19] Like such mothers' groups, Hopper set out to mobilize her millions of women readers into a strong isolationist movement.

"Up to Women to Avert War" headlined one of Hopper's columns in September 1939, the month Germany invaded Poland and England and France declared war, and her readers responded, indicating she had tapped into the isolationist maternalism that built the national mothers' movement. "I'm firmly convinced that the only way we'll keep America out of war is through women," she wrote. "And that can only be done if we organize at once." Utilizing a phrase—"up to the women"—popular in women's magazines and writings of the era, and drawing on maternalist rhetoric and stereotypes about the power of women's nurturing care and moral superiority, Hopper called for action.[20] "We've heard that the hand that rocks the cradle rules the world," she declared in late September. "All right, let's use that slogan and see if we can make it come true." To those who believed foreign policy "has no place in a movie column," she argued, "they are right, of course, but I was a mother long before I was a columnist." "Hurray for you, Hedda Hopper!" exclaimed a woman from Beverly Hills. "I'm with you all the way." A Pasadena woman "could hardly believe my eyes" when she saw Hopper's appeal. "Your idea of an organization of women to keep America out of war was what I had been talking-talking-talking ever since the European war started."[21] The quantity and passion of the responses from her readers surprised and pleased Hopper. "I had no idea you women would come through so quickly after my feeble plea for peace the other day," she admitted. "I put on an extra secretary to answer your grand letters." She later addressed "all you women . . . trying to keep our boys from marching 'over there.' Let's put our power together, our wealth, our motherhood . . . and cooperate."[22]

Many of Hopper's respondents already were cooperating toward keeping the United States out of the European war, and they urged her to continue her isolationist agitation. As one reader put it, a "movement of this kind needs publicity and you are in such a grand spot to contribute this." They shared their ideas for political actions as well as the ones they already had undertaken. One southern California woman "had spent days contacting my friends and even perfect strangers" and writing to women's clubs to build momentum for a movement against war, and another sent Hopper a leaflet publicizing a women's pacifist organization. A third wanted to put pressure on local Selective Service boards. "Let the women impress the war boards that they will not let their dearest possessions be taken from them," she urged. "Organize!"[23] Hopper liked seeing her readers "take the initiative and organize"—contending that once underway, "Hollywood will join in and their support will astound you!"—but her readers had other ideas. "In your column," wrote a woman from Los Angeles, "you made an appeal to the women to keep our country out of war and asked for some one to lead in that movement. Might I suggest, that you, yourself take on that responsibility for Hollywood?" "I don't know of anyone better to be at the head of such an organization than yourself," stated an Iowa woman, who believed "any movement of that sort would be more effective if it was started in Hollywood." "We are very fond of our Movie Stars, and look up to them more or less," she pointed out. "They set the styles for us in everything."[24]

But Hopper rejected a leadership role for herself and instead suggested Anne Morrow Lindbergh—the wife of the famed aviator, fervent isolationist, and anti-Communist Charles A. Lindbergh—to "head the women's movement to keep our boys from fighting over there."[25] Charles Lindbergh was the most prominent and controversial isolationist in the United States, and he later joined forces with the country's leading anti-interventionist organization, the America First Committee. While very "few pacifists were drawn" to Lindbergh, he was popular among American women, and Hopper endorsed his writings and speeches in her column and on her radio show. In 1940, she championed one of Lindbergh's major speeches advocating a strong military, with a focus on air defense, to protect the United States, and isolation from the European war. Hopper's public support for Lindbergh's speech came the very same week in May 1940 that President Roosevelt called isolationists "unwitting aids of the agents of Nazism."[26] Such stark differences in opinion appeared in the "Great Debate" over U.S. intervention in 1940–1941 and were mirrored in Hopper's mail. "Congratulations, and thank you, for your advice to your listeners to hear, read, and heed Colonel Lindbergh's speech to the American public," wrote a New York woman, while a Minneapolis man criticized Lindbergh because he "had no word of condemnation for Germany and her heartless aggression in Holland, Belgium, and Norway."[27] Hopper continued to endorse Lindbergh after his famous speech in Des Moines, Iowa, in September 1941, in which he blamed the British, the Jews, and the Roosevelt administration for leading the nation to war, and boosted his reputation for being pro-Nazi and anti-Semitic. "My admiration for Lindy has never diminished," Hopper recalled, "even after he was purged by F.D.R. I believed Lindbergh, not our President."[28]

Hopper also believed U.S. Ambassador to Great Britain Joseph P. Kennedy, another staunch anti-interventionist and anti-Communist. She intensely disliked Kennedy from earlier dealings with him in the motion picture industry, when he had headed Pathé Studios and earned the title "Financial Wizard of

Hollywood." But she "overcame antipathy" to join him in seeking American neutrality in the war. In May 1940, as Nazi Germany rapidly advanced on France and British troops retreated from the European continent, Kennedy urged President Roosevelt to make peace with Germany, and Hopper mentioned that "Joe Kennedy" was doing "much good" for the country.[29] When Kennedy returned to Hollywood in November 1940—just before Roosevelt demanded he resign his ambassadorship—he told movie producers to stop making anti-Nazi films and begin to reconcile themselves to a neutral United States and a Europe dominated by Germany. When Hopper saw Kennedy at a party during his California visit, she "sought him out to urge him never to stop speaking against American involvement in the European struggle."[30]

Although a shared anti-Communism fostered Hopper's isolationist affinity with Lindbergh, Kennedy, and those closer to home, such as Walt Disney, the same could not be said of Hopper's endorsement of the anti-interventionist activities of the Hollywood Left. During the era of the Nazi-Soviet Pact, a non-aggression treaty signed in August 1939 and broken with the German invasion of the Soviet Union in June 1941, members of the Communist Party USA (CPUSA) followed Soviet directives, abandoned their earlier commitment to intervention, and embraced neutrality for the United States. This policy shift irretrievably damaged the CPUSA, including the Hollywood branch, which lost disillusioned members and liberal allies but gained—at least briefly—Hopper's support for their position. In December 1939, she devoted an entire Sunday column to Communist Party member Dalton Trumbo and his recent antiwar novel *Johnny Got His Gun*, a book she recommended to anyone interested in keeping the United States out of war.[31] Three months later, she publicized "an interesting meeting being held tomorrow night" dedicated to discussing "Public Controversy No. 1—Is Roosevelt leading us towards war?" The meeting featured John Howard Lawson, the "most respected Red in the movie industry," according to scholars Larry Ceplair and Steven Englund, arguing the affirmative. "I wouldn't miss it," wrote Hopper. But her anti-Communism made her wary "of our so-called 'peace' organizations (the ones with the pink halos)," and this common ground only lasted as long as the Nazi-Soviet Pact.[32] When the Hollywood Left returned to the interventionist camp in mid-1941, Hopper stayed where she was, on the Hollywood Right.

Hopper's isolationism meant she paid attention to like-minded members of the U.S. Congress, but she objected when they attacked the motion picture industry. In January 1940, the Democratic senator from Montana and leading anti-interventionist Burton K. Wheeler accused Hollywood of making films that advocated intervention.[33] The next year, he sponsored hearings on "war-mongering" motion picture propaganda. According to his colleague D. Worth Clark, an Idaho Democrat, Hollywood movies were being "used to infect the minds of audiences with hatred, to inflame them, to arouse their emotions, and make them clamor for war." Revealing the anti-Semitism of many conservative isolationists, Senator Gerald P. Nye added that those "responsible for the propaganda pictures are born abroad," positing a Jewish conspiracy aimed at pushing the United States into war.[34] Despite testimony praising "how good Hedda Hopper is as a movie gossip," she, as did Parsons, publicly rejected the premise of the Senate hearings. "The claim seems to be that the screen is being used for propaganda war pictures." "Well," she asked, "what's Hollywood supposed to do—close its eyes to the war, with news of it on every front page?" She also believed "movie patrons" were "awakening to the menace of 'isms' and espionage and would be glad to see them exposed," and she strongly supported anti-Nazi films, including Warner Brothers' *Confessions of a Nazi Spy* (1939).[35] When the isolationist senators targeted the film, Hopper condemned the "avalanche of protests from pro-Nazis, 'liberals,' propagandists, and peace outfits [that] crashed down on it." With European markets closed off to American movies, and Hollywood experiencing the "Boxoffice Blues" domestically through mid-1941, Hopper tempered her criticisms of industry products generally.[36]

A prominent exception, and where Hopper wholeheartedly agreed with the isolationist senators, was Charlie Chaplin's most popular film, *The Great Dictator* (1940). Due to her long-standing personal and political objections to the filmmaker and actor, she regarded his films with great suspicion. For the FBI, *The Great Dictator* was "nothing more than subtle Communist propaganda."[37] For Hopper, Chaplin's pro-intervention, satirical attack on Adolf Hitler in the film was an affront. As she contended, "with the condition of the world at present, no one feels like laughing at any dictator." Chaplin's final speech in the film, which scholars consider an "impassioned six-minute attack on the dehumanizing material and spiritual conditions that have led to fascism," left Hopper "colder than an icicle."[38] When Chaplin delivered the final speech at a concert celebrating President Roosevelt's third inauguration in 1941, this performance confirmed Chaplin's ties to an administration Hopper loathed. Hopper commented on these political connections while *The Great Dictator* was in production, claiming that Secretary of the Interior Harold L. Ickes, known for his strong condemnations of Hitler and later the America First Committee, "was backing Charlie Chaplin in his dictator picture."[39] Due to Chaplin's independence as a filmmaker, Hopper could criticize *The Great Dictator* without hurting the struggling major movie studios and, at the same time, possibly undermine the Roosevelt administration.

For Hopper, the Roosevelt administration and liberal activists, rather than the movie industry, were primarily responsible for conveying the interventionist message. "It isn't a good sign when we feel we must prepare ourselves for America's entrance into a war we don't belong in," she worried. "Let's spend our time fighting against it instead of preparing for it."[40] As late as October 1941, a majority of Americans joined Hopper in favoring neutrality, but with the Japanese attack on Pearl Harbor on December 7, 1941, the "logic of preparedness prevailed," and the isolationists were discredited. The Senate hearings on motion picture propaganda ended, and the America First Committee "closed its doors" four days after Pearl Harbor.[41] Yet Hopper remained unbowed. After the war, she indicated her belief in conspiracy theories popular on the extreme Right and published in Robert McCormick's *Chicago Tribune* that Roosevelt knew about the imminent attack on Pearl Harbor but allowed it to occur to justify U.S. entry into the war. "I hope I'll still be here when the real truth of Pearl Harbor is told by the President's best friend," she wrote McCormick in 1947.[42] But by that time, Hopper had signed on to a new war, the Cold War.

In her transition from pre–World War II isolationist to strident Cold War interventionist, Hopper faced a political and ideological challenge in changing her approach to foreign policy. Along with prominent conservative isolationists in Congress, such as Arthur Vandenberg, a Michigan Republican, and Robert Taft, Hopper needed to rethink the place and responsibilities of the United States in the world. While Vandenberg "renounced his earlier isolationism in favor of the internationalism" of the Cold War era, Taft remained "suspicious" of international commitments and opposed a larger role for the United States abroad.[43] Hopper's affinity remained with Taft, as her support for his presidential ambitions in 1948 and 1952 made clear, and she did not easily embrace America's foreign entanglements and "global responsibility" that were part of the "broad public consensus that supported Cold War foreign policy."[44] Yet her long-standing political ideas and beliefs soon translated into a new position with regard to U.S. intervention abroad. By the late 1940s, her fierce anti-Communism combined with her fervent belief in American national greatness to make her an advocate of an aggressive foreign policy aimed at protecting the United States from global Communism. Throughout the rest of her career, Hopper took a militant stance wherever in the world the Cold War turned "hot."

Civil Liberties in Times of War

From world war to Cold War, Hedda Hopper also changed her position on civil liberties while maintaining her ideological and political commitments. Consistent with her libertarian and antistatist principles, which in this case dovetailed with Quaker traditions, Hopper strongly defended the civil liberties of the actor and World War II conscientious objector (CO) Lew Ayres "to protect private conscience from the state."[45] On March 31, 1942, just four months after the United States declared war, Ayres announced that his Selective Service Board had accepted his appeal for CO status. A popular Hollywood actor whose first movie success had been the antiwar *All Quiet on the Western Front*, Ayres became the most famous CO during the war, and he "astounded his Hollywood colleagues with his decision."[46] At the time of his announcement, he was starring in the successful Dr. Kildare movie series. Within the first week, the Boston City Council unanimously voted to revoke the license of any theater showing an Ayres film. A theater in Hackensack, New Jersey, withdrew *Dr. Kildare's Victory* after receiving 130 telephone calls within twenty-four hours from members of the American Legion threatening a boycott. MGM considered Ayres "washed up" as a film actor and, at an additional cost of $100,000, decided to reshoot the latest movie in the series with a new actor as Dr. Kildare.[47] While motion picture producers and exhibitors were taking action, articles and editorials both supporting and condemning Ayres's decision appeared in newspapers and magazines across the country, and the public answered with letters both pro and con. This debate concerned the legitimacy, meaning, and consequences of conscientious objection for the wartime United States and played out in "Hedda Hopper's Hollywood."

From the very start of the controversy, Hopper expressed support for Ayres in print and on air, and most letters from her readers and listeners agreed. Of letter writers expressing criticism of Ayres, men constituted the majority, reflecting the "gender gap in public opinion," with women more tolerant of COs than men.[48] Hopper always liked Ayres and offered positive coverage of his professional career and personal life in her column. She had played his mother in the gangster film *Night World* (1932), and, asserting her expertise as an industry insider, "I knew what kind of man he was."[49] Together with the majority of her respondents, she helped to forge the broader public consensus of tolerance toward Ayres and his antiwar convictions that emerged over the next few months. Central to Ayres's philosophy was the Christian creed of nonresistance to evil. He told his draft board that he believed "it is degrading and extremely harmful to the moral and spiritual progress of the soul to kill," and "we will never stop wars until we individually cease fighting them, and that's what I propose to do."[50] He benefited from new liberalized criteria under which up to one hundred thousand men became COs during World War II. In 1940, Congress expanded the definition of conscientious objection from membership in a pacifist church, such as the Quakers, to include individuals like Ayres who opposed "participation in war in any form," on grounds of "religious training and belief." The guiding norm for granting appeals during World War II became "the sincerity of individual conviction not formal adherence to a creed," and the question arose—was Ayres a "sincere objector" and "worthy of state authorization," or a "slacker" evading service to his country?[51]

Hopper and most of her respondents treated his pacifism as a sincerely held conviction, reinforcing the legitimacy of private religious belief as a basis for CO status rather than public membership in a pacifist church alone. Her critical respondents doubted Ayres, viewing him as "just afraid," "selfish," and hiding "behind the much abused . . . 'religion.'" In contrast, Hopper contended, "Lew Ayres, the man, has dedicated himself to God." One of her New York respondents, a CO himself, felt "a deep kinship with Lew Ayres as an upholder of Absolute Truth."[52] Hopper and her respondents looked to Ayres's film roles, particularly in *All Quiet on the Western Front*, as evidence of the sincerity of his beliefs and the legitimacy of his actions as an objector. A woman from Indiana believed Ayres as she had "studied him upon the screen," and the New York CO felt "that Lew has a Mission in life and his greatest role is yet to be played as a fulfillment of the promise he revealed in *All Quiet on the Western Front*."[53] Indeed, Ayres's role as the "war-embittered" soldier Paul Bäumer profoundly affected him as well as his audience. "The role was a powerful influence in my life," Ayres told his draft board. "I was twenty when I played the part of the German soldier who abhorred war and I thoroughly believe that the picture had much to do with my later thinking and my present step. War is as abhorrent to me in real life as it was in the screen play nearly 15 years ago."[54] Hopper publicized Ayres's statement, confirming that *All Quiet* made Ayres "a sincere believer in Pacifism and gave him a soul-searching hatred of war."[55]

All Quiet on the Western Front occupied a significant place in American screen memory, as Hopper and her respondents indicated. By 1942, the film was known as "the celluloid Bible of pacifists." Although not a pacifist, Hopper called the film "one of the greatest documents against war ever put on the screen" with a "grim lesson."[56] Directed by Lewis Milestone and scripted in part by Gordon Kahn—both of whom would be targeted in the anti-Communist alarm and attacks that constituted the postwar Red Scare—and released in 1930, the film was a major box office success, won Academy Awards for both best picture and best direction, and made a star out of Ayres. Unlike most war movies, *All Quiet*, like the original novel, exposed World War I as "futile, horrible, and destructive," and, as a result, its release was controversial. The film affected a whole generation's thinking about war, as film critic Judith Crist wrote. "We were the disillusioned who were learning that the world had not been made safe for democracy; we learned our lessons from *All Quiet on the Western Front*."[57] The film was rereleased in 1934 and then again, with added commentary and newsreel footage on the rise of Nazism, in 1939. This version of the film "was vigorously anti-Nazi," yet "it was also strongly isolationist, with emphasis upon peace in America," hence its popularity with Hopper. Critics, most prominently Erich Maria Remarque, author of the novel, questioned the use of a film about one war to justify opposition to all war. "It is too bad the story had this effect on Ayres," he stated.[58] Nevertheless, Ayres, Hopper, and most of her respondents justified their stances in support of conscientious objection within the moral framework of the movie.

Hopper and her respondents not only debated the legitimacy of Ayres's decision but also the meaning of his action for wartime America. This debate represented an extension of the public discourse about the "problem" of conscientious objection that dated back to the nation's beginning. At issue was how to balance the power of the federal government to call men for military service against the right of individual citizens to decide whether to serve.[59] For one of Hopper's critical respondents, Ayres was "not worthy of his birthright of American citizenship." For another, Ayres's action said, "To Hell with my country." But Hopper and most of her letter writers believed he had a right to conscientiously object to war. "I'm not defending Lew Ayres's convictions," she emphasized in her radio address. "I'm defending his right of conscience." "It was his perfect American right to do what he did," one of Hopper's female letter writers asserted, because "the country," wrote another, "recognizes a person's right to serve as his conscience permits."[60] Indeed, they felt this right was one of the "things we're fighting this war for," reflecting the prominence of freedom of worship and freedom of speech in President Roosevelt's 1941 inaugural address, "The Four Freedoms." "I am in here fighting so that such people can stand up for such principles," wrote one serviceman to Hopper. These supporters of Ayres used the same moral arguments in his defense that were used to justify the war effort.[61]

The debate over Lew Ayres in "Hedda Hopper's Hollywood" also concerned the consequences of his action for U.S. national security and definitions of wartime masculinity. Ayres's critics condemned the actor for not measuring up to the ideals of American manhood, of which military service and defense of nation were hallmarks. "For shame Lew Ayres—hiding your supposed! manhood," wrote one of Hopper's critical respondents. Another called Ayres a "conscientiousless coward" whose decision was "the equivalent to saying he would stand idly by or no doubt run away if his mother or sister was being ravaged by a sex degenerate." For critics, Ayres refused to uphold the moral obligations of the male protector or the political obligations of the male citizen, and his conscientious objection constituted a betrayal of the nation.[62] Supporters, however, believed Ayres's critics posed more of a danger to democracy than he did. One woman from Seattle saw the reaction against him as an example of "oppression, inhumanity, and intolerance." "Evidently," noted a Massachusetts respondent, "we, as well as our Axis enemies, need to learn and practice toleration." Supporters also commended Ayres for his courage and bravery in standing up for his convictions. "By so many Americans, he was thought of as a coward," Hopper stated, but "I knew he wasn't." "I think it takes a greater form of heroism to stand by one's principles," stated one of her respondents, "than it does to shoulder a gun."[63]

In her commentary, Hopper pointed out that Ayres had been "willing to serve his country in any way except carrying a gun into battle," and, although first assigned to a Civilian Public Service camp, he eventually won reassignment to the U.S. Army Medical Corps. Ayres's celebrity status helped him to secure a noncombatant military service position that did not assist other soldiers in killing, a precedent-setting achievement.[64] Hopper enthusiastically endorsed this development, and she and other commentators could not help but link Ayres with his screen role as Dr. Kildare. The *Los Angeles Times* noted that Ayres, "who as Dr. Kildare, performed medical miracles on the screen," always wanted to do medical work. One of Hopper's respondents considered this work apt for Ayres: "Witness his characterization of young Dr. Kildare in which there has always been a feeling of realism and sincerity." After Ayres's induction into the Army Medical Corps, Hopper too noted that, "like Dr. Kildare, he's tending the wounded, the sick, and the helpless."[65] Ayres's reassignment provided what the media and the military considered a resolution to the case. As one commentator noted, "There is some feeling . . . that with Ayres to be spotted in the Medical Corps of the Army, much of the sting will be taken out of the situation." Indeed, Ayres served overseas for two years, participating in three invasions in the Pacific war, and Hopper later wrote of "letters from soldiers in the South Pacific testifying to his courage under fire. He came home a hero."[66]

Hopper's support for Ayres set her apart from mainstream Hollywood yet fit with American public opinion. Hollywood "did a stupid thing," she recalled in her memoirs, in its "sanctimonious" condemnation of Ayres.[67] Members of the motion picture industry took action against the actor and his films in anticipation of box office pressure, badly misreading audience reaction. Few movie audiences protested with hissing or booing Ayres films. Instead, public condemnation, boycotts, and threats of boycotts came mostly from veterans groups, like the American Legion, which demanded adherence to their version of patriotic male citizenship, were "pockets of organized hostility" against COs, and later would become Hopper's strong allies in Cold War anti-Communism. When MGM conducted a comprehensive survey of audiences in twenty-one cities, the studio found little adverse criticism of Ayres.[68] Even so, after the war Ayres never regained his former popularity with audiences or the favor of the movie industry. "Hollywood never forgave Ayres the embarrassment he had caused them," film historian Colin Shindler has argued. Hopper remained a supporter, however, and Ayres reciprocated. Upon returning to Hollywood after the war, with various media outlets clamoring for an interview, he promised his first one to Hopper.[69] Moreover, she received many compliments for her stand in support of Lew Ayres. Most of her respondents praised her—although one canceled his subscription—and one woman doubted that Hopper's rival Louella Parsons would take such a stand. She also won the respect of public figures such as the *New Yorker* cartoonist James Thurber, who published an antiwar graphic novel, *The Last Flower*, in 1939. "You've won the admiration of a free-thinking American public," he wrote her.[70]

But Hopper inaccurately claimed, "I was the only one in town that came to his defense." In fact, a group of prominent actors and filmmakers, including Humphrey Bogart, John Huston, and Olivia de Havilland, sent a letter to *Time* arguing that "the abuse being heaped on Ayres was a sorry comment on the rights of democratic life." Their concern for and commitment to democracy meant most of them also took a stand for civil liberties during the Cold War.[71] Hopper, however, would not join them. Her respect for Ayres's civil liberties did not apply to every American, revealing her limited vision of U.S. wartime unity. For the Roosevelt administration, liberal intellectuals, progressive activists, and many Hollywood moviemakers, World War II provided an opportunity to expand the circle of citizenship and put aside racial, ethnic, religious, political, and class conflicts. Hopper, however, never embraced the new pluralistic vision of American society projected during "the Good War." When the war provided an opportunity and a catalyst for African Americans to advance the struggle for black equality in society and for "dignity in cinema," for example, she resisted the demand for change in filmic representations or race relations.[72] She also fiercely maintained her political antagonisms to racial change, the Democratic Party, organized labor, and the political Left, and, as became clear during the Cold War, she had little concern for or real understanding of civil liberties. She defended Ayres's right to private conscience because she liked and agreed with him and it fit with her isolationism and antistatism. She did not defend this right, and supported state incursions of private conscience when she disliked or disagreed with the person. Americans deserved civil liberties unless the person was "doing harm to his country"—as she understood it. In those cases, she asserted, "I'm agin' you."[73] And without a doubt, she was against Charlie Chaplin.

Chasing Charlie Chaplin

Hedda Hopper never liked Charlie Chaplin. Although she admired the film artistry of his early career—"I bow to his talent, which verges on genius"—he did what a Hollywood gossip columnist could not tolerate: he ignored her. Chaplin's worldwide fame and extensive economic resources gave him an extraordinary measure of independence within the motion picture industry, so he did not have to "truckle to gossip columnists."[74] Unlike other filmmakers, he never complained about being left out of Hopper's column and never responded to her praise or criticism. "It was galling," her biographer George Eells noted. "Hedda was like a big kid," a Hollywood publicist remembered. "Chaplin had slighted her."[75] Hopper's personal dislike translated into a decade-long campaign against Chaplin that extended from world war to Cold War and worked on three fronts: the professional, the personal, and the political. She consistently criticized his films of the 1940s and early 1950s—not just *The Great Dictator* (1940) but also *Monsieur Verdoux* (1947) and *Limelight* (1952)—his personal life, including his status in the United States as a resident noncitizen and his sexual and marital relationships with women, and his political support for liberal and leftist causes. For the nativist Hopper, Chaplin always had represented an alien threat, but she also saw him as a moral and political threat and, together with her readers and her allies in government and on the political Right, aimed to ruin his career in Hollywood.

Hopper strongly disapproved of Chaplin's real and alleged sexual and marital relations with women, particularly with young women, and she used her column to build a reputation for him as a "moral subversive." As it turned out, "charges of immorality" had "dogged" Chaplin since the 1920s.[76] Married unsuccessfully three times, his fourth marriage, with Oona O'Neill, daughter of the famous author and playwright Eugene O'Neill, was a lasting one. Chaplin met his future fourth wife when she was seventeen, and although the pair waited until her eighteenth birthday to marry, the thirty-six-year gap in their ages appalled Hopper—despite or perhaps because of a similar age gap between her and her former husband, De Wolf Hopper.[77] Over the years, Hopper accused Chaplin of using and abusing young women through casual sexual affairs and "casting-couch promiscuity": giving or promising the woman a leading role in his latest film, having a sexual relationship, and then dropping her from the film and his life. In late 1943, Hopper reported on the "many screen tests of girls whom he's discovered, which have never seen the light of day." She also emphasized the young age of the women in his life, introducing "little Oona O'Neill, Chaplin's latest lady, who just passed her 18th birthday," and recalling the story of an actress "who was a youngster hardly out of pigtails, busy with her schoolbooks, when her Chaplin chance came along."[78]

But Hopper dealt her greatest damage to Chaplin's moral reputation on June 3, 1943, when she facilitated and then broke the story of actress Joan Barry's paternity lawsuit against him, a scandal that led to three trials during World War II and proved "a turning point in the unraveling of Chaplin's star image."[79] One day, as Hopper recalled in her memoirs, "a girl walked into my office. I'd never seen her before; nor had I ever seen anyone as hysterical. From her wild eyes, I knew she was on the borderline of something desperate." The "girl" was the twenty-four-year-old Barry. In 1941, Chaplin met Barry, cast her briefly in a film, had a sexual affair with her, and then broke it off in 1942. Barry, who had a history of mental illness, continued to pursue him and in May 1943 sought to confront Chaplin with her pregnancy, claiming he was the father, but Chaplin refused to meet with her.[80] Hopper "was outraged" and, together with her fellow celebrity writer Florabel Muir, encouraged the paternity lawsuit against Chaplin, publicized Barry's side of the story, and supported her throughout the first trial and a retrial. "At stake was the life of an unborn child," Hopper later dramatized.[81] "I am not responsible for Miss Barry's condition," Chaplin declared, and blood tests proved him right. Yet they were inadmissible in California courts, and, after the first jury deadlocked in late 1944, the jury at the second trial in mid-1945 decided he was indeed the father and obligated to pay child support—a decision one Los Angeles attorney considered "a landmark in the miscarriage of justice."[82]

In the meantime, federal authorities, with help from Hopper, used the Barry-Chaplin scandal to indict Chaplin for violating the Mann Act, popularly known as the White Slave Traffic Act, which "made it illegal to transport a woman across state lines for immoral purposes."[83] Chaplin had paid for a roundtrip Los Angeles–New York City train fare for Barry in October 1942 but denied having sexual relations with Barry at that time. Hopper's role in the federal indictment, as with the paternity suit, again proved important. She provided information on Chaplin's relationship with Barry to the FBI during its investigation, served as a popular media outlet for the FBI's alleged findings, testified before the grand jury that indicted Chaplin, and publicized the charges and subsequent 1944 trial in her column. Hopper worked hard to foster sympathy for Barry and enmity for Chaplin among her readers by publishing stories about a "very nervous" Barry testifying in court and an incident when Barry "collapsed completely." And she succeeded. "I wish to congratulate you on your stand in the Chaplin matter," a Chicago woman wrote. "Apparently you are the only columnist who isn't afraid of him because the others either avoid it altogether or handle it with gloves." "P.S.," she added, "we don't think C. Chaplin is a genius."[84] "Just a few lines to let you know that one American woman appreciates the efforts you have made in your fight for Joan Barry's Civil Rights," wrote another reader, who saw Hopper's defense of Barry as integral to American involvement in World War II. "This case in the paper brings home to us all of the things we are fighting for and sacrificing much. That one small girl can't be pushed around by a lot of people with authority and influence is just one more good example of our American way."[85]

During and after the Barry-Chaplin scandal and trials, Hopper's coverage of Chaplin and letters from her readers made his private life and behavior into a public policy concern. The Justice Department and the U.S. Attorney in Los Angeles later admitted they had "flimsy evidence" against Chaplin stemming from the Barry affair, but when Chaplin won an acquittal in the Mann Act trial, Hopper remained silent about his victory and continued her personal attacks, undermining his vindication.[86] Most damningly, she linked his alleged immorality with his status as a noncitizen, and during the scandal she quoted an unnamed source on "moral turpitude as good and sufficient grounds for the deportation of an alien." Similarly, in 1945 Senator William Langer of North Dakota sought Chaplin's deportation, emphasizing "his unsavory record of lawbreaking, of rape, or the debauching of American girls 16 and 17 years of age."[87] An "indignant reader" of Hopper's spared no ugliness in agreement: "Ye Gods cannot that Chaplin beast be thwarted? . . . Moral turpitude has landed some . . . in Ellis Island and worse places and that nasty repulsive little enemy alien flies high . . . He should be ridden out of this America which he so scorns. Get busy you grand person and show him up."[88] By seeing the private Chaplin as a public threat and unworthy of residence in the United States, Hopper, her reader, and conservatives, like Langer, anticipated Cold War attacks on Chaplin as guilty of both "moral perversion" and "political subversion."[89]

Chaplin's liberal-left politics and support for progressive causes had long drawn the attention and ire of Hopper and other Hollywood conservatives, as well as state and federal authorities. Jack B. Tenney, a California state senator and chair of the Joint Fact-Finding Committee on Un-American Activities, California's "little HUAC," considered Chaplin "within the Stalinist orbit."[90] Hopper also deeply distrusted Chaplin. When he gave two speeches during World War II calling for a "second front" against Germany in western Europe to aid the Soviet Union's fight in the east, she argued he had preempted and undermined authorities, as "that front had already been arranged by the British and American governments." During the Cold War, Chaplin's "second front" speeches looked like "procommunist subversion" to Hopper and her allies, as did his interactions with Soviet artists and diplomats, his friendships and associations with the Hollywood Left, and his defense of the civil liberties of Communists.[91] When Hopper falsely charged Chaplin with contributing $25,000 to the Communist Party, the charge made it into Chaplin's FBI file; an investigation into whether Chaplin indeed ever had joined or financially supported the CPUSA concluded in November 1949 that he had not. But Hopper never wavered in her belief that Chaplin, as a foreigner and political progressive, upheld "an ideology offensive to most Americans and contrary to the principles that have left this nation the last refuge of freedom-loving people," an ideology he was "fostering" through his activities and his films.[92] Hopper's assumption that Communists in the movie industry inserted propaganda into Hollywood films meant she regarded Chaplin's films with great suspicion.

After *The Great Dictator* (1940), Chaplin released *Monsieur Verdoux* (1947), which also advanced a progressive, antifascist view of politics and society and provided fodder for his enemies, including Hopper. The film's black humor and Chaplin's role as a French Bluebeard who married and murdered wealthy women for their money marked a distinct "departure from Chaplin's aesthetic contract."[93] Hopper could not have been happier. "Poor dears," she called the publicists for the film's distributor United Artists, because "they're expected to perform miracles in reclaiming Chaplin's lost popularity and prestige with Mr. and Mrs. America." "I've witnessed a historic occasion," Hopper quoted an unnamed industry executive about a screening of *Monsieur Verdoux*. "I've just seen Chaplin's 'last' picture."[94] This comment was not far off the mark. Despite an innovative marketing strategy by the "brash" freelance publicity agent Russell Birdwell that played up the film's controversial content—even Hopper received Birdwell's promotional telegrams—*Monsieur Verdoux* was a box office failure and panned by critics in the United States. Even more, the film was subject to picketing, boycotts, and bans, and the FBI labeled it "Soviet propaganda."[95] Hopper reported positively on the protests, received material from the FBI, and sought to link Chaplin to Communism—to "Red-bait" him—by publicizing enthusiastic reviews of *Monsieur Verdoux* that appeared in left-wing publications. This "hate campaign," to borrow film historian Tino Balio's apt term, was directed at Chaplin and his film because his financial independence made him invulnerable to the punishment soon to be meted out to other filmmakers accused of Communist sympathies during the Cold War and strongly supported by Hopper: the blacklist.[96]

This hate campaign culminated in the cancellation of Chaplin's reentry permit in 1952, a few months before U.S. national elections returned Hopper's Republican Party to the White House after two decades of Democratic control. In the intervening years, Hopper continued to work against Chaplin. In 1950, when Chaplin decided to rerelease his 1931 classic *City Lights* as a way to reconnect with American audiences, Hopper sought to undermine him. "Charlie Chaplin's fearful about reissuing his picture, 'City Lights' here. Thinks there's too much ill feeling against him personally."[97] She also strategized with her U.S. senator (and soon-to-be vice president), Richard Nixon. "I agree with you that the way the Chaplin case has been handled has been a disgrace for years," Nixon wrote Hopper in May 1952. "Unfortunately, we aren't able to do much about it when the top decisions are made by the likes of Acheson and McGranery," referring to the secretary of state and the attorney general in the Democratic Truman administration. But a Republican victory in November could change that situation.[98] To help achieve this victory, Hopper sought to associate Chaplin's image of alien, moral, and political subversion with the Truman administration. When Chaplin and his family planned a trip to Europe in September 1952, Hopper reported that "Charlie's arrangements were made through the Justice Department, and their permit to re-enter America was obtained through the same source," implying collusion between Chaplin and the executive branch. "I've had a very close check on that for months," she later claimed, which was probably accurate given her relationship with the FBI.[99]

But U.S. Attorney General James McGranery cut short Hopper's partisan political attack when, two days after Chaplin left the country, he rescinded Chaplin's reentry permit and ordered the Immigration and Naturalization Service (INS) to hold him for hearings upon his return. Hopper crowed. Chaplin had thought he had "the right to go against our customs, to abhor everything we stand for, to throw our hospitality back in our faces." "I've known him for many years," she continued. "I abhor what he stands for, while I admire his talents as an actor. I would like to say, 'Good riddance to bad company.'"[100] Hopper's "vituperative" condemnation "was one of the worst press lashings Chaplin ever received," according to one of his biographers, Charles J. Maland, and received a wide audience when *Time* magazine included it in their coverage of Chaplin's immigration troubles. Hopper later revealed her access to inside information when she reported that Chaplin "never would have allowed his dancing feet to wander away from our shores" if he had known about the decision of government officials, who "were so afraid he'd get wind of their plans they practically held their breaths for two months."[101]

Although at first Chaplin said he would return to the United States to answer charges, in April 1953 he surrendered his reentry permit in Switzerland. A second massive hate campaign directed against his new film *Limelight* (1952) had occurred after his departure from the United States, supported by Hopper's allies in the American Legion and Catholic War Veterans, as well as her respondents. One male reader wanted Hopper to send her "good riddance" column "to all American Legion and other 100% American groups." "There are so many people," a Connecticut woman wrote, "that will not attend his pictures, they have absolutely no respect for him at all." The hate campaign destroyed the box office chances for *Limelight*, with it playing in only about 150 of the 2,000 theaters in which it was originally booked.[102] This poor reception indicated that Chaplin had no future in the United States as a filmmaker and actor. Blaming the "lies and vicious propaganda by powerful reactionary groups who by their influence and by the aid of America's yellow press have created an unhealthy atmosphere in which liberal minded individuals can be singled out and persecuted," Chaplin broke his American ties.[103] Hopper had achieved her aim of ruining his career in Hollywood.

Hopper's involvement confirms Maland's finding that the campaign against Chaplin involved a number of American institutions, including the FBI, Congress, the Department of Justice, the INS, and the press, cooperating formally and informally.[104] As it turned out, the INS had a "paucity of evidence against Chaplin," and it was "highly likely" he would have been readmitted to the United States if he had returned, but, to Hopper and her allies' great satisfaction, he did not. When the FBI could not provide reliable evidence of connections between Chaplin and the Communist Party, the INS had no political grounds to detain Chaplin, and thus his alleged immoral behavior came to be seen as "key to the case."[105] Certainly, Attorney General McGranery emphasized the morality issue. "If what has been said about him is true, he is, in my opinion, an unsavoury character" who "had been publicly charged with being a member of the Communist party, with grave moral charges and with making leering, sneering statements about the country whose hospitality has enriched him."[106] Rumor and unverifiable accusations, as well as memories of the Barry-Chaplin scandal and the image of Chaplin as a moral subversive, dominated McGranery's statement and the U.S. government's case against Chaplin. The innuendo and intertwining of public and private talk that characterized the Hollywood gossip of Hopper and her readers had found an audience and an endorsement from the highest law official in the United States.

For Hopper, chasing Charlie Chaplin out of the country was part of her larger fight against the Cold War at home and abroad, but her campaign against him began during World War II. In this way, Hopper anticipated the domestic Cold War even as the United States was fighting "the Good War." She also anticipated a Red Scare in Hollywood by aiding the formation of the Motion Picture Alliance for the Preservation of American Ideals (MPA) in 1944. A charter member of the organization and later a committee member and an officer, Hopper was joined over time by many prominent Hollywood conservatives, including Cecil B. DeMille, Walt Disney, Robert Taylor, and John Wayne. "We believe in, and like, the American Way of Life; the liberty and freedom which generations before us have fought to create and preserve," the MPA declared, and it pledged to fight the Communist subversion in Hollywood that members considered rampant.[107] Senator Robert R. Reynolds, a North Carolina Democrat and strong anti-Communist, praised the new organization for counteracting "the flagrant manner in which the motion picture industrialists of Hollywood have been coddling Communists." Not all observers were happy, however. For screenwriter Elmer Rice, the organization followed "orthodox Red-baiting and witch-hunting lines," and its members' views were "tinged with isolationism and anti-unionism and off-the-record of course . . . anti-Semitism and Jim Crowism."[108] Rice's description accurately captured Hedda Hopper's less than tolerant views and strident political tactics during the Cold War, which she and the MPA would fight in the name of "Americanism."

Hedda Hopper, "The Gossipist," makes the cover of *Time* magazine, July 28, 1947. (Courtesy of Time.)

Cold War Americanism,
Hopper Style

"My dear Miss Hopper," wrote one of her readers in September 1953. "Every morning my husband, who is 90 years of age, and a very young fellow at that, says to me—read me Hopper." The reader went on to praise Hedda Hopper's honesty and added, "We like your way of speaking out against subversion and policies detrimental to our form of Government." "I want to thank you," she finished, "for being pure grass roots American."[1] In describing Hopper as a "pure grass roots American," this reader used exactly the terms Hopper herself would have chosen. She presented herself as ideologically pure, holding to a conservatism untainted by any outside ideas, and a believer in absolutes. As in the case of her contemporaries on the far Right, she rejected—at least on a rhetorical level—"ambivalence" and "mixed feelings." One of her insults, in fact, was to call someone "a middle-of-the-roader."[2] Hopper also valued the second word in her reader's description, although she most often conveyed the idea of the grass roots by using the phrase "the public." She considered her politics to represent average Americans and, thus, reflected the "populist persuasion" in American history. She used the language of populism to defend American citizens against threats to their rights and liberties, threats she saw as emanating from government elites and foreign enemies. Hopper's populist rhetoric revealed how populism had changed from a political language of the Left—with banks and corporations posing the greatest danger to "the people"—to that of the Right by the 1950s.[3] But it was the last word in "pure grass roots American" that meant the most to her.

Hopper's writings were filled with "American," "Americans," and "America," revealing the importance of the nation—as she imagined it—and feelings of nationalism to Hopper. In her mind, American national greatness was a given.[4] Moreover, "Americanism" was the term she herself used to convey—in shorthand—her political perspective and positions during the Cold War. Americanism has been variously analyzed as an ideology, ideal, culture, way of life, and, by historian Gary Gerstle, "political language," but it functioned as an ideology—even if without a consistent internal structure—for Hopper.[5] When Hopper contrasted Americanism with Communism, as she often did in the Cold War era, it was with the assumption that the terms conveyed two opposing sets of principles, even belief systems, and the correlating practices, rather than two languages. "The search to define and affirm a way of life, the need to express and celebrate the meaning of 'Americanism,' was the flip side of stigmatizing Communism," argues historian Stephen Whitfield.[6] The ideological content of Hopper's writings and speeches during the Cold War indicated that by then conservatives owned the concept of Americanism. Although Gerstle and other scholars are correct that Americanism historically sustained "a multiplicity of political visions," the Cold War Americanism of Hopper, her respondents, and her allies in the Motion Picture Alliance and elsewhere carried "profoundly conservative political impulses."[7]

The ideological positions encompassed by Hopper's Cold War Americanism shaped the content and contours of her political advocacy and activism and deeply resonated with her audience at the height of her career in the late 1940s and into the 1950s. During this time, she achieved an estimated readership of 32 million for her newspaper column. She continued with her radio and film work and began to appear on television as both an actress and "herself." She had two different radio series, *This Is Hollywood* and *The Hedda Hopper Show*, hosted television episodes of series such as *Playhouse 90*, explored a television series of her own, and published her first, best-selling set of memoirs, *From Under My Hat*. She earned an annual income close to $250,000 (the equivalent of about $2 million today) and made the cover of *Time* magazine on July 28, 1947.[8] A *Time* cover was something Walter Winchell and Louella Parsons never achieved. Winchell "must have had a fit when he saw it" and Parsons "must be burning," wrote publishing colleagues, but then neither had the favor of *Time*'s publisher, Henry Luce.[9]

Yet Hopper's career high point occurred as the motion picture industry reeled from a series of post–World War II shocks: sharply declining movie attendance as Americans moved to the suburbs and bought televisions, increased foreign taxation on Hollywood imports when overseas receipts could make or break a film, bitter labor conflict in 1945 and 1946, government investigations of Communism in the movie capital beginning in 1947, and the Paramount decision, which divested the big studios of their theater chains in 1948. Although Hopper's gossip career looked solid and successful, the industry she depended on did not. As the Cold War began, Hopper and Hollywood did not share Americans' "grand expectations" for the postwar period, a situation that exacerbated Hopper's Cold War fears and fueled her conservative Americanism.[10]

Selling Americanism

In early 1947, Hedda Hopper expressed alarm about a proposal to prohibit exporting Hollywood films that "may offend the political beliefs of other nations." Her alarm was both economic and ideological. "Since when has it become a sin," she asked, "to sell Americanism?"[11] For Hopper and others, ranging from Eric A. Johnston, the head of the industry's trade association, the Motion Picture Association of America (MPAA), to the foreign policy adviser and diplomat George F. Kennan, Hollywood marketed not just a product, the movies, to a world audience, but also the United States of America, its culture and political economy. "This was salesmanship of a high order," John Elsom has argued.[12] But Hopper had long believed such salesmanship was one of the functions of the motion picture industry. In mid-1939, she commended *Land of Liberty* (1939), a film that presented Hollywood's vision of "the story of America" through clips from over one hundred historical epics and documentaries about the United States compiled by Cecil B. DeMille for the New York World's Fair. Hopper described *Land of Liberty* as an excellent example of "Americanism for the screen" and urged the industry, "Let's get together and sell America to Americans!"[13] What changed between 1939 and 1947, with World War II and the Cold War, was a shift in Hopper's focus from looking inward to looking outward, from the domestic audience to the world audience, from isolationism to interventionism. What remained consistent was selling Americanism.

For Hopper and her allies, "Americanism" expressed belief in, endorsement of, and preference for American ideals and institutions—as they defined them. In 1951, when Hopper was an officer, the MPA introduced an award called the "Americanism award" to honor those who espoused and worked toward the organization's brand of conservative Americanism. Hopper also used Americanism to indicate her approval of others' politics. "Congratulations on your Americanism," she wrote one of her fans in 1961. Fans complimented her in return. "Once again, Miss Hopper, thank you for your bravery and Americanism." "Dear Hedda," wrote another. "Always admired your solid stand for Americanism 100%."[14] Hopper's easy use of Americanism to convey what she understood to be the ideals and institutions of the United States contrasted with the difficulties faced by the U.S. government to provide a "positive ideology" and "ideological unity" for overseas propaganda efforts during the Cold War. In the Cold War's "ideological and symbolic" struggle, it was felt at the time that the United States had a "serious propaganda handicap" because it could not offer a "counteracting inspirational concept" to that of Communism.[15] One important attempt at imparting ideology and inspiration was the "People's Capitalism" campaign designed for a series of trade fair exhibitions in the 1950s, but Hopper always considered Americanism a more compelling "grammar for the nation's message" than this advertising slogan. In the end, the United States fought the Cold War not in the name of capitalism or democracy "but in the name of America."[16]

Hopper's affiliation with the American Legion confirmed her Americanism. The American Legion, with its Americanism Commission to promote "the true spirit of Americanism," was at the forefront of U.S. domestic anti-Communism from its founding in 1919 by World War I veterans through the Cold War, and Hopper maintained close contact.[17] In 1950, the national commander of the American Legion, Erle Cocke, appeared on the first broadcast of *The Hedda Hopper Show*. "We of The American Legion," he informed her, "have long admired the courageous battle you have waged in behalf of Americanism and against Communism." Five years later, Hopper's local American Legion post presented her with their annual Americanism award.[18] Hopper corresponded with Legion officials and read the *American Legion Magazine.* "I love your magazine and applaud your stand," she wrote the managing editor. "We've got to stick together, or we'll all fall together." "The Reds hate you but we love you for your stand against Communism," read one telegram from the Legion to Hopper. She attended and addressed Legion functions, and she covered Legion news in her column. "'Red, White, and Blue"—an American Legion fund-raising show—"promises to be the biggest thing since the atomic bomb," Hopper reported in mid-1950.[19] She never missed a chance to comment on Hollywood stars affiliated with the Legion. "There'll be some bowing and scraping at Fibber McGee and Molly's household in Encino," she commented in 1954. "Their cook, Albert Alvez, was elected Commander of the Encino American Legion Post, which means Alvez outranks his boss who's a mere Legion member." With 3.2 million members, a million in its Women's Auxiliary, and 17,000 posts in 1947, together with its magazine and other publications, the American Legion played a "crucial, opinion-setting role" in the early years of the Cold War.[20]

The Americanism of Hopper, the Legion, and their allies overarched a constellation of ideas and beliefs, and informed and motivated their political activism. Hopper articulated her Cold War Americanism in various venues during the late 1940s through the early 1960s, including her short-lived radio series in the early 1950s, *The Hedda Hopper Show* on NBC. The weekly half-hour radio program closed with an "editorial" in which she commented on the issues of the day. These radio editorials provided room for more extensive political commentary than did her gossip column, and letters and telegrams from Hopper's respondents showed they appreciated and approved of them. Although the editorials were ghostwritten by L. D. Hotchkiss, an editor at the conservative *Los Angeles Times*, and contained more, and more specific, evidence to support a political argument than Hopper ever marshaled, their ideological content differed not at all from Hopper's column. Indeed, Hopper thanked him for putting the thoughts of her readers and herself "so brilliantly into words."[21] Because the show ran from October 14, 1950, to May 13, 1951, during some of the harshest and darkest days of fighting in the Korean War, when many Americans feared that "World War III was at hand," Hopper, aided by Hotchkiss, devoted most of the editorials to making the case for her brand of Americanism.[22]

Liberty and freedom were at the heart of Hopper's Americanism. She used these words to convey the basic right to live one's life free of external restraints and to privilege independence and individualism over social qualities or collective interests. In 1960, her anti-Communist campaigns in defense of the "Free World" earned her the label "fighter for freedom," and her fans supported these campaigns, as "good Americans can help this country keep the freedom we hold dear."[23] For Hopper, it was up to the American people to win the Cold War. "Yes, the diplomats may decree, the generals plan and direct," she editorialized on her radio program, *The Hedda Hopper Show*, in early 1951. "But it's the little people who win or lose wars. The little people—the everyday citizens—like you and me."[24] Moreover, popular sovereignty—the power and authority of the people to govern—was exactly what Hopper saw as at stake in the Cold War. "For what is government but the people—their voice?" she asked. "And why should we drop the most successful way of life in the history of civilization for this foreign ideology which says government is everything—people nothing?"[25]

In discussions of freedom and liberty, Hopper and her respondents looked backward and referenced both facts and myths about American history, particularly the American Revolution, the Founding Fathers, and the birth of the republic. These references allowed them, as it had earlier purveyors of Americanist language, "to legitimate their particular goals by linking themselves to the revered causes of the nation's past."[26] In expressing her anti-Communist views, one reader listed her extensive Americanist credentials: "My grandfather familiarized me with the Declaration of Independence. He also read to me many times the Bill of Rights which his maternal ancestor drew up . . . . My husband's great great grandfather and great uncle both signed the Declaration of Independence. . . . And we have tried to be good Americans."[27] Hopper similarly made links with the past. For example, on her radio program in 1951, she asserted, "The Commies yell loudest for peace, while attempting to take over the world by subversion and force of arms. But that's not the kind of peace we Americans can accept." Then she quoted the American revolutionary Patrick Henry, ending with, "As for me, give me liberty or give me death."[28] By nostalgically invoking the words and actions of early Americans, Hopper sought to justify her political perspectives; in turn, she, along with other Hollywood insiders like Walt Disney, contributed to a Cold War development in which Americanism, according to historian Michael Kammen, "came to connote a love of continuity and respect for the past" in contrast to Communism's "repudiation of and break with the past."[29]

The meaning of freedom or liberty Hopper highlighted most was economic freedom—the opportunity promised by capitalism or, in the American Legion's favorite phrase, "the free-enterprise system"—which she still felt threatened by "big government."[30] "This nation was built on the theory of individual liberty," she commented on her radio show, "on the premise that success or failure was up to us." As a result, the United States was "the greatest business country in the world. In fact, our great business ability is a major source of our strength."[31] Hopper's emphasis on economic freedom affirmed capitalism and the economic status quo and fit with her antistatism. She still resented the income tax, but then she was not alone. A 1952 Gallup survey found that seventy-one percent of those polled felt taxes were too high.[32] She also maintained that the welfare state eroded American liberty and undermined the self-reliance and work ethic of citizens. "There's been too much talk about being taken care of from the cradle to the grave," she declared. Americans were relying too much on government. "We are depending more and more on subsidies and allowing Washington to do our thinking for us."[33] She kept a vigilant watch on what she considered "creeping socialism," as did her readers. One Chicago woman wrote about a play in which Bing Crosby opened a newspaper with the headline "Health Program Gains Supporters." "There was nothing else on the front page . . . to read except that propaganda." "He'd better be more careful after this," Hopper's reader threatened, "unless he is for these socialistic measures, and if he is that's the last picture of his I'll go to see." By opposing and labeling as "socialistic" social welfare measures, Hopper and this reader wielded "an effective bludgeon" and aided the larger anti-Communist effort to fight the expansion of the New Deal welfare state.[34]

Intrinsic to Hopper's Americanism, along with freedom and liberty, were her pride and patriotism in being an American. She loved her country and assumed her politics expressed her loyalty. In addressing complaints about the political content of her radio show, Hopper defended herself. "They accused me of being a flag-waver. I AM a flag-waver. I'm proud of it. And I'll wave Old Glory every time I get a chance until Gabriel blows his trumpet." She put great store in the power and public expression of patriotic feelings, strongly believing, as she said in late 1950 while United Nations forces fared badly in Korea, that it was patriotism—"love of country and the will to defend it to the last man and woman"—that would "save any nation in this topsy turvy world."[35] Meanings of patriotism are multiple, as historian John Bodnar has argued. For Hopper, given her conservatism and great fear of Communist domination, patriotism in the Cold War years became about self-sacrifice and service in defense of the nation. Her pride in the United States focused on maintaining national greatness within a global context. She rarely expressed "the liberal version of patriotism," with its "appeal of egalitarianism and the promise of democracy." Instead, she advocated what the "reality of the Cold War" reinforced: "the power of illiberal patriotism" with "its devotion to individualism."[36]

As part of her national pride and patriotism, Hopper preferred all things American—no matter how insignificant, including women's fashions. In 1947, when the French designer Christian Dior introduced what came to be called the "new look"—a term later applied to President Dwight D. Eisenhower's nuclear strategy—Hopper was aghast. "The Battle of the Bulge is being repeated between French and American fashion designers," she declared, referring to the famous World War II battle.[37] According to historian Sara Evans, instead of the "simple, loose-fitting, square-shouldered" clothing of the World War II era, Dior proposed "a dramatically new silhouette"—long skirt, narrow waist, and a prominent bust line, with padded bras and reinforced girdles "to add and subtract where necessary" to complete the new look.[38] Dior's style of femininity was traditional, but Hopper did not welcome its return, despite her endorsement of traditional morality and family life as properly "American." "After the years spent streamlining our figures, I hope it's not thought that we women will pad our hips and show our sloping shoulders because French designers want us to." Hopper tried to discourage this fashion trend among her readers. "Our smartest women are following the styles of Adrian—rather than Paris—this year." Adrian, who had retired from his position as MGM's chief costume designer to open his own fashion salon in Beverly Hills, kept shorter skirts and his famous square shoulder line, as did Hopper.[39] "Any woman with good legs should show them, regardless of her age," she instructed. "Ahem, I'm showing mine." Although she was fighting a losing battle, Hopper criticized stars wearing Paris fashions and complimented those wearing American designs throughout the 1950s.[40] At stake for Hopper was not just a dress style but national pride.

Hopper also believed Hollywood films should promote national pride. She praised films that "teach the meaning of democracy" and in 1946 proposed a Best Picture Oscar for "a wonderful picture of democracy at work," rewarding patriotic content regardless of its merit as a motion picture. Darryl Zanuck wrote to criticize her proposal, arguing that the Academy Award should recognize "production achievement" not "flag waving." The producer believed a new, separate award more appropriate for "pictures that sell Americanism."[41] Hopper's strong support for films that "waved the flag" extended the following year to anti-Communist films. "Our producers are finally waking up to the perils of Communism," she reported in April 1947. "It's high time." She lauded Zanuck's plans for the first postwar anti-Communist film, *The Iron Curtain* (1948), a Cold War spy thriller about Communist subversive activities in Canada, and agreed with his aim of "impressing on the public mind the dangers we are faced with." When the film came out, she reviewed it as "a picture everyone will want to see."[42]

Hopper similarly endorsed her MPA ally John Wayne's *Big Jim McLain* (1952), in which he plays a HUAC investigator who travels to Hawaii to run "Operation Pineapple" and uncovers a Communist conspiracy. When the *New York Times* film critic Bosley Crowther panned *Big Jim McLain*, Hopper retorted that the film, "which everyone expected to die a horrible death in New York, is doing a smashing business at the Paramount. Good!"[43] In these ways, she supported the aims of what would become in 1955 a top-secret government campaign called "Militant Liberty." The campaign, which enlisted the support of Hopper's MPA colleagues Wayne and Ward Bond, designed "to insert the theme of 'freedom' into American movies" to explain what was at stake in the Cold War, convey a sense of the Communist threat, and motivate people to combat that threat.[44] Hopper and her allies shared these goals and supported such films—despite their failure at the box office—as a demonstration of their and Hollywood's patriotism.

Hopper's patriotism meant she refused to believe her country was anything less than perfect. Where this "superpatriotism" found its fullest expression was in her opposition to films she believed presented an unflattering picture of the United States, such as "social problem films" that took as their subject a problem or conflict in society.[45] One movie in particular raised Hopper's ire: *Blackboard Jungle* (1955), which she considered the most brutal film she had ever seen. Produced by MGM when Dore Schary was head of production and starring Sidney Poitier, *Blackboard Jungle* told of a vocational high school "terrorized" by juvenile delinquents. It was a story "torn from the headlines," as the media, including Hopper, devoted much attention to the "problem" of juvenile delinquency in the mid-1950s.[46] When a Senate subcommittee, chaired by Senator Estes Kefauver, investigated the influence of motion pictures on youth violence, Schary was the first to testify. Asked if he and others at MGM had "acted responsibly" when making *Blackboard Jungle*, Schary defended his film. But one witness, a film critic for *Catholic Tidings*, disagreed, stating the film "contain[ed] too much brutality to be seen by young viewers," and the British Board of Film Censors rejected the film.[47] In fact, the movie's portrayal of juvenile delinquency as "cool" and "anti-authoritarian," combined with the first time use of a rock and roll song as a movie theme (Bill Haley and His Comets' "Rock Around the Clock"), proved a hit with young audiences—a market studio executives were seeking—and even caused theater riots, which Hopper covered in her column to criticize the film.[48]

Hopper especially objected to *Blackboard Jungle* and other "pictures that show the worst side of American life" when they were exported. During the Cold War, the United States Information Agency also sought "to reduce the negative impact abroad of U.S. commercial films," which Hopper considered huge in the case of *Blackboard Jungle*. The film showed "dreadful, dreadful people" and "went all over the world and did a great deal of harm," she argued.[49] She supported Clare Boothe Luce, then U.S. ambassador to Italy, in her protest against the screening of the film at the Venice Film Festival in 1955. Moreover, Hopper enlisted her readers and the American Legion in the campaign. "Mrs. Clare Booth[e] Luce is to be congratulated for her good judgment in banning *The Blackboard Jungle* from the Venice Film Festival," one of Hopper's readers wrote directly to Dore Schary. "I agree with Hedda Hopper that this picture <u>should never</u> have been made."[50] Although Luce did not have the power to censor or ban the film, she succeeded in pressuring the distributor to pull the film out of the festival, because she believed "films are often viewed as the 'face of America,' as we ourselves wish it shown abroad," and feared the film "might give comfort and assistance to the Communists here." Hopper agreed that movies always "should reflect the best side of America" and, in this way, "could be our greatest ambassador of good will."[51] Hopper had a clear understanding of the importance and uses of what historians of U.S. foreign relations call "soft power"—the global appeal of American popular and consumer culture—as distinct from, yet a crucial counterpart to, the "hard power" of U.S. military might.[52]

But in her fight for Americanism and against Communism Hopper did not neglect "hard power" either, and she took a militant stance on the Korean

War. In keeping with her residual isolationism and distrust of Democrats, and like the politician she most admired, Robert Taft, she had misgivings about the Korean War. Both criticized waging the war under the auspices of the UN. Hopper had attended the 1945 founding meeting of the UN in San Francisco as a correspondent for CBS and believed the organization ineffective. "And where is the peace that was promised?" She later believed it dangerous and supported a conservative women's successful grassroots anti-Communist campaign to ban "foreign, antinationalist" UN-sponsored materials in the Los Angeles schools.[53] In Korea, she was most concerned about how the UN constrained the United States' "free hand" or unilateralism in foreign affairs:

> We're fighting a war in Korea under direction of [the] United Nations. Our principal enemy is Communist China, and to date these Reds have killed, wounded, or caused to be missing, more than 40,000 of our boys. American boys! . . . If we have to fight a war, let's fight it our way. Let's issue the orders in Washington. . . . Let's not pull our punches while the diplomats palaver and stall in the United Nations. Let's tell the world that 40,000 American boys are 40,000 too many to sacrifice on the altar of diplomatic double-talk. And that from now on we mean business! Our business![54]

For Hopper, the Korean War—a "crucial fulcrum upon which the Cold War pivoted"—needed to be fought hard and won. In this way, she lent significant support to the "extraordinary overall escalation" in American military spending and in Cold War fear and hysteria that the war wrought.[55]

Achieving and maintaining U.S. military superiority and backing and publicizing the armed forces were top priorities for Hopper. During the Korean War, as during World War II, she included items in her column about soldiers and veterans connected to Hollywood and about the motion picture industry's aid to the war effort. "It's high time our town mobilize," she wrote in early 1951, and in the next months she reported on the production of a Marine Corps training film and the opening of "Hollywood's new USO." "The place was packed. I haven't seen so many servicemen in town since the last war." She attended and wrote about military parades and Cold War patriotic pageants, including new American holidays such as Armed Forces Day and Loyalty Day, held on May 1 to rival the Soviet May Day.[56] She accompanied Bob Hope on USO tours in 1954, 1956, 1957, and 1958, traveling to entertain military troops in Hawaii, the Pacific Islands, Alaska, Germany, Italy, and Scotland. She received military recognition, invitations, and awards, including a Department of Defense "Certificate of Esteem," and corresponded with military personnel. "Major David Crocker has named a weapon carried in Korea 'The Hedda Hopper,'" she reported. "It carries machine guns, mortars, and other deadly weapons. I hope the Commies get a bang out of it."[57] Most meaningfully, Hopper expressed gratitude and respect for military personnel and their sacrifices in fighting America's Cold War, particularly in Korea. "American casualties are approaching 55,000," she reported in March 1951. "Somehow our share of death seems a little heavy. But perhaps that's in proportion to our love of freedom."[58]

To Hopper, Americanism meant nothing without strong, stanch opposition to global Communism. Before and after the Korean War, she believed the Soviet Union and its allies posed a grave military and ideological threat and that the United States needed to fight aggressively to "roll back," not just contain, Communism in the world. In these beliefs, Hopper stood squarely in the mainstream of her political party. The 1952 Republican Party platform rejected the Truman administration's policy of containment—pursued since the 1947 beginning of the Cold War and aimed at limiting Soviet expansion—as "negative, futile, and immoral." "The idea of 'rolling back' communism and freeing the Soviet satellites seemed much more appealing than merely containing the Soviets," historian Lewis L. Gould notes. Rollback was difficult if not impossible to achieve, however, as became clear after President Eisenhower took office. In addition to settling for a truce and a divided country in Korea in 1953, the Eisenhower administration decided not to support militarily or diplomatically the Hungarian Revolution in 1956, despite Secretary of State John Foster Dulles's declaration of "liberation" as the goal of U.S. foreign policy. "The concept of liberating captive nations faded away in the face of the reality of Soviet power in that region," Gould continues.[59] For Hopper—and especially other conservative anti-Communists who had encouraged eastern Europeans to revolt—this was a betrayal and, when Soviet tanks rolled in and crushed the rebellion, a tragedy. Hopper's anger at the U.S. failure to aid the Hungarians remained fierce for years. "We behaved shamefully toward the Hungarian people," she wrote in 1962. "When they called for our help we gave them the back of our hands."[60]

Hopper expressed her anger, as did other conservative anti-Communists, about the Soviet suppression of the Hungarian "freedom fighters" and the administration's lack of action when Soviet Premier Nikita S. Khrushchev accepted Eisenhower's invitation to visit the United States in 1959. This visit resulted from a thawing in Cold War tensions in the late 1950s that included cultural exchanges. Although U.S. officials saw, as did Hopper, "militarization as the dominant paradigm of postwar American diplomacy," the "cultural diplomacy" of Khrushchev's visit and other exchanges was an important dimension of the Cold War.[61] Unlike some conservatives who feared cultural exchanges allowed "Red agents" in the country, Hopper strongly supported these contacts after a 1958 U.S.-Soviet cultural agreement, revealing that her anti-Communist stance did not extend to all things Russian. For example, she raved about a performance of the Moiseyev Dance Company in May 1958. "You don't have to visit Moscow. The best of Russia is at our Shrine Auditorium. I'd seen their dancers before at the New York Met; I could see them again; you never weary of perfection." But Khrushchev's visit was of a different order and very controversial. "Letters, telegrams, and petitions flooded Congress opposing the visit," Donald Critchlow describes, "while conservative periodicals lashed out against the visit of Stalin's former lieutenant, the man . . . who had sent troops into Budapest."[62]

In protest, Hopper refused to attend any functions honoring Khrushchev during his visit to Hollywood in September 1959, and a number of her respondents, all from southern California, supported her stance. "I compliment you upon your courageous stand while bloody butcher K was here." "You show true Americanism," wrote another. "Now today, in our country's darkest hour in our time . . . our president has seen fit to invite the most debase cruelest man in the world to visit our country." One reader, perhaps inspired by the suggestion of some anti-Communist organizations to wear black armbands in objection to the visit, shared with Hopper her own protest: draping her front door with black crepe and lowering her American flag to half mast.[63] Hopper also vehemently criticized members of the movie industry who participated in the Khrushchev visit, particularly those in attendance at a luncheon sponsored by 20th Century-Fox, and her readers joined in the criticism. "We watched the disgraceful episode on T.V. and to see these people . . . fawn over this 'butcher of Budapest' was so nauseating I could not eat my lunch on Saturday." For another reader, missing lunch was the least of it; she threatened a boycott and deportation. "After viewing the disgusting performance by the so-called stars, have decided they are not worth patronizing in any of their future shows or pictures, maybe someone will give them a one way ticket to Russia!" Although one reader cautioned, "We do owe politeness and dignity to him as a guest of President Eisenhower," she was the exception. The rest encouraged Hopper and, since the majority of Americans approved of Khrushchev's visit, defended her to any critics. "I pray the red mob won't deluge you with vulgar insults. God Bless You," ended one letter.[64]

As this letter indicated, religion shaped and buttressed Hopper and her respondents' Americanism. According to one reader, "my family since its beginnings in America has felt that to be an American, a good American, was being aligned to God," revealing Americanism as "a cross between ideology and religion" or a even a "civic religion." Expressions of religious faith became more prominent in Hopper's writings and speeches with the Cold War, as happened in Hollywood generally. This "public spirituality" appeared in films such as *David and Bathsheba* (1951) and *The Ten Commandments* (1956).[65] Hopper's new religiosity reflected less her own belief system than the image of "a bipolar world divided between God and Satan" that dominated the era; "as we find ourselves arrayed against this ideology of Godlessness," she editorialized, "we are turning more and more to the teachings of the man who showed the way nearly 2,000 years ago." Even Hopper's casual references to God— "God bless you," "God help us"—increased, but then, as Frances Stoner Saunders comments, "God was everywhere" during the height of the Cold War.[66] Congress made "In God We Trust" the nation's official motto in 1956, and it began to appear on dollar bills and coins. When Hopper discovered a dollar bill without the motto in 1961 during the Democratic Kennedy administration, she expressed fears of a government conspiracy to remove the phrase. One of her readers responded, exhibiting the belief of many anti-Communists that Christianity was a bulwark against Communism. "May God bless you for printing that article," he wrote. "A Godless country is a Communist country."[67] For Hopper and her respondents, God was on America's side and America on God's side in the Cold War, and anyone less than devoted to God, the United States, or fighting the Cold War became a suspect "un-American."

Fighting the "Un-Americans"

In articulating and acting on her Cold War Americanism, Hedda Hopper defined what and who was "un-American." She fervently believed that she stood and spoke for "real" Americans, so anyone who disagreed with her was, by definition, un-American. As her biographer George Eells argues, "She increasingly equated difference of opinion with disloyalty." She also increasingly lacked respect for free speech, despite her own use of that very right every day in her gossip column. In one of her radio editorials in late 1950, near the end of a great controversy over loyalty oaths and academic freedom at the University of California, she warned, "Let's make certain that misuse of this term 'academic freedom' does not lead us down a cockeyed alley from which there is no return. The alley to Moscow!"[68] With no toleration of diverse political perspectives or minority points of view, Hopper judged people as either with her and American or against her and un-American.

Hopper not only conveyed an "us" versus "them" mentality, but she also set out to rid the United States of the influence of those she opposed. "The quest for 'Americanism,'" historian David Caute notes, always involved "the hunting down of 'Un-Americans.'" Hopper thus deployed her Americanism to both include and exclude. As she avowed on *The Hedda Hopper Show* in early 1951: "This is the moment of Americans for America. The moment we all must stand and be counted. And let's boot out the chiselers, the doubters, and the disloyal now."[69] Along with her anti-Communist allies, she considered the most disloyal and dangerous un-Americans to be members of the Communist Party USA and Communist sympathizers or "fellow travelers." She would have concurred with Senator Joseph McCarthy, who emerged as a leading anti-Communist in February 1950 after accusing the State Department of harboring Communists, that "the Communists within our borders have been more responsible for the success of Communism abroad than Soviet Russia."[70]

This "specter of the enemy within" gave anti-Communists like Hopper a way to explain and understand the series of dramatic global developments over 1949 and 1950 that made "the communist menace . . . an even more frightening presence."[71] In 1949, the Soviet Union exploded an atomic bomb in August, and Chinese Communists declared the People's Republic of China in October. The next year, the North Koreans invaded South Korea, starting the Korean War. That year, Hopper spoke about Americans fighting World Wars I and II, and "now we prepare for a third," while a public opinion poll showed fifty-seven percent of those surveyed believed they were "actually in World War III." At the same time, public revelations occurred about the existence of spies in the United States. In 1949, the case of Alger Hiss, a former high State Department official accused of Communist Party membership and espionage, became a "national sensation," ending with his conviction for perjury in January 1950.[72] The next month Klaus Fuchs, a British physicist who had worked on the Manhattan Project, confessed to passing on atomic secrets to the Soviets during the 1940s, and his confession led to further arrests, including those of Julius and Ethel Rosenberg in July 1950. Domestic Communism, it appeared to Hopper and others, had contributed to successes for global Communism, and anti-Communists were able, as historian M. J. Heale argues, "to tap the vein of suspicion that traitors in government were selling out the United States to the Soviet Union."[73]

These developments reinforced the conviction among Hopper and others that the Cold War needed to be fought at home as well as abroad, a fight that was both an end in itself and served other ends. "Why send millions to other countries to fight Commies," she asked in 1947, "when we let them run riot under our noses in America?"[74] This conviction intensified the reach and impact of domestic anti-Communism beyond that of card-carrying Communists to all progressives and liberals. Hopper, J. Edgar Hoover, and other anti-Communists indicted as un-American anyone who doubted or questioned any aspect of the anti-Communist cause, methods, or effect, accusing them of "coddling the commies" and being just as traitorous. While Hopper sincerely believed in the cause of anti-Communism—her long-standing commitment indicated sincerity—she also was cynically aware of how this fight served the interests of her and her conservative political allies. The deployment of anti-Communism against more Americans than the relatively few members of the Communist Party USA—estimated at seventy-five thousand at its height in 1938, although high membership turnover meant a larger number associated with the CPUSA over time—provided real material gains, enabling various government agencies, private organizations, and public figures to expand their power; McCarthy and Hoover's FBI are just two examples.[75] Hopper also joined with anti-Communists in Red-baiting any challenges to the status quo, and by wielding accusations of Communism they successfully stymied most social reform and social movements until the 1960s.

At a time of intense competition between the two main political parties, members of the Republican Party, from Hopper to Nixon, McCarthy to Eisenhower, benefited from accusing Democrats of being "soft" on Communism. In a booklet issued during the 1950 congressional elections, the Republican National Committee urged candidates to run on this issue, stressing that the "red brand of Communism has been stamped on the Democrat record. Whitewash can not hide it."[76] That year, Nixon ran a California Senate campaign against his opponent, the "Pink Lady" Helen Gahagan Douglas, which not only resulted in his "smashing" victory but also signaled the success of the Republican electoral strategy of Red-baiting. As a member of Women for Nixon, Hopper spearheaded and starred in a radio commercial that exemplified the strategy. The commercial began with the sound of a fierce rainstorm. Four women waiting to catch a bus sought shelter and began to discuss the upcoming election. One woman, a "venomously sarcastic cynic," supported Douglas because the liberal candidate opposed sending aid to countries to help fight Communism. Another woman, played by Hopper, explained this was why she intended to vote for Nixon and then went on to accuse Douglas of having "un-American" ideas. Douglas wanted to "give away our atomic secrets" and curtail investigations of domestic "subversion." "If you stand too close to a red lamp," Hopper's character added in a Red-baiting fashion, "you're bound to get burned."[77] Nixon's Senate win in 1950 positioned him to be Eisenhower's pick for Vice President in 1952, and Hopper rejoiced in their victory, attended the inauguration, and devoted three columns to the "big event." "The general feeling around town is one of glorious rebirth," she reported from Washington, "so let's hope it is."[78]

Such real, material interests served by the anti-Communist movement were never part of Hopper's public discourse, however; the emphasis instead was on ideology. Political ideology is often seen by scholars as the defining characteristic of those considered un-American in this new Red Scare. This emphasis on ideology marked a change from the first Red Scare of the World War I years and the 1920s, when race, ethnicity, nationality, and religion defined the un-Americans, and can be attributed to developments in the 1940s when Americanism itself came to convey "a commitment to intergroup tolerance and harmony."[79] Hopper, for example, made a distinction between personal characteristics and what she perceived as dangerous, un-American ideas when pursuing her targets. As she declared in her column, "There's a great difference between Russians and Communists."[80] But prejudices and "images of otherness" based on these personal characteristics, along with homophobia or fear of sexual deviance, antifeminism, and opposition to organized labor, intertwined with ideology in historically old and new ways during the Cold War, gained more force in the 1950s, and influenced Hopper's choice of target.[81] Still, a professed dedication to Americanism and anti-Communism by an African American, immigrant, or labor leader could trump these prejudices, at least "on the record," for Hopper and other anti-Communists, as she publicly embraced anyone with the correct political ideology as allies and included them in her circle of "Americans."

At a time when her allies in the FBI equated blackness with "subversiveness and whiteness with Americanism," Hopper trusted very few African Americans and targeted many more, with the twin aims of furthering anti-Communism and hindering the struggle for black equality.[82] Among black Americans, Paul Robeson stood out, and she "rushed to her own set of barricades" to attack him during the Cold War, according to Robeson biographer Martin Duberman. Hopper opposed Robeson for both his fight against racism and his friendliness toward Communism. At the beginning of her career, she embraced Robeson as a performer, arguing that his singing of "Ol' Man River"—a song in the black spiritual tradition from the Jerome Kern–Oscar Hammerstein II musical and then film Show Boat (1936) with which Robeson became identified—had never "been surpassed."[83] Robeson made "Ol' Man River," despite its lack of authenticity, part of his repertoire. As a "political performer" who wove "his politics into his performances," over time he changed the lyrics to the song.

He removed offensive terminology, such as "nigger," and ostensible black dialect, including "dere's" and "dat's," and began to emphasize black resistance—"I must keep fightin'"—rather than resignation—"Ah'm tired of livin'"—to white oppression. Hopper found these changes objectionable and could not understand how the original lyrics "might offend the Negroes."[84]

Robeson's appearance in Los Angeles in March 1947 heightened Hopper's hostility.[85] "When Paul Robeson sang the Communist 'People's Battle Song' here and dedicated it to Gerhardt Eisler, some members of his audience walked out," reported Hopper in her column. As the song included the line "I am a firm deep friend of the Soviet people," and Eisler was a known Communist, Hopper firmly supported the walkout. "Why one remained is beyond me." One of Hopper's readers felt so angered by the "propaganda on Communism inflicted on concert audiences by Paul Robeson" and appreciative of Hopper's "courage," she sent her letter directly to the editor of the *Los Angeles Times* rather than to Hopper.[86] While Hopper, her readers, and like-minded others emphasized Robeson's sympathy with the Soviet Union and Communism as the reason for their objection, Robeson's unsparing attacks on American apartheid before international audiences made him "the most prominent target of Cold War travel restrictions"—his passport was cancelled from 1950 to 1958—and contributed to Hopper's continued opposition.[87] In late 1950, after folk singer Josh White, under pressure and hoping to clear his name, testified before HUAC and mentioned Robeson, he appeared on Hopper's radio show, where Hopper lauded him as a "fine American."[88] Hopper's antagonism toward Robeson dovetailed with her friendliness toward White, an African American who took a public anti-Communist stance during the Cold War.

As with Robeson, Hopper linked civil rights activism and Communism and at times tied them together with what she considered sexual deviance. Such intertwining occurred when she targeted the Actors Laboratory Theater, which brought new acting techniques from the leftist Group Theater in New York to California and "prided itself on having opened its doors to students of all races."[89] In 1948, Hopper launched an attack on the theater group:

> The Actors Lab made no friends when they gave an open-air barbeque, which included dancing between Whites and Negroes. They used a parking lot on Sunset Blvd. for their dancing space where one and all could see. This group's corny idea of being liberal will eventually lead them into trouble. The situation has nothing whatever to do with racial prejudice or discrimination; every man in the world is as good as he is in his heart, regardless of race, creed, or color. But that doesn't mean they have to intermix.[90]

The Actors Lab already had encountered the "trouble" threatened by Hopper. That year, it found itself under investigation by California's "little HUAC" and eventually listed as a Communist front organization.[91] "It was when the Lab started taking Black students that they called the Actors Lab *communist*," actress Juliette Ball asserted. Within this context, Hopper's attack made liberalism and racial tolerance indistinguishable from Communism. Moreover, her strident reaction to the possibility of interracial intimacy or sexual relationships—long a staple of white racist campaigns against racial equality—belied her claims of being without racial prejudice.[92] Hopper's condemnation of the Actors Lab "drew upon a variety of cultural narratives that had long constructed communists and civil rights activists as sexual deviants," and revealed heightened anxieties around racial integration, Communism, and departures from normative white heterosexuality that abounded during the Cold War era.[93]

Homosexuality was one prominent departure, but Hopper did not publicly engage in a "Lavender Scare." The popular understanding that homosexuals posed a "security risk" because Communists or Soviet agents could blackmail or manipulate them into engaging in espionage or other subversive activities did not appear in Hopper's writings, although it resulted in "eliminating thousands of suspected homosexuals from government," as historian David K. Johnson found.[94] But Hopper did understand how what would come to be called "gay-baiting"—accusing a person of being homosexual—could be put to partisan political use, especially as "subversion and perversion came to be linked in the political—and eventually public—mind." In personal correspondence, she claimed that fears of homosexuality contributed to the defeat of liberal Democrat Claude Pepper in the 1950 Florida Senate campaign and wondered "why somebody doesn't reveal the fact that one of Harry S. Truman's greatest friends is a homosexual." They could "dig up all the dirt and it would make wonderful reading."[95] Publicly she sought to "emotionalize and polarize issues" by "mapping" gender and sexual differences onto partisan differences. "Oh, politics! POLITICS! Where are the men? WHERE ARE THE MEN?" she exclaimed, criticizing the Democratic Party's leadership. She singled out the defeated 1952 and 1956 Democratic presidential nominee, Adlai Stevenson, whose sexuality had been the subject of rumor and gossip and whose "reputation for effeminacy" critically damaged his electoral chances.[96] "Stevenson? I would have turned Stevenson out to pasture years ago. Of course I never call him anything but Adeline," although on occasion she used "Adelaide," as did one of her newspapers, the *New York Daily News*. Hopper exemplified how "the hunt for homosexuals," according to Johnson, "was less about national security than about partisan politics."[97]

Hopper also expressed malice in her nativist attacks on immigrants and foreign visitors, as in her campaign against Charlie Chaplin, but her Cold War nativism could be mollified if the non-American became an American citizen and anti-Communist. She never missed a chance to report on Hollywood denizens gaining American citizenship, and she often noted their contributions to the nation or conveyed their appreciation for the honor of naturalization. Pola Negri, a silent film actress and Rudolph Valentino's last lover, expressed her own gratitude when she appeared on *The Hedda Hopper Show* in 1951. "My citizenship is the greatest," Negri intoned. "I've had my rich share of precious possessions. This piece of paper is the most priceless thing I own." "God bless you, Pola Negri," Hopper replied.[98] In this way, Hopper's nativism accommodated civic notions of shared political values across ethnic differences as a basis for the nation—provided the politics were hers.

Similarly, shared politics could override Hopper's anti-Semitism in her relationships with Jewish Americans, although she also expressed anti-Jewish sentiment during the Cold War, most prominently in controversies over loyalty and loyalty oaths in Hollywood. In place in unions and the federal government by the late 1940s, the loyalty oath spread to other sites of employment, and by 1953 one-fifth of the U.S. workforce, or 13.5 million Americans, had gone through some sort of loyalty or security check.[99] Over these years, definitions of disloyalty expanded from specific crimes such as espionage, advocating overthrow of the government through force or violence, or serving a foreign government to "a general test of loyalty to American ideas and institutions"—a broader and vaguer definition that opened up more people to investigation and appealed to anti-Communists like Hopper.[100] She believed loyalty oaths should be required of all motion picture industry employees and urged their adoption. In turn, she associated any opposition to loyalty oaths with Communism and failed to object when both were conflated with Jewishness, as happened in a controversy over whether loyalty oaths should be instituted in the Screen Directors Guild (SDG).

During a heated 1950 debate at a guild meeting, Cecil B. DeMille presented an anti-Semitic speech, and Hopper supported him in print. While DeMille was a strong proponent of loyalty oaths, SDG president Joseph L. Mankiewicz was not, and so DeMille organized both the passage of a guild loyalty oath and a recall movement against Mankiewicz. When the motion to recall the guild president came up for discussion, DeMille took the stage to argue his case and criticize his opponents. DeMille attributed the lack of sympathy for the loyalty oath among Mankiewicz and his supporters to sympathy for Communism, rather than a stance for civil liberties. Moreover, he believed Jewish directors, like William Wyler, were more susceptible to Communism, hence their opposition to the loyalty oath. In his speech, DeMille hatefully adopted a Yiddish accent and read a list of his opponents' names: "Mr. Villy Vyler . . . Mr. Fleddie Zinnemann . . . "[101] When this performance contributed to the defeat of DeMille's motion to recall Mankiewicz, Hopper defended DeMille—without criticizing his speech or his anti-Semitism. "It's terrifying when a man like DeMille," she wrote, "is let down by a group of young whippersnappers."[102] Although the recall motion went down to defeat, the guild loyalty oath stood, ostensibly "voluntary," but in practice required; even Mankiewicz signed it. In the end, despite this skirmish, Hopper and her allies, like DeMille, won the war, and loyalty oaths spread throughout the motion picture industry.

Similarly, Hopper drew on familiar ideological associations to link the U.S. labor movement with Communism in her opposition to unions. While Hopper's populism led her to claim to identify with labor—"I believe nine-tenths of Americans are sympathetic with labor—for at least that number of us are laborers"—she remained hostile to unions—"I do not believe that one-tenth of Americans sympathize with the methods labor is using to attain its ends."[103] One of those methods was the strike, and when labor unions in the movie industry participated in the great post–World War II strike wave, Hopper sided with studio management rather than striking workers. A series of vicious, violent strikes and conflicts in 1945 and 1946 pitted the Conference of Studio Unions (CSU), a federation of craft unions run democratically with militant leadership, against the film studios as well as its union rival, the mob-led and management-oriented International Alliance of Theatrical Stage Employees (IATSE). "Now the strike is upon us," Hopper asserted in September 1946, "so you can look for it to be the biggest and bloodiest, with the blackest headlines ever seen." That month, the strikes culminated in a lockout of CSU, a move by the studios that successfully prevented CSU members from working and eventually decimated the union.[104] These dramatic confrontations divided employees in the motion picture industry. The Screen Writers Guild strongly supported CSU, and a number of prominent SAG members also honored the picket lines. But IATSE portrayed itself as a "bulwark of Americanism," and in early October SAG voted decisively to cross CSU's picket lines. Hopper cast her vote with the majority. She believed picket lines "violated the constitutional rights of any American to work if he wants to" and felt "mighty proud of my fellow actors" for SAG's decision.[105]

The "class struggle in Hollywood," as it played out over 1945 and 1946, propelled Ronald Reagan, a CSU critic, into the SAG presidency in mid-1947;

it also provided fodder for Cold War anti-Communists like Hopper and Reagan as the movie studios and IATSE accused CSU and its leader, Herbert Sorrell, of Communism. "Labor is suffering incredibly from not having thrown out Communistic elements from its ranks years ago," Hopper wrote. "Now even legitimate labor causes are being identified with Moscow." She and others, such as IATSE leader and her fellow MPA member Roy Brewer, helped Americans make the identification. According to historian Gerald Horne, however, Sorrell was not a Communist, nor did he have the support of the Communist Party for CSU's 1945 strike.[106] There was Communist influence among the unions in the CSU federation, but, as was true of Communists and the motion picture industry generally, the amount of Red-baiting and Red-bashing that occurred was out of proportion to the number of actual Communists or even fellow travelers. With the Communist label securely affixed to militant trade unionists in CSU, and images of brutal battles between strikers, scabs, studio "goons," and police involving chains, clubs, batons, fire hoses, and tear gas, Hollywood labor conflict contributed to the growing anti-Communist, antiunion mood in the country. It also significantly shaped the antiunion Labor-Management Relations Act passed in 1947.[107] Popularly known as the Taft-Hartley Act after the cosponsors—one of whom was Hopper's political hero, Senator Robert Taft—the legislation "recast the legal context for labor relations in the United States" in ways "designed to constrain unions." The "anti-labor motif" of Hopper and other anti-Communists crucially strengthened their movement and critically weakened the labor movement.[108]

As Hopper articulated and acted on her definitions of Cold War Americanism and un-Americanism, she helped to link "all expressions of liberalism and radicalism to communism." This linking, as Larry Ceplair and Steven Englund persuasively argue, "required a massive and unremitting campaign, conducted on several fronts by numerous groups and individuals, from both the public and private sectors. Anti-communism became a full-time business."[109] As one of these individuals and working in tandem with groups such as the American Legion, Hedda Hopper waged an anti-Communist campaign throughout the Cold War era. Although her campaign was not a full-time business for her, it took up a significant part of her life, affecting all aspects of it—professional, political, and personal. This was particularly true as she focused on fighting what she saw as Communist subversion in Hollywood films by purging from the motion picture industry any filmmakers she considered un-American and keeping them out through a blacklist.

Hedda Hopper at her office, 702 Guaranty Building, Hollywood Boulevard, 1945. (Courtesy of the Academy of Motion Picture Arts and Sciences.)

Blacklisting Hollywood "Reds"

In September 1947, Hedda Hopper planned to appear on a radio broadcast to debate the topic "Is There Really a Threat of Communism in Hollywood?" The very next month HUAC would hold its first post–World War II hearings to investigate Communism and subversion in the motion picture industry. These October hearings would feature the "Hollywood Ten" and lead to the establishment of the Hollywood blacklist to ensure that no persons espousing or supporting leftist, or even liberal, political ideas and efforts were employed in the motion picture industry. The months preceding the hearings were part of the "prelude to repression."[1] Hopper's Red Scare politics contributed considerably to this repressive atmosphere, and her planned participation in this radio debate confirmed her prominence and power as a gossip columnist and an anti-Communist activist. She was to argue the affirmative position—that indeed there was a Communist threat in Hollywood—but the show's producers were having trouble lining up her opposition. Arguing against the claim of Communist subversion in the motion picture industry would, according to news reports, "lend a pink tinge, but more important, no star yet approached wants to oppose Hedda Hopper."[2]

Despite this fact, Hopper always felt on the political defensive, expected a hostile reception, and sought to buttress her position by practicing her gossip trade: making private talk public by exposing Communist beliefs among members of the film industry. In preparation for her appearance, she appealed to J. Edgar Hoover for "some facts to hurl back at the angry mob in the audience." She hoped the FBI director would give her the names of Hollywood Communists, despite the fact that such information would have violated their civil liberties and right to keep their political affiliations private. "Naturally, I won't be able to accuse certain stars of being registered Communists, as even those who are deny it, always have and always will." But she believed "naming names," and thus publicizing private information, was "the only way we'll ever get rid of them." With the aim of getting the confidential information she sought, Hopper wrote a letter to Hoover that was, at once, fawning, flattering, and sincere. "You're so wise and have so many facts at your finger tips that I feel that I can call upon your friendship for help." Hoover sent her a stack of articles in return, but they were hardly the confidential information she sought. Instead, they were all drawn from "records available to the public."[3]

This exchange between Hopper and Hoover was only one of many between the gossip columnist and the FBI director, but it was characteristic of how the public and the private intersected in anti-Communist efforts and indicated the importance of gossip and its purveyors to those efforts in Hollywood, particularly the blacklist. The FBI leaked items about actual or accused Communists to Louella Parsons, Ed Sullivan, Walter Winchell, as well as Hopper, and Hopper was not the only Cold Warrior in celebrity journalism. Among her gossip colleagues, Winchell embraced "fashionable Red-baiting conservatism." As Neal Gabler argues, "the image of Winchell as a journalistic Joseph McCarthy, slashing and burning his way through the American left," dominated the 1950s.[4] Like Hopper and Winchell, Ed Sullivan mobilized his readers and viewers in various anti-Communist campaigns. But Hopper's main rival, Louella Parsons, was not nearly as involved in domestic anti-Communism. Although Parsons expressed concern about "the danger of the 'Red Tide'" and supported the Hollywood blacklist, she also cautioned that "care must be taken that good Americans were not falsely accused." With the support of the vast majority of her respondents, however, Hopper never worried about false accusations as she worked to establish, extend, and enforce the blacklist, busying herself with "exposing Reds in the name of patriotism."[5]

Establishing the Hollywood Blacklist

In her gossip column, Hedda Hopper devoted much attention to justifying a blacklist in the motion picture industry. Although Americans were fired or not hired due to their actual or assumed political opinions or associations in a wide range of areas, including all levels of government, the military, industry, public and higher education, and radio, television, and theatrical entertainment, the Hollywood blacklist received the most publicity and became the most famous. Its establishment in late 1947 not only signaled the stifling of social criticism and political dissent in Cold War America, but the accompanying national publicity meant it had a political and symbolic significance well beyond the motion picture industry. The blacklist built on several premises shared by Hopper: that Communists and Communist sympathizers constituted a significant presence in the film industry, that they had successfully inserted Communist propaganda into motion pictures, and that the industry needed—and had a right—to fire or not hire anyone suspected of having Communist views or affiliations to prevent them from having access to such a powerful medium for molding public opinion. Through her column, her activism in the MPA, her work with other anti-Communists (including those in HUAC, the FBI, and the American Legion), her machinations behind the scenes in Hollywood, and, most important, her readers' response and mobilization, Hopper helped to establish the Hollywood blacklist.

"The main threat of communism in Hollywood today is that Red propaganda has been put over in some films," Hopper wrote in the fall of 1947, just as HUAC, working with the same assumption, was gearing up—with help from the FBI—for its October hearings about Communism in the motion picture industry.[6] Hopper's anti-Communist allies agreed. Articles in the *American Legion Magazine* included such titles as "Does Your Movie Money Go to Commies?" and revealed Legion members' fears that "left-wing subversives" controlled Hollywood. Meanwhile, the MPA—by repeatedly issuing invitations for an investigation—had played a key role in bringing HUAC to Hollywood in the first place, and also had developed criteria for determining whether a film contained Communist propaganda, criteria utilized by the FBI for its film content analyses.[7] On September 3, 1947, Hopper dedicated her entire column to the issue of Communist propaganda, which, like the FBI, she found not only in films that presented the Soviet Union positively but also in films that portrayed any aspect of the United States negatively:

> The Commies are trying to destroy the faith of the American people in the institutions and principles of the United States. They make subtle attacks upon our government and upon free enterprise. Their aim is to destroy our confidence in our system of government, our system of economics. . . . It is an insidious program, and it has been well directed.[8]

In a dramatic move intended to reinforce her point that Communists had infiltrated Hollywood, Hopper included a quote she attributed to V. I. Lenin: "You must always consider that of all the arts, the motion picture is for us the most important."[9]

As for specific examples, Hopper first focused on three films made during the war that she considered to be "definitely pro-Soviet."[10] Warner Brothers' *Mission to Moscow* (1943) was so diplomatic about Soviet actions, such as the purge trials and the 1939 Nazi-Soviet Pact, that it was nicknamed "Submission to Moscow" by critics. Based on the memoirs of Joseph E. Davies, President Roosevelt's ambassador to the Soviet Union from 1936 to 1938, the film had the strong support of the U.S. government and was designed to convey sympathy for the U.S. ally at a critical point in the war. "Its goal," Hopper reported while the film was in production, "to sell America on Russia. We already bow to their fighting spirit." But later she agreed with those who labeled the film "pro-Communist" and "sloppy history."[11] *North Star* (1943) was a Samuel Goldwyn film about a Ukrainian village resisting German invaders, with no mention of Communism. But the movie was based on a script by Lillian Hellman, a Communist Party fellow traveler soon to be targeted by HUAC, and the FBI considered the project to be "subversive."[12] Metro-Goldwyn-Mayer's *Song of Russia* (1943), Hopper dryly noted, "seemed to prove that Russian industry was based on a five-year plan devoted exclusively to the production of violins." Robert Taylor, a fellow MPA member, starred in *Song of Russia*, and he later considered the film's ending—with the Russian flag superimposed over the American flag—as positive "proof that Hollywood was trying to indoctrinate the people that Russia was about to take over the United States."[13]

These films, especially *Mission to Moscow*, were patent political propaganda, aimed at persuading American public opinion. Yet this was true of much of Hollywood's output during World War II. As Thomas Doherty argues, filmmakers and audiences emerged from the war understanding "cinema for what it was: a powerful delivery system for ideology."[14] Although such film propaganda aimed to present the U.S. wartime ally in a favorable light, it did so not at the command of the Communist Party, as MGM's Louis B. Mayer testified before HUAC about *Song of Russia*. Instead, public figures encouraged wartime enthusiasm for "Joe" Stalin and the Soviet Union as part of the war effort. Hopper herself had generously praised Stalin for keeping theaters open twenty-four hours a day during the 1942 siege of Stalingrad, the turning point in the European war.[15] Now, in the postwar climate with the wartime alliance shattered, Hopper and many others wanted to forget about such endorsements.

Along with naming films that showed the Soviet Union in a positive light as Communist propaganda, Hopper's September 3, 1947, column, as well as later columns, alleged Communist propaganda in movies that had nothing to do with the Soviet Union but "followed the party line" by highlighting negative aspects of the United States. Frank Capra's *Mr. Smith Goes to Washington* (1939) "implied that there were only two honest men among the 96 members of the Senate of the United States," and his *Meet John Doe* (1941) presented "an American industrialist . . . as possessing his own private uniformed army, . . . ruthlessly breaking up an orderly assemblage of citizens." The FBI also singled out Capra's films and considered *Mr. Smith Goes to Washington* "decidedly socialist in nature."[16] "There are two schools of thought on such pictures," Hopper admitted the next month during the October HUAC hearings. "The lefties argue that by inspiring social reform through such mediums we may prevent the Communists from taking over. Others claim that such pictures are paving the way for the Reds to takeover our country."[17] In articulating this fundamental difference between liberals—mislabeled "lefties" here—and conservatives, Hopper made it clear she agreed with the latter group, and she condemned such message or social problem films for "pointing up our racial problems, political corruption in government, the evil of wealth, men driven to crime because of the supposed pressure of the capitalist system." "Emphasizing the negative," she continued, "can be just as effective as waving the Red flag."[18]

In declaring the motion picture industry guilty of "waving the Red flag," Hopper and other anti-Communists overstated the number of Communists in Hollywood, the power of individual artists within the industrialized context of film production, and the clarity with which a film's message may have been received. Perhaps 300 people (about one percent of the motion picture industry workforce) had at one time been members of the Communist Party, including 50–60 actors, 15–20 producers, and close to 150 screenwriters.[19] Still—lending credence to anti-Communist accusations—these small numbers fail to convey the extent of Communist influence, as not everyone on the political Left joined the party. Rather, the Hollywood branch, as was true of the CPUSA nationally, was "a mobilizing center" for a wider range of causes and activists.[20] The charge of Communist subversion in Hollywood recognized that films have political messages, but disregarded the fact, wellknown to Hopper, that film production is a collaborative process and subject to a range of forces—studio policy and financing, box office receipts, government and interest group pressure—which work against one or even a group of individuals exercising complete control. While there were prominent exceptions—the liberal director William Wyler was one—Communists and others interested in social critique and reform often complained about "the virtual impossibility" of bringing their politics "to the screen." Scripts, in particular, were continually subject to revisions, cuts, and censorship. Lillian Hellman, for example, was "so incensed at the changes" made in her script for *North Star* that she decided to buy out her contract with producer Samuel Goldwyn.[21] Moreover, not every filmgoer interpreted film in the same way.

Indeed, a film could be labeled both "Red propaganda" by the conservative *Hollywood Reporter* and "capitalist propaganda" by the Communist Party's *Daily Worker*—as happened with John Huston's *We Were Strangers* (1949).[22]

But these caveats did not undermine Hopper's public conviction that the Communist threat in Hollywood was real and sinister and that she needed to do all she could to expose and combat it, beginning with full and fulsome support for HUAC. In 1947, as she had in 1940 with its forerunner, Hopper gladly welcomed HUAC, now a permanent committee in a Republican-controlled Congress, to Hollywood. So did her MPA colleagues Adolph Menjou, Robert Taylor, and Walt Disney. In March, the same month an emboldened HUAC commenced its first post–World War II investigation of the motion picture industry, Hopper wrote, "We have dawdled long enough. It seems to me the time has come for facts, not vagaries; action, not lethargy. If, as they have so often been accused, 'Communist front' organizations have a direct link with a foreign government unfriendly toward our way of life, let it be proved once and for all by our government."[23]

HUAC's premises and purposes in launching its Hollywood investigation were consistent with Hopper's anti-Communist campaign. HUAC sought to expose Communist propaganda in the movies and, as part of the effort to conflate liberalism with Communism, the connection between the Roosevelt administration and wartime films about the Soviet Union—a connection Hopper later made with *Mission to Moscow*. "I was told at the time F.D.R. told Jack Warner to make it. It would give Americans a more kindly feeling toward Commies," she later wrote, forgetting her own kindly feelings during the war.[24] HUAC also aimed to destroy the Communist Party, undermine the film industry's interest in making films that criticized any aspect of the United States, and set the stage and gain publicity for its Cold War pursuit of "un-American activities."[25] Hopper backed all these aims, as did her allies in Hollywood. In May 1947, HUAC held hearings in Los Angeles and heard testimony from fourteen witnesses deemed "friendly" because they, like Hopper, endorsed the HUAC investigation; most of these "friendlies" were her allies in the Motion Picture Alliance. Hopper's support for HUAC's investigation predated that of the studio executives and producers in the MPAA, who only went on record in support of an "objective and fair investigation" by HUAC in June.[26]

As the October 20, 1947, starting date for the hearings in Washington, D.C., grew closer, Hopper hoped HUAC's investigation would expose the private political views of Hollywood filmmakers to public scrutiny, to "reveal the names of actors, writers and directors who have Commie inclinations," and thus "clea[r] up a great deal of our smoggish red glare." SAG past and present officers, including the new president Ronald Reagan, were set to testify as friendly witnesses before HUAC, as was IATSE head Roy Brewer.[27] But Hopper was more interested in the "unfriendly" witnesses. Even before HUAC issued its subpoenas for the hearings in late September, Hopper published an item, not entirely accurate, about who would be targeted. "Despite protests, Charlie Chaplin, Paul Henreid, Peter Lorre, John Howard Lawson and Clifford Odets will soon be making a trip to Washington, D.C., for that Commie investigation." Of these, only Lawson testified as an unfriendly witness, while Henreid, a liberal activist, and Lorre, who had fled Nazi Germany, were never listed with the other subpoenaed witnesses.[28] With the phrase "despite protests," Hopper anticipated HUAC's confrontation with the unfriendly witnesses, who disagreed in principle with the investigation and would testify unwillingly, refusing to answer questions about their political affiliations. Initially, nineteen unfriendly witnesses received subpoenas, eleven eventually were called to testify, one of whom was Bertolt Brecht, who left the United States after testifying, and ten, famously, remained: writers Lester Cole, Dalton Trumbo, Albert Maltz, Samuel Ornitz, John Howard Lawson, Alvah Bessie, and Ring Lardner, Jr., directors Edward Dmytryk and Herbert Biberman, and producer Adrian Scott.

Before and after the October 1947 HUAC hearings, Hopper condemned the men who became the Hollywood Ten. In her condemnation, she never admitted how, in 1940 before U.S. entry into World War II, she had found common political ground with them—despite differing motivations—on support for American neutrality.[29] By October 1947, however, the lines were clearly drawn between Hopper and the Hollywood Ten. She objected to their politics. All were or had been members of the Communist Party, and Hopper could not understand why a successful screenwriter like Trumbo— one of the highest-paid screenwriters in Hollywood—"could be a Commie." They contributed financially through donations and fund-raising—Hopper later reported a figure of $10 million "into Communist Party coffers" from Hollywood since 1940—and were important, effective progressive activists. Most recently, Lawson, Trumbo, Maltz, and Scott had honored picket lines at Warner Brothers during the CSU strikes.[30] The seven of the ten who were members of the Screen Writers Guild also incurred Hopper's wrath when the guild criticized the Red-baiting and Red-bashing of the MPA as "harmful" and "irresponsible."[31] The Hollywood Ten's work on socially conscious films further maddened her. Motivated by their political commitments and perhaps their own personal backgrounds—more than half of them were Jewish Americans—they sought to make motion pictures that contributed to social change and reform. "They wanted to improve the plight of poor and working people, especially minorities, and to end racism and discrimination," and they were able to express these aims to a certain degree in their films. Indeed, their efforts to improve representations of African Americans—with John Howard Lawson and Albert Maltz singled out for their respective screenplays *Sahara* (1943) and *The House I Live In* (1945)—led the NAACP to lend early, if short-lived, support to the Ten.[32]

Of all their films, two 1947 films in particular raised the hackles of Hopper, HUAC, and the FBI: *Crossfire* and *So Well Remembered*. Produced by Adrian Scott and directed by Edward Dmytryk at RKO when Dore Schary was studio head, *Crossfire* powerfully criticized American racism and anti-Semitism through a story of murder motivated by hatred. It was an important film, ended up with five Oscar nominations, and, according to the film scholar Jon Lewis, "struck a lot of people on the right as a harbinger of things to come." Hopper believed *Crossfire* would "receive more conflicting criticisms than any picture that we've made in ages" and "may backfire in its intent." In the end, *Crossfire* contributed to Scott's and Dmytryk's targeting by anti-Communists.[33] The two men also produced and directed RKO's *So Well Remembered*, a film that examined British class relations in which the hero was a socialist and labor leader "fighting for the rights of the working class." Hopper labeled the film "Exhibit A"—evidence proving the Hollywood Ten guilty of spreading Communist ideology—because "capitalism is represented as decaying, corrupt, perverted, unfeeling." "I urge you to see it," Hopper told her readers. "Then decide for yourself whether or not Hollywood is capable of inserting leftie propaganda in its films."[34]

For Hopper, most objectionable of all was the Hollywood Ten's refusal to answer HUAC's questions about their Communist affiliations. They cited their First Amendment rights to freedom of speech and assembly, but this defense of the right to private political conscience "outraged" Hopper, as did their "outrageous, abusive, and rude conduct as witnesses," which also offended others.[35] Hopper refused to respect the right to privacy in these cases. They "duck behind the Bill of Rights," she exclaimed, "crying their rights to freedom of political thought." She believed in "the public's right know" and lamented that "no one can look into a man's mind or heart and evaluate his loyalty." Moreover, the unwillingness to testify about their political affiliations only further convinced her of the ten men's Communism. In her view, appeals to privacy, whether about one's political or sex life, always implied guilt, as she considered declaring one's politics "no invasion of privacy to a true American."[36] Her respondents agreed. A Des Moines, Iowa, reader regarded the Hollywood Ten with suspicion, because they "have made no attempt to clear their names." A Chicago area reader could not understand why HUAC's investigation violated constitutional rights. "Why do people become so angry when asked if they are Communists?" Over time, a few readers would write Hopper urging her to respect "political sanctity," but the vast majority believed "those people who really are reds, should be known," which was exactly what Hopper believed.[37]

Hopper's ardent opposition to the Hollywood Ten led her to denounce their most prominent film industry allies, the Committee for the First Amendment (CFA). Formed just before HUAC's October hearings, with a leadership and membership drawn from the ranks of Hollywood's non-Communist liberals, plus national figures such as Eleanor Roosevelt and Senator Claude Pepper, the CFA sought to support the civil liberties of the unfriendly witnesses without endorsing their left-wing politics.[38] The organization, as screenwriter Philip Dunne put it, "was in the business of supporting *rights*, not causes." Sylvia Kaye, another CFA member, recalled their efforts as "a protest against the procedures and tactics of the House Committee, not a defense of the nineteen" unfriendly witnesses.[39] The "star-studded" CFA organized a national radio broadcast titled "Hollywood Fights Back," newspaper advertisements that called any "investigation into the political beliefs of the individual . . . contrary to the basic principles of our democracy," and a charter airplane to fly a group of members, including Lauren Bacall, Humphrey Bogart, John Huston, Danny Kaye, Gene Kelly, and William Wyler, to Washington, D.C., to attend the HUAC hearings.[40]

Despite these carefully delineated actions—for the First Amendment, against HUAC, and in defense of the film industry but not the unfriendly witnesses—CFA members became targets too. They were accused of being fellow travelers and "fronting and stooging" for Communists.[41] Bogart came under so much pressure from his studio, Red-baiters, and celebrity journalists like Ed Sullivan—who told him "the public is beginning to think you're a Red!"—that he withdrew from the political arena after declaring his anti-Communist position in *Photoplay* magazine. Paul Henreid recalled "a campaign of innuendos launched in an attempt to frighten and discredit us—a very successful attempt."[42] Hopper joined in, referring to these mostly liberal Democrats, like Melvyn Douglas, Katharine Hepburn, and Edward G. Robinson, as "Demmies" to sound like "Commies," and confronting those who had participated. "But why did you go in the first place?" she demanded of Judy Garland. In print, Hopper warned stars that their HUAC protests "didn't endear them to the American public."[43]

Hopper also mobilized her readership, and they responded with a boycott of all films associated with the Hollywood Ten and the CFA. Mobilization began on October 29, 1947, when she reprinted a telegram from Gertrude Smith, a Milwaukee woman who listened to the CFA radio broadcast, "Hollywood Fights Back," and determined to boycott:

> May I present to you a group of people who have just listened to this broadcast—my own family, three sisters, three brothers, their wives, husbands, and children, their relatives and friends—in all 50 of us. We are plain American citizens, who are deeply appreciative of the American way of living . . . and who are bitterly opposed to Communism or any taint of it. . . . We are for this investigation and strongly behind any move to rid our country of anyone Communistically inclined. If the movie box office suffers, there is only one remedy: Remove the Communists from Hollywood and we will be only too happy to return to our favorite entertainment—the movies. But not until we can attend them with a clear conscience, knowing we are not contributing to the support of any peoples who are not for our way—the real American way—of life, Hedda.[44]

Hopper had prepared the ground for a boycott. During the summer of 1947, she began a cross-country trip to meet "a cross-section of America" and "let America tell me what they think of Hollywood, what they want from their pictures, and what they expect from their stars." Although she only made it to Kansas City, along the way she spoke to six thousand members of the American Legion Auxiliary of Women and urged boycotts of movies made with anyone who had Communist connections.[45] Then, over the fall of 1947, Hopper reported often on the HUAC hearings, the testimony of friendly and unfriendly witnesses, and her respective support and opposition. As a result, readers who backed HUAC's investigation, like Gertrude Smith of Milwaukee, felt they could turn to her.

As did others. Hopper claimed she received hundreds of letters, and she reprinted excerpts in her column; her entire November 7, 1947, column consisted of such excerpts. Letters came from readers in Boston, Hartford, Hackensack, Long Island, Chicago, Minneapolis, Des Moines, Iowa City, Seattle, and Los Angeles, and, with only one exception, they were all committed to a boycott. "I will not see any more pictures featuring those sympathizers of Commies." "Don't these players realize their success is in the hands or the dollars of the public? I admire Katie Hepburn as an actress, but it's thumbs down on her until she recovers from her present phase."[46] "I wouldn't see one of Bogie's pictures if he stuck his smoking rod into my ribs." "From now on we will know what movies not to see. All those actors and actresses who yapped at Congress will be boycotted."[47] The use of nicknames such as "Katie" and "Bogie" revealed the intimacy and personal relationships spectators felt they shared with movie stars, making the stars' perceived political betrayal a personal betrayal and even more egregious for spectators. Readers further explained their boycott as a stand for Americanism. "I don't recall hearing one person who protested the investigation claim a definite preference for our American form of government to Communism," contended a Seattle reader. "Therefore, I believe they must lean toward Communism and not toward Americanism."[48]

Hopper's respondents understood their participation in the boycott not only as an individual action but also as part of a broader anti-Communist effort. They saw themselves as joining together with other readers of Hopper's column. "I agree with Gertrude Smith and her Milwaukee family," wrote a reader from Fostoria, Ohio. "Until writers and actors become real Americans, I shall never attend another movie with any actor or actress who protested the Un-American Activities Committee investigation."[49] "Our family wants to add its voice," declared a resolute reader from Fort Leavenworth, Kansas. "We will attend no more movies made by those who are not happy to say they are not Communists, but honest-to-goodness Americans. I am typing this with a broken right arm, but I feel I must send you the message." They also sought to organize others in a wider boycott. "Our clubwomen are going to boycott each one of the clique that went to Washington to protest against sincere Americans," avowed a Long Island reader. "My family and a group of friends are buying 50 postcards each, and mailing them to our local theaters, with this message: 'We will not attend any pictures showing those who have sympathized or are connected with the Communist activities in Hollywood.' I hope people all over the States will do the same thing."[50] These readers, apparently all women, were "kitchen table" activists, who took it on themselves to extend the boycott beyond their immediate circle of family and friends, thus engaging in the type of political action characteristic of conservative women during the 1950s.[51]

To make certain they did not patronize films with any of the Hollywood Ten or CFA members, Hopper's readers began keeping lists. "Many people have made a list of the actors and actresses who took the plane trip and have made it a rule not to attend pictures in which those persons appear, and it will be some time before they are reinstated in the public opinion."[52] One reader from Colorado Springs shared her family's list-making procedure: "We hung a huge sheet of paper on our kitchen wall. Each time new names were made public in the un-American activities investigation, we wrote those names in with red crayon. Before attending any movie, we check cast, writers, directors against those names and, unless the picture has a clean bill of health, we cancel out."[53] This reader, then, had a "red list" at the consumption end of the film industry before studio financiers, executives, and producers instituted a blacklist at the production end. But the Hollywood blacklist was soon in coming, and the protest and boycott by anti-Communist moviegoers, like Hopper's respondents, contributed.

Hopper had long advocated firing or not hiring "Red sympathizers" in the motion picture industry, but her advocacy became more strident during 1947. She wanted to "weed out Red writers, directors, and actors who are offending most of the people in this country with their political beliefs." The Truman administration and Congress prepared the way.[54] On March 22, 1947, President Truman issued an executive order establishing loyalty review boards to investigate federal employees; if found guilty of "disloyalty"—to be defined in the investigation—the employee was fired. In addition, one provision of the Taft-Hartley Act required all union officers to sign affidavits swearing they were not members of the Communist Party; without these loyalty oaths their unions would be excluded from legal protections.[55] Thomas Schatz argues that the Hollywood blacklist was "only a step beyond the loyalty oaths already mandated by Taft-Hartley." Hopper confirmed this logic when she endorsed congressional actions aimed at preventing "Communists from holding leadership positions in American labor unions." "And," she further asked, "why keep only labor Communists out of the film business—why not all Communists?"[56]

As a consequence, Hopper was delighted by her readers' boycott, as an example of grassroots anti-Communism, a sign of her political influence, and a catalyst for the blacklist. She believed it would have an impact on filmmakers who continued to employ anyone suspected of having Communist views or affiliations. As she wrote in early November, "They will change their minds when such action starts hurting at the box office."[57] Eleven days later, she again made the connection between box office boycotts and the need for a blacklist. "The paying customers will gladly sacrifice an evening's movie entertainment rather than support what they consider the Commie menace." She urged the real power in the industry—corporate ownership in New York as opposed to management in Hollywood—to "clean our own house of that element which has shaken the faith of the theater audiences." The American

Legion made a similar distinction and, to great effect, "applied its pressure in New York rather than in Hollywood."[58]

One week later, on November 24 and 25, 1947, industry ownership and management gathered at a conference at New York City's Waldorf-Astoria hotel and, after hearing a presentation by MPAA head Eric Johnston that emphasized protests and boycotts, decided to blacklist the Hollywood Ten. Of the six reasons given by Johnston for instituting a blacklist, three had to do with boycotts or protests similar to those of Hopper's respondents: the American Legion threatened a boycott, boycotts were being instituted in Glendale, California, and Independence, Kansas, and an audience in Chapel Hill, North Carolina, had protested when CFA member Katharine Hepburn appeared on the screen. According to one story, the audience "had stoned the screen," while an FBI informant reported that Hepburn "was booed from the audience, persons saying, 'She is a Communist; that one I won't see.'"[59] At the end of the conference, Johnston, on behalf of the industry leaders, issued what came to be called the Waldorf Statement. "We will not knowingly employ a Communist or a member of any party or group which advocates the overthrow of the Government of the United States by force or by illegal or unconstitutional methods," the statement read in part.[60]

Although the studios could not fire a worker for political reasons, they could for private behavior. Most studio contracts "had a 'morals clause' forbidding scandalous behavior; they had only to invoke that."[61] This invocation indicated the way in which both politics and morality were subject to public exposure and censure in Hedda Hopper's Hollywood. Studio and industry heads were aided by contempt of Congress citations—spearheaded by Richard Nixon and opposed by Helen Gahagan Douglas—issued on November 24 against the Hollywood Ten for not cooperating with HUAC. Scholars agree the blacklist was a political act motivated by economic concerns, ranging from "fear of adverse box office" to the need to restructure the movie industry and film production along more flexible lines.[62] Later public opinion polls released on November 29 and December 17 showed that Americans were evenly split over whether the Hollywood Ten should be punished. According to a Gallup poll, "the public has little awareness of possible Communist influences, if any, in pictures being produced today."[63] The same could not be said of readers of Hopper's gossip column. At an early, key point in time, the grassroots anti-Communist activism of moviegoers like Hopper's readers, who were convinced of Communist infiltration of Hollywood, contributed to industry arguments in favor of punishment and of establishing the blacklist.

Hedda's Black (and Gray) List

With the blacklist now established, and five of the Hollywood Ten with studio contracts either fired or suspended—Dmytryk and Scott from RKO, Cole and Trumbo from MGM, and Lardner from 20th Century-Fox—Hedda Hopper and her respondents should have been happy. They were not. "The producers, with their usual blithe spirits, think they have done a wonderful job in getting rid of five Commie writers," Hopper wrote in a December 1947 letter, "and hope the public will forgive the misguided stars" in the Committee for the First Amendment.[64] Hopper was not in a forgiving mood. Instead, she aimed to extend the blacklist of Communists or ex-Communists beyond the Hollywood Ten and engender a "graylist" of filmmakers and performers with "left or liberal associations"—rather than actual membership in the Communist Party—who now would be marked as "controversial" and have difficulties finding work. Over time, both aims were achieved, with the help of others in Hollywood, including IATSE, the MPA, and SAG under the leadership of Ronald Reagan.[65] Forgiveness was not forthcoming from Hopper's respondents either. Of CFA members, one reader asserted, "it will be some time before they are reinstated in the public opinion." "Time will prove just where those misguided actors and others in the movie business stand," she continued, "but until then why not give the star roles to the many versatile actors who have never faltered in their Americanism?"[66]

Hopper and other respondents agreed with this suggestion and reacted strongly when a casting controversy involving Lauren Bacall, a prominent CFA member, and the film *The Fountainhead* (1949) emerged in early 1948. Adapted by the vehement anti-Communist Ayn Rand for the screen from her best-selling novel, *The Fountainhead* tells the story of Howard Roark—an architect representing "pure individualism"—defiantly following his vision in the face of criticism from his mediocre opponents—representing "society"—even to the extent of dynamiting one of his own buildings. Bosley Crowther of the *New York Times* considered Rand's ideas "reckless," and the *New Yorker* saw the film as expressing "a point of view that was probably popular in Cro-Magnon days."[67] But the novel influenced a new generation of conservative intellectuals, and Hopper respected Rand's anti-Communist credentials. A novelist, screenwriter, and MPA member, Rand wrote the *Screen Guide for Americans* on behalf of the MPA. The guide commanded filmmakers to take a pro-business, anti-labor stance—"Don't Smear the Free Enterprise System," "Don't Deify the 'Common Man,'" "Don't Glorify the Collective," read some of the guidelines—and to "not hire Reds to work on your pictures." Rand was also a friendly witness at the October 1947 HUAC hearings.[68] As a consequence, Hopper was very interested in the film's production and reported on plans for *The Fountainhead* several times in 1947. In one column, she noted that Barbara Stanwyck had insisted that Jack Warner purchase the movie rights to the 1943 novel. "Since its purchase, value of the yarn has increased enormously," Hopper wrote.[69] Stanwyck, an MPA member who publicly supported the HUAC hearings, along with her husband and friendly witness Robert Taylor, was slotted to play Roark's love interest, Dominique Francon.[70]

But Hopper's February 23, 1948, column told of cast changes for *The Fountainhead*. "After waiting four years to make it, Barbara now learns that Lauren Bacall will play the part promised her."[71] For Hopper and her respondents, the conflict between Bacall's liberal politics and Rand's tale of ambition, will, and heroic individualism was galling. "WHAT A MISERABLE MISTAKE to cast her for the part," exclaimed a New York reader. "The thought of her as Dominique is revolting." This reader had clearly read the novel, as she added that Bacall "does not have any of the requirements and attributes that a Dominique should have." Asked a female reader from Los Angeles, who also wrote to Jack Warner, "Can't a thing be done about the terrible injustice being done to 'The Fountainhead'? Is public opinion too impotent to do any thing about it?" "They are ignoring the feelings of the AMERICAN theater-going public," emphasized a Chicago woman, who threatened another boycott. "Actions speak for themselves and I am sure the box office receipts will manifest our views, more emphatically than words."[72] In the end, these protests were quelled with the casting of newcomer Patricia Neal as Dominique. With these letters, Hopper's respondents demonstrated a continuing concern about the political views of cast and crew of Hollywood movies.

This reader interest dovetailed with Hopper's commitment to exposing the privately held political views of film performers and filmmakers and extending the Hollywood blacklist, which she and her anti-Communist colleagues succeeded in doing when HUAC returned its focus to the movie industry in March 1951. The 1951 hearings occurred in the aftermath of the explosion of the Soviet atomic bomb, the establishment of Communist China, and the prosecution of the Fuchs, Hiss, and Rosenberg spy cases, and amid the Korean War. The previous year, Senator McCarthy had gained fame by, and given his name to, smearing and silencing targeted Americans with unsubstantiated accusations of Communist sympathies. Closer to Hollywood, Richard Nixon had won his election with his Red-baiting campaign against Helen Gahagan Douglas. In Hollywood itself, the years between 1947 and

1951 took the Hollywood Ten from "blacklist to prison," as their contempt of Congress citations led to indictments, trials, failed appeals, sentencing, and prison terms.[73] The movie studios did not extend the blacklist while these legal cases were still in process, but once the Supreme Court upheld the Ten's contempt convictions in the spring of 1950—a decision Hopper's MPA marked with full-page advertisements in industry trade papers—"an inquisition in Hollywood could begin in earnest."[74]

As usual, Hopper lent HUAC her full-fledged support in 1951. In March, the month the first group of subpoenas went out for the new HUAC hearings, Hopper reported positively on a request from an industry spokesperson for "the co-operation of our studios and guilds with the Un-American Activities Committee . . . to aid the nation's fight against Communism."[75] As it turned out, far more people were affected during this second round of hearings than during the first round in October 1947, in part because HUAC shifted its focus from trying to prove that film content was politically subversive and instead aimed to prove the same of individual filmmakers. In 1951, private beliefs, not public acts, were enough to prove Communist subversion, and Hopper's arguments followed suit. HUAC issued more subpoenas and called more witnesses, and the blacklist grew. Those subpoenaed who refused to testify about themselves or about others cited their Fifth Amendment protection against self-incrimination, rather than invoking the First Amendment and risking contempt of Congress citations and jail time, as had the Hollywood Ten. But these "Fifth Amendment Communists," as Hopper and others dubbed them, did not escape the blacklist.[76] Those witnesses who cooperated with HUAC, hoping to avoid the blacklist by recanting their earlier beliefs and activism, could not limit their testimony to their own lives and politics. Once they chose to cooperate, they had to answer any and all questions put to them, including providing information about the political involvements of former friends and colleagues; such informing came to be called "naming names." As it turned out, just having one's name mentioned in a HUAC hearing could get someone blacklisted, and a 1952 HUAC report included 324 people named as Communists by cooperative witnesses.[77]

Hopper and her anti-Communist allies encouraged this "naming names" of present and former Hollywood Communists and sympathizers. In the wake of HUAC's return to Hollywood, the agenda for an important meeting of the MPA included Hopper and a "call again for anyone who has been misled into joining front organizations or who has aided the Communist Party to come forward and denounce them and give any information he can to the F.B.I."[78] This call to inform was answered by a majority of those subpoenaed

(58 out of 110), prompting Lillian Hellman to remember the blacklist era as "a scoundrel time."[79] But "naming names" did not provide HUAC with any information the committee did not already have. Instead, it was a ritual of confession and hoped-for forgiveness that contributed to "the devastation" wrought by the hearings in 1951 and later.[80]

For Hopper and her colleagues, the hearings and the lists were necessary to expose and rid Hollywood of the "Red menace" and, in turn, necessitated private information—information about anyone with real or suspected, current or former ties to the Communist Party. Government hearings provided this kind of information, as did lists from private organizations such as the American Legion. In 1949, local "Red hunter" Myron Fagan began issuing the pamphlets *Red Treason in Hollywood* and *Documentation of the Red Stars in Hollywood*, which listed "pals and helpers and agents" of Soviet Communism and included an endorsement by Hopper. "I'm all for you!" read her testimonial, which appeared alongside those of J. Edgar Hoover, Ed Sullivan, and Adolphe Menjou, a friend, actor, and MPA member who had testified willingly before HUAC in 1947.[81] Whether Hopper actually endorsed Fagan's work, or if he just used her name and invented her quote, is difficult to tell, as she certainly disavowed him later on. In an exchange of letters in 1961, she called Fagan's pamphlets "absolutely unreliable." "We know there are a great many Communists in Hollywood," she wrote, "but many of those listed in the little red pamphlet are loyal Americans."[82] As it turned out, the "most authoritative source" of information for anti-Communists, according to Thomas Doherty, was the official newspaper of the Communist Party USA, the *Daily Worker*, where a "favorable review or a tangential mention in its pages tarred the recipient with subversive residue."[83] But gossip, rumor, and innuendo also supplied names, and here Hopper played a key part.

For those she suspected of Communism or any form of disloyalty or un-Americanism, Hopper worked hard to identify and expose them. She and her staff conducted research and gathered information on various suspects. Her files included the kinds of reports that circulated among anti-Communist blacklisters, such as the "Voting Record of Helen Gahagan Douglas on Significant Measures Involving Un-American Activities, Internal Security and National Defense," and one titled "JOSE FERRER," a mimeographed record of political activities Ferrer sponsored, organizations in which he participated, and letters he signed in the *Daily Worker*.[84] Hopper corresponded with and received information from various anti-Communist organizations, including the Anti-Communism Voters League, the Americanism Educational League, and the Committee to Proclaim Liberty, as well as her associates in the MPA, such as Adolphe Menjou.[85] Industry insiders also wrote her, often anonymously, with their suspicions and accusations. In November 1947, the "Faithful Employees" of RKO sent her a list of more than seventy RKO employees they accused of Communism, which Hopper passed on to the president of RKO, and in May 1950 a letter claimed that an associate of Darryl Zanuck, vice president in charge of production at 20th Century-Fox, "is smooth—check his commie status with someone."[86]

Hopper's readers, too, researched and offered information. One southern California reader wrote about Charlie Chaplin, actor John Garfield, and their wives being entertained on a Soviet ship docked in Long Beach and urged Hopper to look into it; this event later showed up in Chaplin's FBI internal security file.[87] When Hopper mentioned Howard Duff in her column, a male reader in Colorado Springs sent details of his "affiliations, associations, collaborations, and/or cooperations with five Red fronts or organizations" based on HUAC reports. Implicating Duff was not enough, however. At the time, Duff starred in *The Adventures of Sam Spade* on the radio, a program, this reader commented, "created by Dashiell Hammett who has citations much longer than those of Duff."[88] Another respondent objected to the casting in a film of Howard Da Silva, "a known communist sympathizer, if not actually a card holder." "I've hoped for some rampaging from you on this matter," she wrote Hopper in 1950, "but since there has been no mention of it in your column, I assume it has not been brought to your attention." The following year, Da Silva received a HUAC subpoena.[89] These readers had conducted research, and they backed up their accusations by citing their sources, which ranged in credibility from the mainstream, if conservative, *Los Angeles Times* to published HUAC reports to the disreputable Red-baiting magazine *Alert*—billed as "A Weekly Confidential Report on Communism and How to Combat It."[90]

Hopper's close relationship with J. Edgar Hoover and the FBI also provided her with private information. The FBI had been intensely investigating Communist infiltration of the motion picture industry since 1942, and the bureau maintained a strong presence in Hollywood with agents and informers on the ground "haunt[ing] everybody even remotely suspected of harboring left-wing views" and gathering information. "All our producers need to do before hiring a questionable character," Hopper wrote in her column, "is to phone the FBI for information." Hoover and the FBI also had a "huge public relations budget to supply gossip, information and misinformation" to media outlets.[91] An undated report from "Operative 888" about Edward Dmytryk can be found in Hopper's personal papers. The report claimed that

Dmytryk had been caught in a lie to his studio head and compelled Hopper to write about the incident in her column.[92] Hopper wanted more than small items, however, and she directed her requests to Hoover. "I loved what you said about Commies in the motion picture industry," she wrote "My dear Edgar" in April 1947. "But I would like it even more if you could name names and print more facts. Who's keeping the truth from the American public?"[93]

Although answers to these specific questions were not forthcoming, Hoover and his employees clearly considered Hopper an important part of the effort to persuade Americans that Cold War Communism posed an overwhelming threat to U.S. national security, and she reciprocated. For example, when Hopper missed the "anti-American propaganda potentialities" of a film she reviewed favorably, an FBI contact met with her, pointed these out, and reported that "she now realizes the damage that foreign distribution of such a picture could do to the efforts our American government is making to sell democracy abroad."[94] Hopper's enthusiastic cooperation with the FBI meant not only publishing items fed to her, changing her opinion of a film, or declaring that "this country is in a state of emergency." It also meant serving as a witness for FBI investigators, as she did in the cases of Charlie Chaplin and John Garfield. For the FBI, Hopper was both a source and outlet for information. "Hoover to Hopper, Hopper to Hoover, this was all gossip," Otto Friedrich has noted, but the gossip had serious consequences.[95]

Hopper acted as a source for others as well. She gained a reputation for having access to private information about Communists, fellow travelers, and sympathizers in Hollywood. At one point, for example, an FBI informant assumed that she had "seen a photostat copy of a Communist Party membership book in the name of John Garfield." She had not, but on the assumption that she had concrete evidence of Garfield's Communist affiliation, an FBI investigator paid her a home visit.[96] Readers relied on Hopper to know who was and who was not a Communist in Hollywood. One reader sought "any pertinent facts" about actor Albert Dekker and his wife, Esther, as rumors about them had "sharply divided" her village after Mrs. Dekker was nominated to be president of the local Parent Teacher Association. "I have lived here 12 years," Hopper's reader wrote, "and never have we had a tempest like this." In response, Hopper claimed the Dekkers had "played ball with many organizations that have been cited by the Attorney General as Communist, communist dominated, and/or subversive," adding "I know of no actions by the Dekkers or recent associations that show any change in their left-wing thinking."[97] Journalist colleagues similarly directed their queries about possible Communists to Hopper. "Dear Hedda," wrote A. M. Kennedy of the *Chicago Tribune*. "Our reference room has no information on Howard Duff. Do you know if he is a pinko?"[98]

While people came to her for information, she also went to them when she had an item of interest. Hopper wrote the editor of the *American Legion Magazine*, for example, about Nelson Algren when his novel about drug addiction, *Man with the Golden Arm*, was being made into a movie. Hopper believed Algren's story was dangerous because it glorified "the dope habit" at a time when "dope is being used by the Commies as a weapon of war." In her letter, she accused Algren of having "a long Commie record going back to 1935, and extending up to [the] time of [the] Ethel and Julius Rosenberg defense in which he participated. He was also a writer on the *Daily Worker*." Although Hopper does not include the source of these accusations, they are consistent with what the FBI believed about Algren.[99] By feeding these accusations to the American Legion, Hopper could hope for some action—either toward inclusion in the Legion's many publications or against the film, given the group's reputation as "the most credible threat to picket theaters playing non-conforming movies" and as having "a direct effect on the studios."[100] But her efforts to pass on information were not always successful, as when she forwarded letters accusing certain Fox employees of being Communists to Darryl Zanuck. He rejected her overture and returned the letters, as "he was not interested in playing this game." "Usually, the so-called exposures are based on petty or personal grievances," he wrote Hopper.[101]

Once Hopper believed—accurately or not—a Hollywood denizen was implicated in Communist attitudes, affiliations, or activities, she went after them, making their private political lives public. "When Hedda was on her pinko purge," commented a magazine editor, "she never let up."[102] Her main weapon was her column, but she also used her other media outlets. She could be subtle about those she wished to implicate, as when she simply dropped a few hints in her column. Of course, by hinting often enough, industry insiders would pick up on it, her target would come to be known as "controversial," and the studios would steer clear.[103] Leonard Spigelgass, a Screen Writers Guild activist, recalled how she operated:

> What she used to do was to run an item saying that the Hollywood Ten and other Communists have been given film assignments. Paragraph. Leonard Spigelgass has been assigned to write *Gypsy*. There was never anything I could put my finger on. She could say it was just a news item that followed the other by chance. But the column had that kind of continuity.[104]

One need not have been an insider, however, to pick up on Hopper's hints, as one reader objected, "You have made insinuation after insinuation, and nasty snide remark after remark. . . . If you have information . . . then stop hinting and trot it out."[105] Hopper also could be quite direct, as on her radio show when she listed the top ten box office draws among Hollywood stars in 1951. She named John Wayne, Bob Hope, Bing Crosby, and Betty Grable, among others, and linked their popularity among movie audiences to their non- or anti-Communist politics, commenting, "There isn't a red herring—or a tinge of red—connected with one of them. Could be that's the reason they're on top."[106]

Dore Schary, although never a Communist, received some of Hopper's most direct accusations. For example, when he left RKO to take over as production head at Metro-Goldwyn-Mayer in 1948, and Hopper observed that "the studio will be known as Metro-Goldwyn-Moscow," he threatened to sue. The item was removed from future editions of her column, but that failed to stop her. "Dore Schary's in the pink after five weeks at Arrowhead," she wrote the following year, after Schary returned from a vacation. Although the phrase "in the pink" could be read innocently, Hopper's use of "pink" and "red" almost always had political connotations.[107] She was forthright about her reasons for disliking Schary. She believed he had displaced and disrespected her friend Louis B. Mayer at MGM. But more important, she characterized Schary's liberal politics as "pinko sympathies" and considered social problem films made under his studio leadership, like *Crossfire* and *Blackboard Jungle*, as "downbeat pictures" that go "right along, in a sense, with the Communist Party line." Most egregious for Hopper—although judicious for many—was Schary's initial refusal to fire the Hollywood Ten members Edward Dmytryk and Adrian Scott from RKO.[108] "I defended them," Schary later wrote, because "(if they were Communists) they had a right under the law to think as they wished to think." This was a civil liberties argument Hopper would never accept, and she delighted in Schary's final dismissal from MGM in 1956, naming the day Schary was fired as one of the "happy days in my life." "I've always liked making people happy," Schary riposted.[109]

Hopper not only used her column but also worked behind the scenes to pursue and punish those she considered "subversive," as she did with Carl Foreman. When Foreman received a HUAC subpoena as part of the 1951 hearings, he was writing the script for the western film *High Noon* (1952). His script featured Hadleyville, a town in peril due to both an external threat and an internal weakness, and the film could be read—as Foreman intended— as a critique of both HUAC's investigations and Hollywood's capitulations.[110]

While the film was in production, Foreman appeared before HUAC. He testified that he was not currently a Communist—having left the party in the early 1940s—but refused to testify about any earlier involvement, invoking his Fifth Amendment right not to incriminate himself. As a result, Foreman was considered an "uncooperative witness," and "when it was over," he recalled, "I was finished in Hollywood." John Wayne, at the time the president of the MPA, attacked Foreman, and Hopper joined him, demanding that he be fired immediately and "never be hired here again."[111] Behind the scenes, they went after Henry Rogers, a publicist working with the screenwriter. "You've got yourself mixed up with that Commie bastard Carl Foreman," Hopper yelled at Rogers. "That washes you up in this town. I'm going to see to it that you're driven out of business." Rogers received calls from many in the MPA, including Wayne, Ginger Rogers, and Ward Bond. "It was," Henry Rogers said later, "a calculated plan of terror." This opposition to Foreman contributed to his blacklisting and move to London. "I'll never regret having helped run Foreman out of this country," Wayne proudly stated, a variation of a western idiom he had used many times in his movies.[112]

Enforcement Efforts

After having helped to establish and extend the blacklist, Hedda Hopper also intervened behind the scenes to enforce it, as when William Holden wanted to appear in a film coscripted—although without official credit—by Carl Foreman, *The Bridge on the River Kwai* (1957). "Bill, you can't do it! We can't let those Commies get their feet back in the industry now," she pleaded.[113] As in this instance, once a former employee of the motion picture industry was on the blacklist or graylist, she worked hard to keep them there. For the most part, no process of rehabilitation was enough to overcome her skepticism. She strongly believed that economic need rather than genuine conviction motivated blacklistees to clear their names. Adolphe Menjou agreed, asking, "Isn't it strange that economic pressure makes patriots (?) of the strangest people?" In addition, Hopper trusted few people on or threatened with the blacklist to tell the truth. With actors, she could not resist commenting on their testimony or confessions as "acting." One actor's HUAC appearance was "far beneath his screen acting," she nastily wrote, while another "read the best script of his career."[114] There were exceptions, particularly when a rehabilitee energetically worked to ingratiate him- or herself. Hopper lauded screenwriter Martin Berkeley, who managed to fit 161 names into his HUAC testimony and joined the MPA, as "the most co-operative witness to testify" and "the only former Communist to receive a citation from the American Legion." Carl Foreman also eventually "won her over," although he did not go out of his way to curry favor and never became an informer.[115] Despite her exceptional treatment of Foreman, Hopper generally refused to forgive and forget.

Hopper's unforgiving attitude particularly shaped her enforcement of the blacklist and treatment of members of the Hollywood Ten, especially Dalton Trumbo. In April 1950, she accused MGM of continuing to employ Trumbo. Eddie Mannix, a studio executive, insisted she retract her false statement, which "is calculated, of course, to do us great damage with the public."[116] It also was calculated to warn other studios to maintain the blacklist. Years later, Trumbo, still blacklisted, needed to hide his identity when he wrote the Oscar-winning script for *The Brave One* (1956), so he used the pseudonym "Robert Rich." When the winners of the Academy Awards were announced, and Hopper heard a name she did not recognize, she was immediately suspicious. "Who the hell is Robert Rich and why are we giving him an Oscar?" she demanded, and she began looking into the situation and putting pressure on those protecting Trumbo.[117] She took more public action against Trumbo when he received screen credit for *Spartacus* (1960), a sign that the blacklist was no longer in force. Support for the film came from across the political spectrum. President John F. Kennedy attended a screening, *Time* magazine praised "longtime Far Leftist" Trumbo for his script, and the Daughters of the American Revolution named the film a "Lesson in Freedom." But Hopper, along with her allies in the American Legion, held strong, and she took out a paid advertisement in *Daily Variety* to express her opposition to "one of the worst pictures I've ever seen." "The script was written by a Commie," she wrote, "so don't go to see it."[118]

Trumbo did not receive the worst of Hopper's mistreatment, however; that distinction belonged to Larry Parks. Parks became a star with his Oscar-nominated starring role as showman Al Jolson in *The Jolson Story* (1946), followed by the sequel and box office hit *Jolson Sings Again* (1949). Parks was one of the original "unfriendly nineteen" subpoenaed by HUAC for the October 1947 hearings, but the hearings adjourned before he was called to testify. When he testified during the March 1951 hearings, he admitted his membership in the Communist Party but did not want to "name names." He conveyed his emotional anguish about being forced "to really crawl through the mud to be an informer," but under pressure from HUAC he eventually complied.[119] With his confession, Parks hoped to avoid the blacklist, and even John Wayne felt Parks had been punished enough. But Hopper did not agree. She was angered by that fact that Parks had waited from 1947 to 1951 to come forward and testify. "A Stool Pigeon Sings Too Late" was the title of her "scathing" column after Parks's testimony.[120] Hopper also castigated Parks at an MPA meeting, placing his belated confession within the context of the war in Korea and asking whether the families of dead soldiers "will be happy to know their money at the box office has supported and may continue to support those who have been so late in the defense of their country?"[121] Wayne criticized this speech, but Hopper, he recalled, "gave me fifteen minutes of the roughest go. 'Our boys are dying in Korea and the whole bit.' Real enough. And I had to take it."[122] In the end, Hopper's speech contributed to the blacklisting of Parks.

But there was a backlash brewing against Hopper and her extreme anti-Communism. The very next month, April 1951, she issued criticisms of HUAC for "attempts to whitewash" and, as reported in the *Hollywood Citizen News*, claimed she knew of Communists and Communist sympathizers who had denied their guilt before HUAC. This "blast" at HUAC earned her an interview with the committee chairman, John Wood. Although Hopper privately retracted her statement, Wood later went public, threatening, "If she ever prints or broadcasts such a statement again, we'll subpoena her fast and make her tell what she thinks she knows." He also compared Hopper's statements to "crackpot letters."[123] When Hopper appeared in May as a mistress of ceremonies at the American National Theater Academy's annual show in New York, she was met with "catcalls, boos, and foot stamping" and "instrumental raspberries in the form of hoots and toots from the orchestra pit," and forced to retreat; the New York audience had put "Hedda Hopper in her place." *Variety* attributed the audience's antagonism to "her general rightwing political sympathies," and filmmaker Nunnally Johnson cheekily considered "her 188 per cent Americanism" to blame.[124] Then in a major defeat for her, *The Hedda Hopper Show* was not renewed, and the last show of her last radio series aired on May 13, 1951. Public reprimands increased over the decade, most damagingly from George E. Sokolsky, a Hearst syndicate columnist whom Hopper could not easily dismiss. Sokolsky was among the "anti-Communist writers who have proved themselves to us," according to an internal FBI memo. In 1953, Sokolsky told *Variety* he considered Hopper and her allies "very dangerous people for us anti-Communists. They hurt us all over the country by taking an almost blood bath attitude. They give the cause of anti-Communism a bad name."[125]

Sokolsky's attempt to rein in Hopper, as with HUAC chairman John Wood's earlier effort, revealed a concern among anti-Communists about the extremism of their "counter-subversive" compatriots. The very next year, for example, public and political opinion turned decisively against Senator Joseph McCarthy and his methods, and in December 1954 the Senate voted to condemn him—after considering the more serious action of censure—for "bringing discredit upon the chamber."[126] Yet, when other colleagues deserted him, a determined Hopper defended him. "Since when has it become violative for the U.S. Senate to investigate persons and organizations that would destroy our country by force?" she asked. After his death, she still stood by him, because "he more than any other man in America has alerted this nation to the dangers of Communism." While these pro-McCarthy comments placed Hopper on the right of the political spectrum, she was not there alone, as many conservatives in the later 1950s and 1960s missed McCarthy as one of the "stalwarts" and "spokespersons of the Right."[127] Moreover, criticism of Hopper and her Red Scare politics was much belated. "The intimidation of Hollywood, a process begun in 1947, was successfully completed in the early 1950s," writes M. J. Heale.[128] Hopper, her anti-Communist allies in Hollywood, and her supportive respondents were less extreme than effective.

By using her column to publicize private lives and political beliefs, Hopper aided the Red Scare and the blacklist in Hollywood. In turn, these developments justified additional public incursions into private lives and crucially contributed to the anti-Communist consensus of the 1950s. At a critical point in the early Cold War, the HUAC hearings into Communist "subversion" in the motion picture industry garnered national media attention for domestic anti-Communism, consolidated the power of HUAC, and established "the machinery of McCarthyism," including the use of economic sanctions against unfriendly or uncooperative witnesses.[129] These developments affected both the content of film and the lives of filmmakers. Socially conscious films became harder to make, and all liberal and social reform efforts—not just left-wing political activity—became harder to undertake in Hollywood.[130] Such outcomes of Hopper's anti-Communist activism dovetailed with the aims of her campaigns around another significant issue on the post–World War II conservative political agenda: curtailing African American civil rights activism. One of the forms civil rights activism in the 1940s and 1950s took in Hollywood—changing racist film representations of African Americans— also became a target of Hedda Hopper's Red Scare politics.

Hedda Hopper with the actresses Irene Dunne and Louise Beavers at a Republican Party function, 1950. (Courtesy of the Academy of Motion Picture Arts and Sciences.)

Representing Race in the Face of Civil Rights

When Hedda Hopper appeared in the Women for Nixon commercial during the 1950 U.S. Senate race, she not only used the Republican Party's Red-baiting campaign tactics and advanced the party's electoral prospects. She also revealed her conservative racial attitudes. In planning for this radio broadcast, Hopper wanted a black actress involved. Until the 1930s, the majority of African Americans able to exercise their voting rights—mostly those who lived in the North—cast their ballots for Hopper's Republican Party. By the 1950s, however, most enfranchised African Americans fell into the Democratic column, making Hopper's task more difficult. She first asked Hattie McDaniel, famous for her Oscar-winning role as Mammy in *Gone with the Wind*. Although apologetic, McDaniel turned down the request. "I have made it a rule, never to openly endorse a candidate or work in a political campaign for any personality." In the end, Louise Beavers, who had "perfected the optimistic, sentimental black woman whose sweet, sunny disposition and kindheartedness almost always saved the day" in films like *Imitation of Life* (1934), appeared in the radio commercial.[1] A "kindly old Negress," the character played by Beavers, had several lines. She declared her support for Nixon—"Ah'm votin' foh him too"—and her membership in a "group dat is workin' hard fuh to elect Mr. Nixon," an organization for black women separate from Women for Nixon.[2] In using Hollywood's false and demeaning black dialect for Beavers's character, the script reinforced racist images of African Americans as ignorant and inferior to white Americans. Hopper approved of this script despite the fact that black actors, actresses, and civil rights activists had been attacking the use of such dialect and what it signified for years. Indeed, a year later Beavers would play the television role of "Beulah," a black maid to a white family, without "any trace of dialect."[3]

Hopper's endorsement of false black dialect for Louise Beavers's character in the campaign commercial revealed her belief in and comfort with white superiority. Hopper was known within the motion picture industry as "deeply bigoted," but she eschewed virulent expressions of racism in public.[4] For Hopper, such expressions of racism were unrespectable. Moreover, they were unfitting for a member of the Republican Party—the "party of Lincoln"— and Hopper, unlike many white Republican women, did seek to involve African American women in her political efforts and activism, as her work on the Women for Nixon radio broadcast indicated. Her efforts were less than effective, however, when she decided to tell "an offensive joke" at a Women's Division banquet at the 1956 Republican National Convention. "The principle character of the anecdote," reported the Chicago Defender, "was a Negro maid whose dialect has long since been dead and buried."[5] Yet, "if anyone had accused her of prejudice, she would have been astounded, arguing that she liked Hattie McDaniel, Butterfly McQueen and Stepin Fetchit." The African American actors of whom Hopper approved were all performers associated with racially stereotypical and often demeaning roles, and her interactions with them were characterized by paternalism and condescension, demonstrating her beliefs in black inferiority and inequality.[6] For blacks in the post–World War II period who challenged Hollywood's old stock stereotypes, offered new images of African Americans, and refused her paternalism, such as Sidney Poitier, Hopper's support came much more slowly, if at all. In her racial beliefs and actions, Hopper was no different from most of white Hollywood. Her gossip rival Louella Parsons only stopped using the word "pickaninnies" in her column after World War II and only after receiving criticism.[7]

Where Hopper differed from her colleagues was in her very public efforts to "keep blacks in their place," both in Hollywood and the United States generally. As civil rights activists sought to build on the momentum toward racial equality and more positive movie portrayals of African Americans gained during World War II, Hedda Hopper's column became a site for a discussion of what cultural studies scholars have come to call "the politics of representation."[8] Two key events in this discussion were Hopper's successful Oscar campaign for James Baskett, who portrayed Uncle Remus in Walt Disney's Song of the South (1946), and a less successful 1947 defense of Hattie McDaniel's typecasting as and portrayals of "mammies," most famously in Gone with the Wind but also in Song of the South and other films. In taking on these campaigns for Baskett, McDaniel, and the characters they played, Hopper launched a defense of white superiority and an attack on civil rights efforts, just as the Cold War began and the modern Civil Rights Movement took shape. With this timing, Hopper's conservative racial politics gained traction, as she joined with her anti-Communist allies in the motion pic- ture industry, such as Walt Disney, to link proponents of racial change on the film screen and in American society with Communism, bringing together her Red Scare politics with her anti-civil-rights agenda. The relationship between civil rights and the Cold War, according to recent scholars, resulted in both repression and reform for African Americans, but repression was the result Hopper sought.[9] Unlike reformers who used the Cold War to expose the contradiction between U.S. democratic ideals and racist realities, Hopper and her Hollywood allies deployed Cold War anti-Communism to head off racial progress.

Hopper's endorsement of racist stereotyping in Hollywood film and Red- baiting of filmmakers and activists concerned with civil rights did not go unnoticed by her African American readers or by younger actors, such as Poitier. While Hopper and many of her mostly white respondents sought to keep African Americans in a stereotyped, subordinate position in the motion picture industry, as in the wider society, Hopper's African American respon- dents responded with powerful arguments about why Hollywood's racial representations must change. At stake in the conflicts among Hopper and her readers, Hollywood filmmakers, and civil rights activists was whether motion pictures would contribute to or hinder the larger struggle for racial equality in the United States.

An Oscar for Uncle Remus

At just the historical moment when civil rights activists, much of the black press, and many black filmgoers heightened their campaign against the use of degrading images of African Americans in films, Walt Disney Studios released *Song of the South* (1946) to great acclaim from Hedda Hopper. For Americans seeking changes in race relations and racial representations, 1946 was a decisive year. The first year of peace following the end of World War II was also the year in which Hollywood would either further "the war-driven, nuanced changes in racial depiction" or "restore its prewar racial order."[10] The production and reception of *Song of the South*, Disney's first postwar film, not only indicated a move toward restoration but also that any changes or chal- lenges would be Red-baited. When the NAACP, which had opened a Holly- wood bureau that year to more closely monitor how movies presented black characters, and the National Urban League issued strong protests against the way the film caricatured blacks, Walt Disney attributed this condemnation of racist stereotypes in his movie to the "rising of the red menace."[11] Hopper agreed with Disney and blatantly ignored the vociferous criticism of the film's black caricatures, especially that of Uncle Remus, played by James Baskett. Instead, she reinforced and celebrated such caricatures when, together with a group of mostly white readers, she controversially and successfully campaigned for a special Oscar for Baskett in 1948.

Coming from a studio where "'good' Disney stories adhere to a hierarchy in which white reigns supreme over black," *Song of the South* perpetuated the racially demeaning stereotypes that met with Hopper's approval. Baskett's Uncle Remus came with the all too familiar "toothy smile, battered hat, grey beard, and a profusion of 'dis and 'dat talk."[12] The Uncle Remus stereotype was one of the dominant images of blacks to appear on U.S. motion picture screens. Donald Bogle, an important scholar of blacks and American popular media, has catalogued the set of stereotypical characters, the "mythic types," that Hollywood filmmakers drew on to represent African Americans. Most prominent was the "tom," initially a slave who remains loyal to his white master and "hearty, submissive, stoic, generous, selfless, and o-so-very-kind." A second stereotype of black men was the "coon," the "Negro as amusement object and black buffoon," made famous in the 1930s by Stepin Fetchit, the stage name for Lincoln Perry. Bogle considered Uncle Remus as "a variation of the coon" and "a first cousin to the tom." "Harmless and congenial," the Uncle Remus "distinguishes himself by his quaint, naïve, and comic philosophizing." *Song of the South*, Bogle argues, along with *Green Pastures*—which Hopper also loved—brought the Uncle Remus type "into full flower."[13]

Hollywood's black stereotypes, like many of the industry's storytelling conventions, derived from an earlier cultural form, in this case minstrelsy. Minstrelsy, where white performers in blackface caricatured enslaved and free African Americans through speech, song, and dance, emerged in the nineteenth century before the Civil War as "the cultural dimension of white supremacy" and the United States's first mass popular entertainment.[14] Minstrel performers spoke and sang in mangled English, presented as black dialect, and used racist humor while wearing the "grotesque, demeaning, animalistic blackface mask" to reinforce racial hierarchy, justify slavery in the South, and discrimination against free blacks in the North.[15] Although recent scholarly readings of nineteenth-century minstrelsy have contended that "just as minstrelsy can be used to serve racist ends so can it be used to resist racist discourse," for many commentators Hollywood's use of minstrel stereotype closed off the latter possibility. "The silver screen was for many years Black America's daily betrayal before millions of people," wrote the poet Langston Hughes and his coauthor Milton Meltzer.[16] Walt Disney and filmmakers at his studio continued this betrayal with *Song of the South*, their first film to feature an African American in a prominent role.

Hopper covered the film while it was in production. Disney and his colleagues based the screenplay for *Song of the South* on the work of Joel Chandler Harris, a white southerner who began collecting and publishing traditional slave tales about animal tricksters, such as Brer Rabbit, beginning in 1880 with *Uncle Remus: His Songs and Sayings*. Drawing on his experiences with slaves he knew growing up in antebellum Georgia as well as with watching minstrel productions, Harris—in an instance of "literary minstrelsy"—invented Uncle Remus as his storyteller to young children.[17] *Song of the South* follows this plot with Uncle Remus befriending Johnny, the sad and lonely grandson of his white plantation mistress, telling the little boy stories that teach him life lessons, and ultimately saving his life. Joel Chandler Harris has been criticized for misappropriating and distorting African American folklore, but literary scholar Peggy A. Russo compares the original stories favorably to Disney's film. Harris made Uncle Remus a "teacher," passing "on the inherent wisdom of the folktales," while Disney made him an "entertainer," "an 'oldtime darky' who takes care of his master's child." Moreover, the film's mix of live action and animation, which was considered innovative at the time, places Uncle Remus frolicking with animated creatures against backdrops that made Baskett look like a cartoon himself.[18] The novelist Alice Walker recalls listening to the Brer Rabbit and Brer Fox stories as a child with her siblings. "But after we saw *Song of the South*, we no longer listened to them. They were killed for us."[19]

As a consequence, while in production Disney's *Song of the South* received strong criticism from African Americans inside and outside the motion picture industry, although not from Hopper. "Walt," she reported, "is doing raves over James Baskett, famous Negro actor who's playing the title role."[20] But African American filmmakers and civil rights activists feared a filmic portrayal of Uncle Remus would undermine their efforts to secure more realistic and human representations of blacks in film, which they saw as part of the larger struggle for black equality in the United States. Walter F. White, executive secretary of the NAACP, first read about Disney's proposed film in Hopper's July 7, 1944 column, titled "Disney Bows to 'Uncle Remus.'" "The picture will be rich in the humor of the lovable old Negro philosopher," Hopper informed her readers. White soon wrote to Walt Disney. "I was very much interested in seeing in Hedda Hopper's column that you plan to make 'Uncle Remus.' I would like very much to know the treatment you plan to give it." Walt Disney responded, saying he was willing to work with White and other critics.[21]

This failed to happen, however. When the literary scholar and philosopher Alain Locke became a consultant on the film, he suggested scholarly readings on the "harsh history" of slavery to correct the sentimentality and nostalgia for the Old South in the Uncle Remus stories. But the studio rejected a script based on this historical scholarship.[22] Hired later on to help with scriptwriting, actor Clarence Muse also was rebuffed when he made "suggestions for upgrading the image" of the black characters in the film. He resigned, saying the movie would be "detrimental to the cultural advancement of the Negro people." Similarly, Rex Ingram turned down the role of Uncle Remus, believing the film would "set back my people many years."[23] "These good people," stated a Production Code Administration memo to Disney in 1944, "have become most critical regarding the portrayal on the motion picture screen of the members of their race," but even this industry warning went unheeded.[24]

Criticism from the black press and activists continued after the film was made with James Baskett in the leading role, although African American heterogeneity meant there was no "monolithic black party line on the issue of black cinematic representations."[25] Herman Hill of the *Pittsburgh Courier*, for example, complimented "the truly sympathetic handling" of race in the film and believed *Song of the South* would "prove of inestimable good at furthering of interracial relations."[26] But Hill's opinion was decidedly a minority one among African American commentators. Many considered the film "a throwback." Hope Spingarn of the NAACP saw in *Song of the South* "the old clichés," while her colleague Gloster Current felt Baskett's Uncle Remus personified "the Negro stereotype of docility."[27] The National Urban League joined the NAACP in protest, objecting to the film's "perpetuation of the stereotype casting of the Negro in the servant role," while the National Negro Congress called the film "an insult to the Negro people" and picketed in Los Angeles, San Francisco, and at New York's Palace Theater hoping to "run the picture out of the area." Richard B. Dier, writing in the *Afro-American*, considered the film "as vicious a piece of propaganda for white supremacy as Hollywood has ever produced," and Matthew Bernstein, editorializing in *Ebony*, made the explicit connection between the black struggle for civil rights and filmic stereotypes of African Americans: "*Song of the South* cannot but retard America's biggest minority in its battle to get a square deal."[28]

These protests and criticisms angered both Hopper and Walt Disney. Disney refused to see any merit in objections to *Song of the South* and—conflating civil rights, antiracism, and Communism—blamed them on Communists.

According to his most recent biographer, Neal Gabler, Disney suspected that the black newspapers leading the protests against his movie were "Communist-controlled" and wanted the FBI "to find out why the black community was harassing him."[29] Similarly, Hopper later attributed protests against *Song of the South* to "several Commie groups."[30] For anti-Communists like Hopper and Disney, any American concerned with changing racist representations of African Americans was a Communist; for FBI chief J. Edgar Hoover, any departure from black stereotypes in film was a sign of successful infiltration of Hollywood by Communists.[31] HUAC operated on these assumptions the following year during its hearings on Communist subversion in the motion picture industry when Disney testified as a "friendly" witness with the enthusiastic support of Hopper. From Hopper's perspective, then, endorsement of black stereotypes in *Song of the South* was consistent with the crusade against Communism.

Hopper and her respondents praised precisely what civil rights activists condemned about *Song of the South*. Upon its release, Hopper gave a glowing tribute to the film, James Baskett's "sensational" performance, and the character of Uncle Remus. Later on, a number of her readers were similarly enthusiastic, heaping Uncle Remus with praise and highlighting his good qualities. "He was sweet!" wrote one woman from Florida.[32] "Dear Miss Hopper," wrote another from Chicago. "I saw the picture 5 times, (twice with my grandchild). . . . So many mothers have told me that their children have come home from the movies . . . and raved over Uncle Remus's kindness and sweetness. They said he was the kindest old man they knew. Many parents took their children several times to see the picture—the magnet which drew them was Uncle Remus." "Uncle Remus," she added, was "a kindly, humble, lovable old man, who tried to make others happy, especially little children by being their friend." These apparently white readers contributed to *Song of the South* becoming one of the country's favorite films of the immediate postwar years and a major moneymaker for Walt Disney Studios.[33]

Why did the Uncle Remus stereotype appeal so much to Hopper, these readers, and the white audience in general? Relevant here are studies of minstrelsy and the very popular radio show *Amos 'n' Andy*, which aired from 1928 to 1960. The radio show drew on minstrel stereotypes and told the adventures and mishaps of two black characters, Amos and Andy, "known for being bumbling, stumbling, dim-witted souls who had problems thinking straight and who constantly misused the English language."[34] As with the audiences for minstrelsy in the nineteenth century and *Amos 'n' Andy* in the twentieth century, the audience for *Song of the South* "needed to see black people as buffoons" and "took comfort in having their racial imagination confirmed"; such works of popular culture, as historian James Oliver Horton has argued, "provided white America with the image of black people . . . that most wanted to believe."[35] In the face of a strengthening civil rights presence and voice for black equality, Hopper and her white fans liked *Song of the South* because it gave them what they wanted: a portrayal of African Americans free of "overt racial hostility" and "non-threatening in presenting the simple 'darky.'" In fact, one of Hopper's readers argued that Baskett's portrayal of Uncle Remus "has been a force for good in race relations."[36] Although the southern critical and popular response may have been expected—"Dixie Reviewers Have Praise for 'Song of the South,'" "super," "definitely one of the best pictures ever made"—Hopper and most of her respondents on *Song of the South*, all but one from the North, also gravitated to the film's fantasy of American race relations, one that combined white "benevolent dominance" with black "grateful submission."[37]

That white Americans found their desired portrayal of black life in a film set on a plantation in the Old South did not escape the notice of African Americans. Nostalgia permeates *Song of the South*. "Out of the humble cabin, out of the singing heart of the Old South," the film begins, "have come the tales of Uncle Remus, rich in simple truths, forever fresh and new."[38] In keeping with Harris's original stories, Walt Disney Studios claimed they set the film in the period after the Civil War, with Uncle Remus ostensibly a free man. But this fact was obscured in the film, as the use of "Old" rather than "New" South indicated, and many viewers left the movie theater with the impression that *Song of the South* depicted the era of slavery. The *New York Times*'s Bosley Crowther was one, as was Hopper, who recalled Baskett as playing "a slave," and one of Hopper's readers, who referred to Uncle Remus as having a "Master."[39] Walter White also understood the film in this way, and objected to the film's presentation of "a dangerously glorified picture of slavery" that gave the "impression of an idyllic master-slave relationship which is a distortion of the facts."[40] Indeed, this impression was apparent when Uncle Remus sings the film's theme song, "Zip-a-Dee-Doo-Dah," which includes a line about "everything being satisfactual," hardly an accurate statement coming from an African American character living in either the pre– or post–Civil War South. The ambiguous time period, combined with the use of the Uncle Remus stereotype, allowed *Song of the South* to function as a justification of white supremacy. As Donald Bogle contends, "Remus's mirth, like tom's contentment and the coon's antics, has always been used to indicate the black man's satisfaction with the system and his place in it."[41]

Within this context of criticism of the Uncle Remus stereotype and its political function, Hopper extended her praise for James Baskett's performance to nominate him for a special Academy Award. Disney joined her, writing to Academy president Jean Hersholt that Baskett had brought to life the "immortal folklore character" of Uncle Remus.[42] For Hopper, Baskett was "a special actor, and deserves a special award," as she wrote in her February 20, 1948, column. Because *Song of the South* combined live action and animation, Hopper argued Baskett could not be "classed as either star or supporting actor," thus his performance did not fit the established categories for Academy Awards and necessitated a special Oscar. Baskett also won Hopper's favor with his criticism of black protest over the film. "I believe that certain groups are doing my race more harm in seeking to create dissension, than can ever possibly come out of the *Song of the South*," he stated publicly. Hopper concluded by noting that Baskett "is a great, warm-hearted gentleman" who "has been ill for months." "Let's give him the recognition due him now."[43]

Readers eagerly and enthusiastically responded—many on the day the column came out. "Letters are pouring in from all over," Hopper happily reported. "Dear Miss Hopper, I'd like to be one of the many fans to cast a vote for James (Uncle Remus) Baskett."[44] Like this woman from Detroit, Hopper's readers understood they were joining with others to advance this Oscar campaign. Most letters also included generous compliments for Hopper herself. A male actor noted, "It is a splendid and a beautiful thought of yours to beg Academy members give a special award to James Baskett for his outstanding and warmhearted performance as Uncle Remus." "'Orchids to you!'" sent her correspondent from Florida. "If there is <u>anything</u> you can do to help James Baskett receive recognition for his portrayal of 'Uncle Remus,' you are an angel!"[45] Most of the letters to Hopper in support of an Oscar for Baskett appear to come from white Americans, and their investment in the minstrel stereotype of Uncle Remus implies a civil rights conservatism. But letters came in from schoolchildren as well, expressing their sincere affection for Uncle Remus and thanking Baskett for playing the role. Hopper reported their sentiments and promised to forward their letters onto the Academy.[46]

For African American activists, intellectuals, and audiences, discomfort with Baskett's humiliating stereotypical role tempered their admiration for his acting in *Song of the South* and their excitement about the possibility of an Oscar. Although Uncle Remus was Baskett's only major film role, he had been an important figure on the vaudeville stage and had played the role of Gabby Gibson, a "slick-talking" lawyer on the *Amos 'n' Andy* show.[47] Like *Amos 'n' Andy*, *Song of the South* posed a contradiction for African Americans. Both the radio program and the movie reinforced racist stereotypes and sparked anger among African Americans, but, as film scholar Mark A. Reid has strongly argued, "reception is not constructed so simply. Audiences have the ability to overlook the obvious racism and seize the humane properties of the overtly racist discourse." In fact, *Amos 'n' Andy* had a large audience among blacks, because they saw in the program "glimmers of African American humor and traditions, even if through a distorted lens."[48] As a consequence, with *Song of the South*, Baskett's performance in a starring role earned him credit as well as criticism from African Americans. Gloster Current of the NAACP was a good example. Although he had censured the Uncle Remus stereotype, he also found Baskett's performance "artistic and dynamic." Another African American expressed anger at *Song of the South*'s white audiences, not Baskett, for "laughing and chuckling" at Uncle Remus. The singer Etta James helps to explain how African Americans viewed actors like Baskett in the mid-twentieth century. "All the black actors were heroes. They might play fools on the screen, but the folks in the neighborhood knew it took more than a fool to break into lily-white Hollywood."[49]

In keeping with this view, the letters of the few blacks writing to Hopper about *Song of the South* were very positive toward Baskett and the special Academy Award. The only African American writing to Hopper or in the media to compliment Baskett without reservations, however, was Charles E. Butler. A "Motion Picture Artists' Agent, Specializing in Colored Agents," as his letterhead stated, Butler ran an essentially segregated division of the Central Casting Corporation. Given his profession, his fulsome praise for Baskett's Uncle Remus made sense. In his letter to Hopper, Butler lauded Baskett for bringing "great happiness to millions of people as he certainly did a fine piece of work."[50] Dr. Charles W. Hill of the Phi Beta Sigma Fraternity, an African American collegiate association, also championed Baskett, but he made it clear that Baskett's acting repertoire was not limited to playing the humble, happy "darky." He paid tribute to "Jimmy" as "one of the finest versatile actors to ever trod the American stage," and he informed Hopper that "Jimmy sings the classical arias with a rare, rich, mellow baritone voice." Hill's elaboration on Baskett's talents challenged the association between role and actor, between racist stereotypes and actual people, between filmic representation and lived reality. By focusing on Baskett apart from Uncle Remus, he countered the idea that for a black actor acting out a minstrel stereotype there is "no presence or identity behind the mask."[51]

African Americans' mixed feelings about Baskett and his film role meant civil rights groups never mobilized a "coherent campaign" against Hopper's drive for a special Academy Award.[52] Even so, criticism of *Song of the South* did influence some board members of the Academy of Motion Picture Arts and Sciences, and they opposed giving Baskett an award. But Jean Hersholt, an actor who served as Academy president from 1945 to 1949 and a social activist who helped form the Motion Picture Relief Fund in 1939 to supply medical care to those motion picture industry employees who could not afford it, silenced the opposition by speaking out against the "racism of the academy." As a result, despite different motivations, Hopper and Hersholt won out, and the Oscar, presented as part of the 1947 Academy Awards, recognized James Baskett for his "able and heartwarming characterization of Uncle Remus, friend and storyteller to the children of the world."[53] Baskett's correspondence with Hopper revealed his sincere gratitude for her praise of his performance in *Song of the South*, her concern for him during his illness that came after the making of the film, and her campaign to win him a special Oscar. "You are responsible for my happiness," he wrote following the presentation of the award in March 1948—a quote Hopper quickly got into print—and he died just a few months later, in July. For Hopper, the Oscar for Uncle Remus was a great success and a symbol of her power in the motion picture industry. So important to her was this accomplishment that she discussed it years later in both of her autobiographies.[54]

In Defense of Mammy

During the same period, Hedda Hopper exercised her power in defense of Hattie McDaniel and the stereotypical role for which she was known: the black mammy. Most famous for her Oscar-winning role as "Mammy" in *Gone with the Wind*, McDaniel also appeared in *Song of the South*. She "praised the script" after taking the role of a happy domestic servant "joyfully bouncing about the kitchen laughing and baking pies to the everlasting pleasure of the household and Uncle Remus."[55] Like Baskett's Uncle Remus, McDaniel's servant received criticism upon the film's release, but the criticism aimed at McDaniel was sharper and more vociferous, due to her long, illustrious career in Hollywood as well as to the particular black stereotype, the mammy, she brought to life in more than one hundred roles.[56] As a consequence, in April 1947 Hopper published a letter from McDaniel defending her film roles, which Hopper disingenuously introduced with "Hattie McDaniel must be confused by those people picketing *Song of the South*." Eight months later—and two months after the October HUAC hearings in Washington, D.C.—Hopper dedicated an entire Sunday article to a defense of McDaniel and a condemnation and Red-baiting of her critics, including leaders and members of the NAACP. The NAACP had contributed, Hopper claimed, to McDaniel's "siege of career trouble"—a recent twenty-one-month period without work in the motion picture industry.[57] Hopper's December 1947 article sparked a strong response from readers, with many letters from African Americans who sought to educate Hopper on the interconnections among the politics of representation, the image of the mammy, and civil rights.

"I have known and admired Hattie, both as an artist and an individual," Hopper noted in her defense of McDaniel, "since we did *Alice Adams* together twelve years ago." In *Alice Adams* (1935), McDaniel played a servant, a portrayal Hopper described in what she considered positive terms as "a female Stepin Fetchit cook." The role of servant was one of the few stereotypical roles—along with the related mammy and the sexualized jezebel—open to black women in Hollywood movies at the time.[58] By that point in McDaniel's film career, which began in 1931 following her stint on the black vaudeville circuit in the 1920s, she already had become typecast as the mammy-maid. "A powerfully built woman," according to Donald Bogle, "she weighed close to three hundred pounds, was very dark, and had typically Negro features." As such, McDaniel fit the physical description always ascribed to the mammy: "large, deep brown in color," "big, fat," "sexless, cheerful, maternal."[59] "Mammy" originated as the name given to enslaved African American women in the pre–Civil War South who nursed children, and a popular image of the mammy as a nurturing servant, either tending to children, the stove, or housework, proliferated through American culture after the Civil War. The mammy character had a turn on the nineteenth-century minstrel stage, played by white men in blackface, apron, and bandana. As Aunt Jemima she sold pancake mix beginning in the 1890s, and in the twentieth century she became the film role—"dressed by the studio in gingham and rags and made to speak a 'dem and dose' dialect"—that "Hattie McDaniel was to perfect."[60]

Hopper failed to see McDaniel's typecasting in the roles of mammy and maid as a problem, because such portrayals, she added patronizingly, "are the kind at which Hattie excels. It was her mammy role in *Gone with the Wind* that got her an Oscar."[61] By playing a mammy actually named "Mammy" in the 1939 historical melodrama about a white slaveholding family just before, during, and after the Civil War, McDaniel did achieve her greatest fame and acclaim. At the time, Hopper cheered McDaniel's success. After *Gone with the Wind*'s Los Angeles premiere in December 1939, Hopper gave the film and McDaniel a glowing review—even if she spelled her name wrong. Hopper complimented the performances of the film's other luminaries, such as Vivien Leigh, who played Scarlett O'Hara, and Clark Gable's portrayal of Rhett Butler. "But it was Hatty MacDaniel," she stated, "as the colored mammy, who broke my heart."[62]

McDaniel's presence and prominence in *Gone with the Wind*, however, made her a controversial actress. *Gone with the Wind* enjoyed phenomenal box office and critical success, but it also received biting criticism from the black press and civil rights activists for its glorification of the Old—slave—South and portrayal of enslaved and later free African Americans as "happy house servants."[63] "A slanderous anti-Negro picture inciting racial hatred" was the consensus of four leading black newspapers. Melvin B. Tolson, a prominent leftist writer with the *Washington Tribune*, considered *Gone with the Wind* "dangerous." By telling the story of the Old South from "the viewpoint of the white masters," the film conveyed the idea that "the North was wrong in freeing the Negro." As a result, *Gone with the Wind* topped the list of "excessively 'anti-Negro'" films compiled for the NAACP's Walter White.[64] Despite accolades in the black press for McDaniel's performance—Tolson commented that she "registered the nuances of emotion, from tragedy to comedy, with the sincerity and artistry of a great actor"—by the early 1940s, she was seen as one of a group of black actors in Hollywood most responsible for perpetuating, in the words of the *Pittsburgh Courier* columnist George S. Schuyler, "the grinning darky stereotype."[65]

Hopper expressed dismay that McDaniel "had been attacked by certain members of her own race simply because she had tried 'to earn an honest dollar' by playing roles those critics thought degrading to Negroes." "The parts, almost strictly those of 'mammies' and maids," Hopper insisted, "were not criminal."[66] No one regarded McDaniel's roles as "criminal," but Hopper sought to undermine the legitimacy of the criticism and the critics with this exaggerated misrepresentation of black objections to the mammy stereotype. She also revealed her ignorance of the historical significance and implications of the mammy image, for African Americans had long condemned the image and what it symbolized. In the late nineteenth and early twentieth centuries, prominent white southerners made the mammy the favored image of the faithful, loyal slave, more dedicated to her white family than her own and, in the 1920s, even proposed a monument to the black mammy to be built in Washington, D.C. With an understanding of how the mythic mammy "diluted the brutal reality of slavery" and supported the claims of the defenders of slavery—that slavery was a benevolent institution and that race relations in the Old South had been "harmonious"—African Americans criticized the image and campaigned against the monument.[67] The supreme dedication and loyalty to whites of the mammy character found full expression in *Gone with the Wind* when Mammy remains, along with other former slaves, with the O'Hara family after black emancipation at the end of the Civil War. The film's message was, as filmmaker Carlton Moss put it, that Mammy "loves this degrading position in the service of a family that has helped to keep her people enchained for centuries."[68]

Gone with the Wind's controversial success linked McDaniel even more firmly to the mammy image and made her, according to Hopper, "a pet target" for Walter White and the NAACP. By 1942, White and other black activists were on a "crusade against 'Mammyism'" as part of the effort to remove racist caricatures of blacks as "clowns, heavies, moronic servants or as superstitious individuals scared of ghosts" from the movies.[69] Although Louise Beavers and Ethel Waters received criticism for playing mammy-maid roles, McDaniel was singled out as the most famous and recognizable mammy of them all. She had become nearly synonymous with her role in *Gone with the Wind*. She was often billed as Hattie "Mammy" McDaniel, and Hopper referred to her as "Mammy Hattie McDaniel," which implied McDaniel approved of a stereotype disdained by most blacks. She also had won an Academy Award as Best Supporting Actress for her performance, the first African American to be nominated for an Oscar and the first to win. Although many blacks were proud of her acting achievement—the California branch of the NAACP gave her a special award for her work in *Gone with the Wind*—others urged her to refuse the Oscar as a protest against Hollywood's racism.[70] For such critics, McDaniel's celebrity made her mammy and maid roles even more damaging, and they assumed her "star power" could be wielded to change representations. But her ability to challenge the demeaning treatment or typecasting of black film actors was negligible. She herself was prohibited from attending the 1939 Atlanta premiere of *Gone with the Wind*, due to segregation laws, and forced to sit at a rear table at the Academy Award ceremonies that honored her. Moreover, despite the widespread recognition of her talent, "iron-clad" typecasting limited her to servant roles throughout the 1940s.[71]

By 1947, McDaniel's film career was in steep decline, and she was on the defensive. Between 1934 and 1938, she had averaged ten films a year, but in the 1940s she only made two or three films a year. Within this context, McDaniel felt her livelihood threatened by the crusade against Mammyism and "bitterness" toward Walter White, feelings that were complicated by intra-racial class differences.[72] She was not the only member of black Hollywood to feel this way. African Americans within the motion picture industry, rightfully fearing for their jobs and careers based on playing stereotypical roles, had organized in opposition to the NAACP's and other activist efforts to change racial representations in film. Due to her prominence, McDaniel emerged as a leader and, together with Clarence Muse, "bitterly attacked" White and his activism in Hollywood.[73] By the late 1940s, White believed criticism and campaigns about Hollywood racism had achieved some success, aided by the post–World War II popularity of social problem or "conscience liberal" films, like *Pinky, Home of the Brave, Lost Boundaries*, and *Intruder in the Dust*, all released in 1949. But resistance from southern censors, like the "notorious" Lloyd T. Binford, head of the Memphis Board of Censors, and theater owners who "refused to exhibit movies that depicted blacks as anything but subservient to whites" meant these films made up only a small proportion of Hollywood's total output over these years. These films also failed to provide work for black veterans of Hollywood typecast to play the old stock stereotypes, like McDaniel.[74] When combined with an overall loss of industry jobs due to economic pressure, as the studios dealt with declining movie attendance, the 1948 Supreme Court Paramount decree ordering divestiture of theaters, and export limitations in the international marketplace, McDaniel's career was in peril.

Seeing McDaniel's story as a way to attack White, the NAACP, and the goal of more realistic filmic representations of African Americans, Hopper ignored such industry factors as falling revenues, racial typecasting, and racist southern censors and exhibitors, and put the full blame for McDaniel's career slump on black protest. "Because of the pickets and protests," Hopper wrote, "Hattie believes—and so do I—that producers hesitate to hire Negro actors. Studios certainly need their talent, and they would love to give them work, but they don't want the trouble stirred up—not by censors like Lloyd Binford of Memphis, but by elements of the Negro race itself."[75] The African American critic Robert Jones made the same point earlier that year. "The solution to protests against stereotyping the Negro has been quite simple for Hollywood; cut them out altogether." But he held the industry responsible, insisting that, rather than eliminating black roles, it make the changes demanded by protestors.[76] In contrast, Hopper supported McDaniel by assailing civil rights activists and the demand for more realistic racial representations. McDaniel's cooperation with the racially conservative Hopper was based on a common agenda about film roles and racial representation, but also revealed how desperate McDaniel was less than a decade following her ostensible triumph in *Gone with the Wind*.

McDaniel's desperation evoked sympathy from Hopper's white respondents but failed to do the same with African Americans—with the notable exception of Charles E. Butler. As he did with James Baskett during the Oscar debate, Butler complimented both actress and columnist. "Thanks again for your story about Hattie. She deserves it and is a swell person and a good trouper." Butler aside, the racial divide among Hopper's respondents mirrored that among audiences for a personal appearance tour taken by McDaniel in 1940, following *Gone with the Wind*. Rejected by black theatergoers, McDaniel was enthusiastically embraced by white audiences. As film scholar Victoria Sturtevant has argued, "White audiences created and sustained McDaniel's fame; it is white audiences who were invested in the notion of Mammy."[77] Similarly, in the letters to Hopper, it was two white women who expressed compassion for McDaniel. "I felt so badly after reading your column," noted one. "I had wondered a number [of] times why we do not see her in pictures any more. She is so good, it is a shame." In a letter addressed directly to McDaniel, she added, "It is a shame you are not working in pictures. . . . What would *Gone with the Wind* be without you? You have lots of friends. I am afraid the N.A.A.C.P. is doing more harm than good. I don't understand them."[78] But the majority of letter writers were African American, and they communicated unwavering criticism of, and anger about, McDaniel's career. "Your endeavor to help Hattie McDaniel was well meant but a little misdirected," wrote one to Hopper, "and I hope you will be patient enough to read what another Negro woman thinks about Hattie's portrayals of the past."[79] Such letters emerged out of an "implied actor-audience contract," as scholar Anna Everett puts it, where black public opinion should matter to black Hollywood. Readers admitted their letters might sound "bitter" and "vindictive" but did not apologize. One Chicago man felt so strongly he wrote two letters, just days apart.[80]

This intensity of opinion about McDaniel from Hopper's black letter writers included passionate support for ridding Hollywood movies of racist stereotyping. "We are damn tired of seeing ourselves portrayed on the screen in stereotypes," asserted one Los Angeles man.[81] The man from Chicago held nothing back in his description of the dominant film image of African Americans as "the exceptionally ebony, white-eyed, chalk livered lipped personage typically characterized as a dialected frightened fool." "I get so darn tired of going to a movie," he declared, "and being embarrassed and humiliated by such performances (if you can call them that) and stereotypes."[82] In making their case against stereotyping, these African Americans argued that representations were important. Black audiences and actors knew the stereotypes were a performance; as McDaniel had written to Hopper, "the part is the thing." But they feared white audiences understood the film image to represent actual African Americans, and Hollywood's stock black characters were egregious distortions. "With Hattie McDaniel's type of acting others may get the idea that all Negroes are on the same level that she portrays in her pictures," wrote one reader.[83]

These respondents joined in the "hue and cry"—reported and commented on negatively in Hopper's article—"against roles that depict Negroes as members of the servant class." One woman objected to McDaniel's "depiction of the servant on the screen." "Her pictures have all taken us back to the old slave days and while we know that situation existed, I think it would be good policy to let us forget it if we can. It is not pleasant to be reminded that we were slaves nor should I think it good for your race to be reminded that they held us in bondage."[84] As this letter writer understood, images of blacks in servant or servile positions reinforced racist beliefs in white superiority and justified continuing inequality for blacks. In her analysis of the mythic mammy—the "first controlling image applied to U.S. Black women"—the black feminist theorist Patricia Hill Collins makes this point as well, finding the mammy image "used to justify the economic exploitation of house slaves" in the nineteenth century and "sustained to explain Black women's long-standing restriction to domestic service" in the twentieth century.[85] Moreover, if black women have functioned as white women's "Other" in American history and culture, then the most famous pairing of social and physical opposites comes from *Gone with the Wind*, where the devaluation of Hattie McDaniel's Mammy increased the estimation of Vivien Leigh's Scarlett.[86]

Hopper's African American respondents also agreed with those who criticized "the use by Negro actors of 'outmoded dialects.'" Not only did this dialect convey ignorance and inferiority, argued one woman; even worse, it was employed for comedic purposes. "It is true to laugh is good, but why laugh at illiteracy? Better to be ashamed that such a wonderful nation as ours permitted and still permits it to exist."[87] In fact, such dialect hardly existed at all and was largely an invention of white scriptwriters. According to McDaniel's biographer Jill Watts, "Hollywood's stereotypical black speech was so foreign to such a large number of African-American players that, in some cases, studios hired white speech coaches to instruct them on their lines."[88] McDaniel herself, Hopper reported, "even got the permission of producers to speak good English," to which the same reader replied, "If, as your article said, the studio 'permits' Hattie to use 'good' English and you really want to help her, then tell her instead of feeling sorry for herself to take advantage of the 'permission' and use it [and] portray the type of Negro woman her race is proud to own."[89]

In their criticisms of stereotypical roles and dialect, Hopper's African American respondents knew representations affected social and political reality. "Each time Hattie McDaniel goes on the screen or radio the Negro race takes one tiny step backward," observed one man. "The type of characters created on the screen for the various races have long tended to establish good-will for some and continuous stereotyped humiliation and disgrace for others," wrote the Chicago man.[90] Consequently, they demanded more realistic, accurate, and human portrayals of themselves. "On the screen a Jew, an Italian, a Mexican, an Irishman, a Swede, can be a doctor, lawyer, scientist, etc. but a Negro, no!" "Negro doctors, lawyers, scientists, medical students, law students, etc." should be portrayed in the movies, one reader argued, as should blacks who spoke standard, proper English. "Sure there are many Negroes that use dialect," wrote another. "There are also many Negroes that have educated themselves and their children," and Hollywood should portray them on-screen as well.[91] Another reader pointed out that even when playing servant roles "Hattie and other Negroes can still maintain a semblance of dignity and self respect." "I should know," she continued, "for I am in domestic service and love my work and my employer but the reverse would be true if I had to don a handkerchief on my head and use the dialect of the old slaves." These letter writers reinforced what black intellectual Lawrence Reddick asserted in 1944: "The overwhelming desire of the Negro people, as expressed through their critics, is to have Negro actors on the screen treated 'like everybody else.'"[92] Yet Hopper's respondents were not waiting for African American critics to express their desires; they were voicing their own views directly.

Moreover, these respondents believed that more realistic portrayals were possible, as they had seen them before. The Chicago reader lauded "the previous and continued fine performances of contributable persons like Canada Lee, Ethel Waters, Lena Horne, Paul Robeson, and a very few others," and held the film industry responsible for choosing to perpetuate stereotypes. "It is up to the producers, directors, etc., to stop inserting the traditional stereotyped role."[93] This reader recognized, as film historian Thomas Cripps argues, that "black roles remained in bosses' hands," and that filmmakers could offer more accurate representations of African Americans, such as those roles played by Lee, Waters, and others, if they so chose.[94]

For these African Americans, then, Hattie McDaniel was a harmful anachronism. "In your write up of Hattie McDaniel," one letter writer addressed Hopper, "you said, 'she has always been a credit to her race.' I would like to ask you a simple question. How has she been a credit to her race?"[95] For McDaniel, who upon accepting her Academy Award expressed her hope "that I shall be a credit to my race and to the motion picture industry," this question would have been heartbreaking. She saw herself as a "race woman," as someone who expressed racial pride and solidarity. "I do not feel that I have disgraced my race by the roles that I have played," she emphasized in personal correspondence to Hopper. McDaniel regarded her portrayal of Mammy in *Gone with the Wind* not as another "handkerchief head role," as some critics would have it.[96] Instead, inspired by the biographies of nineteenth-century black heroines such as Harriet Tubman and Sojourner Truth, she considered Mammy "an opportunity to glorify Negro womanhood." McDaniel also supported reform efforts. She joined with other prominent members of black Hollywood to establish the Fair Play Committee— which advocated improved film roles for blacks—and to fight against racially restrictive covenants in Los Angeles housing. The latter legal struggle led to a local victory in 1945, three years before the Supreme Court's famous *Shelley* v. *Kraemer* (1948) ruling banned restrictive covenants throughout the nation.[97] But these challenges to the racial status quo went unnoticed among Hopper's respondents.

Also unnoticed were McDaniel's efforts to manage the conflict she faced as a black woman in white Hollywood. Throughout her career, she confronted what Clarence Muse called in his 1934 pamphlet "The Dilemma of the Negro Actor."[98] To work and earn a living in Hollywood meant playing racially stereotypical roles that came with an emotional and political cost, but trying to change or refusing such roles meant risking or very probably ending a Hollywood career. In a famous remark, McDaniel pointedly captured this conflict and revealed her choice, given her limited employment options as an African American woman: "Hell, I'd rather play a maid than be one!"[99] Hopper's respondents also grasped this dilemma. "We know that casting Negroes in pictures is difficult, for stories are not woven around Negro life," wrote one. Nevertheless, they believed black actors like McDaniel should refuse to work in Hollywood rather than play caricatured parts, choosing integrity over money and fame. "If the Colored actors and actresses can't perform roles which are complimentary to the merits of Art and Hollywood, then I say down with any sort of characterization that belittles."[100] Early in her career McDaniel attempted to reconcile this dilemma by imbuing the characters she played with "attitude." As Donald Bogle argues, McDaniel's mammies and maids, including Mammy in *Gone with the Wind*, were "cantankerous," "headstrong," and "audacious." "In front of the camera," Jill Watts notes, "McDaniel created a maid that she knew in real life would be fired in an instant."[101] Over time, however, she found less room for such maneuvering, "gradually killing off the rebellious . . . character and becoming a near-parody of complacency and sweet agreeableness."[102]

McDaniel also increasingly compromised with and appeased white power brokers in the motion picture industry like Hopper. In one instance, in 1940 after *Gone with the Wind*, McDaniel had resisted the studio's demands that she cooperate with publicity for fan magazines by offering cooking advice and recipes. She knew what was expected of her: recipes for stereotypical black dishes, such as greens and fried chicken. But, seven years later, when Hopper gave her a Christmas present that revealed similar stereotyping, McDaniel's defiance was gone. "I also haven't forgot the Catfish and corn-bread which I shall fry myself."[103] Making her capitulation to white Holly-wood even more evident was McDaniel's denial of racism in the industry, as reported in Hopper's December 14, 1947, article. "So far as racial prejudice goes," she told Hopper, "I wish that my critics could work on movie sets. I have found no discrimination there."[104] And, in one last ditch effort to save her dying career, McDaniel adopted a stance as a Cold Warrior, which won her kudos from the Hopper and other industry leaders but criticism from African American readers. "Hattie loathes communism and regrets that a few prominent members of her race have acquired the red tag," wrote Hopper. By 1947, McDaniel had violated a tenet of black stardom: she was more attached to white Hollywood than to black audiences and communities.[105] This was the McDaniel with whom Hopper's African American respondents took issue.

Although not identifying as civil rights activists or countering Hopper's criticisms of the NAACP, these respondents situated their demands within the context of the struggle for black equality and disavowed Hopper's link between civil rights activism and Communism. Movies with racist carica-tures, contended one, "do nothing for better race relations toward which we all should strive to the utmost to attain." They saw this effort as crucial and these years, the late 1940s, as a key historical moment for achieving a more equitable and just society. "Negroes all over the U.S. are educating themselves and doing everything in their power with the help of some white people to advance themselves."[106] Taking issue with Hopper's Red-baiting and equation of dissent with treason, one reader warned against "branding people promis-cuously of communism. . . . Lately everyone, black or white who tries to aid any minority group is branded a communist. It is neither wise nor fair." Walter White also weighed in against the "dangerous error of labeling 'subversive' honest American doctrine of freedom, justice and equality," a label that "haunted" the NAACP from 1946 with help from Hopper.[107]

What was the solution to the problem of demeaning representations of African Americans in Hollywood film? For McDaniel, African Americans, including the NAACP, should invest in film production and make films they deemed worthy. "Once we make a sound investment in the film industry, we can talk policy without appearing ridiculous," she told Hopper.[108] One reader agreed. "The N.A.A.C.P. or some other Negro source should advance money into production of Movies. If I had the money I would do it myself." Challenging Hollywood's "propaganda monopoly," as another reader put it, fell into a long tradition of black independent filmmaking and reflected an understanding of the interrelationships among images and representations, social and economic inequalities, and access to and participation in cultural production.[109] Charles Butler's suggestion reflected his belief that audiences fundamentally shaped the content of motion pictures. "I have been telling the colored Press that the colored people will never get anything out of pictures till they send in fan mail to show that they contribute something to the product and to Democracy."[110] Similarly, just a year earlier, the *Chicago Defender* suggested that the NAACP "might emulate the Catholic Legion of Decency" and demonstrate "the box office value of good productions from a race relations standpoint." But market power eluded African Americans, as they constituted only fifteen percent—at the most—of the postwar movie audience.[111] Other respondents advocated what scholar Francis Couvares terms "good" censorship—"I would clip out entirely blasphemous scene[s] showing any . . . ster[e]otype"—or suggested banning altogether those performers who took stereotypical roles. If McDaniel did not change the types of roles she played, one woman wrote, "then her race would be extremely grateful if she would stay off the screen."[112]

Due to Hopper's censorship, the content of these very critical letters about race and representation in the movies never appeared in her column. This silence contrasts with her reports about letters in support of her Oscar campaign for James Baskett, revealing her strict control over whose views were represented in her column. It also does not appear that Hattie McDaniel received copies of these letters. Upon thanking Hopper for her supportive writings, McDaniel only mentioned having "received some lovely comments on account of them."[113] But Hopper's writings did not rejuvenate McDaniel's film career. Already at the time of Hopper's defense, McDaniel had made the move to radio, playing the lead character on *Beulah*, a show about a black maid employed by a white family. "*Beulah* became a radio hit with McDaniel," according to Donald Bogle. But Beulah was another mammy role—a happy, loyal servant whom McDaniel described as "everybody's friend"—and again proved controversial. In 1949, for example, the *Kansas City Call*, a black newspaper, included McDaniel on a list of things that "Must Go."[114] Hattie McDaniel played Beulah on radio until her early death from breast cancer in 1952.

Meanwhile, Hopper could feel satisfied about her efforts on McDaniel's behalf, just as she did with her support for James Baskett. For Hopper, these campaigns were less about furthering the careers of a particular black actor and actress than about promoting the characters they played. From Hopper's perspective, Uncle Remus and Mammy were ideal images of African Americans, allowing for "painless racial harmony" rather than the conflict and contest of the 1940s, a decade known as "a transition period in American race relations."[115] Moreover, these campaigns reflected Hopper's paternalism toward the African American actors of whom she approved. She sought to guide and protect these performers, with the racist assumption that she knew what was best for them and could speak for them. How McDaniel and Baskett truly felt about Hopper and her efforts ostensibly on their behalf is unknown, as certainly their warm letters to her must be understood as written within the context of a power and racial structure in Hollywood and the United States that privileged Hopper and disadvantaged them. But never again would Hopper have the opportunity to exercise her racial, and racist, paternalism so prominently.

Presenting Poitier

As a new generation of African American performers, led by Sidney Poitier, emerged in Hollywood in the late 1940s and 1950s, they sidestepped a paternalistic relationship with Hedda Hopper and, together with growing pressure from the Civil Rights Movement, strengthened the challenge to Hollywood's racist images by the 1960s. For some scholars, such as Donald Bogle, the success of this challenge already can be seen in the "more adult and serious representations of African Americans" that appeared in the social problem films of 1949 and after.[116] Others, however, emphasize the incremental or even superficial nature of the change represented by these few, albeit prominent, films. Thomas Cripps calls such films "conscience-liberal movies," as they were made by white filmmakers who considered themselves racial liberals. These movies presented the message that a color-blind, integrated society was best for all Americans, black and white. But "conscience-liberalism" in Hollywood was essentially a white and, thus, limited vision of race relations. White filmmakers "could not create complex and fully realized black characters," and these films featured these still-stereotyped black characters in white environments where they taught whites the damage done—as much to whites as to blacks—by racism, as well as the value of racial integration.[117] In the 1950s, such characters were most famously played by Sidney Poitier, beginning with *No Way Out* (1950). Although critics and scholars would later lambaste Poitier for playing such "harmless types," he and his films signaled a dramatic change for a racial conservative like Hopper.[118]

Sidney Poitier posed a challenge for Hopper. When Hopper finally devoted an interview and Sunday article to Poitier in 1958, he had just made *The Defiant Ones* (1958), which earned him an Oscar nomination for Best Actor. A film about two prisoners, escapees from a chain gang, one black, one white, and their eventual capture, *The Defiant Ones* functioned as a metaphor for American race relations. The men, played by Poitier and Tony Curtis, are chained together, and so have to confront their prejudice and pride and learn to get along to make their escape. An example of conscience-liberalism, the film was directed by Stanley Kramer, who made his name as a producer-director of social problem films—exactly the type of message films Hopper disliked. Rather than attacking the antiracist message of such films, however, she criticized such films generally, arguing—disingenuously, given her endorsement of anti-Communist films—the "only message" she favored in movies "is that of entertainment."[119] Like other racially themed social problem films, the conflict in *The Defiant Ones* is resolved through the greater humanity and magnanimity of the character representing the oppressed minority, in this case Poitier's character, Noah Cullen. By 1958, Poitier had perfected such roles, playing "restrained Black men who endure the indignities and injustices of racism with cool patience and dignified strength." By 1958, he was also a star and widely viewed by producers as a box office draw.[120]

But more than an actor or a star, Poitier was, in the words of his most recent biographer Aram Goudsouzian, "popular culture's foremost symbol of racial democracy," making Hopper even more wary. Poitier's success in Hollywood indicated to many Americans, particularly middle-class blacks and whites, that racial progress was occurring in the 1950s and 1960s.[121] Early in his career, he criticized stereotypical roles for blacks—"Hollywood as a rule still doesn't want to portray us as anything but butlers, chauffeurs, gardeners or maids," he said in 1951—and he turned down roles on Broadway and in Hollywood because the characters were "too passive" or "bereft of dignity." For Donald Bogle, "Poitier was a near revolutionary figure—the first black man who did not sing, did not dance, did not clown. He was educated, sophisticated, articulate."[122] Within the context of a growing and increasingly effective Civil Rights Movement, Poitier and his roles reflected and effected a shift in the cinematic image of African Americans away from the minstrel stereotypes brought to life by earlier performers, such as James Baskett and Hattie McDaniel.

Hopper had trouble coming to terms with this shift, however, as is evident in the following exchange from their 1958 interview:

HOPPER: Did you sing? So many of your people do.
POITIER: I couldn't sing for beans.
HOPPER: You're the first one I've ever met who says he can't sing. I've never known any of your people who couldn't sing.
POITIER: (smiling): Sorry to be the exception, but here I am.[123]

Hopper's insistence that as a black actor Poitier must also be a singer reflected "white culture's perception of African Americans as fun-loving, 'rhythmic' people," as well as "Hollywood's propensity for representing African Americans with and through musical performance."[124] With Hopper and in his choice of film roles, Poitier sought to undermine the association of blackness with music. This effort fit with his rejection of the minstrel stereotype, as minstrelsy was predominantly "an affair of song and dance."[125] It proved difficult, however, and Poitier not only took a role in the film musical *Porgy and Bess* (1959) but also sang in other films, including a blues song in *The Defiant Ones*.

Hopper's condescension and resistance to change exemplified what Poitier was up against in Hollywood. Her declaration of African Americans as "your people," for example, separated white Americans from black and distanced herself from Poitier based on skin color. Poitier's bemused reaction revealed his familiarity with racist stereotypes as well as discriminatory treatment by Hollywood figures such as Hopper. He also tactfully handled her queries about why he initially refused the role of Porgy. Rather than pointing out that *Porgy and Bess* "portrayed blacks as singing, dancing, clowning darkies of old" or that his character expressed acceptance of poverty and inequality when singing "I got plenty of nothin', and nothin's plenty for me," Poitier responded gracefully. "I thought if it were improperly handled it might be questioned by Negroes, myself included. I am not the conscience of the Negro race but being one myself I have certain responsibilities to myself."[126]

Given the historical moment and the struggles and achievements of the Civil Rights Movement, racial politics figured in Hopper's coverage of Poitier. In 1958, she asked, four years after the landmark *Brown v. Board of Education*: "Do you think it a wise decision the Supreme Court handed down on desegregation?" Unsurprisingly, Poitier strongly endorsed *Brown*. "I think it was overdue for many years." Making connections between civil rights and the Cold War, as did other prominent black and white Americans, Poitier called segregation "a blight on our democracy," "one of the cracks in our jewel," and a hindrance to U.S. efforts in the Cold War. He confirmed the idea proffered by liberal anti-Communists as well as the U.S. State Department that the *Brown* decision dealt a "Blow to Communism." U.S. Ambassador to Italy Clare Booth Luce, for example, believed the court decision "cut the ground out from under the anti-American propaganda put out by Communists on this point." "We are a great strong and young country and have absolutely nothing to sell but democracy," Poitier went on to tell Hopper. "Let's not give the other fellow an edge so he can say—you sell a hypocritical kind of democracy."[127]

By pointing out how segregation and racial discrimination undermined U.S. efforts to present itself as the world's bastion of freedom and democracy against the totalitarianism of the Soviet Union, Poitier brandished "a potent discursive weapon" of the Civil Rights Movement and challenged Hopper's use of Cold War anti-Communism to stymie civil rights reform.[128] Poitier's challenge came exactly a decade after Hopper's campaigns for Baskett's Oscar and McDaniel's career labeled as "Communist" civil rights activism and calls for new filmic representations of African Americans. Although Hedda Hopper slowly came around to see and endorse Poitier as Hollywood's first African American star, she never agreed with his analysis of racial progress as key to fighting the Cold War. Instead, racial conservatism, like sexual conservatism, remained her priority as a means to defend America and Americanism.

Hedda Hopper posing with household products from her radio show sponsors, 1940s. (Courtesy of the Academy of Motion Picture Arts and Sciences.)

"Family Togetherness" in
Fifties Hollywood

On December 12, 1949, Hedda Hopper was notably scooped by Louella Parsons, who announced that Ingrid Bergman was pregnant and by a man, Italian director Roberto Rossellini, who was not her husband. "I spent the day of the announcement rubbing egg off my face," Hopper recalled, "because six months before I'd interviewed Bergman at the scene of the crime." She had traveled to Rome, where Bergman and Rossellini were living while making *Stromboli* (1950), to confront Bergman about newspaper reports of a pregnancy. Bergman denied them. "Hedda, look at me. Do I look like I was going to have a baby?" "I've never seen her give a finer performance," Hopper remembered. At the time, Hopper reported, "Ingrid declares she will bring suit against the Italian papers which said she was going to have a baby. I don't blame her; there's not a word of truth in it." After Parsons broke the true story, Hopper barely acknowledged it. The next day she dedicated an entire column to Rossellini's filming of *Stromboli*, with only a veiled reference to his romance and impending parenthood in her last line, "He sure got Bergman."[1] Hopper's anger at being lied to, losing a major story, and an actress's sexual transgressions meant she took the side of Bergman's wronged husband in the ensuing divorce proceedings, gratified that after the property settlement "I don't believe Ingrid will have enough left to pick up a check for a cup of coffee." Then, when baby Robertino was born two months later in February 1950, Hopper contentiously claimed "the morals clause in every player's contract can now be deleted." She referenced *Gilda* (1946) star Rita Hayworth's nearly simultaneous adultery and pregnancy with Prince Aly Khan, and concluded bitterly, "With Rita's travels before becoming a princess and later a premature mother, and now Ingrid, that clause should be clipped."[2]

Hopper's fury contributed to a heated controversy over Bergman's actions, which created "a state of panic in Hollywood." Initially, executives at RKO chastised Bergman and claimed her scandalous behavior would destroy her career and their finances, and her publicist warned her of protests and boycotts from pressure groups, such as the Catholic Legion of Decency. But then the studio decided to capitalize on Bergman's notoriety in the advertising for *Stromboli*, which prompted Senator Edwin C. Johnson, Democrat of Colorado, to condemn her from the halls of Congress as "a powerful influence for evil." Johnson also proposed legislation to police the private lives of motion picture performers to protect the public good, naming both Hayworth and Bergman as "Hollywood's two current apostles of degradation."[3] To many observers, Bergman's adulterous affair and illegitimate pregnancy were particularly shocking given her most recent starring role in *Joan of Arc* (1948). "Having seen Ingrid on the screen in Joan of Arc," Hopper noted, "they'd come to imagine that some of that sainthood had rubbed off on her. She just couldn't commit such a common sin!" Yet Hopper, as well as Parsons, had contributed to making Bergman a star, enthusiastically reviewing her film performances and contributing to her "canonization" as an ideal wife, mother, and homemaker after her arrival in Hollywood from Sweden in 1939.[4] Public knowledge of Bergman's private transgression stripped the happy façade from her family life, betrayed the "moral security" she offered audiences as Joan of Arc, and provided Hopper's readers with a reference point—"the morals of Bergman and Hayworth"—to assess bad behavior among stars.[5] The resulting controversy also revealed fears about the strength and security of the American family generally, as Cold War tensions grew in 1949 following the "fall" of China and the fallout from the Soviet nuclear explosion.[6]

In print and over the airwaves, Hopper helped to establish connections between the American family and the nation during the Cold War. While experienced in the private sphere, the family is defined in the public sphere and images of the family have political significance.[7] These connections between personal, familial lives and public matters had long been a feature of U.S. culture, politics, and society. But in the latter half of the 1940s and during the 1950s, anxieties about the state of the American family and what it meant for the nation as a whole heightened, as historian Elaine Tyler May and others have argued.[8] In the immediate postwar years, the family was perceived to be in crisis due to the stresses and disruptions of World War II, then "the uncertainties of the ensuing peace" gave way to fears of the internal and external threats posed by Communism. During these years, the well-being of the American family and its role in "nurturing national health and 'American' values" became a major topic of concern and commentary.[9] Hopper agreed with government officials, political figures, media commentators, and average Americans that successfully fighting the Cold War at home and abroad required fostering "family togetherness," the ideal family life heralded by the women's magazine *McCall's* in 1954. Family togetherness met Americans' felt needs to recuperate from the damages of the Great Depression and World War II, a familial practice evidenced in demographic developments, including a dramatic drop in the age of marriage for both women and men and the resulting "baby boom." As new national and international conflicts developed, the family became seen as a retreat from, a defense against, as well as vulnerable to these conflicts. Strong, happy families provided safety from Cold War dangers, while fragile, miserable families imperiled Americans.[10]

Hopper endorsed the importance of what she called "home life and good citizenship" and, together with the rest of the motion picture industry, worked hard to promote movie star families as the postwar American ideal of domestic comfort and happiness. She did this by pressing the "master plot of celebrity journalism" into new service, demonstrating how stars sought "true success," or self-fulfillment through home and family life, in the new Cold War context. Yet high-profile Hollywood sex scandals and star divorces, such as Bergman's, belied this era as one of successful family togetherness, and, for Hopper, further justified her incursions into private life as a way to defend the American family.[11] In two major controversies during the 1950s, Hopper, together with most of her readers, vociferously championed the cause of the "abandoned" wife and condemned "the other woman"—when Frank Sinatra left his wife, Nancy, for Ava Gardner in 1950 and when Eddie Fisher dropped Debbie Reynolds for Elizabeth Taylor in 1958. The Sinatra situation and the Liz-Debbie-Eddie incident provoked an intensity of interest among Hopper's readers that increased over the decade of the 1950s, indicating that all was not well with the American family. By exposing private truths and challenging Hollywood's happy domesticity, these and earlier sex scandals, such as Bergman's, prompted readers to evaluate the choices made by movie stars in their private lives. In the process, readers discussed their own personal choices and revealed their own familial disruptions and discontent. Hopper's columns and her readers' letters about these controversies revealed contradictions and ambivalences in Cold War domesticity hidden by apparent American consensus on the fifties family.[12]

Hopper's "Home Life and Good Citizenship"

In her coverage of stars' ostensibly factual—although often fictional—private lives, Hedda Hopper embraced the conservative "privatization discourse" that prioritized business, consumerism, and traditional family values and reached "fever pitch" at the height of the Cold War.[13] Similarly, Cold War pressures prompted the Screen Actors Guild to jettison its politically progressive and activist image "by turning the stars' imagery from public to private life." In a series of SAG-sponsored talks to civic groups, "stars now embodied the rejuvenated family life unfolding in the suburbs," with stable, companionate, and child-centered marriages.[14] In the 1940s and 1950s—until threatened by television's ascendance as the most popular form of U.S. culture—the motion picture industry was the dominant purveyor of cultural meanings, including a "family-centered definition of national identity." Along with movies and the gossip of Hopper and others, the private lives of Hollywood stars, particularly women, became carriers of those meanings.[15]

Marriage was the heart of the ideal postwar family, and Hopper relentlessly promoted it. Originally more patriarchal in structure, marriage by the 1950s was characterized as companionate but obligatory, and couples were encouraged to find self-fulfillment in family togetherness. Hopper pressed her mostly female audience to marry and stay married. If an aspiring actress was not a star by the age of twenty-four, Hopper advised in print, "she'd better start searching around for a husband while her youth and beauty last." In private, she told one actress, "Get married. Don't wind up an old lady in a big house like I am."[16] Hopper presented all single women as searching for good husbands. In July 1948, when Rita Hayworth was in the midst of her second divorce, Hopper wrote that "her one hope is someday to meet and marry the right man." As it turned out, that very month Hayworth met her future, albeit short-term, husband Aly Khan in Europe. Despite her own divorce, Hopper praised stars who kept their marriages together. "It is obvious that her idea of marriage is for all time and eternity," she complimented Dorothy McGuire, an Academy Award Best Actress nominee for *Gentleman's Agreement* (1947).[17] Betty Grable, the perfect symbol of American womanhood during World War II—her pinup poster was the most popular among American servicemen—came to represent the American ideal of "family unity and marital harmony" in Hopper's column after she wed bandleader Harry James. Grable, wrote Hopper, devoted "most of her spare time to raising two beautiful daughters, and making a home for her kids and her everloving husband, Harry James."[18]

By the 1950s, under the influence of new theories of sexuality, pleasurable sex for both partners had become a cornerstone of—but also had to be contained within—marriage, and Hopper policed the boundaries of licit and illicit sex in Hollywood. For sexual conservatives, like Hopper, "sex appeared as an uncontrollable force that spawned social chaos when its power was let loose."[19] Yet the publication of the Kinsey reports on male and female sexuality in 1948 and 1953 made sex a legitimate topic of public discussion—even for Hopper—and revealed a mismatch between private behavior and public mores. American women, for example, were not "models of sexual propriety": one-half of Kinsey's respondents had engaged in premarital intercourse, and one-quarter had pursued extramarital affairs. Hopper was "repelled" by the report and "felt no decent woman would have agreed to answer the questionnaire." When she asked an actor what he thought about the "newest Kinsey report" on women's sexuality in 1953, his response pleased her: "Most women lie, and why do you think they'd tell the truth to Kinsey?" While she doubted and disliked Kinsey's findings, she also feared what their truth might mean: the weakening of the nation's morals and, thus, its fight against Communism.[20] Hopper also disapproved of overt displays of women's sexuality. Even though she still lamented Hollywood's loss of glamour, she approved of actresses who rejected in their private lives the "exoticism and eroticism" associated with glamour as opposed to "middle-class domesticity."[21] "There are two Rita Hayworths," Hopper contended, "the girl you meet at her home is a complete switch from the sexy silk-and-satin Latin lady," and she admired Dorothy McGuire as "the first young star to toss over the idea that an actress must dress glamorously." Betty Grable also was "no glamour girl," and, thus, was "the kind of girl with whom any woman would trust her husband."[22]

Where the marriages of Grable, McGuire, and Hayworth publicly departed from the postwar ideal, as had Hopper's own marriage and others in Hollywood, was in women's wage earning. In the late 1940s and 1950s, Americans experienced a reassertion—following the wartime destabilization—of traditional gender roles and polarized images of masculinity and femininity. Men were cast in the breadwinner role, and, in what feminist writer Betty Friedan later called "the feminine mystique," women were to devote themselves to home and family and find their ultimate fulfillment in the role of housewife and mother. The return to rigid gender divisions in the family was essential to maintaining the Cold War consensus; this "domestic containment," according to Elaine Tyler May, paralleled the foreign policy of containment of Communism abroad and aimed to provide security against Communist subversion at home.[23] This conservative domestic ideology was powerful but partial; not all American women could or would conform, and Hopper knew it. As a consequence, "ambivalence" characterized the attitude of Americans toward wage-earning women, with the lives, priorities, and achievements of career women both questioned and validated in the wider culture.[24] In her column, Hopper launched a strong defense of women working outside the home. Her stance stemmed from her own personal history of continuous wage work, her location in an industry with prominent women workers, and her understanding of the economic imperatives steadily pushing married women into the workforce. As the "family wage" ideal, where a breadwinner husband earned enough to support an entire family, increasingly failed to match reality, the proportion of married mothers working for wages outside the home increased, and by 1960 thirty-nine percent of mothers with school-age children were earning wages.[25]

As part of her defense of wage-earning women, Hopper took on psychiatrist Marynia Farnham in 1947. That year, Farnham published, with Ferdinand Lundberg, *Modern Woman: The Lost Sex*. Although Hopper misspelled Farnham's name, she did not mince her words. "Mariana Farnsworth," Hopper wrote, "gives me a big fat pain." Under the heading "MIND HER BUSINESS," Hopper took issue with Farnham's claims that "feminine careerists" experienced emotional disorders and had difficulties with motherhood and homemaking. "Well, for her information," Hopper argued, "the career women I've known—and I've known quite a few—make their homes the center of their lives." She also pointed out that many women work "to keep their homes from falling apart" and are "too busy taking care of their homes, families and jobs—yes, even husbands—to spend their time at . . . psychiatrists' offices."[26] In her defense of wage-earning women, Hopper joined "the storm of controversy" raging over Farnham's arguments, which, according to historian Joanne Meyerowitz, were "rejected more often than embraced." Hopper's defense, then, placed her in the mainstream of American culture. Similarly, she made it clear that, consistent with societal expectations, women should be the primary caretakers of children and households, even if they were wage earners.[27]

For Hollywood and the United States, Hopper touted parenthood and domestic life as essential to marriage; childcare and homemaking as vocations for women; and both as key to the country's Cold War struggle. "She adores that bright charming little girl and spends more time with her than with anyone else," Hopper wrote of Rita Hayworth and her three-year-old daughter, and she believed Dorothy McGuire "has a far more solid view of things much of which comes, I think, from being a mother." Both women assured Hopper they wanted more children, and they both, in fact, did. Both women also enjoyed homemaking, which Hopper often equated with selecting and purchasing consumer goods. Indeed, a year before the famous 1959 "kitchen debate" between Vice President Richard Nixon and Soviet Premier Nikita Khrushchev at the American Exhibition in Moscow, which linked the Cold War, consumerism, and women's domestic roles, Hopper published an item about international fairs and exhibitions as superb sites to "show our super markets, electric refrigerators, washing machines and dryers, all the things to help make the housewife's life easier and happier."[28] For Hopper, as for Nixon, unprecedented affluence, an abundance of appliances, and the image of the happy homemaker demonstrated the superiority of Americanism over Communism, and she favorably noted how Hayworth set "comfortable furniture against a background of cool, clean pastels," and how McGuire "thought wrought-iron furniture with glass-topped tables was lovely." Betty Grable also ostensibly lived up to postwar maternal and domestic ideals. Yet Hopper's story on Grable included comments about caring for her children "when not working" and during "her spare time," revealing how demanding acting careers limited maternal dedication.[29]

The wifely dedication of female stars also had limits, of which Hopper was well aware. With the ideal postwar wife "subordinate, understanding, and passive" while her husband dominated, Hopper did not necessarily endorse these gendered characteristics among Hollywood stars. In response to an actor's claim that eighty percent of women want to be dominated by males, she exclaimed, "That word! Why is it, whenever anybody tells you women want to be dominated—a man always says it?"[30] Yet she also gave John Wayne, her anti-Communist colleague in the Motion Picture Alliance, favorable coverage when he was in the midst of a messy divorce from his second wife in 1952. Although Wayne's estranged wife accused him of domestic violence and sought a restraining order against him, Hopper praised him. "Under the circumstances, I think he has controlled his temper beautifully, and that's no temper to tamper with, as the Mrs. will learn before this divorce is finished."[31] That Hopper found no fault with Wayne's temper or even the threat of physical violence in his private life fit with the positive reception of the hard-edged masculinity Wayne projected on-screen in his roles as cowboys and war heroes. Despite the 1950s "gender paradox that required a 'hard' masculinity for defending the nation and a 'soft' masculinity as the foundation of the home," Hopper always endorsed vigor and virility and excused violence among men.[32] In 1947, when Frank Sinatra punched newspaperman

Lee Mortimer for ostensibly using an ethnic slur—insulting "my race and my ancestry," Sinatra told Hopper—she dismissed his behavior. "We've been having fights here for years."[33] Similarly, a wife's expression of gendered characteristics, such as submission and subordination to her husband's authority and assertiveness, allowed Hopper to forgive a multitude of sins.

Indeed, in 1953 when Lucille Ball, then starring in the top-rated television show, *I Love Lucy*, became ensnared in a controversy over her 1936 voter registration for the Communist Party, her husband and costar, Desi Arnaz, became her spokesman and defender, and Hopper sided with the couple. Hopper's uncharacteristic, even hypocritical action, given the truth of Ball's Communist affiliation, can be explained by Ball's clearance by HUAC after two rounds of questioning, held in private, in 1952 and 1953. The immense popularity of Ball and her show and her friendship with Hopper also helped. Hopper later appeared on Ball's television programs, lived in the same Beverly Hills neighborhood, and left the actress her Rolls-Royce in her will. Most important, however, with each of these audiences—HUAC, the American public, and Hopper—was Ball's star persona as a happy, if scatterbrained, wife and mother subject to her husband's discipline in public and private. On television as Lucy Ricardo, she demonstrated "childish incompetence" next to her husband Ricky's "authority and control," in a show that comically centered on but always contained domestic conflicts.[34] Off-camera, she presented herself to Hopper and the rest of the media as a woman who longed for a traditional family life, put her children before her career, and focused on her husband's happiness. "I'm just a typical housewife at heart," she told *Cosmopolitan* magazine earlier that year.[35]

Ball's "exaggerated allegiance" to Cold War domesticity shaped her and Hopper's responses to the revelations about her radical past. She had been considered a "longtime left sympathizer, invaluable host for fund-raisers, and general Party ally," and had supported the Committee for the First Amendment during the 1947 HUAC investigations. By the early 1950s, however, within the context of the Red Scare and the Hollywood blacklist, she retreated from politics and demonstrated an "obvious apoliticism" in her appearances before HUAC.[36] Ball explained her registration as a silly attempt to please her socialist grandfather and therefore less about political convictions than personal relationships. She repeated this explanation publicly and then remained silent while Arnaz took the lead, issuing forthright declarations of her innocence. "Lucille is no Communist!" "Lucille is 100 percent American," he argued and, most adroitly, called her "my favorite redhead—in fact that's the only thing red about her and even that's not legitimate."[37]

The controversy quickly subsided following Arnaz's passionate defense of his wife when it became clear that the television audience and sponsor would not desert *I Love Lucy*. Although Ball had supporters among Hopper's respondents, the majority expressed shock and disappointment at the revelations and Hopper's neutral stance. "So the only thing RED about Miss Ball is her hair, eh? Hedda, how can you be so taken in?"[38] Readers declared personal boycotts against Ball's television program, and many felt betrayed by the revelations, particularly as the intimacy and immediacy of television fostered a strong sense of familiarity between performer and audience. "It came to me as a great shock," admitted one woman, "as no doubt it did to millions of American families who have each week taken her into the center of their family life. We learned to love her—and now this."[39] Supporters accepted Ball's use of her personal life and relationships to explain a political act. Readers who believed Ball's political innocence believed in her happy home life. Others questioned the sincerity of her publicized personal life and the stability of her actual private life, casting doubt on her and her husband's political statements. Certainly, Hopper's coverage of the Ball-Arnaz marriage detailed a series of separations and reconciliations. "About once every six months someone notifies me that Lucy and Desi Arnaz are separating," Hopper noted, and the couple eventually divorced in 1960. "Their TV show is tops," a male reader acknowledged earlier in 1953, "but, it will go the way of all successful Hollywood teams: we will read in the Hopper column that Miss. Hopper is shocked to hear that the Arnazs are separated—wish to make up—then a stink over who owes who in the settlement. It is the Hollywood pattern."[40]

In fact, Hopper herself had to admit there was a "Hollywood pattern." As much as she sought to promote Hollywood as a typical American town, she and her readers knew the industry town was anything but typical, which was precisely why she could make a career out of gossiping about it. The term "Hollywood marriage" emerged to describe the phenomenon of short, movie star marriages, and the continuous series of rifts, separations, reconciliations, divorces, and remarriages in the movie capital kept Hopper, her gossip colleagues, her readers, and local judges busy. "The divorce mills are so heavy laden in this town," she reported in early 1945, "that another judge is being appointed."[41] In the immediate postwar period, the U.S. divorce rate was at an all-time high, and, with fears of personal and familial disorder interconnecting with anxieties about national and global events, divorce came under even greater public scrutiny during the Cold War. In 1947, the Motion Picture Research Society, a private organization, "set up to fight the divorce evil so rampant in the movie colony with a view to bettering the condition all over the country—believing as we do that the stars in Hollywood set the pattern for the rest of the country." Five years later, a local American Legion chairman founded the "Crusade Against Unjust Divorce" with similar aims.[42] Although divorce rates declined nationally during the 1950s, the decade was the great exception in more than a century of rising American divorce rates. Explanations for divorce included women's desire for "emancipation," as it was women who most often sought divorce, as well as high expectations for happiness and fulfillment within marriage; Hollywood movies have been implicated in encouraging both of these developments.[43]

In the era of family togetherness, opinions about "Marriage and Divorce— Hollywood Style" among Hopper and her respondents ranged from condemnation to toleration.[44] While Hopper's respondents nearly unanimously disapproved of divorce, and Hopper did not hesitate to denounce the partner at fault in an acrimonious marital split, her own life experience meant she accepted divorce by mutual consent. "The old storybook ending of 'They lived happily ever after' doesn't seem to apply to Hollywood stars," Hopper wrote in September 1958, and she mainly attributed the absence of fairy-tale families in Hollywood to the prevalence of dual-career couples.[45] Although she also blamed "nagging" housewives who wanted more attention from their tired, hardworking husbands for marital conflict, she joined other celebrity journalists in questioning "whether marriages and careers mixed. They should," Hopper argued, "but, unfortunately, they usually do not." Professional jealousies provoked personal conflicts between the partners. "One thing leads to another, and most roads lead to Reno," the city in the state of Nevada known for providing speedy divorces.[46] Hopper's own marriage foundered on professional issues and fragile egos. Her husband "had insisted when I married him that I give up my career." She did not, and when her salary matched her husband's he was outraged: "You're not worth it!" "He had a point there," she recalled, but "only to myself would I admit it." "Right there I began to fall out of love with him," and many "times in Hollywood I've seen this bit of domestic difficulty repeated."[47]

Differences in professional success affected Ronald Reagan's first marriage to Jane Wyman, and when their marriage foundered Hopper strongly supported Reagan. Married in 1940, they were considered an ideal couple. "I always thought Jane and Ronnie Reagan were one of the best-balanced, merriest, feet-on-the-ground couples around town," Hopper enthused.[48] In the postwar period, however, Wyman's career took off while Reagan's stagnated. Hopper warned Wyman to pay attention to her home life, because husbands "like hers are not easy to find in this—or any other—town." Politics soon became a marital issue as well. With time on his hands, Reagan stepped up his activism in the Screen Actors Guild, eventually becoming SAG president in 1947 and serving until 1952 and then again in 1959, during the height of the blacklist years. Wyman had little interest in politics but also felt her ideas "were never considered important" by her husband.[49] Pressures built during the production of *Johnny Belinda* (1948). Wyman's Oscar-winning performance as a deaf-mute woman, assisted by Lew Ayres in his most prominent postwar film role, was demanding, and Hopper criticized Wyman for putting her career before her family and even her own health. "By the time she wobbled off the last scene, she looked like a ghost, her eyes large in their sockets." "If this comes to a divorce," Reagan told Hopper, which it did in 1949, "I think I'll name *Johnny Belinda* co-respondent."[50] In most star divorces, however, the correspondents were actual, flesh-and-blood people and targeted by Hopper and her readers as "home-wreckers."

The Sinatra Situation

"Did you ever hear Frankie Sinatra sing," Hedda Hopper asked her readers, "'I'm not much to look at, nothing to see, but I've got a woman crazy for me'? That's a thing of the past, his wife Nancy told me yesterday."[51] With this opening to an October 1946 news story, Hopper informed her readers not only of the Sinatras' separation but also that she was siding with the abandoned wife. Usually, as with the Reagan-Wyman marriage, Hopper took the husband's side when a relationship ended, but the singer-actor's two separations and eventual divorce from his wife of fourteen years were clearly his doing, aided only in the last instance by actress Ava Gardner. Even so, both Hopper and her readers held nothing back in condemning Gardner for being the woman that finally got Sinatra into divorce court and back to the altar in 1951. As for Sinatra, his first separation from Nancy in 1946 occurred just after the readers of *Modern Screen* had voted him the "most popular star of the year." A singing sensation during World War II—although detested by enlisted men, who questioned his ineligibility for military service—Sinatra was dubbed "the Voice" and famously mobbed by his zealous teenage fans, or "bobby-soxers," whenever he performed. He took his swooning fan base with him when he added film to his recorded music and radio career with an MGM contract that year. Childhood sweethearts in New Jersey, the Sinatras relocated to Los Angeles with their two children, Nancy and Frank, Jr., and they eventually had a third child, Christina. From their working-class roots to fame and fortune, the Sinatras were seen as living the American Dream, and American audiences identified with them and their upward mobility. "Having pulled herself up by her bootstraps she has lots of solid sense," one friend said of Nancy.[52]

Although the Sinatras held to traditional gender roles, with a breadwinning husband and a caretaking wife, the absence of professional conflicts did not make their marriage any easier. "Fireworks usually start to sizzle in a marriage when the husband pulls himself ahead and the wife lags behind," Hopper recalled. "But Nancy, the plasterer's daughter from Jersey City, kept pace with Frank's growth as an entertainer"—at least at first. When the marriage fell apart, Nancy won praise for fulfilling her obligations as a good wife and mother. "I'd call Nancy the perfect wife," a male friend of the family told Hopper. "As a mother and home-maker, she's wonderful." Nancy also exhibited the understanding and selfless support of her husband valued in Cold War America for ensuring domestic stability. "She's maintained her patience and her dignity over the years, saying not a malicious word about any of the women who've cluttered up Frank's life," Hopper asserted.[53] "She's a wonderful woman," wrote one New York woman to Hopper, "and if I were she, I doubt that I should have been able to put up with so much far so long." She considered newspaper photos of Sinatra "with a blonde" at a public event especially egregious. A Wisconsin woman sympathized with Nancy Sinatra, assuming she "felt insecure and inferior in that town of so many beautiful talented and creative people." Others agreed that Nancy "couldn't compete with the glamour girls." But this situation angered readers, who felt domesticity should supersede glamour in valuing a wife's contributions. "I think a good wife and mother is sometimes one of the most talented and creative of persons," contended the Wisconsin reader, but she felt this fact was rarely recognized—even in a postwar American society that ostensibly glorified domestic life.[54]

In contrast, Sinatra was much criticized for his failings as a husband and father, particularly—as Hopper noted—because his fans liked "to think of Frank as a happy family man. Their protests against Sinatra's leaving home were vehement." Hopper reported receiving a letter with "a piece of shattered record on which Sinatra had crooned 'Cradle Song' and 'Nancy with the Laughing Face.'" "All that ballyhoo about him being such a wonderful husband and father makes me sick," muttered one reader.[55] Other readers had more measured responses. In a Hollywood marriage with only one star, one reader argued, it was "up to the publicized member of such a team to be sure to give the other his due, keep them secure in their love. We can see that Frank failed here miserably."[56] Hopper and her readers also reminded Sinatra of his parental obligations. "Day Frank Sinatra left home," Hopper reported in an item designed to evoke sentiment and sympathy for his abandoned wife and children among her readers, "Nancy had just presented him with ivory cuff links. One bore the carved likeness of his son's face; the other, his little girl's."[57]

As in the case of other star scandals, fans associated Sinatra's personal and professional lives, and some announced to Hopper their personal boycotts of his recorded music, radio program, and films. For many, the intimacy of radio listening—with Sinatra's voice and music coming right into the home—created a familiar closeness with him, as television would with Lucille Ball. Similarly, this intimacy made his personal behavior seem even more objectionable to Hopper's readers and spurred them to take action.[58] "My husband and I are avid listeners to the Sinatra program," penned a New York woman, "but now whenever we hear 'Frankie' we think of Nancy Sr., Jr., and Frank Jr." A group of ten Sinatra fans in Chicago felt that "Frank did a contemptible thing walking out on his wife and children," and decided to switch their allegiance to a singer who "is a fine husband and father."[59] Another reader from New York wrote: "The mothers in our apartment house have all gotten together and forbid all our children, little ones and big ones, from going to see any Sinatra pictures or even to listen to his radio show. He is no help to children. He is a very bad example." For fellow Catholics, like these mothers, the Sinatras' Catholicism made their marital crisis a spiritual one as well. They pointed out that divorce was not permitted in their church, asserted that Sinatra "has no faith in God," and insisted his "own priest should take him hand."[60]

Hopper and her readers found Sinatra's actions during his first marital separation in 1946 especially galling within the context of his liberal-left politics and public service efforts. At the time, Sinatra was "unabashedly liberal" and a strong supporter of the Democratic Party. In 1945, Sinatra won regard for his endorsement of wartime unity and tolerance in the song and special Oscar-winning short film *The House I Live In*. In the film, which was written by the future Hollywood Ten member Albert Maltz, Sinatra preaches to a gang of white youths about the need to overcome bigotry and prejudice, and ends with the title song, which invokes an America shared by "all races, all religions."[61] For Hopper, Sinatra's political views and personal actions were not only highly objectionable, they also made him a hypocrite. "Last year Frank Sinatra got an Academy Award for the song, 'The House I Live In.' Evidently that house wasn't large enough for Nancy and the children." Hopper's readers agreed. "And those speeches he made, he should be booed off the air if he tries it again."[62] Sinatra's outreach efforts to young people during the wartime crisis about juvenile delinquency were similarly undermined by his martial separation. "For how can he go on making talks to us on 'Intolerance' and 'Delinquency, etc.,'" asked one California reader, "when he is really being delinquent himself?" "He has no right to go out and preach to young boys," wrote a group of New York mothers. "Does he want those boys to grow up and get married and then leave a good wife and two beautiful children?"[63] For these readers, Sinatra's damaged personal reputation delegitimized his political and charitable efforts.

The perceived conflict between Sinatra's personal and political lives did not arise in Hopper's column or elsewhere when he finally left his wife for Gardner in 1950. By then, like Lucille Ball, he had retreated from progressive politics in the wake of the Red Scare and blacklist; instead, it was Gardner who received the brunt of the criticism for their "romance of the century." Hopper called her the "woman who came within an ace of wrecking Frank Sinatra," because of his passion and jealousy for her.[64] One of MGM's top box office draws, and with two failed marriages behind her, Gardner was known as a beguiling, bewitching beauty when she became involved with Sinatra. Her studio head, Louis B. Mayer, was not happy. "Have you read the papers? Do you know what Hedda and Louella are saying about you? Have you read your fan mail? They're calling you Jezebel," he reportedly lambasted her. "A homewrecker."[65] Indeed they were. "As for Ava G.—shame on her! When will some frustrated females learn it is far wiser to pick on the single men and let the husbands alone?" "If she were . . . any part of a lady, she would not break up a home, where there are three lovely children," insisted one of Hopper's Chicago readers.[66]

But Gardner was not one to let public or private condemnation stop her, and she went on with the affair and over time gained support, even from the likes of Hopper. In her initial stories and columns announcing the Sinatras' final separation in 1950 and divorce negotiations in 1951, Hopper presented Nancy Sinatra sympathetically, quoting Nancy on her "unhappy and almost unbearable" married life, and casting Gardner as the woman Sinatra wanted to "be free to marry." Yet, as Nancy held out on finalizing a divorce, Hopper claimed fans were beginning to criticize her and, in a comment credited with prodding Nancy toward a resolution, said it was time she "considered the children after a year and a half of sizzling publicity and bitter arguments."[67] While the Sinatras battled over a property settlement, Gardner was cast in *Show Boat* (1951) as Julie, a stereotypical mixed-race character that only exploited and exacerbated Gardner's image as amoral and aggressively sexual. One of Hopper's readers found it appalling that one of Gardner's songs in the film, "Can't Help Lovin' Dat Man," expressed Julie's devotion and dedication to her husband. "How untypical of Ava that would be," Hopper's reader exclaimed.[68] Still, the film received good reviews and box office returns, securing Gardner's professional status despite her personal turmoil and tumultuous relationship with Sinatra, which continued after their wedding in November 1951. "I figured that Ava Gardner and Frank Sinatra would be back together within a week of their cold war, and so they were," Hopper later observed in 1953. "With those two highly strong, hot-tempered people, we can expect future rifts and reconciliations."[69] And she was right, until the couple divorced in 1957.

By labeling one of Sinatra and Gardner's many fights a "cold war," Hopper conflated personal and global conflicts, as did many of her readers who felt more was at stake in the scandal than the personal lives of a few people. Still, some readers emphasized the personal, reading their own lives in the scandal. "You know," one woman told Hopper, "there are millions and millions of women like me, wives and mothers who have had to make sacrifices for their husband and children, and when we see one of our own kind, Nancy Sinatra, receive such a deal because of a person like Ava it hurts us to the soul."[70] One of the few men who wrote Hopper supported Sinatra, confessing, "I too have gone through what he has and still am chained. I have great sympathy and understanding for him." "One of the greatest crimes in our times," he declared, "is this one of keeping two people in unendurable bondage."[71]

More readers, however, explicitly equated the private and the public in their criticism of Sinatra and made connections between personal behavior and American citizenship. "Wake up Frankie, go home to your Nancy and children and become a good decent citizen."[72] "I feel you are both a good American and a decent human being," a reader wrote anonymously to Hopper, and "as a decent human being and an American I'm fed up to the ears about a certain personality." Another reader believed that without "decency" in private life, Sinatra and Gardner "are not responsible enough to accept the dignities and obligations of public life." And most revealingly, one woman lamented the entire situation within the context of the Cold War and anxieties of the atomic age. "Life is complicated enough with these wars and would be dictators."[73] For this reader, marriage and the family should be a place of stability and security in an uncertain world.

What to do, then, about such scandals? For Hopper and most of her readers, the problem lay with the principals, with most of the blame on Sinatra and Gardner, although a few readers faulted Nancy Sinatra. "I sincerely believe it takes <u>two</u> to break up a marriage," wrote a California woman. Still, a number of readers believed Hollywood was the source of the trouble. "Hollywood sure is difficult on matrimony."[74] One reader felt Sinatra had been a devoted husband and father. "But after he went to Hollywood he seemed to change, as so many of them do. We began to read stories of his carrying on, his violent temper, and his walking out on Nancy and the children so often." Yet it was not just the pressures of Hollywood that readers pointed to; they also believed the motion picture industry promoted and profited from such scandals. Of Gardner, a reader asserted, "this notoriety enhanced her box office."[75]

Just like earlier female reformers involved in the Woman's Christian Temperance Union's pro-film-censorship campaigns from the 1890s to the 1930s, and Colorado Senator Edwin S. Johnson in the wake of the Bergman and Hayworth scandals, Hopper's readers demanded moral reform from the industry.[76] "If the movie industry would enforce some restraint, these affairs would be reduced to a minimum," insisted one woman. But the continued appearance on the motion picture screen of scandal veterans, such as Gardner and Hayworth, was "conclusive proof that they are not interested in promoting high morality and clean living." The industry had a "moral responsibility" not to put "a sense of glamour on tawdry affairs and doings" through promotion and publicity of the transgressors, wrote another woman.[77] Hopper's readers also called on her to exercise moral responsibility and refuse to cover the doings of Sinatra, Gardner, and others in her column. "Look how Ingrid Bergman turned out, also Rita Hayworth. Such people should be snubbed, not recognized," urged one reader. "Best never to put their names in print."[78] Such arguments from readers to Hopper only grew more urgent over the decade of the 1950s, as the Liz-Debbie-Eddie incident demonstrated.

The Liz-Debbie-Eddie Incident

On September 11, 1958, Hedda Hopper published an exclusive interview on the front page of the *Los Angeles Times* with one of the principals of the romantic triangle Hollywood had been whispering about for weeks. The triangle involved "Hollywood's ideal" married couple, Debbie Reynolds and Eddie Fisher, and the "other woman," Elizabeth Taylor, Hopper's interviewee.[79] From this "damning" article in September, through Taylor and Fisher's wedding in April 1959, to Taylor's suit the following December against a tabloid that claimed she had "stolen" Fisher from Reynolds, this incident received a sensational amount of media and popular attention. Taylor and Fisher "shared headlines" for months, the popular women's magazine *McCall's* gave Reynolds the space to tell "Her Story," and Fisher lost his television show "in the furor over his divorce."[80] The issues of love and marriage, sex, betrayal, and divorce raised in this incident grabbed the attention and appeared to resonate even more deeply with Hopper and her readers in the late 1950s than they had a decade earlier with the Sinatra situation. "I've had more letters," Hopper reported, "than I've had since Charlie Chaplin's outrageous affair with Joan Barry. They're pouring in by the hundreds." This late 1950s Hollywood sex scandal and star divorce occurred when "the baby boom and the cold war were both at their peak" and revealed other changes as well.[81] Hopper's readers continued to see the private lives and actions of stars as public concerns, but Hollywood and Hopper came in for much more of the blame with the Liz-Debbie-Eddie incident than the Sinatra situation.

"I've known Elizabeth Taylor since she was nine years old—always liked her; always defended her," Hopper began her first article about the Liz-Debbie-Eddie incident. She recounted Taylor's three marriages—to hotel heir Nicky Hilton, actor Michael Wilding, and producer Mike Todd—and how Taylor won "the sympathy of the world" when Todd died in an airplane crash earlier that year. "But I can't take this present episode with Eddie Fisher. I've just talked with Liz to ask her what this is all about. Her reply was unprintable." Hopper printed Taylor's other replies, however. When Hopper accused Taylor of causing the marital breakup between Fisher and Reynolds, of "taking him away from Debbie," Taylor refused to take the blame—"he's not in love with her and never has been"—or show any remorse—"you can't break up a happy marriage. Debbie's and Eddie's never has been." "Well, let me tell you this, Liz," Hopper concluded the conversation. "This will hurt you much more than it ever will Debbie Reynolds. People love her very much because she's an honest and wonderful girl," characteristics, she implied, missing in Taylor. Hopper ended her article by lamenting Taylor's loss of girlhood innocence, as the adult no longer resembled the child. "Where, oh where has she gone?"[82] Five years later, Hopper published Taylor's "unprintable" reply in her memoirs: "What do you expect me to do? Sleep alone?" Even without this sexually explicit comment, Taylor's damning statements sparked popular criticism, and "the mail started arriving in stacks, all in Debbie's favor." As for Taylor, Hopper contended, the "women of America" were "ready to all but stone her," an ancient punishment for female moral transgressors.[83]

Hopper's front-page story presented an influential interpretation of the Liz-Debbie-Eddie incident that put full blame on Taylor, sympathized with Reynolds, and deemphasized Fisher's role. Almost universally, other commentators and Hopper's respondents followed her lead. In the two initial stories on the scandal carried by the *Los Angeles Times*, including Hopper's, Fisher had no interviews or quotes, and even over the life of the scandal his public comments were few. He acknowledged marital difficulties with Reynolds and his primary role in catalyzing the divorce. "Debbie and I are having a misunderstanding," he said early on in the controversy, and it turned out Hollywood's ideal couple had been "squabbling for a year."[84] Later, Fisher admitted "it was all his fault" for wanting out of the marriage, but few commentators, including Hopper, held him primarily responsible for the scandal. Even Reynolds let him off the hook, at least in public. "I love Eddie and don't blame *him* for what's happened."[85] Similarly, Hopper's readers considered it difficult "for a man to resist a siren" such as Taylor and believed one should defend "any man such a beauty might set out to capture!"[86] Such excuses rendered Fisher passive, powerless, and emasculated. Reynolds considered Taylor "the strong one in this situation," and letter writers to Hopper described Fisher as weak: "he must be a very weak individual," "weakling Eddie," "this weak-kneed jerk." "It's too bad that Mr. Fisher is so weak minded as to be swayed by such a woman," wrote a California woman.[87] Such characterizations of Fisher contrasted sharply with those of Frank Sinatra, and neither Sinatra's moral and marital responsibility nor his masculinity were ever questioned in the midst of his scandals.

Even when Fisher displayed little concern for public propriety and openly showed his sexual and marital desire for Taylor, media, popular, and Hopper's attention concentrated on Taylor as sexual temptress and Reynolds as betrayed wife. After Reynolds filed suit for divorce, Fisher flaunted his freedom by sharing "champagne and caviar at a Beverly Hills bistro" with Taylor, and, in a gig in New York before his divorce was final, he openly sang songs such as "Makin' Whoopee!" about "another bride, another June, another sunny honeymoon" to Taylor sitting in the audience.[88] A few of Hopper's readers condemned Fisher for his "disgraceful conduct" and urged Fisher to "ask Debbie's pardon and honor his marriage vows," but most focused on the two actresses. "Taylor is even worse than Bergman," wrote a Chicago reader, and a Los Angeles woman suggested Taylor "join Ava Gardner"—who was then in Spain—"they should make a good pair!"[89] Some truly hateful letters were directed at Taylor, while Reynolds received sympathy: "My heart aches for her as if she were my own child." "Everyone feels so sorry for her," contended a Denver woman. "She is a brave little thing but her husband's treatment of her must hurt her to the depths." "Debbie is a very lucky girl in my book to be rid of such a guy," wrote a Phoenix reader, reflecting a common sentiment among Hopper's respondents. Anti-Semitism also shaped the responses of a few readers, as Fisher was Jewish. One reader told Reynolds to "marry a Christian" next time.[90]

The focus on Taylor and Reynolds by Hopper, her readers, and the wider media reflected social and cultural expectations that women would—and should—be primarily responsible for postwar domestic stability as well as emotional and sexual relationships between the sexes. "I feel it remains the part of women to uphold the moral and ethical standards," one of Hopper's readers declared, and another exclaimed, "I always feel it is up to the woman to keep a man in his place!"[91] These readers believed women should be more sexually virtuous and morally pure than men, an assumption also held by Hopper that harked back to earlier ideals and ideologies of womanhood. Attention to Taylor and Reynolds made further sense given the greater prominence and popularity of the actresses and Fisher's declining career as a singer. Both women appeared in the list of top ten movie box office stars in 1960, and Reynolds also made the list in 1959, and by 1965 both had won a Best Actress Academy Award.[92] Finally, they drew most of the media and popular attention because the Liz-Debbie-Eddie incident was understood and framed as a classic "cat fight," a spiteful, malicious competition over a man between two very different women. As Hopper put it to Reynolds a few years later, "You are as unlike as a primrose and a tiger lily; each has its place but the climate in which one blooms is no good for the other. What one thrives on will eventually destroy the other."[93]

Indeed, in their appearance and attire, film roles and off-screen personalities, Elizabeth Taylor and Debbie Reynolds represented a dichotomy in the popular image of American women in the 1950s. The polarization of women into good girls and bad girls, domesticated housewives and voluptuous sex symbols, characterized this dichotomy and, respectively, Reynolds and Taylor; even their coloring connoted the difference between innocence and sexuality. Reynolds was the girl next door—blonde, blue-eyed, and freckled, sunny and innocent—while Taylor was dark and sultry, "a 'man's woman'" with "apparent sexuality."[94] While Taylor always was described as beautiful, Reynolds was considered pretty, and Hopper's readers objected to the contrast between Taylor's physical perfection and Reynolds's more moderate attractiveness. "I wish they would quit talking about that luscious Liz for 'Beauty is as Beauty does.' One look at that sweet face of Debbie and there is no comparison." "The thing that burns me up the most," wrote a California woman, "is the fact that the papers or certain rumors keep referring to Liz as so glamorous, etc. Personally, have talked to a lot of people and they all think that Debbie is the desirable one, pretty, talented, lovely, adorable."[95] The fashion choices off-screen of Taylor and Reynolds reinforced these differences. The photographs of the actresses that appeared in the media coverage of the scandal consistently showed Taylor bejeweled and in skimpy, revealing dresses, while Reynolds appeared in gingham shirtwaist dresses or, as in one well-publicized shot, in pigtails and pedal pushers. Taylor flaunted her sexuality; Reynolds did not. "Liz is an indecent woman," wrote one of Hopper's Chicago readers, "you hardly ever see a picture of her that her dress isn't cut so low her breasts are falling out."[96]

The recent screen roles of Reynolds and Taylor drew on and reinforced their contrasting image and styles. After her *Singin' in the Rain* (1952) musical fame, Reynolds appeared in sweet romantic comedies, including *Bundle of Joy* (1956), in which she costarred with Fisher, whom she had wed the previous year, and *Tammy and the Bachelor* (1957), for which she recorded a smash pop music single, "Tammy." Meanwhile, Taylor's portrayal of Maggie, the rejected wife trying to win back her cold and hostile husband through sexual display, in MGM's hit *Cat on a Hot Tin Roof* (1958) appeared on movie screens and won her excellent critical reviews amid the scandal.[97] Hopper's readers immediately connected the actress and the role. For one California woman, the scandal revealed that "Liz . . . obviously is a cat on a hot tin roof, and badly in need of a man," while another asked Hopper to "deliver the enclosed package to 'Maggie the Cat' when you see her. It's a piece of cheese for the 'rat' she trapped."[98] A Mississippi woman reported to Hopper that at a local screening of *Cat on a Hot Tin Roof* Taylor "was booed and ridiculed during the performance," with "snide" remarks made about "tramp Taylor." As a consequence, Reynolds was the more popular actress among women. She was "all right—a trifle corny, but cute and fun," according to film scholar Molly Haskell, while Taylor lost women's loyalty "when she grew intolerably voluptuous."[99]

Although both women were hardworking actresses, Reynolds and Taylor further diverged in their apparent dedication to motherhood and domesticity. Reynolds seemed to adhere to the feminine mystique to a far greater extent than Taylor. Her marriage to Fisher was her first, and they soon had two children. Photographs of "homespun," "home-loving" Reynolds with her infant son, two-year-old daughter, and a diaper pin stuck on her shirt appeared in media coverage of the scandal. She demonstrated self-sacrifice by transforming her "once-formal living room" into a playroom for her children, and ostensibly had considered giving up her career.[100] When she publicized the fact that Fisher had asked her to wear sexier clothing, "like Liz,"

Hopper's readers defended her. "Maybe she doesn't stand in front of a mirror and dress to the hilt all the time," contended a Chicago woman. "Perhaps she would rather spend such wasted time with her children." Hopper's readers praised Reynolds's "devoted duty to her children which is a very admirable trait."[101] In contrast, Taylor was photographed alone or with Fisher, never with any of her three children. Her multiple marriages—"Always a bride, never a bridesmaid," quipped one observer—her jet-setting lifestyle, her pursuit of self-fulfillment at the expense of those around her, and now her public affair with Fisher contradicted the ideology of domestic containment. "Multiple marriages flaunt the sanctity and permanence of the marriage sacrament, with the ensuing tragic effect on children," argued one of Hopper's readers. "Liz Taylor is a no good mother. Why doesn't she stay at home and take care of her children?" asked a Chicago reader. "She is a disgrace to motherhood and women."[102]

Taylor's status as a recent widow also won her no sympathy in the controversy. As a widow living beyond male control and protection, Taylor appeared "both more vulnerable and more empowered than 'ordinary' women." Despite initial concern for the mourning Taylor and compassionate stories from Hopper and others about her shock and grief over Todd's sudden death, widowhood only heightened her image of excessive eroticism and disorderly potential, soon to be realized in the scandal.[103] As Mike Todd and Eddie Fisher were good friends, the two couples socialized together, and the two actresses were considered friends. Upon Todd's death, Fisher rushed to Taylor's side and attended the funeral with her, while Reynolds took care of Taylor's children—making Taylor's betrayal even worse. In fact, Reynolds never trusted Taylor's loyalty to female friendships. "Elizabeth has no girl-friends. She's not a woman's woman." In turn, Taylor disdained Reynolds's good girl image, referring to her as "that little Girl Scout."[104]

Once news of the Taylor-Fisher affair came out, compassion for "the Widow Todd" quickly turned into mockery, and Hopper did not help. In her initial article, Hopper claimed she asked Taylor what her deceased husband, Mike Todd, would think of her new romance, and invented Taylor's response, "Mike is dead and I'm alive." This fictional quote helped Hopper paint a portrait of Taylor as a "spoiled, materialistic, callous woman" rather than a grieving, sympathetic widow.[105] "She needs at least a full year of dignified conduct, if her love for Mike Todd was real," argued one of Hopper's readers. Rumors of an Academy Award nomination for Taylor's performance in *Cat on a Hot Tin Roof* led another reader to suggest "she certainly should get one for her performance at the time of Mike Todd's death." "I nominate," added another,

"Elizabeth Taylor, for her recent role as the grief-stricken widow."[106] Other readers were angered that her widowhood had drawn their sympathy. "My heart went out to her when her husband died, but this is indecent, immoral," wrote "a former fan." "I cried for the horror of empty grief which Liz was suffering, because I, too, five years ago, suffered like that," admitted another. "Makes you feel like a sort of idiotic fool to have her pop up six months later with Debbie's husband."[107]

Like this woman, many of Hopper's respondents linked the issues raised in the Liz-Debbie-Eddie incident to those in their own lives, many more than had in the Sinatra situation. Readers gave Reynolds advice—via Hopper—on going through a divorce. A New Orleans woman urged Hopper to "tell little Debbie that time heals all wounds," while another woman insisted that Reynolds not make "kind, lackadaisical generous arrangements" about finances, as she mistakenly had. "Maybe you never had Eddie Fisher's love—but at least demand his respect."[108] Both women, as did others, told their own stories of adultery and divorce, with a mix of happy and unhappy endings, but readers unanimously condemned men who abandoned marital fidelity and familial responsibilities. When men, in the words of one woman, "who have married wonderful women who have borne them children and shared and sacrificed to help them up the ladder to success," attain fame, "their wives were thrown aside for a more glamorous or pretty faced younger woman." "<u>That</u>," she exclaimed, "is a crime!"[109] Many of Hopper's respondents indicated their status as housewives dependent financially on a breadwinner husband, and their letters revealed fears of marital unhappiness, abandonment by husbands, and economic vulnerability. Indeed, not all American men were living according to the breadwinner ethic or providing women and children with the support and protection promised. By defending Reynolds and condemning Taylor and Fisher, these women asserted their interests within "the heterosexual paradigm of the Cold War" in the face of male betrayal and threats and competition from financially independent, sexually liberal women.[110] The intensity of these assertions, and interest in the Liz-Debbie-Eddie incident more generally, indicated cracks in the façade of fifties family togetherness.

As happened with the Sinatra situation, Hopper and her readers not only made connections between their private lives and those of Taylor, Reynolds, and Fisher; they also made public issues out of these private matters. Reynolds's apparently morally upstanding and respectable life made her a "real American girl," while Taylor's behavior threatened the nation. "By the purity of its women shall a nation rise or fall has been true all thru history," warned one woman. A number of readers expressed despair about the moral direction of the country. "What in the name of heaven is happening to these people?" "What is this world coming to with Bergman . . . and now this mess?"[111] Readers also expressed concerns about international opinion on the scandal, indicating understanding of the U.S. global role and responsibilities during the Cold War. One woman feared "many Europeans feel all Americans are the same" and would assume Taylor and Fisher were typical U.S. citizens.[112] Another reader lamented the huge amount of money spent on and earned by Hollywood stars rather than on "programs benefiting American youth and people at large." In the wake of the Soviet launch of the Sputnik satellite the previous year, this woman believed U.S. priorities were skewed. "No wonder Russia and other countries are way ahead of us in the field of educational and cultural potential."[113]

The concern for the national and international implications of the Liz-Debbie-Eddie incident—particularly for children—led Hopper's respondents to pledge to boycott Taylor's films and Fisher's television show and his sponsors, including Coca-Cola and Chesterfield cigarettes. "If Eddie could look over my shoulder and read the letters coming in about him, he'd be shaking in his boots and so would his sponsors," Hopper reported in late September. In these letters, agitated readers expressed concerns about the influence of Hollywood stars' "bad" behavior on young people and the need to do something about it. "I'm sure many other mothers of daughters like myself were made by sick by the sight of your story of the interview with brazen Liz," wrote a California woman.[114] Another worried mother questioned, "If she gets by with this thing, with our youngsters watching to see what happens, how are we going to say the good girl eventually wins and the bad girl loses?" "Eddie Fisher has no respect for his family, himself, or his public, and it seems sad," stated another reader, "that the young people of America should be exposed to this sort of immorality on television, which comes right into the home."[115] A family in Omaha, Nebraska, determined not to buy "<u>anything Eddie Fisher</u> has on his program and will not listen to him or see any pictures or buy any records or see any pictures of E. Taylor either!" Similarly, a woman reader announced, "We are switching to Pepsi-Cola!!"[116]

Yet, revealing a shift from the response to Frank Sinatra's separations and divorces, Hopper's readers went beyond personal action to call for a collective response and mass boycott of Elizabeth Taylor and Eddie Fisher, and Hopper supported them. "If enough people would do this," an "irate moviegoer" from Chicago believed, "we would have a cleaner Hollywood."[117] This call was echoed and acted on by other readers, demonstrating the ways in which gender conservatism in the 1950s did not contain wives and mothers within the private sphere. Instead, women's traditional roles—as they had in the past—could provide a basis and a justification for public activism during the Cold War, be it grassroots moral reform or anti-Communism. "After all, we the women, can use our phone and don't underestimate our power to combine," promised a woman from Oklahoma. "Eight mothers" collaborated on a letter to Hopper. "We are a group of eight women and . . . we won't be looking at Eddie's t.v. show this season."[118] "No Eddie Fisher show in our living rooms and no products of any of his sponsors," declared a Hollywood woman. "There are oodles of us behind this scheme." Hopper's readers went further, writing angry letters to Fisher's network, NBC, and his sponsors, and urging Hopper to "bundle all the letters you have received" and send them on as well. This campaign by Hopper's respondents fit with the maternalist activism of earlier women reformers, as they used their roles as guardians of children to "mother the movies"—or, more precisely, movie culture. And they could claim victory when NBC and Coca-Cola canceled Fisher's television show.[119]

Taylor's career suffered little setback, however, and what became increasingly clear to Hopper's readers was how the movie industry and its publicists, including Hopper, created and capitalized on movie star scandals. While many readers complimented Hopper on her "very courageous stand" and "strength of character and fortitude" in the scandal, just as many—and far more than in the Sinatra situation—criticized Hopper's star gossip, especially about Taylor. "Don't you know how to write a column anymore without mentioning her name?"[120] A New York woman criticized stars committing sexual transgressions "who get the newspaper headlines. . . .Why you give them any notice, I fail to understand." "The lower one gets in Hollywood the more they are glamourized," contended "a disgusted Eddie Fisher fan," and Hopper contributed to that process. "You make your living glamorizing the tramps in Hollywood," accused one reader.[121] Although the Liz-Debbie-Eddie incident dashed Taylor's chances of winning an Academy Award for her performance in *Cat on a Hot Tin Roof*, within two years she costarred with Fisher in *Butterfield 8* (1960) and won an Oscar, after a serious illness sparked the sympathy of her industry colleagues. "Hell, I even voted for her," recalled Debbie Reynolds, not sounding much like a Girl Scout.[122] As Taylor straddled the decades of the 1950s and 1960s, she negotiated commitment and independence by converting to Judaism and marrying Fisher in April 1959, but her faithfulness—sexual and religious—failed to last. Soon she was involved in another act of husband stealing; this time the object of her affections was Welsh actor Richard Burton. That Elizabeth Taylor's stardom only grew greater with this second scandal confirmed what many of Hedda Hopper's respondents were already thinking. As a reader from Missouri suggested, "Maybe we could do well without a place called Hollywood."[123]

Hedda Hopper and Walter Winchell exchange their famous hats at the Republican National Convention, San Francisco, July 13, 1964. (Courtesy of the Academy of Motion Picture Arts and Sciences.)

Taking on "Hollywood Babylon"

In January 1962, the filming of 20th Century-Fox's costly *Cleopatra* (1963) resumed in Rome, with scenes of Elizabeth Taylor as "the temptress-queen" and Richard Burton as the Roman general Marc Antony together for the first time. Their tumultuous affair soon began and became known to the production crew, their respective spouses (Eddie Fisher and Sybil Burton), the international press, and the wider public. "The rumors are flying again," Hedda Hopper reported in March. "Heigh-ho!"[1] Once again, she and her readers expressed strong opinions about the latest Hollywood sex scandal. They had little sympathy for the cuckolded Fisher—"When you leave home and hearth, you can expect the worst"—and great concern for Sybil Burton. "I feel so sad for Sybil Burton," wrote one reader. "I think she has a sweet face but it does cover a multitude of grief."[2] Richard Burton came in for his share of clobbering. In Hopper's column, she referred to him as "Wicked Richard" and less publicly as "an absolute louse." But it was Taylor who received the brunt of the outrage from Hopper and others. "She has done more to degrade the women of this world," Hopper argued, "than any mistress of any king." The Vatican's weekly newspaper also weighed in, warning that "the sultry actress was headed for 'erotic vagrancy.'"[3] Connecting personal and international affairs, Georgia congresswoman Iris F. Blitch averred in May that Taylor "lowered the prestige of American women abroad, and damaged goodwill in foreign countries, particularly Italy." Although her efforts came to naught, Blitch called on the U.S. attorney general "in the name of American womanhood" to "determine whether or not Miss Taylor and Mr. Burton are ineligible for re-entry into the United States on grounds of undesirability."[4]

For Hopper, her readers, and other commentators, Taylor's current starring role fit with her scandalous love life. "I have no desire to see the picture if I was given the best seat in the house," a San Francisco reader contended in light of the Taylor-Burton affair. "I have never thought Cleo was much of a character in history. She could not get and keep her own man either."[5] *Cleopatra*'s producers, however, hoped the connection between actress and historical figure would attract audiences. "Any similarities between the personality of our Cleopatra and Miss Taylor are coincidental," claimed one producer. "Although," he added happily, "there are parallels obviously." Less circumspect was 20th Century-Fox's chief Peter Levathes: "She's above material; she IS Cleopatra."[6] Hopper dedicated an entire Sunday column in August 1962 demonstrating that the role of Cleopatra, "queen of the Nile" and "ancient glamour girl," was "tailor-made for Elizabeth." Like the actress playing her, Cleopatra had "terrific magnetism" and was "a born wheeler-dealer" but also had an "insecure" childhood and several children fathered by different men. Although at the end of the film Cleopatra kills herself by allowing herself to be stung by an asp, Hopper predicted that Taylor would come out of the film and the scandal unscathed. "I wonder who'll get the asp?" she quoted in her column. "I wager it won't be Elizabeth." Indeed, the following year Hopper argued of Taylor: "She has become Cleopatra to the life now, and the world is her oyster. What she wants, she takes, come hell or high water—and this includes Richard Burton."[7]

Like other sex scandals in the movie capital, Hopper and her readers' commentaries about the Taylor-Burton affair went beyond the personal morality, lives, and actions of the principal figures. They pointed out the implications for national and international politics—"it is injuring the country," wrote one reader—but it was the faults and failures of the U.S. motion picture industry that dominated their writings.[8] Over the 1940s and 1950s, Hopper's respondents increasingly targeted Hollywood as the source of scandal, but it was in the 1960s in the wake of Taylor's latest public affair—coming just four years after the Liz-Debbie-Eddie incident—that Hopper joined them in blaming the industry. "In the old days the scandal of the past four years would have killed her professionally," Hopper noted. "In these changed times it seems only to help her reputation." Indeed, in the 1960s, Taylor "became the most important woman, with the most financial clout, in Hollywood."[9] The $1 million salary she drew for *Cleopatra* was the highest yet paid to a movie star, indicating Taylor's individual star power and appearing to reward her for a disreputable personal life. Hopper also felt Richard Burton undeservedly benefited from the adulterous affair. She was "furious" to see Burton's top billing "only because of a world scandal," and believed "his one object of making love to Liz in the first place was money," citing as evidence a rise in his typical salary from $150,000 to $500,000. Hopper's readers conveyed their belief that the industry encouraged and benefited from such scandalous behavior, blaming "the executives who . . . insist on such rotten conduct for Liz and Richard to keep the publicity going" for *Cleopatra*.[10]

The Taylor-Burton affair, together with *Cleopatra*, proved to Hopper and her readers the complete moral and institutional decline of Hollywood and the United States by the early 1960s, and nostalgia for old Hollywood and an earlier America permeated their increasingly sharp and strident commentary. The studio system—in place since the 1920s when Hopper made Hollywood her permanent home—was under increasing pressure. With the loss of control over film exhibition following the 1948 Paramount antitrust decision, a shrinking domestic audience due to competition from television, and the growth of independent productions, the major studios were struggling—RKO-Pathé closed in 1958—and producing fewer films each year. In the year of *Cleopatra*'s release, 1963, only 143 films were produced, a historical low. In addition, *Cleopatra*, the expected "blockbuster," was "a highly publicized, enormously expensive flop," failing to turn a profit domestically.[11] For Hopper, the making and unmaking of *Cleopatra* in the early 1960s signaled the fading of her old, beloved Hollywood—and her power and influence within it—and the arrival of a decadent and scandalous substitute, a "Hollywood Babylon."[12] At the same time, her equally beloved Republican Party was in transition. Although Hopper could take comfort in the emergence of a New Right, which espoused and energized her conservative political agenda and fit with her politics of nostalgia, she died in early 1966 and did not live to see her party achieve a major electoral victory.

A Career's End

Over the 1950s and early 1960s, as the old Hollywood system of major studios controlling the production, distribution, and exhibition of motion pictures gave way to a less integrated, more fluid motion picture industry, Hedda Hopper's function as a gossip columnist changed dramatically. Although never just an industry shill, she built her career on publicizing and popularizing the industry's products—its stars and the movies. The studio system provided her with regular and consistent products as subject matter for her column, with the "behind-the-scenes" access to films and film stars that gave her column cachet and made it more than just another studio press release, and with a large, national movie audience potentially interested in reading it. With the decline of the studio system Hopper's subject matter and potential readership narrowed. Hopper's power and relevance worked in tandem with the major studios, and she saw her power and relevance shrink over time. She and her readers lamented the changes all around them as the old Hollywood, besieged and breaking up, became something new. She and her readers not only appeared anachronistic and wielded less sway during this time, but Hopper also died too soon to see the "New Hollywood" that resulted.

Compared with rival contemporaries Louella Parsons and Walter Winchell, Hopper's career as a gossip columnist looked strong in the early 1960s. In 1963, Hopper's daily column was still in 130 newspapers, including the *Los Angeles Times*, while that year Parsons had only seventy newspapers and the *New York Mirror*, home to Winchell's flagship column, folded. Her readership remained an estimated 32 million readers.[13] The Chicago Tribune–New York News Syndicate continued to promote her column—"Hedda Hopper the number-one reporter of a fabulous industry" and "Smart hat . . . smarter head!"—and privately to compare it favorably to Louella's column, which a syndicate representative characterized as "pretty bad (no pep and no news)." In 1964, Parsons suffered a hip injury and retired the following year. "NOW THERE IS ONLY HEDDA," *Daily Variety* headlined.[14] Hopper's fans remained mostly women, and they continued to express their loyalty and daily reading of her "very entertaining and enjoyable" column and to criticize Parsons. "Louella used to try to play God so much, telling actors and actresses to lose so many pounds and do this and that, that I stopped reading the movie gossip."[15] Hopper's fans still flocked to her lectures. Of a 1962 lecture, Hopper wrote, "in Pittsburgh I spoke at the Sports Arena to 13,000 women and 3 men." Hopper also reaped a range of honors over the preceding decade, with a "Woman of the Year Award for Outstanding Achievement" from the *Los Angeles Times*, a "Golden Flame Award for Outstanding Journalism" from the Press Women of the State of California, and "Hedda Hopper Days" in her hometowns of Altoona, Pennsylvania, and Los Angeles.[16]

One reason for Hopper's longevity was that she gravitated to the new medium of television, even as it threatened the success and stability of the motion picture industry. She recognized and fretted over television's contribution to Hollywood's decline—"That bastard, television," she once muttered—yet she still sought a place in the industry. In contrast, Winchell "belonged to radio," admitted to stage fright, and made his "long-awaited, much-resisted television debut" in 1952, while Parsons, "insecure about her appearance and performing talent," hesitated to do a live television show until 1958.[17] Still a confident actress, Hopper tried unsuccessfully to secure her own television series, *This Is Hollywood*, in the mid-1950s with the help of the television impresario David Susskind, and she made guest appearances on a range of television shows, just as she did on radio.[18] During the 1950s and 1960s, she performed in top-rated situation comedies, including *I Love Lucy* and *The Beverly Hillbillies*, interview talk shows such as *Small World*, and game shows like *What's My Line?* She provided the voice of "Hedda Hatter," the female counterpart to the Mad Hatter, for a cartoon version of *Alice in Wonderland*, aired in prime time in 1966.

An entire episode of *I Love Lucy* was built around Hopper. "The Hedda Hopper Story" aired on CBS on March 14, 1955, and featured Desi Arnaz and Lucille Ball playing musician Ricky Ricardo and his wife, Lucy, attempting to win Hopper's attention and, thus, coverage in her column during a visit to Hollywood. Hat jokes and gags filled the episode. "Craziest hat you've ever seen and Hedda will be underneath it," Ricky declares, leading to a situation where they mistake a platter of fruit carried by a waiter for a Hopper hat. As part of a series of Hollywood episodes, "The Hedda Hopper Story" helped to bring *I Love Lucy* back to first place in the national television ratings.[19] Hopper benefited from the mid-1950s "paradigm shift" in American television led by *I Love Lucy*, in which production moved from live to filmed performances and from New York to Hollywood, a shift that also benefited her son, Bill Hopper, when he took the role of the private detective Paul Drake in the television series *Perry Mason*.[20]

Hopper not only frequently appeared on television; she also recognized early on the power of the new medium. In 1940, she dedicated a Sunday column to the emergence of television as "something to hope for," and that hope was soon realized. "Television is here, but Hollywood doesn't know it yet," she wrote in December 1947, contributing to what would become a popular misconception about the film industry's ignorance of, or even hostility toward, television. "The situation is reminiscent of the time when sound came in. Warners was the only studio that believed sound was here to stay, and the other organizations didn't wake up until they were caught with their priorities down."[21] In fact, by the time Hopper weighed in on the significance of television, the major studios already were playing "a central role" in the development of television broadcasting. Only when rulings by the Federal Communications Commission in the wake of the Paramount decision thwarted studio ambitions in television did the majors—although not independent producers—disengage from the new industry, allowing Hopper to presume wisdom greater than that held by studio moguls.[22]

Hopper consistently covered the television industry and its growing influence, particularly its political influence, and detailed film industry changes needed to accommodate the new medium. "This is one medium that I don't believe Hollywood can give the old runaround," she wrote in 1950, "so we might as well take the teevee producers by their little hot hands and co-operate." NBC sought to reprint her column, "as it packs a real wallop." Thus Hopper pleased the network she would soon join with her new radio show in October.[23] Her column included items on television shows, stars, ratings, and contract negotiations, an important inclusion as film's female audience "dispersed into television viewing." She urged the studios to share talent they had under contract at the same time the Federal Communications Commission issued a similar warning, and she recommended they move into television production. "Instead of ruining our industry, I believe such a change would help."[24] And she recognized the political power of television and encouraged conservative actors, like Ronald Reagan, to go into politics. "Since so many elections are won on TV," Hopper wrote, actors have "an edge on their competition. After all, they know how to put on their make-up and they're sure not camera shy." Unlike many of her contemporaries, Hopper did not look askance on these developments. Just as she had brought politics into entertainment, she never questioned the advent of "the age of show business" in American political life.[25]

Hopper's positive stance toward television as it became the most popular mass medium in the United States helped to sustain her career and celebrity status into the 1960s, and she demonstrated that she still had star power. Her syndicate encouraged her to continue to include herself in her column, because "readers want to keep abreast of your latest doings, much as movie fans like to follow the activities of their favorite stars," and "readers would like to have your views and opinions, rather than an actor's or actress's." Her newspapers also sought special features from her on topics such as how she entertained, including food preparation and "hostess talk."[26] More prominently, Hopper hosted *Hedda Hopper's Hollywood*, a television special on NBC that presented Hollywood in a glowing, sentimental light. "This is my town," she began. "There's no town like it." The special won an impressive share of the television audience when it aired in January 1960, demonstrating that there was an audience for golden age Hollywood nostalgia.[27] Hopper also published her second set of memoirs in 1963. *The Whole Truth and Nothing But* followed Parson's *Tell It to Louella* (1961), and Hopper claimed Parsons had called to ask what the book was going to be about. "I'm just going to tell the truth," Hopper replied. "Oh, dear," she reported Parsons exclaiming, "that's what I was afraid of." *The Whole Truth and Nothing But* was excerpted and strongly promoted in *McCall's* women's magazine, sold 750,000 copies in paperback, and appeared on best-seller lists.[28]

Yet both Hopper's television special and her memoirs provoked great controversy and cast a shadow over her late career. For the television special, Hopper persuaded a number of Hollywood luminaries to appear for minimum union-scale wages, a situation the New York–based Ed Sullivan could not tolerate. Hopper's special had been scheduled opposite Sullivan's popular Sunday night variety show for which he paid his guests top wages, and he publicly accused her of populating her special with stars for less than ten percent of his costs. "This is the most grievous form of payola," he sputtered, prompting some of Hopper's major guests, including Joan Crawford, Bette Davis, and Charlton Heston, to pull out. Sparked by personal grievance, ratings rivalry, and an east-west coastal competition for television production, Sullivan kept up his attacks, belittling her as a woman who "used to hang around the fringes of show business." "She's no actress. She's certainly no newspaper woman," he contended. "And yet she's established a reign of terror out there in Hollywood."[29] According to a friend, Hopper broke into tears when Sullivan's attacks appeared in *Time* magazine, and she wrote an angry letter to the president of *Time* protesting the publication.[30]

Hopper's second set of memoirs, however, caused her far greater problems. *The Whole Truth* was a very different book than *From Under My Hat*, published eleven years earlier. Rather than a lighthearted look at herself and Hollywood, *The Whole Truth* was far more strident in tone, offering scathing information about the industry and its stars. "She knows the stars better than their mothers and lovers," claimed the promotional materials for the book. "They have told her their secrets and now frank, adult, astringent, she tells us."[31] In fact, one such secret resulted in a successful libel suit against Hopper. Despite warnings from others, she wrote that Michael Wilding had a homosexual relationship with a famous star before he became Elizabeth Taylor's second husband in 1952. In response, Wilding filed a multimillion-dollar libel suit, claiming her statements "had been made in a reckless and wanton disregard of his rights and feelings and with intent to injure his feelings." Hopper was forced to settle when she could not secure a witness to testify to Wilding's homosexuality. "The first loyalty of her gay friends was not to her but to one another," William J. Mann notes. Wilding's win included a $100,000 settlement and the removal of the material from subsequent printings of the book, while Hopper's loss meant financial damages and public humiliation. "It was one of the most dramatic incidents of her career," one of her assistants recalled, "and a sorry one."[32]

These two controversies late in Hopper's career revealed changes in the culture of movie celebrity and Hopper's role in it by the 1960s. Sullivan's attacks and Wilding's suit demonstrated that Hopper no longer was seen as all-powerful within the film industry or celebrity journalism, and the outcomes—stars pulling out of her television show and the loss of the libel suit—further confirmed that. Moreover, the placement of her column in newspapers became less prominent over time, and she complained about her column being dropped from papers or cut by editors. "I wish the *Tribune* would run a little more of my daily columns, so little of the copy is used; it seems like such a waste," she wrote the editor of the Sunday *Chicago Tribune*. "I work so hard to get my material." She chafed at any sign of disrespect or indication of her weakening position as a columnist and writer. When her publisher, Doubleday, delayed the publication date of *The Whole Truth*, Hopper began calling the company "double-crossing Doubleday."[33]

Hopper and her gossip contemporaries also faced growing competition from other news media. Although movie attendance dramatically decreased in the postwar period, celebrity news coverage and outlets notably increased. "Maybe our readers didn't go to the movies as often as before," declared a fan magazine publicist in 1954, "but they still maintained their loyalty to the stars." In addition to fan magazines, mainstream magazines, radio, and television expanded their celebrity coverage, aided by the increase in the number of Hollywood publicists providing the press with access to and seeking exposure for their star clients.[34] The relentless publicity of the Taylor-Burton affair over 1962 and 1963, for example, provoked one of Hopper's readers. "It is getting sickening all of these sick [head]lines screaming from every magazine stand in every department store, supermarket and newsstand." For Hopper, the couple had made headlines "ad nauseum [*sic*]," while one newspaper questioned the "the judgment of the wire chiefs and news editors" for making the affair "the biggest news story since the Armistice."[35]

New outlets for celebrity news appeared at both the low and high ends of journalism, crowding Hopper's column. Tabloid magazines, such as *Confidential*, which debuted in 1952, took advantage of waning studio power to control both star behavior and information about it to focus exclusively on exposing and sensationalizing star scandals. These magazines were incredibly successful, particularly at skirting libel, privacy, and obscenity laws.[36] Their existence greatly angered Hopper. Privately, she blamed "the smear magazines and *Confidential* . . . with everybody trying to sink Hollywood," and publicly she called them "horrible" and "doing our stars more harm than anything that's ever happened to them." Demonstrating her allegiances, she worked with one up-and-coming star, Rory Calhoun, to release and frame positively information about his youthful crime record to head off a *Confidential* exposé. When *Confidential* hired private detectives to investigate Hopper, they gave up after six months. "They couldn't find anything on me," Hopper declared. "There's nothing to find."[37] Meanwhile, traditional newspapers expanded their celebrity coverage to such an extent that during the

Taylor-Burton affair one local newspaper included a sardonic editor's note: "Due to an abundance of legitimate news, there is no Elizabeth Taylor–Richard Burton story in today's Saturday Special."[38]

The growth of celebrity journalism had a profound effect on Hopper's work at the end of her career. Her information was neither as exclusive nor as explosive as what appeared in other forms of media, and the competition put pressure on her to reveal more of what she knew about the private lives of stars, despite her criticisms of tabloids like *Confidential*. In 1958, she sought only to suggest Rock Hudson's homosexuality in a feature story on his ex-wife, Phyllis, for *Motion Picture Magazine*. "Of course, she won't say he is a fag, and name his lover, but we can hint at that," she confirmed to the editor.[39] Five years later came her explicit, and libelous, discussion of homosexuality in the case of Michael Wilding in *The Whole Truth*. Moreover, expanding celebrity journalism demanded a greater supply of photographs and photographers of movie stars, since images, not text as with Hopper's column, sold the magazines and newspapers. The increasing importance of images affected Hopper's work, as when the *Chicago Tribune* held up a number of her Sunday stories because the editors needed good photographs to run them.[40] More threatening to her career was how the revelation of Taylor's affair with Burton in 1962 owed much to the new phenomenon of "paparazzi" photography, which created candid photos of celebrities taken without regard or respect for privacy, and less to Hollywood gossip. In contrast to Hopper's exclusive, influential interview with Taylor in 1958 about her affair with Eddie Fisher, she had to admit in 1962, "I have not spoken with Elizabeth Taylor since she has been in Rome" filming *Cleopatra*. While this admission meant Hopper could not be criticized for sparking a scandal, it also revealed the declining significance of her, her column, and her readers.[41]

This decline owed as much to her age and sensibility as to changing conditions and context, and Hopper definitely was showing her age. When her television special *Hedda Hopper's Hollywood* aired in 1960, she was seventy-five years old. The show's makeup artist worked with "clips and rubber bands" to transform her appearance, thrilling Hopper. "My God, I look forty!"[42] But her transformation did not go unnoticed. "Miss Hopper," the *Herald Tribune* critic John Crosby snickered, was "wearing a face that I suspect Loretta Young loaned her for the afternoon." She wrote articles about how to "stay glamorous after 40," and in her column commented on the advancing years and their effect on her mind and body, particularly her growing forgetfulness. "Youthful memories seem to last longer," she mused. "Perhaps they are more important than the things we learn today."[43] In the mid-1960s, she talked about retirement and deplored post–World War II music and art. "Hate this modern stuff," she wrote, "which I avoid like poison." She found especially distressing the decline of hat wearing among women. "I can walk six blocks today in any city and see nothing more than hair or a scarf covering anybody else's hair but mine."[44] Hopper also began complaining about young people and youth culture, and younger Americans noticed her age as well as her negative attitudes. Although she made an effort to embrace Elvis Presley and later the Beatles, Hopper never bridged the "generation gap" or adapted to the new conditions in Hollywood before her career abruptly ended with her death in early 1966.

Reporting on a Fading Hollywood System

In her reporting on the film industry and fulfilling her functions as a gossip columnist over the 1950s and into the 1960s, Hedda Hopper consistently revealed herself to be out of step with changing times. A negative refrain came to characterize her reportage as she strained against a new, unfamiliar emerging Hollywood and bemoaned the passing of old Hollywood. Her readers noticed. "In the so-called Golden Days of motion pictures to which you refer so much," wrote a San Francisco man, who was less enamored of the past than Hopper. She sadly reported on the deaths of the industry leaders and stars of her generation, including those of Louis B. Mayer in 1957 and Cecil B. DeMille in 1959.[45] She blamed the decline of the old studio system on their replacements rather than competition from television or the effects of the Paramount decision, and she believed that by prioritizing realism in film they had brought about the "death of glamour" and "dream stuff" in Hollywood. "Our town was built on it, but there's scarcely any trace left now." She attributed MGM's downturn to Mayer's successor, Dore Schary, for "putting pictures on screen that distorted our way of life" and for a more realistic and less glamorous approach at a studio well-known for its big stars and lavish productions.[46] As with Schary, Hopper generally viewed the new generation in Hollywood with disdain. She privately called new actors "young degenerates" and believed that few "of today's young stars will reach the statures of those who really sell tickets at the box office." She disliked the postwar popularity of "method acting," a realistic style adopted by younger actors like Marlon Brando, and agreed with an actress "tired of their deliberate naturalness." Hopper also faulted younger scriptwriters, producers, and studio heads for "doing everything possible to kill one of the greatest industries ever put into the hands of man."[47]

For Hopper, "everything possible" included dramatic changes in film content, including greater realism, and she used her column's agenda-setting function to oppose those changes. "The only scripts coming in are about drunkards, dope addicts, neurotics, psychotics, nymphomania, and just plain ignorance. Aren't there any normal people around any more?" In *The Whole Truth*, Hopper deplored the industry for "churning out pictures reeking of violence, prostitution, perversion, and decay." "Of course, we always knew there were such things as sewers," she argued, "but never before have audiences had their noses pushed over so many gratings."[48] In addition to ascribing changes in film content to a new generation in Hollywood, Hopper blamed Communists. She held to her Cold War politics throughout her life, repeating in the months before her death her belief that film was the "greatest propaganda medium" and that the "Commies thought so, too," and so had infiltrated Hollywood. "We're still suffering that infiltration." In 1964, she devoted a column to an anti-Communist screenwriter who contended, as did she, that films depicting the underside of American life—not just explicitly political films—were a result of Communist infiltration. Their aim, the unnamed screenwriter argued, was to use the movie industry's "world influence" to "get the American image into disgrace."[49]

But Hopper also saw male domination in Hollywood as responsible for the 1960s "sea change" in film content.[50] In a 1963 column dedicated to the topic, she argued that early in the industry, "back in the days when females got an even break in Hollywood," women "held their own" as stars and screenwriters. But this situation was no longer true. "Stories are written by men, produced, directed and acted by men," she contended, "and they wonder what happened to Hollywood." As a consequence, film content had changed. "There are no more tender love stories," claimed her friend, screenwriter Frances Marion. "Today these men write from the belt buckle down." This development led to a glut of women's roles as "hussies" and "baby-faced killers," according to Hopper, and she missed the strong female characters played by actresses like Rosalind Russell. "The type that Roz played," she grieved, "has disappeared from the screen lately."[51] Hopper, and Marion, correctly perceived the decline of women's power and presence in the industry and "the substitution of violence and sexuality . . . for romance" in film content, as Molly Haskell has noted. But it is less likely that these changes contributed to the disintegration of old Hollywood, as Hopper argued, than emerged out of the reorganization of film production and industry attempts to capture new audiences, particularly young men.[52]

Hopper held to her argument, however, and condemned what she saw as the increasingly violent, sexual, and political content of film and its impact on Hollywood and beyond. Still appalled about the violence in *Blackboard*

Jungle (1955) three years after the film came out, Hopper contended "any 10-year-old can walk into a hardware store and buy" a switchblade knife like those featured in the film. She also exchanged views on media violence with the film's star Sidney Poitier, who worried about children "seeing mayhem and learning about crime."[53] She attacked Tennessee Williams, one of the most prominent and provocative playwrights of the era, whose successful plays *A Streetcar Named Desire* and *Cat on a Hot Tin Roof* became Oscar-nominated movies in 1951 and 1958. He also wrote the script for *Baby Doll* (1956), a film condemned by the Catholic Church and the Legion of Decency that Hopper stated "had the censors tearing their hair." What scholars consider his "powerful and transgressive view of sexuality" and "major role in breaking down" film censorship led Hopper to excoriate his work as "the substrata of the sewer" and to confront him personally.[54] "The last time I was in Hollywood a famous lady columnist with a way-out taste in millinery . . . got me on the phone one morning and lit into me," Williams recalled in 1960. "'I want to know why you are always plunging into sewers!' she demanded." His response—that his work came not from the sewers but from "the main stream of life"—failed to convince her. Hopper was further "horrified" by the content of political films such as *Dr. Strangelove* (1964), believing no "Communist could dream up a more effective anti-American film to spread abroad than this one."[55]

For Hopper, the moral decline and political messages of recent films posed a danger to audiences, particularly children, to U.S. society, culture, and standing in the world, and to Hollywood. In the mid-1950s, she decried "so many films about murder, alcoholics, gangsters, blood, gore, dope and depravity of all kinds—pictures made for sensationalism and a quick buck—without thought of the harm they are doing to our country." She worried about film exports destroying America's "good image around the world." "Today it's like the fall of Rome," she wailed in the early 1962. "Shouldn't there be some consideration as to what is good for the children and for our country?" She was not alone. A few months later, Congressman Walter Rogers, a Texas Democrat, advocated congressional investigation of the motion picture industry, because "as a father of six children and as a legislator he is indignant at what he called concentration on sex and obscenity in films."[56] Hopper's readers were equally concerned and began staying away from the movies. "Dear Miss Hopper," asked a Los Angeles woman, "do you realize there is not a new decent movie?" She "had a flood of letters from people complaining that Hollywood is not making movies they can take their children to," and one man wrote to criticize films that "wash our dirty linen in public."[57] While many in Hollywood saw the new film content as a way to compete with tamer television offerings, Hopper considered it benefiting television. "People would rather sit home and look at old pictures on television," she wrote in 1950. "That proves what the American family wants," she declared in 1963, when eight of the top-ten television shows were situation comedies. "There's not a downbeat, psychological, sinful or horror story in the lot."[58]

As was her practice, Hopper did not rest with criticizing the new film content but campaigned to correct what she called "Hollywood's Shame." When "downright depravity creeps in," she argued, "we should have some way of stopping it." She first looked to the industry's system of self-censorship, but the Production Code Administration was under pressure from an industry seeking less screen censorship and in transition following Joseph Breen's retirement in 1954.[59] In her column, Hopper covered the debate about whether the Production Code should be revised. "We're having to re-examine the code," she quoted MPAA head Eric Johnston saying the following year. While the majority of industry insiders wanted "a more adult interpretation" of the code, others, including Hopper, believed "the code should be enforced."[60] They were fighting a losing battle. Johnston himself was not very "interested in issues involving morality," and Supreme Court decisions in the 1950s opened the way for greater cinematic freedom. Two sets of code revisions came in quick succession in 1954 and 1956. Even so, by 1958 *Time* magazine noted "the much-publicized Production Code, which once bulldogged producers and exhibitors, is being observed these days about as often as the whooping crane," and most moviegoers were not bothered.[61] Exactly a decade later, under pressure from inside and outside the industry, the MPAA replaced the Production Code with the current ratings system, which instead of regulating the content of film regulates the age of the audience for film. Hopper did not live to see, and could not have imagined, the end of the Production Code, and she continued to advocate strict regulation of film content.

Even more, Hopper once again aimed to mobilize her readership. She urged her readers to write Johnston about films they felt violated the code, and "he may get off his fat you-know-what and do something," she exclaimed.[62] In a 1964 column titled "Women on the Warpath for Clean Pictures," Hopper reported on "an underground movement by mothers of this country." "The women, convinced that unsavory films affect the morals of their children, are on the march." Their motivations recalled those of U.S. women's organizations, which sought to "mother the movies" and protect "the safety and the purity of the child viewer" through pro-censorship campaigns earlier in the twentieth century. They were planning a boycott, which Hopper urged her readers to join, adding, "If you don't think they can deal the movies a mighty blow with their planned boycott, you don't think."[63] The next year she reported on state and federal censorship bills prohibiting "morally corruptive matter" for children. "The mothers of this country got through to their lawmakers, and if one of those bills passes, censorship is here." Although Hopper's libertarian, anti-state-censorship stance remained, she no longer believed the film industry was serious about self-censorship. "Producers can't say they haven't been warned."[64] Hopper's mail indicated support for her campaign for "clean pictures" among her readers. An Arkansas woman believed Hopper "alone had managed to maintain a true sense of values through the years [and] wage a fight against immoral movies." "And my hat's off to you for having an awfully lot of more nerve than the average Hollywood reporter," wrote a Massachusetts reader. But this campaign was unsuccessful, contributing to Hopper's reputation by the early 1960s as a "modern-day Carrie Nation," flailing dramatically but fruitlessly against an institution she sought to change morally and politically.[65]

Hopper and her readers had little luck reforming Hollywood's film content, and they had even less luck reforming the stars. The post–World War II period in Hollywood history brought about a new kind of movie star, one who needed and respected gossip columnists like Hopper much less than had earlier stars. With the major film studios now in decline, stars had greater freedom, independence, and negotiating power. In contrast to the old system of studio contracts and control, movie stars could more easily set the terms of their employment and lead their own lives. High star salaries like Elizabeth Taylor's in *Cleopatra* demonstrated the increased sway held by "A-list" actors and actresses, who did not need to bow to the demands of the studios, Hollywood publicity, or Hopper. "In the old days when the real producers were alive, the stars were forced to attend the premieres [and] all the important social functions," Hopper recalled.[66] But stars need no longer be obedient or loyal to their employers, and although Hopper continued to fulfill one of her functions as a gossip columnist—disciplining noncompliant employees through criticism in her column—she had little effect. The decline of studio control, combined with the expansion of celebrity journalism, meant stars were less protected but also less dependent on studio publicity and gossip columnists. Hopper was aghast at her first interview with Marlon Brando when he was making his first film, *The Men* (1950). Brando had little interest in publicity and disinterestedly and characteristically grunted at her. "Do you care to answer my questions?" finally asked an exasperated Hopper. "I don't believe so," Brando replied. She refused to interview him again and based her later coverage on information gathered from those around him, saying, "I can't be insulted twice." Hopper's "approval or disapproval meant little," noted her biographer George Eells, to "a Brando."[67]

Marlon Brando was not alone in recognizing the diminution and rejecting what was left of Hopper's star-making power. By the 1950s, according to Joshua Gamson, stars became "proprietors of their own image." "I am my own industry," Elizabeth Taylor famously said. "I am my own commodity." With this control, stars became less concerned with what the old studio system had sought and Hopper still supported: apparent consistency between stars' on-screen roles and off-screen lives.[68] "The public gets a certain idea about you and insists that you live up to it constantly," Robert Mitchum complained to Hopper in 1947, the year before his arrest for marijuana possession sparked a major Hollywood scandal. "It gets mighty monotonous." By distinguishing between the two aspects of the star persona, and refusing to appear to be like the characters they portrayed on-screen, the new Hollywood stars joined the trend in celebrity journalism toward calling attention to the artifice of older star images and substituting new "markers of authenticity."[69]

These stars also asserted that their obligations to employers and audiences were limited to professional work as actors and did not include maintaining traditional moral standards in personal life or behavior. "I can't be that hypocritical to protect my public," Taylor argued in the wake of her affair with Richard Burton. "What I am is my own business." Brando felt that "the only thing an actor owes his public is not to bore them."[70] Film audiences seemed to agree, tolerating the social and sexual transgressions of stars that Hopper and her readers found intolerable. Hopper's readers considered "the waywardness of one Robert Mitchum" to be more "proof of immorality in Hollywood." Even so, as a consequence of his marijuana possession, "Bob Mitchum served a term in jail and came out to find his career unaffected," Hopper regretfully admitted in the early 1950s.[71] Already by then her moral outrage no longer meant as much.

Although Hopper's contribution to the construction of star personas mattered less in the 1950s and 1960s than under the old studio system, her column still provided information and judgments about stars on- and off-screen. In assessing the screen presence of various stars, she finally accepted the star persona projected by Sidney Poitier after his Oscar-winning role as Homer Smith in *Lilies of the Field* (1963). An unemployed construction worker whose car breaks down near a farm run by Catholic nuns in refuge from Communist eastern Europe, Smith ends up staying, helping them, and overcoming myriad differences to forge a friendship. Hopper loved the film, felt as if "I had taken a spiritual bath," named Poitier "one of our great, great actors," and claimed "he's got my vote for the Oscar."[72] *Lilies* appeared just as the modern Civil Rights Movement reached its point of most effective pressure and protest, and the success of the film's racial representations and Poitier's performance indicated the triumph of Hollywood's conscience-liberalism by the 1960s. But, as scholars argue, "the nature of the change [was] more cosmetic than substantial," because Poitier's character acted "not as a black man, but as a white image of what a black man is." This fiction, this new racial and racist stereotype, was what finally won Hopper over, bearing out her racial conservatism. She complimented Poitier's "modesty" and "example," and called him, as she had Hattie McDaniel in the 1940s, a "credit to his race."[73] Letters about Poitier in *Lilies* exist from Hopper's white but not black readers; African Americans apparently no longer saw her column as relevant to issues of racial representation. Indeed, Poitier was the "first and only black star of a dying system," and, with the changing politics of representation in 1960s Hollywood, his star persona and genre of movies became, like Hopper, anachronisms.[74]

Despite her fairly extensive and favorable coverage of Poitier's screen roles in the 1950s and 1960s, Hopper paid most attention to white women's roles, and she did not like what she saw. While she approved of wholesome, "good girl" characters and the actresses who played them—"She's as American as ham and eggs," she said of Doris Day—she criticized sexy or immoral characters and the actresses who portrayed them with requisite sexual display.[75] "Our actresses who have been so anxious to take off their clothes on-screen and for magazines must be crazy," she wrote in 1964 and informed them of a time when women were considered "more seductive when covered." She was aghast at Carroll Baker's costuming in a "shortie nightgown" in Tennessee Williams' *Baby Doll* and disapproved of French actress Brigitte Bardot, "whose on-screen commodity is strictly sex." In 1958, the year Bardot made the list of top-ten moneymakers due to such hits as *And God Created Woman* (1956), Hopper seethed, "I'm fed up to the teeth with stories and pictures of Brigitte Bardot. Ugh!"[76] As in the General Federation of Women's Clubs nearly simultaneous antipornography campaign, Hopper and her readers considered film's increasingly sexual representations of women as harmful to youth and degrading to women.[77] "The sexy pictures they are trying to choke down our neck is not good for the teenagers," declared one of Hopper's readers. And Hopper bemoaned media coverage of actresses' "frontal fortifications instead of their talent, which appalls me." "But then I come from the era when Fanny was a girl's name," she added, revealing an understanding that her time had passed.[78]

Hopper's coverage of stars on-screen was matched by her coverage of them off-screen, and, since the movie stars and industry worried less about apparent consistency between their "reel" and "real" lives, she increasingly explored and exploited the gap between the two. This development particularly affected her reporting on the lives of troubled stars, most prominently Judy Garland, who attempted suicide in 1950, and Marilyn Monroe, who died in 1962, apparently of suicide. In her columns following Garland's attempt and Monroe's death, Hopper offered interpretations of their self-destructive acts that presented the personal "truth" behind the stars' public façades. Although both women were at low points in their careers, Hopper paid tribute to their attributes and accomplishments. "Hers is the greatest talent ever developed in this city," she complimented Garland. "None in my memory hypnotized the camera as she did," she wrote in her obituary for Monroe. But recently both women had been fired from films due to their absenteeism and tardiness, and their studio contracts and relations were in jeopardy. Hopper still promoted Garland's career, however, and recognized her "talent" as the basis for her stardom, moves encouraged by Hopper and Garland's shared affiliation with the same studio: MGM. It was Monroe whom Hopper judged harshly, as she saw Monroe's stardom as less about talent than celebrity. She also disapproved of Monroe's liberal-left politics and commented that the actress "knew the end of her acting career was waiting for her."[79]

While Hopper noted several such external pressures on the actresses, her function as a gossip columnist meant she confirmed, along with the rest of the Hollywood press, the industry's framing of star suicides and suicide attempts as due to the problems of individual stars rather than the star system itself.[80] Thus Hopper emphasized internal reasons for Garland and Monroe's suicidal actions, pointing out both women's long-standing problems with self and psyche. The emotional difficulties of both actresses had appeared in the Hollywood press before their suicide incidents. Of Garland, Hopper reported on an earlier "crack-up" and her "confused nerves," and Louella Parsons "played up" Monroe's "well-known tragic childhood as an orphan."[81] Hopper presented these suicide incidents as internal crises within a psychological context. "The little girl, who's been sick so many years, couldn't take any more," she wrote of Garland, while "Marilyn Monroe seemed to be touched by forces impossible for any human being to bear, and life became a nightmare of broken dreams, promises, and pain." That Hopper drew on psychological ideas and practices in her discussions of Garland and Monroe indicated how the popularization of psychology after World War II had permeated the private talk of her gossip column, just as it had the rest of the popular press, Hollywood publicity, and her readers' letters.[82]

Hopper's readers responded in great numbers to both tragic events, declared their love, loyalty, and distress as fans of Garland and Monroe, and joined Hopper in offering psychological explanations. "We, her fans, are anxious about Judy's recent illness and attack of nerves." Garland "is nervous," declared a Los Angeles woman. "I can understand for I have a daughter of the same type."[83] For Garland, they recommended psychiatric institutions and care. "She should be confined in a hospital until she is completely recovered." "Try, Compton Sanitarium," suggested one reader.[84] Another reader offered the name of "a counselor [who] does analysis work." This reader's letter demonstrated her awareness of key psychological concepts, such as the role of a trained practitioner in bringing about a cure for emotional problems. "Sometimes," she noted, "we do need help from someone who believes in you and has faith." She also had adopted the "therapeutic ethic," particularly its injunction to "self-actualization." "It hurts to see people who are trying to mature having to go through such intense emotional disturbances. But that is life. We must have the problems in order to acquire character and maturity."[85] In the case of Monroe's suicide, readers saw her as "insecure" and "frightened." They understood her emotional symptoms as rooted in her difficult childhood and early family relations, another important psychological assumption, as well as her unhappy marriages and two miscarriages. "I always felt sorry for Marilyn with her mother in a mental institution and her sad fate to have no children," wrote a Nebraska woman. "I don't think [she] ever had a home or knew much of a mother's love." Monroe was a "woman who could not find peace of mind," believed a New York reader. She was a "woman whose beginnings were tragic, who was never allowed to forget these beginnings."[86]

A significant group of letter writers departed from Hopper's interpretation of star suicide, however, and refused to put the blame primarily on the internal defects of Garland and Monroe. Instead, they focused on external factors related to the movie industry and celebrity culture, and understood "the star as victim of the Hollywood system."[87] Hopper's readers used their letters to point out what they believed was missing from the public discussion, which film scholar Adrienne McLean has called the "institutional sources of some of the psychic pain and suffering that contributed to the suicides [or suicide attempts] in the first place."[88]

In the case of Garland, Hopper's readers blamed working conditions in the movie industry and, in particular, singled out MGM. Although Hopper detailed in her column the enormous amount of pressure on Garland due to her demanding work schedule, battles with her weight, and subsequent drug use, she used the passive voice to avoid directly criticizing her former studio. "Instead of giving her benzedrine to keep her going, and sleeping pills to quiet her nerves at night," Hopper wrote about Garland's suicide attempt, "she should have been sent to the Menninger Clinic." She goes on to mention but does not name Garland's "boss," Louis B. Mayer.[89] Hopper's readers did not share her qualms about assigning blame. They were fans of Judy Garland and had helped to make her one of the top-ten box office draws during World War II and MGM's main asset by 1948, enjoying her in popular films such as *The Wizard of Oz* (1939), *Meet Me in St. Louis* (1944), and *Easter Parade* (1948).[90] "Angry fans are calling Metro 'the house that Judy built,'" wrote a woman from New York. "They are saying they will never attend another Metro movie, unless Metro does the right thing by her." For another New Yorker, it seemed "a pity, that a person who made millions for her boss, should be so treated." One of Hopper's Maryland readers addressed MGM directly, sending her letter also to Hopper. "I blame your studios for her illness and attempted suicide. I believe you are . . . driving her to her death."[91] For these readers, Garland's emotional problems were the result of her studio's exploitation of her talent.

With Monroe's suicide twelve years later, readers of Hopper's column held celebrity culture responsible, indicting Hopper in the process. Changes in the movie industry by 1962 meant Monroe was not under the same kind of studio control as Judy Garland had been in 1950, and no reader argued that Monroe was overworked. But celebrity culture had expanded, and they contended that the emotionally vulnerable actress found the exposure and exploitation difficult to withstand. In the past, wrote one reader, "the stars were not so much in the public eye as they are today. Now, nearly all the people's lives are publicized to the most intimate and minute details."[92] Indeed, press coverage of Monroe, following the peak of her film career with Billy Wilder's *Some Like It Hot* (1959), showed a woman and an actress in decline. While making her last completed film, *The Misfits* (1961), she was "working in a constant stupor from drugs and alcohol," gaining a reputation, with help from Hopper, as "irresponsible and unreliable," and appearing "burdened by her celebrity." Hopper hinted as much herself, in her obituary for Monroe. "In a way we're all guilty," she admitted. "We built her up to the skies, we loved her, but left her lonely and afraid when she needed us most."[93]

The majority of Hopper's respondents on Monroe's suicide scoffed at her belated admission and blamed her, along with the rest of celebrity journalism, for exacerbating Monroe's psychological problems and contributing to her death. A Mississippi woman wondered "why you used your advantage through the newspapers to constantly needle poor Marilyn Monroe who never had a chance, coming from twelve foster homes."[94] Unlike other events in Hopper's career, most of the extant letters on Monroe's suicide come from male readers, confirming scholarly conclusions that men, not women, constituted Monroe's fan base. "You knew Marilyn was sick, but you never gave her any sympathy," sputtered a South Dakota man. "Do you sleep well Hedda?" "What effect did you think those harsh words would have on her sensitive and unstable mind?" another San Francisco reader asked Hopper. "But it made good copy, it Sold!"[95] These male respondents were readers but certainly not fans of Hopper, and their letters contain the harshest criticism toward her, particularly when making connections between Hopper's negative coverage of Monroe and her contemporary Elizabeth Taylor. "Now you've killed Marilyn with your dirty journalism. I suppose the campaign is on until Liz kills herself too." Monroe's suicide and the hate mail Hopper received afterward reinforced her alienation from new Hollywood and her nostalgia for old Hollywood. With the "stars to hell and gone," she feared there was no one "to give Hollywood the color and the excitement that it needs."[96] At least she did not have to feel similarly about Republican Party politics in the 1960s.

From Old to New Right

For Hedda Hopper, the 1960s brought exciting changes to her beloved Republican Party. The conservative grassroots movement and leadership she had supported throughout the Cold War era finally came to power with the party's nomination of Barry Goldwater for president in 1964. That year, Hopper's political ideology of anti-Communism, antistatism, militant foreign policy, anti-civil rights, antiunion, and traditional morality captivated the Republican Party, and the audience her conservative, mostly female respondents represented became an important Republican Party constituency. These changes were developments she had longed to see, and they energized American conservatism, created what would come to be called the New Right, and transformed U.S. party politics by 1980, with the presidential election of Ronald Reagan.[97] But Hopper did not live to see a significant conservative electoral Republican victory. Although George Murphy, another actor turned conservative politician, won a California Senate seat in 1964, Goldwater lost the 1964 presidential election to President Lyndon B. Johnson, and Hopper died in early 1966, before Reagan's California gubernatorial victory that November. In between defeat and victory, the Republican Party jettisoned the extremist style of conservatism represented by Hopper and Goldwater for Reagan's successful sunny, moderate approach, though it kept the ideological content of their conservatism.[98] The Republican Party's "right turn" in the 1960s validated Hopper's lifelong political advocacy and activism and demonstrated continuity between the Old and New Right.

Hopper's dedicated fight against Communism at home and abroad, anti-statism, and militant foreign policy continued, with support from her readers, throughout her life, and these ideological positions served to unify conservative Republicans in the 1960s. Even after the FBI closed their investigation of Hollywood in 1958, Hopper persisted in her Red Scare politics in the movie capital. In 1959, on prime-time television, she proclaimed her hard fight against Communist infiltration of the movie industry: "I will fight to my dying breath to keep it out." She still strongly supported the Hollywood blacklist, although filmmakers slowly were bringing it to an end and compensating victims. She was appalled when twelve writers and actors blacklisted during the 1950s received a settlement of $80,000 from the MPAA in 1965.[99] Her reputation for having access to information about Communists or Communist sympathizers remained. "I know you were and I suppose are well acquainted in anti-Commie circles," the editor of the *New York News* wrote her in 1962, asking for information about the Nobel Prize–winning chemist Linus C. Pauling. "He's a one worlder from way back," Hopper answered, referring to Pauling's peace activism. "He's a sneaky hombre and very slippery."[100] She kept up her assault against "big government," repeating old criticisms against income taxes and the welfare state, and adding new ones, such as opposition to the Supreme Court's school prayer ban. Unsurprisingly, Hopper strongly supported the Vietnam War through charity work, USO tours, and her column. She published "reports of high morale and military success" in Vietnam from actor Nick Adams. "If we back down in Vietnam," he argued, "the Commies will take all of Asia."[101]

Hopper also remained a steadfast opponent of civil rights legislation, another aspect of the conservative Republican agenda. When Hopper interviewed Sidney Poitier after his Oscar win in the spring of 1964, what would become the Civil Rights Act of 1964 was making its way through Congress. Hopper had long underestimated Poitier's strong commitment to civil rights and black equality; years earlier she had described him as having "no desire to be white," misunderstanding what black activists sought. "You haven't gone deeply into the race question—you haven't lost your head over it like some," she told him, making obvious her contempt and disrespect for civil rights activists as emotional or crazy rather than sensible and rational.[102] Given Hopper's interest in racial politics and strong racial conservatism, a white female reader called on Hopper to intervene with Poitier and discourage him from supporting the civil rights bill. "If you can, why not put Mr. Poitier right on the issue by telling him that this horrendous bill will do for him just what it will do to all of us—take all our rights away."[103] While Hopper joined other conservatives, such as Goldwater, in claiming antistatism and not racism motivated her stance against civil rights for African Americans, she revealed her racial fears in private. "Barry Goldwater has guts, principle and conscience, and that is why he won't vote for the Civil Rights Bill," she wrote privately. "It gives Negroes supremacy over the Whites."[104]

Hopper consistently opposed unions, just like conservative Republicans who sought to erode the power of "big labor." She emerged as the most prominent and publicized opponent of the biggest strike in Hollywood since the post–World War II strike wave: a 1960 strike by the Screen Actors Guild, which closed the major studios, halted production on a number of films, and put thousands out of work. Because the studios were increasingly selling their old films to television, SAG decided as part of contract negotiations to demand residual payments for actors each time their films dating back to 1948 were televised. The union also brought back Ronald Reagan as president to oversee this effort. But the studio heads and producers refused to budge, leading SAG's membership to authorize a strike. Hopper not only voted against what she called "the unwarranted strike" but also accused the union of undemocratic and corrupt practices, implicating, and thus angering, her would-be political ally Reagan.[105] Moreover, she headlined a meeting of a small group of dissident unionists. "I don't think it moral to accept money twice for a single job," she declared, advancing the same argument producers were using against the strikers. But she went further, attributing the SAG strike to a new stage of Communist infiltration in Hollywood now that filmmakers were breaking the blacklist. "Isn't it coincidental that at a time when some of our liberal producers are hiring Communist writers that this strike came up?" And she promised, "I'm going to find out why this strike was called."[106] In the end, SAG settled the strike, and Hopper's Red Scare politics had little effect.

Hopper also expressed her nativist beliefs into the 1960s, despite an ostensible decline in "the antialien impulse" among most conservatives.[107]

She and her readers continued to see immigrants and foreign visitors as a threat to the United States and to criticize foreign actors in Hollywood for taking jobs away from Americans. "We should be giving our own country-men more work instead of going off half-cocked over every foreigner," wrote a Los Angeles reader.[108] Hopper dedicated an entire column to her dismay that foreigners, mostly British filmmakers, dominated the list of Academy Award nominees in 1964. Reminding her readers of the Boston Tea Party in 1773, she proposed "a tea party of our own [to] dump every last statuette into the Pacific . . . rather than see them carried off to England." That was the year Sidney Poitier, who held dual citizenship in the Bahamas and the United States, won Best Actor for *Lilies of the Field*, and Hopper anxiously asked him in a pre-Oscar interview, "Do you realize if you don't get it, not one American will get it?"[109] As with her acceptance of Poitier's dual citizenship, Hopper considered naturalized immigrants as assimilated, "good" Americans and saw their change in citizenship status as newsworthy. "Boyd Will Become American Citizen" headlined a 1963 column, when Irish actor Stephen Boyd decided to "send in his American citizenship papers."[110]

Hopper's nativism became virulent, however, when left-wing politics were involved. To great fanfare from her readers, she flayed the married actors Yves Montand and Simone Signoret during their visits to the United States in the early 1960s. When they came for the 1960 Academy Awards ceremony, Hopper contended that Montand "has been a most active leader in the Com-munist Party in France and Italy" and wondered about "the true purpose of the tour."[111] "You are on the right track in regard to Yves Montand . . . and his German-Jewish wife," wrote a Los Angeles woman, who included in her letter a report on Communism in France from right-wing sources. After Signoret won the Oscar for her role in *Room at the Top* (1959), Hopper linked her to the Soviet Union, commenting that the actress had used an "Old Russian trick of applauding the audience" in her acceptance speech. Signoret believed that her victory was Hollywood's vote both for her and against Hopper's brand of anti-Communism.[112] The next year, Hopper condemned Signoret's opposition to the French war in Algeria and what she saw as the couple's anti-American "insults to our integrity." They "are examples of performers we could do with-out," she fumed. "God love you for having the courage to write . . . about 2 pinks that we could do without very well," wrote a New Jersey couple. "Good for you!" exclaimed a Los Angeles woman. "I would contribute to a fund to send all Commies to Russia to live. It's a disgrace she ever won the Academy Award." "Three cheers for your patriotic stand, taken in to-day's column! We should have people like you in Washington," recommended another.[113]

Nothing would have made Hopper happier than political leadership in the United States that matched her own conservative ideology, and her hope for change came to focus on the 1964 presidential candidacy of Barry Goldwater. She, like other conservatives in the Republican Party, spent much of the 1950s alienated from the centrist policies and "Modern Republicanism" of President Eisenhower.[114] Eisenhower's foreign policy, including his retreat from rollback in eastern Europe, his 1959 invitation to Khrushchev, and his continuance of New Deal programs, confirmed her initial distrust of him and support for Robert Taft in 1952. Even worse was the presidential victory of Democrat John F. Kennedy in 1960. Before the election, Hopper hoped that Kennedy's candidacy would be doomed by a sex scandal, as she had heard he had "a woman in every port." "If that's the case," she wrote privately, "he'll slip some time and that'll help our side." "I won't listen to his speeches nor will I read them," she declared after the election. "He sounds so much like FDR it makes my stomach turn."[115] Yet she also expressed ambivalence toward Kennedy's Republican opponent for the presidency: Richard Nixon. Hopper supported Nixon in 1960 and again in 1962 when he ran for governor of California, refusing to join other California conservatives in deserting him for his centrist positions. Still, his back-to-back electoral defeats concerned her. "The trouble with Nixon is that he won't listen to anyone," Hopper analyzed. "This campaign, as was the last, has been run by amateurs." She was delighted, however, by his attendance at a book party celebrating *The Whole Truth* the next year. "You've made so many appearances for me," Hopper recalled Nixon saying. "It's time I made one for you."[116]

Goldwater's ascendancy to the top of the Republican Party ticket in 1964 delighted Hopper even more. She shared his conservative politics, which fused libertarianism and moral traditionalism, believed he was "good looking enough to be a movie star," and worked hard for his candidacy. She participated in the national conservative effort to draft Goldwater to run for president with a lecture tour in the fall of 1963. "In each place I spoke, I had a Goldwater rally," she reported. She thought the Democrats could be defeated, if "all the Republicans get out and work."[117] Instead, liberal and moderate Republicans tried to derail Goldwater's nomination at the 1964 Republican National Convention, which Hopper attended as a press correspondent. She was furious, but she was under strict orders from her editor. "Don't let your sympathies for Goldwater appear in what you write."[118] In her private letters, however, she held nothing back. She recalled how in the last contested Republican nomination "the 'Establishment' killed Taft" through behind-the-scenes machinations. "Now they're trying the same dirty technique on

Gold[water]." "I am so fed up [with] the whole lying bunch I could spit right in their faces," she seethed, expressing the divisive mood that nearly split the party.[119] Like the rest of Goldwater's supporters, she understood the convention as a fight between the party's conservative grassroots activists and the liberal-moderate national leadership, she admired and identified with the former, and she was thrilled with the outcome. "They were nice, prosperous, middle class people: the heart of our nation, who are tired of being shoved around by the liberals, and at last they spoke loud and clear." Reiterating another conservative woman's message—Phyllis Schlafly's *A Choice, Not an Echo*—Hopper believed the Goldwater nomination meant "we've got a good candidate now . . . we've got a choice. So, let's make the most of it."[120]

Hopper set out from the Republican National Convention to do just this. "I am 100% for Barry Goldwater," she declared. She became known as a "Goldwater Republican" around Hollywood and kept an eye on press coverage of the candidate. "Your paper has done a marvelous job for Barry," she wrote an editor at the *New York News*, "which pleases me no end." Years of mail from respondents convinced her that the Goldwater campaign had a ready constituency. An "uprising among the grass-roots citizens," she contended, meant the "real people are on the march."[121] While Hopper still rooted her conservatism primarily in libertarianism and preferred that the community rather than the state enforce moral standards, she gravitated to the traditional morals and cultural nostalgia Goldwater espoused. She maintained her contacts with Republican Women's Clubs and, along with Ronald Reagan's second wife, Nancy, joined Mothers for a Moral America in support of Goldwater. A "pseudo-grass-roots" women's group—actually organized by operatives in the Goldwater campaign—Mothers for a Moral America "appealed directly to women's maternal instincts and sense of moral righteousness," two notions dear to Hopper's heart. "The people who asked me to join are a wonderful group of women," Hopper noted, "and I thought this was a worthy cause."[122] But when a campaign movie called *Choice* appeared under the organization's name and included a "montage juxtaposing footage of muggers and gamblers with covers of dirty books and material on the new topless bathing suit," both Goldwater and Hopper disavowed it. "We knew nothing about this film that was made and I am so glad that Goldwater refused to allow it on the network," Hopper insisted.[123] The *Choice* controversy was only one of many that hurt the Goldwater campaign during the fall of 1964, but the alarmist content of the film confirmed the extremist image of Goldwater and his supporters, such as Hopper, and the Republicans lost the November election in a landslide.

Despite Goldwater's defeat, conservative Republicans, like Hopper, had only lost the battle, not the war, but she did not know that.[124] They had organizational and ideological control of their party, even as Republicans shed the extremist image associated with conservatism. While Hopper felt marginalized after the 1964 defeat with the purging of Goldwater and right-wing organizations like the John Birch Society, of which she may have been a member, most of her respondents and allies did not. One of Hopper's St. Louis readers feared this development was "about trying to make the Republican Party again a middle of the road party," but other readers wrote about their continuing efforts. A Los Angeles woman reported on the still-active network of anti-Communist study groups established by conservative grassroots women, mostly housewives and mothers, with which Hopper was familiar. "The study groups, lectures and series of forums that have been held and scheduled for the future have taken much time and effort to plan," she informed Hopper. "These women are all busy with their homes and social activities but believe me they have been so dedicated in this field."[125] Moreover, Ronald Reagan emerged as the new face of conservative Republicanism with a national reputation following his televised campaign speech for Goldwater, "A Time for Choosing," which Hopper felt was "the best speech of them all." Shortly after the election, Reagan told Hopper he wanted to be governor of California. "I think the road back for the Republican Party begins in California," he added. "After talking to Ronnie, whom I've known for twenty years," Hopper later wrote, "I'm certain he's going to throw his hat in the ring for Governor." She was less optimistic than Reagan about his electoral prospects, however. "I don't think he can be elected. I told him so."[126]

Hopper's political pessimism after the 1964 election fit with her larger sense of loss, as her career declined and Hollywood changed. Politics had been banned from her column. "I'm not permitted to write anything about politics in my column," she wrote a month after Goldwater's loss. "The syndicate tells me they have their own political writers, and I'm not one of them." Liberal politics also were on the rise in Hollywood, with "the powerful surge of younger Hollywood stars into the Democratic camp during the 1960 and 1964 campaigns," and they did not fear a political attack from Hopper.[127] The politics and morality of the new Hollywood emerging in the 1960s alienated Hopper and her fans. "I agree with you that much of the present so-called entertainment has sunk to portraying violence, dope addiction and general moral depravity," a southern California man told Hopper, "and that many of the current entertainers seem to delight in criticizing every established principle of Americanism."[128] Hopper's alienation was already nearly total when she resigned from the Academy of Motion Picture Arts and Sciences in 1961, the year after Simone Signoret won her Oscar. "I believe I am one of the oldest members in the city," she wrote the industry's most prestigious organization, but "I don't like the way it is going. . . . I think the pictures chosen for awards this year show us in the wrong light all over the world. The actresses nominated, for the most part, played the roles of whores. Last year we honored a Commie." Hedda Hopper's criticisms summed up everything she saw as wrong with Hollywood, and her resignation was "regretfully" accepted.[129]

Hedda Hopper on her book tour for *The Whole Truth and Nothing But*, 1963. (Courtesy of the Academy of Motion Picture Arts and Sciences.)

Conclusion

Movies, Politics, and Narratives of Nostalgia

The scene opened onto an ornate, overstuffed bedroom in disarray with Hedda Hopper, in her mid-sixties, hatted and gloved, seated on an unmade bed, speaking rapidly into a white telephone on the nightstand. "Times City Desk? Hedda Hopper speaking. I'm talking from the bedroom of Norma Desmond. Don't bother with a rewrite man, take it direct. Ready? As day breaks over the murder house, Norma Desmond, famed star of yesteryear, is in a state of complete mental shock." The film was director-writer Billy Wilder's "pessimistic and bitter" *Sunset Boulevard* (1950), and the actress played herself, a movie gossip columnist determined to get the scoop on a tragic Hollywood murder.[1] The perpetrator, Norma Desmond, was a former star of film's silent era played by Gloria Swanson, whose acting career also flourished during that era. Cecil B. DeMille and others from film's early days appeared as "themselves." Hopper's appearance in this iconic Hollywood film acknowledged her place and reinforced her prominence in American cinema during its golden age. Yet the filmmakers originally wanted both Hopper and Louella Parsons in the film, enacting their famous rivalry by competing for the telephone to get their stories out first. Parsons, however, turned the role down. According to her biographer Samantha Barbas, "she felt that the part, as a crooning, predatory press gossip, would tarnish her reputation."[2] Hopper had no such qualms. She also had no qualms about quoting criticism of her performance and her politics from a review in the *Daily Worker*. The Communist newspaper minced no words in describing Hopper and DeMille as "two of the most bigoted, Sybaritic, ostentatious and fraudulent reactionaries in all filmdom," a description Hopper wore proudly. In fact, as Sam Staggs notes, "It's hard to think of a movie with more right-wingers on it than *Sunset Boulevard*."[3]

Nominated for Best Picture and winner of two Oscars for art direction and story/screenplay, *Sunset Boulevard* remains the most respected film in which

Hopper ever appeared, and it offered an unflinching view of the decline of old Hollywood that both criticized and invoked nostalgia. Norma Desmond lived in the past. For the character, the past of movie stardom was infinitely superior to the present of obscurity, and her excessive longing to return to her glory days resulted in delusion, dementia, and, ultimately, death for her much younger lover, failed screenwriter Joe Gillis. "The great theme of *Sunset Boulevard*," film scholar Jeffrey Meyers argues, "is the mad attempt to sustain an impossible illusion."[4] While the film's plot effectively presented nostalgia as "false and disabling," its meditation on old Hollywood also sparked nostalgic sentiments among Hopper and her industry colleagues. "At a special showing of 'Sunset Boulevard,' for movie bigwigs," Hopper wrote, "many of them sat there and wept. Each saw in it a bit of his own life." She went on to recall fond memories of Gloria Swanson's "triumphant" past in silent film, a past Hopper shared.[5]

Hopper's own careers as actress and gossip columnist spanned the past and present of *Sunset Boulevard*, and she, too, expressed "bittersweet yearning for the past, the pang of recognition that accompanies the taste of one's own fleeting mortality."[6] Although her gossip career was as its height when the film came out in 1950, she saw and feared Hollywood's and her own decline. In harking back to the silent era of filmmaking, which ended abruptly with the advent of sound, the film commented on the waning of the studio system in the new "age of television." Moreover, in using performers like Hopper, Swanson, and others who were in their acting prime during the silent era, *Sunset Boulevard* showed Hollywood as "an unstable, rapidly changing place, where creative giants may be forgotten within their lifetimes."[7] A scene that perfectly captured this sense of time moving on and people being left behind occurred when Norma Desmond gathered together three old friends to play cards at her dark, decrepit mansion. These were Desmond's "actor friends," the Joe Gillis character, played by William Holden, observes in voice-over, "dim figures you may still remember from the silent days. I used to think of them as her Wax Works." Years later, Hopper visited a Movieland Wax Museum that included Gloria Swanson in an "elaborate setting" from the film. "There I met many old friends I've worked with through the years," Hopper reported without a trace of irony, "all in wax."[8] *Sunset Boulevard* and the nostalgia it evoked spoke to an industry fearful of the future and with its golden age soon to be accessible only through museums and memories.

Linking longing for the past, disappointment in the present, and fear of the unknown future, nostalgia appeared as a theme in Hopper's gossip throughout her career. Out of her memories, she constructed a past that served multiple purposes as she negotiated the worlds of entertainment and politics. Nostalgia for small-town America, where everyone knew and monitored each other's private lives, informed and justified her mass media gossip about public figures. Nostalgia for the era of her early years of acting in Hollywood helped her distinguish herself in the crowded field of celebrity journalism and benefited her gossip career. Nostalgia for the values and principles of an earlier time in the United States fueled her various campaigns for moral and political conservatism, and nostalgia for both the Hollywood and the United States of yesteryear became a way to bond and build her relationship with her audience. Hopper's nostalgic commentaries romanticized the past and disparaged the present. She claimed early Hollywood, like the idealized island communities of her youth but very unlike her remembrances of life in Altoona, Pennsylvania, was a place where "we never mentioned money and we were all struggling to get a *little* toe inside the door of success. It seems to me we were working for the common good, with a community-family spirit. It was one for all and all for one, instead of every man for himself."[9]

Through her constant references to an imagined, older world, Hopper constructed and repeated a narrative that presented the history of the twentieth-century United States as one of decline, due to the triumph of liberalism in politics and morality, and her readers responded. She generally positioned herself as an opponent in her campaigns, against individual people, social movements, government policies, and cultural change. Patsy Gaile remembered Hopper's office staff asking her every morning, "Who are we fighting today? What's the battle?" "And there would be a crusade," Gaile stated. "About anything—all kinds of things." Hopper would have agreed with the editors of the conservative *National Review* in the 1950s, when they asserted the magazine "stands athwart history yelling Stop."[10] In addition to opposition, repetition was key to understanding Hopper's influence and impact. Just as the repetition of messages across many films can shape the worldview of spectators, every day for twenty-eight years Hopper presented her readers with her "declensionist" view of the world.[11] Many of the extant letters to Hopper indicated a similar nostalgic sense of loss and decline among her mostly female respondents, which they expressed through their participation in Hollywood gossip. Jackie Stacey found in her ethnographic study of female film spectatorship that such a sense was "an important motivator for respondents to express their opinions about historical change in the cinema."[12] Nostalgia, like Hollywood gossip, operates on personal and collective levels and in domains categorized as private and public. When Hopper and her readers linked memories of personal experiences and private emotions to collective events and public symbols, they expressed a powerful set of ideas about past, present, and future.

The nostalgic narrative of "Hedda Hopper's Hollywood" simultaneously criticized, and called for a conservative reaction to, changes in Hollywood and the United States. Attention to the content of Hopper's columns and her readers' letters provides a sense of the "complex appeal and circulation of right-wing ideologies" in mid-twentieth-century America.[13] Hollywood gossip may appear to be an unlikely arena for the circulation of political ideas and values, and certainly Jürgen Habermas expressed pessimism about the fate of the public sphere in the twentieth-century age of mass media. But, as practiced by Hopper and her respondents, mass media Hollywood gossip became such an arena and intersected with the larger public sphere. Their nostalgia also contributed to the public sphere functions fulfilled by her column. Shared popular memory is part of what constitutes a public, and Hopper's reader-respondents produced and consumed nostalgia along with her gossip. As a consequence, during the crucial decades for the development of the grassroots conservative movement that would come to be called the New Right, Hopper's column provided continuity with the Old Right and an outlet for conservative ideas with a popular culture audience of millions. She modeled the divisive style of political rhetoric characteristic of today's Right and, most powerfully, advanced "the multiple and varied dimensions of conservatism's general assault on the public/private divide" that so fundamentally shapes our contemporary political culture.[14] Although Hopper's nostalgic narrative with its pessimistic tone would not win the support of a majority of Americans, in 1980 Ronald Reagan took what he shared with her—Hollywood celebrity, a location in southern California, conservative ideology, and a similar nostalgic narrative—but added a resonant tone of hope, and he took the White House. Hopper, of course, did not live to see the "Reagan Revolution."

In February 1966, at age eighty, Hopper died quite suddenly of complications arising from pneumonia. She had been in declining health, as well as mood, for several years before her death. "I think you will be delighted to hear that I don't discuss politics, no longer lose my temper, and I don't fight with people," she wrote one of her editors in 1964. "I must be nearing the end." Even her joy in her hats seemed to fade. "If you wear a crazy hat," she pointed out, "no one notices the tired old face beneath it." She sought to make amends with her alienated family members, including her son, Bill Hopper, who felt "sorry we didn't get closer sooner. I think I could have got her not to be so sweeping" in her judgments. "God damn it, honey," he remembered telling her, "people's politics and sex lives are their own." Recalling the many personal and professional feuds over her lifetime, Hopper sadly admitted, "There are times when I hate myself."[15] Before Hopper died, Louella Parsons had relinquished her column and retired to a rest home, so within the span of a few months the two "gargoyles of gossip" were gone from the Hollywood scene. In a tribute to Hopper, Molly Merrick noted that the columnist enjoyed going to parties but never was the last guest to leave. "Don't be swept out," was Hopper's maxim. "Go before the glow fades." "She lived up to it," Merrick concluded. "I'm sure if she had a choice in the matter," gossip columnist Pamela Mason wrote, "she would have chosen to go that way, fast and furious, like she lived."[16]

Hopper never titled her memoirs "Malice in Wonderland" as she had promised early in her gossip career, but it fit. As it turned out, a television movie would be made with that name in 1985, starring Elizabeth Taylor as Parsons and Jane Alexander as Hopper. Casting as Hopper the future director of—and defender against right-wing attacks on—the National Endowment for the Arts during the Democratic administration of President Bill Clinton in the 1990s was a historical irony and gap between "reel" and "real" lives the columnist would not have appreciated. Still, the movie portrayed her kindly. Not so her obituaries, most of which commented on her cruel and nasty reputation. "Mrs. Hopper," one stated, "didn't smile when she lacerated her enemies. They were many, since she opposed those who indulged in liberal politics [and] those who transgressed the moral code." But a person without enemies is a person "without character," Charles Champlin of the *Los Angeles Times* observed after her death. "And Hedda had character."[17] If character can be equated with consistency, without a doubt Hopper remained consistent in her moral and political values and held onto her hatreds and enemies throughout her life. In fact, two days before Hopper entered the hospital where she soon would die, she spoke to Florabel Muir, her colleague and collaborator in the Joan Barry–Charlie Chaplin scandal from two decades earlier. "I hear that son of a bitch Chaplin is trying to get back in this country," she was reported as saying. "We've all got to work together to stop him!"[18]

Notes

INTRODUCTION

1. Hopper quoted in Francis Sill Wickware, "Hedda Hopper: She Became a Leading Hollywood Columnist by Telling What She Knew about Her Movie Friends," *Life*, 11/20/44, 63; David Niven, *Bring on the Empty Horses* (New York: G. P. Putnam's Sons, 1975), 71; George Eells, *Hedda and Louella* (New York: G. P. Putnam's Sons, 1972), 23; Geri Nicholas, quoted in Donald Bogle, *Dorothy Dandridge: A Biography* (New York: Amistad, 1997), 245; "Women We Love: The 1940s," *Esquire* (August 1993), Hedda Hopper Clippings File (hereafter HH Clippings), Margaret Herrick Library, Academy of Motion Pictures Arts and Sciences, Beverly Hills, California (hereafter Herrick Library).

2. Hopper quoted in Eells, *Hedda and Louella*, 209.

3. Eells, *Hedda and Louella*, 210.

4. Ibid., 16; Arthur Miller, *Timebends: A Life* (New York: Grove Press, 1987), 439–440.

5. Correspondence from readers to Hopper is in the Hedda Hopper papers, Herrick Library (hereafter HHP). Although these letters are public and not private letters, given Hopper's practice of publishing readers' letters in her column, I am protecting the privacy of these letter writers by using no names in the text and using only initials in citations. For well-known persons, I use their full names in citations and text.

6. Jackie Stacey discusses the difficulties of uncovering "real cinema spectators" from the past, what she calls "the lost audience." Stacey, *Star Gazing: Hollywood Cinema and Female Spectatorship* (New York: Routledge, 1994), 49–79.

7. As David A. Gerber points out, due to such limitations, it is impossible to render "a precise determination about the representativeness of any particular letter or letter-series." Gerber, "Acts of Deceiving and Withholding in Immigrant Letters: Personal Identity and Self-Presentation in Personal Correspondence," *Journal of Social History* 39 (Winter 2005), 316.

8. Eells, *Hedda and Louella*; Neal Gabler, *Winchell: Gossip, Power, and the Culture of Celebrity* (New York: Knopf, 1994); Samantha Barbas, *The First Lady of Hollywood: A Biography of Louella Parsons* (Berkeley and Los Angeles: University of California Press, 2005); Kathleen A. Feeley, "Louella Parsons and Hedda Hopper's Hollywood: The Rise of the Celebrity Gossip Industry in Twentieth-Century America, 1910–1950," Ph.D. diss., City University of New York, 2004.

9. Quotes from Alice Kessler-Harris, "Why Biography?" *American Historical Review* 114 (June 2009), 626. See also Jill Lepore, "Historians Who Love Too Much: Reflections on Microhistory and Biography," *Journal of American History* 88 (June 2001), 129–144.

10. Robin Dunbar, *Grooming, Gossip, and the Evolution of Language* (Cambridge, Mass.: Harvard University Press, 1996), 79.

11. Nicholas Emler, "Gossip, Reputation, and Social Adaptation," in Robert F. Goodman and Aaron Ben-Ze'ev, eds., *Good Gossip* (Lawrence: University Press of Kansas, 1994), 117–118.

12. Gabler, *Winchell*, 256.

13. James C. Scott, *Weapons of the Weak: Everyday Forms of Peasant Resistance* (New Haven, Conn.: Yale University Press, 1985).

14. Hiroshi Kitamura, "Hollywood's America, America's Hollywood," *American Quarterly* 58 (December 2006), 1263.

15. A Gallup poll later proved this assumption wrong. Thomas Doherty, *Projections of War: Hollywood, American Culture, and World War II* (New York: Columbia University Press, 1993), 150.

16. Linda Williams, ed., *Viewing Positions: Ways of Seeing Film* (New Brunswick, N.J.: Rutgers University Press, 1995); Judith Mayne, *Cinema and Spectatorship* (New York: Routledge, 1993); Gaylyn Studlar, "The Perils of Pleasure? Fan Magazine Discourse as Women's Commodified Culture in the 1920s," *Wide Angle* 13 (January 1991), 6–33.

17. This key insight appears in the foundational texts of star studies, including Edgar Morin, *Les Stars* (Paris: Seuil, 1957); Richard Dyer, *Stars* (London: British Film Institute, 1979); Dyer, *Heavenly Bodies: Film Stars and Society* (New York: St. Martin's Press, 1986); and Richard de Cordova, *Picture Personalities: The Emergence of the Star System in America* (Urbana: University of Illinois Press, 1990).

18. Charles L. Ponce de Leon, *Self-Exposure: Human-Interest Journalism and the Emergence of Celebrity in America, 1890–1940* (Chapel Hill: University of North Carolina Press, 2002), 43.

19. Ibid., 41, 45.

20. Jean Marie Lutes, "Into the Madhouse with Nellie Bly: Girl Stunt Reporting in Late Nineteenth-Century America," *American Quarterly* 54 (June 2002), 219.

21. Ponce de Leon, *Self-Exposure*, 204.

22. For two essential studies, see Lisa McGirr, *Suburban Warriors: The Origins of the New American Right* (Princeton, N.J.: Princeton University Press, 2001); and Donald T. Critchlow, *Phyllis Schlafly and Grassroots Conservatism: A Woman's Crusade* (Princeton, N.J.: Princeton University Press, 2005).

23. Eells, *Hedda and Louella*, 16.

24. Michelle Nickerson, "Women, Domesticity, and Postwar Conservatism," *OAH Magazine of History* 17 (January 2003), 18.

25. Donald T. Critchlow, "Conservatism Reconsidered: Phyllis Schlafly and Grassroots Conservatism," in David Farber and Jeff Roche, eds., *The Conservative Sixties* (New York: Peter Lang, 2003), 109.

26. McGirr, *Suburban Warriors*, 167–168.

27. Nancy Fraser, "Rethinking the Public Sphere: A Contribution to the Critique of Actually Existing Democracy" in Simon During, ed., *The Cultural Studies Reader* (London: Routledge, 1993), 519.

28. Jürgen Habermas, "The Public Sphere," in Steven Seidman, ed., *Jürgen Habermas on Society and Politics: A Reader* (Boston: Beacon Press, 1989), 231–236; Miriam Hansen, *Babel and Babylon: Spectatorship in American Silent Film* (Cambridge, Mass.: Harvard University Press, 1991).

29. Justine Coupland, ed., *Small Talk* (Harlow, UK: Pearson Education, 2000), xix.

30. Michael Warner, *The Letters of the Republic: Publication and the Public Sphere in Eighteenth-Century America* (Cambridge, Mass.: Harvard University Press, 1990), x–xi.

31. McGirr, *Suburban Warriors*, 163.

32. Robert H. Wiebe, *Search for Order, 1877–1920* (London: Macmillan, 1967).

33. Margaret Furry Mitchell quoted in Eells, *Hedda and Louella*, 58; Hedda Hopper, *From Under My Hat* (Garden City, N.Y.: Doubleday, 1952); Hedda Hopper with James Brough, *The Whole Truth and Nothing But* (Garden City, N.Y.: Doubleday, 1963).

34. Carolyn G. Heilbrun, *Writing a Woman's Life* (New York: Norton, 1988).

35. Ponce de Leon, *Self-Exposure*, 113.

36. Hopper quoted in Alice L. Tildesley, "Men Are Afraid Women Will Get Ahead of Them," *Sunday Morning Public Ledger*, 7/22/26, HH Clippings; L. D. Hotchkiss speech for Woman of the Year for 1955 event, Woman of the Year folder, HHP; Hopper, *From Under My Hat*, 9.

37. Hopper, *From Under My Hat*, 29, 31; Hopper quoted in Eells, *Hedda and Louella*, 57.

38. Hopper, *The Whole Truth*, 7–8; Hopper, *From Under My Hat*, 21.

39. Hopper quoted in Tildesley, "Men Are Afraid"; Hopper, *From Under My Hat*, 9.

40. Heilbrun, *Writing a Woman's Life*, 23–24; Ponce de Leon, *Self-Exposure*, 115.

41. Hopper, *From Under My Hat*, 35–36; Frances Marion quoted and Charles Brackett paraphrased in Eells, *Hedda and Louella*, 76, 62.

42. Warren I. Susman, "Personality and the Making of Twentieth-Century Culture," in *Culture as History* (New York: Pantheon, 1984), 271–284.

43. Hopper, *From Under My Hat*, 35–36; Hopper quoted in Tildesley, "Men Are Afraid."

44. Heilbrun, *Writing a Woman's Life*, 22, 25; Ponce de Leon, *Self-Exposure*, 129.

45. Eells, *Hedda and Louella*, 63–64, 68; Hopper quoted in Tildesley, "Men Are Afraid."

46. Hopper, *The Whole Truth*, 7; Hopper quoted in Tildesley, "Men Are Afraid."

47. "De Wolf Hopper's Fifth Wife Seeks Divorce; Suit to Begin Today; No Contest Expected," *New York Times*, 7/21/22, 1; "De Wolf Hopper Is Divorced by Fifth Wife; She Gets Son and 30 Per Cent. of His Salary," *New York Times*, 1/30/24, 1; Hopper quoted in Tildesley, "Men Are Afraid."

48. Heilbrun, *Writing a Woman's Life*, 24.

49. Hopper, *From Under My Hat*, 63, 82; Jean V. Matthews, *The Rise of the New Woman: The Women's Movement in America, 1875–1930* (Chicago: Ivan R. Dee, 2003).

50. Kevin Brownlow, *The Parade's Gone By . . .* (New York: Knopf, 1968), 28; Hopper quoted in Eells, *Hedda and Louella*, 79.

51. Hopper, *From Under My Hat*, 115; Hopper quoted in Tildesley, "Men Are Afraid."

52. Ponce de Leon, *Self-Exposure*, 111–113.

53. Eells, *Hedda and Louella*, 20.

54. Hopper, *From Under My Hat*, 105; Jenna Weissman Joselit, *A Perfect Fit: Clothes, Character, and the Promise of America* (New York: Henry Holt, 2001), 44; Sarah Barry, *Screen Style: Fashion and Femininity in 1930s Hollywood* (Minneapolis: University of Minnesota Press, 2000), xviii.

55. Eells, *Hedda and Louella*, 24; Jeanine Basinger, *The Star Machine* (New York: Knopf, 2007), 91, 74.

56. Steven J. Ross, *Working-Class Hollywood: Silent Film and the Shaping of Class in America* (Princeton, N.J.: Princeton University Press, 1998), 198–199.

57. Hopper, *From Under My Hat*, 250.

58. Malcolm H. Oettinger, "Occasionally You Find a Lady," fan magazine clipping, c. 1920s, and untitled newsclipping, [11/18/27], HH Clippings; Hopper, *From Under My Hat*, 229.

59. Hopper quoted in Eells, *Hedda and Louella*, 79; Hopper, *From Under My Hat*, 229.

60. Michael Paul Rogin, *Ronald Reagan, the Movie, and Other Episodes in Political Demonology* (Berkeley and Los Angeles: University of California Press, 1987), 3, 7.

61. Hopper, *From Under My Hat*, 47; Ponce de Leon, *Self-Exposure*, 113.

62. David M. Wrobel, "Paradise Pondered: Urban California, 1850–2000," *Journal of Urban History* 34 (September 2008), 1033–1034.

63. McWilliams quoted in Kurt Schuparra, *Triumph of the Right: The Rise of the California Conservative Movement, 1945–1966* (Armonk, N.Y.: M. E. Sharpe, 1998), xxi.

64. Kevin Starr, *Material Dreams: Southern California through the 1920s* (Oxford: Oxford University Press, 1990), 98.

65. Hopper quoted in Wickware, "Hedda Hopper," 66. Hopper made the same point but worded differently in *From Under My Hat*, 230–231.

66. Eells, *Hedda and Louella*, 130, 133; Hedda Hopper, from Press Book on "Alice Adams" (1935), HH Clippings; Tino Balio, *Grand Design: Hollywood as a Modern Business Enterprise, 1930–1939*, vol. 5, *History of the American Cinema*, ed. Charles Harpole (Berkeley and Los Angeles: University of California Press, 1993), 250; Molly Haskell, *From Reverence to Rape: The Treatment of Women in the Movies*, 2nd ed. (Chicago: University of Chicago Press, 1987), 127.

67. Hopper, *The Whole Truth*, 63; Starr, *Material Dreams*, 70; Cari Beauchamp, *Without Lying Down: Frances Marion and the Powerful Women of Early Hollywood* (New York: Scribner, 1997), 253, 293.

68. Ponce de Leon, *Self-Exposure*, 111; Hopper, *From Under My Hat*, 265.

69. David Niven, *Bring on the Empty Horses* (New York: G. P. Putnam's Sons, 1975), 70.

70. Publicist quoted in "Hedda Hopper Dies in Hollywood," *San Francisco Chronicle*, n.d., HH Clippings; Eells, *Hedda and Louella*, 170.

71. Howard Greer, "Dear, Dead Days," excerpt from *Designing Male* (1952), reprinted in Christopher Silvester, *The Penguin Book of Hollywood* (London: Viking, 1998), 62.

72. Hopper, *From Under My Hat*, 24.

73. Eells, *Hedda and Louella*, 105–106, 102; Hopper quoted in Amy Fine Collins, "Idol Gossips," *Vanity Fair* (April 1997), 360; Gladys Hall quoted in Barbas, *First Lady of Hollywood*, 204.

74. Barbas, *First Lady of Hollywood*, 197, 207; Eells, *Hedda and Louella*, 98.

75. Eells, *Hedda and Louella*, 130.

76. Parsons quoted in Eells, *Hedda and Louella*, 134; Hopper quoted in Myra Nye, "Hoover-Curtis Clubs Formed," *Los Angeles Times* (hereafter *LAT*), 10/16/32, B18; Alma Whitaker, "Sugar and Spice," *LAT*, 9/11/32, B11; Joan Hoff Wilson, *Herbert Hoover: Forgotten Progressive* (Boston: Little, Brown, 1975), 6.

77. Eells, *Hedda and Louella*, 104–105; Beauchamp, *Without Lying Down*, 232, 294.

1. Hedda Hopper, "James Roosevelt Silent on Rumors of Separation," *LAT*, 10/22/39, 1, 10.

2. "Jimmy Gets It," *Time*, 11/6/39, 47–48; Hopper, *From Under My Hat*, 275–276.

3. Collie Small, "Gossip Is Her Business," *Saturday Evening Post*, 1/11/47, 54.

4. Ronald Brownstein, *The Power and the Glitter: The Hollywood-Washington Connection* (New York: Pantheon, 1990), 3; Hopper, "James Roosevelt Silent on Rumors of Separation," 1.

5. Ponce de Leon, *Self-Exposure*, 78–79.

6. Eells, *Hedda and Louella*, 198, 202; "Hedda Makes Hay" *Time*, 5/25/42, 51–52; Barbas, *First Lady of Hollywood*, 235–236.

7. Small, "Gossip Is Her Business," 14; "The Gossipist," *Time*, 7/28/47, 60.

8. Niven, *Bring on the Empty Horses*, 68.

9. Wickware, "Hedda Hopper," 63; Eells, *Hedda and Louella*, 12.

10. On Parsons, see Barbas, *First Lady of Hollywood*, 239, 19–21; insider quoted in Eells, *Hedda and Louella*, 171; Parsons quoted in Dickson Hartwell, "End of a Beautiful Feud," *Collier's*, 6/5/48, 23.

11. Wickware, "Hedda Hopper," 62.

12. Barbas, *First Lady of Hollywood*, 237; Hopper quoted in "Hollywood's Press: Why the Stars Are in Your Eyes," *Newsweek*, 2/22/54, 63. See also Feeley, "Louella Parsons and Hedda Hopper's Hollywood," chap. 3.

13. Parsons and Hopper quoted in Hartwell, "End of a Beautiful Feud," 23; Editors of Time-Life Books, *100 Years of Hollywood* (Alexandria, Va.: Time-Life Books, 1999), 168.

14. Observer quoted in Eells, *Hedda and Louella*, 211, emphasis added; Hedda Hopper, "Hedda Hopper's Hollywood," *LAT* (hereafter HH column, *LAT*), 3/22/48, 14.

15. Hopper quoted in Eells, *Hedda and Louella*, 246.

16. Rochelle Gurstein, *The Repeal of Reticence: A History of America's Cultural and Legal Struggles over Free Speech, Obscenity, Sexual Liberation, and Modern Art* (New York: Hill and Wang, 1996), 7, 148, 163.

17. Gabler, *Winchell*, 134.

18. Hopper quoted in Eells, *Hedda and Louella*, 69; James Quirk, *Photoplay* editor, in "Moral House-Cleaning in Hollywood: An Open Letter to Mr. Will Hayes," *Photoplay* (April 1922), 52.

19. HH column, *LAT*, 3/19/52, C8.

20. Paul Apostolidis and Juliet A. Williams, "Introduction: Sex Scandals and Discourses of Power," in Apostolidis and Williams, eds., *Public Affairs: Politics in the Age of Sex Scandals* (Durham, N.C.: Duke University Press 2004), 3; James Lull and Stephen Hinerman quoted in Janet Staiger, *Media Reception Studies* (New York: New York University Press, 2005), 122.

21. "Hedda Urges Fact Diet on Film Folk," *LAT*, 9/8/46, HH Clippings.

22. Wickware, "Hedda Hopper," 63.

23. "Hedda Hopper, Columnist Dies," *New York Times*, 2/2/66, 32.

24. Eells, *Hedda and Louella*, 264; Chrys Haranis, "Photoplay's Tribute to Hedda Hopper," *Photoplay* (May 1966), 32.

25. Hedda Hoper (hereafter HH) on *Small World* telecast, Edward R. Murrow, moderator and coproducer with Fred W. Friendly, CBS, 12/6/59, Museum of Radio and Television, Beverly Hills (hereafter *Small World* telecast, 12/6/59).

26. Small, "Gossip Is Her Business," 54; Agnes DeMille quoted in Stuart Oderman, *Lillian Gish: A Life on Stage and Screen* (Jefferson, N.C.: McFarland, 2000), 213; "Women of the Year, 1955," *LAT*, 12/18/55, AA; Edwin Emery and Michael Emery, *The Press and America: An Interpretive History of the Mass Media*, 5th ed. (Englewood Cliffs, N.J.: Prentice Hall, 1984), 342.

27. Lutes, "Into the Madhouse with Nellie Bly," 219.

28. Eells, *Hedda and Louella*, 198; Jean Marie Lutes, *Front-Page Girls: Women Journalists in American Culture and Fiction, 1880–1930* (Ithaca, N.Y.: Cornell University Press, 2006), 3; HH column, *LAT*, 8/7/62, C8.

29. "The Gossipist," *Time*, 7/28/47, 60.

30. Ponce de Leon, *Self-Exposure*, 60; Mildren Howe, "Failure to Keep Things under Her Hat Places Hedda Ahead for Keeps," *LAT*, 8/31/52, D4.

31. HH column, *LAT*, 6/22/50, B6, 4/12/51, B10, and 7/26/58, B2.

32. Eells, *Hedda and Louella*, 171; HH column, *LAT*, 2/14/38, 9; Hopper, *From Under My Hat*, 275; "The Gossipist," *Time*, 7/28/47, 61.

33. Richard Griffiths and Arthur Mayer, *The Movies* (London: Spring Books, 1957), 360.

34. Florabel Muir, "Hedda Hopper Defied Ridicule to Stay in Films and Keep Son," *Sunday News* (c. 1940), HH Clippings; Hopper, *From Under My Hat*, 275; Hopper quoted in Eells, *Hedda and Louella*, 173.

35. Small, "Gossip Is Her Business," 58.

36. Gabler, *Winchell*, 139; Hedda Hopper, "The Hats in My Life," *The Woman* (February 1946), 34–37, Hats folder, HHP (hereafter Hats folder).

37. Joselit, *A Perfect Fit*, 102, 111; Wickware, "Hedda Hopper," 64.

38. Robert Molyneux, "Hollywood's Hopper: Like Dempsey, She Wowed the Press Staff," *Pittsburgh Press*, 11/2/47, 20–21; HH to Don Marshall, NYC, 11/20/64, Hats folder.

39. Barbara Klinger, *Melodrama and Meaning: History, Culture, and the Films of Douglas Sirk* (Bloomington: Indiana University Press, 1994), 57–58.

40. "The Gossipist," *Time*, 7/28/47, 64; Haranis, "Photoplay's Tribute to Hedda Hopper"; HH to Maryland McCormick, 12/10/52, Robert McCormick (*Chicago Tribune*) folder, HHP (hereafter McCormick folder).

41. "People," *Time*, 4/2/56, 44, Hats folder.

42. Jack Withers, General Chairman, Air Force Association, to HH, 3/28/63, Armed Forces folder, HHP; "De Mille Lauds Book for Its Zest, Honesty, and Unfailing Humor," *LAT*, 9/7/52, 12.

43. "Hedda Hopper, Columnist Dies," *New York Times*, 2/2/66, 32; Debbie Reynolds, with David Patrick Columbia, *My Life* (New York: William Morrow, 1988), 79–80.

44. "Hollywood: The Scold and the Sphinx," *Time*, 2/11/66, 52; Wickware, "Hedda Hopper," 64; Bob Thomas, AP Movie–Television Writer, untitled clipping, 2/4/66, HH Clippings; Hopper, *From Under My Hat*, 140; various newspaper articles in HH Clippings.

45. "The Gossipist," *Time*, 7/28/47, 64; Small, "Gossip Is Her Business," 15; Molly Merrick quoted in Eells, *Hedda and Louella*, 254; "Louella's Rival," *Time*, 12/16/40, 66.

46. "Hedda Makes Hay," *Time*, 5/25/42, 52; Wickware, "Hedda Hopper," 63.

47. "Billy Rowe's Notebook," *Pittsburgh Courier*, 1/9/43, 20; Michele Hilmes, *Hollywood and Broadcasting: From Radio to Cable* (Urbana: University of Illinois Press, 1990), 63.

48. HH column, *LAT*, 9/15/41, A16; HH to Francis Sill Wickware, 6/16/44, *Life* magazine and *Time* magazine folder, HHP (hereafter Life-Time folder).

49. Eells, *Hedda and Louella*, 168.

50. Balio, *Grand Design*, 250.

51. Small, "Gossip Is Her Business," 58; Eells, *Hedda and Louella*, 168.

52. Ponce de Leon, *Self-Exposure*, 82; Daniel J. Boorstin, *The Image: A Guide to Pseudo-Events in America*, rev. ed. (New York: Atheneum, 1978).

53. Eells, *Hedda and Louella*, 199; "Modern Screen Goes to a Christening," *Modern Screen* (August 1947), 32; Jean Austin, "Hedda Hopper, Collector of Bristol," *American Home* (March 1957), 50.

54. Henrique Moreno, Rio de Janeiro, Brazil, to HH, 9/5/47, Louella Parsons folder, HHP.

55. Syndicate advertisement for Women's Features, Chicago Tribune–New York News Syndicate, 1962 folder, HHP (hereafter Syndicate 1962 folder); *Buffalo Courier Express* advertisement, *New York Times*, 8/14/50, 35.

56. E. J. Strong to HH, 4/20/51, *Los Angeles Times* folder, HHP.

57. Spec McClure quoted in Eells, *Hedda and Louella*, 203; Joshua Gamson, *Claims to Fame: Celebrity in Contemporary America* (Berkeley and Los Angeles: University of California Press, 1994), 63–64.

58. "The Gossipist," *Time*, 7/28/47, 60; Charles Champlin, "Hedda Hopper and Louella Parsons: Private Lives of Hollywood's Powerful Columnists," *Architectural Digest* 47 (April 1990), 114.

59. Klinger, *Melodrama and Meaning*, 118; Christine Geraghty, "Re-examining Stardom: Questions of Texts, Bodies, and Performance," in Christine Gledhill and Linda Williams, eds., *Reinventing Film Studies* (London: Arnold, 2000), 195.

60. Thomas Schatz, *Boom and Bust: American Cinema in the 1940s*, vol. 6, *History of the American Cinema*, ed. Charles Harpole (Berkeley and Los Angeles: University of California Press, 1997), 11; Stephen Powers, David J. Rothman, and Stanley Rothman, *Hollywood's America: Social and Political Themes in Motion Pictures* (New York: Westview Press, 1996), 14–15.

61. Catherine Jurca, "What the Public Wanted: Hollywood, 1937–1942," *Cinema Journal* 47 (Winter 2008), 5–6.

62. HH column, *LAT*, 5/9/38, 10; Niven, *Bring on the Empty Horses*, 67; Bob Hope quoted in Richard Lemon, "The Warrior Queens of Gossip," *People*, 5/13/85, 133.

63. Jaik Rosenstein, *Hollywood Leg Man* (Los Angeles: Madison Press, 1950), 76; Niven, *Bring on the Empty Horses*, 68.

64. Hopper quoted in "Hollywood's Press: Why the Stars Are in Your Eyes," *Newsweek*, 2/22/54, 64.

65. Eells, *Hedda and Louella*, 202–203; "Hedda Hopper, Columnist Dies," *New York Times*, 2/2/66, 32.

66. Barbas, *First Lady of Hollywood*, 114; HH to Francis Sill Wickware, 6/16/44, Life-Time folder.

67. George Hurrell quoted in "Hedda Hopper," *The Hurrell Style: 50 Years of Photographing Hollywood*, photos by George Hurrell and text by Whitney Stone (New York: John Day, 1976); HH to Louis B. Mayer, 3/28/40, Louis B. Mayer folder, HHP (hereafter Mayer folder).

68. Niven, *Bring on the Empty Horses*, 68; Susan Hayward quoted in Kim R. Holston, *Susan Hayward: Her Films and Life* (Jefferson, N.C.: McFarland, 2002), 64.

69. Hopper quoted in "The Gossipist," *Time*, 7/28/47, 60.

70. Simone Signoret, *Nostalgia Isn't What It Used to Be* (New York: Harper and Row, 1978), 280; "Hopping Around Hollywood with Hedda Hopper," *Look*, 9/10/40, HH Clippings.

71. Hopper paraphrased in Laurence Leamer, *As Time Goes By: The Life of Ingrid Bergman* (New York: Harper and Row, 1986), 190.

72. Scott Siegel and Barbara Siegel, "Gossip Columnists," *The Encyclopedia of Hollywood* (Enfield: Guinness, 1990), 177; Sheilah Graham, *My Hollywood: A Celebration and a Lament* (London: Michael Joseph, 1984), 63.

73. Eells, *Hedda and Louella*, 175; Marion Davies, edited by Pamela Pfau and Kenneth S. Marx, *The Times We Had: Life with William Randolph Hearst* (Indianapolis: Bobbs-Merrill, 1975), 246; Champlin, "Hedda Hopper and Louella Parsons," 122–126.

74. Hopper and Gypsy Rose Lee quoted in Eells, *Hedda and Louella*, 22, 260.

75. Eells, *Hedda and Louella*, 204; HH column, *LAT*, 2/16/50, B10.

76. Dore Schary to Ivan Spear, 2/3/48, Dore Schary to Paul Gregory, 8/26/58, and Dore Schary to Hedda Hopper, 10/24/47, folder 12 "Hedda Hopper," box 99, Dore Schary Papers, 1920–1980, State Historical Society of Wisconsin, Madison, Wisconsin (hereafter Schary Papers).

77. On the "agenda-setting" function of movie reviews, which I am adapting to Hollywood gossip, see Robert C. Allen and Douglas Gomery, *Film History: Theory and Practice* (New York: Knopf, 1985), 90; Basinger, *Star Machine*, 55.

78. David Selznick to HH, 10/2/39, David Selznick folder, HHP; Geraghty, "Re-examining Stardom," 191–196.

79. Eells, *Hedda and Louella*, 259; Hattie McDaniel to HH, 1/9/40, Hattie McDaniel folder, HHP (hereafter McDaniel folder); Joan Crawford quoted in John Kobal, *People Will Talk* (New York: Knopf, 1985), 286.

80. Geraghty, "Re-examining Stardom," 189–191. I am expanding this category of Geraghty's to encompass stars as workers.

81. Danae Clark, *Negotiating Hollywood: The Cultural Politics of Actors' Labor* (Minneapolis: University of Minnesota Press, 1995), 25, 75; Hopper quoted in Raymond Strait, *James Garner* (New York: St. Martin's Press, 1985), 66.

82. Ponce de Leon, *Self-Exposure*, 113; HH column, *LAT*, 11/25/54, C10.

83. HH column, *LAT*, 5/17/42, C3, and 12/14/47, H3.

84. Ponce de Leon, *Self-Exposure*, 107.

85. HH column, *LAT*, 3/22/42, C3, 10/4/41, A9, and 5/10/42, C3; Hopper quoted in Stefan Kanfer, *Ball of Fire: The Tumultuous Life and Comic Art of Lucille Ball* (New York: Knopf, 2003), 103.

86. Carrie Fisher quoted in David Ehrenstein, *Open Secret: Gay Hollywood, 1928–1998* (New York: William Morrow, 1998), 124; Sam Kashner and Jennifer MacNair, *The Bad and the Beautiful: Hollywood in the Fifties* (New York: Norton, 2002), 150.

87. Garry Wills, *Reagan's America*, pbk. ed. (New York: Penguin, 1988), 189; Hopper quoted in Eells, *Hedda and Louella*, 15.

88. HH column, *LAT*, 5/19/53, B6; Donald Bogle, *Dorothy Dandridge: A Biography* (New York: Amistad, 1997), 245; Wickware, "Hedda Hopper," 70.

89. Basinger, *Star Machine*, xiii, 11, 72, 91.

90. Reagan quoted in HH column, *LAT*, 12/5/47, 2; Bergman quoted in HH column, *LAT*, 2/29/48, D1; Joan Crawford quoted in Kobal, *People Will Talk*, 287.

91. HH column, *LAT*, 2/27/40, 12.

92. Gamson, *Claims to Fame*, 41; Barry, *Screen Style*, 186; Dyer, *Stars*, 38.

93. HH to Francis Sill Wickware, 6/16/44, Life-Time folder.

94. Richard Clarke to HH, 6/27/64, Chicago Tribune–New York News Syndicate, 1964 folder, HHP (hereafter Syndicate 1964 folder); "N.Y. Daily News Exec Editor Reveals Hedda Hopper Frequently 'Warned,'" *Variety*, 11/18/53, HH Clippings.

95. HH column, *LAT*, 12/26/44, 9, and 1/19/53, B8.

96. Lary May, *The Big Tomorrow: Hollywood and the Politics of the American Way* (Chicago: University of Chicago Press, 2000), 180; Peter Bart, "Liberals vs. Their Movies," *New York Times*, 8/29/65, X9.

97. HH, *Small World* telecast, 12/6/59.

98. Thomas B. Rosenstiel, "Talk-Show Journalism," in Philip S. Cook, Douglas Gomery, and Lawrence W. Lichty, eds., *The Future of News: Television, Newspapers, Wire Services, Newsmagazines* (Baltimore: Johns Hopkins University Press, 1992), 74.

99. Ralph Daigh, Fawcett Publications, to HH, n.d., *Motion Picture Magazine* folder, HHP; Powers, Rothman, and Rothman, *Hollywood's America*, 18; Brownstein, *The Power and the Glitter*, 177.

100. Robert Gottlieb, Mark Valliantos, Regina M. Freer, and Peter Dreier, *The Next Los Angeles: The Struggle for a Livable City* (Berkeley and Los Angeles: University of California Press, 2005), 11, 16; McGirr, *Suburban Warriors*, 273; Emery and Emery, *The Press and America*, 430.

101. Hedda Hopper to Richard Clarke, 7/19/60, Chicago Tribune–New York News Syndicate, 1960 folder, HHP (hereafter Syndicate 1960 folder).

102. Barbas, *First Lady of Hollywood*, 271; Eells, *Hedda and Louella*, 242; Gabler, *Winchell*, xiii, 193.

103. Hopper, "Republican Women Speak Up," 6, Motorcade for Ike folder, HHP.

104. Schatz, *Boom and Bust*, 13–14, 20; HH column, *LAT*, 4/13/40, 14.

105. Julian E. Zelizer, "The Uneasy Relationship: Democracy, Taxation, and State Building since the New Deal," in Meg Jacobs, William J. Novak, and Julian E. Zelizer, eds., *The Democratic Experiment: New Directions in American Political History* (Princeton, N.J.: Princeton University Press, 2001), 276.

106. Eells, *Hedda and Louella*, 253; Hopper, *From Under My Hat*, 32.

107. HH column, 2/15/40, collected in "Scrapbook #4—1940 Daily and Sunday Columns," HHP; HH column, *LAT*, 6/23/39, A10, 5/19/40, C3, and 1/1/43, A11.

108. Neal Gabler, *An Empire of Their Own: How the Jews Invented Hollywood* (New York: Crown, 1988), 352–353.

109. HH column, *LAT*, 2/22/40, 12.

110. Schatz, *Boom and Bust*, 34.

111. HH column, *LAT*, 11/24/40, C3.

112. Lary May, "Movie Star Politics: The Screen Actors' Guild, Cultural Conversion, and the Hollywood Red Scare," in May, ed., *Recasting America: Culture and Politics in the Age of Cold War* (Chicago: University of Chicago Press, 1989), 128; May, *Big Tomorrow*, 181–182.

113. Clark, *Negotiating Hollywood*, 59–60.

114. HH column, *LAT*, 1/13/45, 5, and 9/23/39, A7.

115. Justus D. Doenecke, *Not to the Swift: The Old Isolationists in the Cold War Era* (Lewisburg, Pa.: Bucknell University Press, 1979).

116. HH column, *LAT*, 10/19/39, A11.

117. John E. Moser, "Principles Without Program: Senator Robert A. Taft and American Foreign Policy," *Ohio History* 108 (Summer–Autumn 1999), 185; HH column, *LAT*, 5/6/39, A7.

118. Gabler, *An Empire of Their Own*.

119. Hopper quoted by Debbie Reynolds, with David Patrick Columbia, *My Life* (New York: William Morrow, 1988), 218; Eells, *Hedda and Louella*, 195–196; Otto Friedrich, *City of Nets: A Portrait of Hollywood in the 1940s* (Berkeley and Los Angeles: University of California Press, 1997), 356–357; HH to Robert McCormick, 7/28/44, McCormick folder.

120. John Sbardellati and Tony Shaw, "Booting a Tramp: Charlie Chaplin, the FBI, and the Construction of the Subversive Image in Red Scare America," *Pacific Historical Review* 72 (November 2003), 496, 514, n. 67.

121. HH column, *LAT*, 6/3/43, 17, and 9/22/52, B8; Hopper's 6/3/43 column in the *Chicago Tribune* quoted in Charles J. Maland, *Chaplin and American Culture: The Evolution of a Star Image* (Princeton, N.J.: Princeton University Press, 1989), 209; this content was cut from the version of her column that ran in the *Los Angeles Times*.

122. HH column, *LAT*, 9/24/52, B8, and 3/22/47, A5.

123. Hopper, *From Under My Hat*, 73; Hopper quoted in Eells, *Hedda and Louella*, 258.

124. Donald Bogle, *Bright Boulevards, Bold Dreams: The Story of Black Hollywood* (New York: One World/Ballantine Books, 2005), 180; Thomas Cripps, "'Walter's Thing': The NAACP's Hollywood Bureau of 1946—A Cautionary Tale," *Journal of Popular Film and Television* 33 (Summer 2005), 119; HH column, *LAT*, 2/3/40, A7.

125. Steven Mintz and Susan Kellogg, *Domestic Revolutions: A Social History of American Family Life* (New York: Free Press, 1988), 108–109, 112; Frances Marion quoted in Eells, *Hedda and Louella*, 109.

126. Gary Alan Fine, *Difficult Reputations: Collective Memories of the Evil, Inept, and Controversial* (Chicago: University of Chicago Press, 2001), chap. 4.

127. Ponce de Leon, *Self-Exposure*, 68; Eells, *Hedda and Louella*, 328; Charles Higham paraphrased in Ada Calhoun, "Hollywood Chronicle," *New York Times Book Review*, 12/6/09, 38; William J. Mann, *How to Be a Movie Star: Elizabeth Taylor in Hollywood* (Boston: Houghton Mifflin Harcourt, 2009), 137–138.

128. Fine, *Difficult Reputations*, 137; Small, "Gossip Is Her Business," 58.

129. Catherine E. Rymph, *Republican Women: Feminism and Conservatism from Suffrage through the Rise of the New Right* (Chapel Hill: University of North Carolina Press, 2006), 86; HH column, *LAT*, 5/16/40, A10; "50 Teachers Walk Out on Hedda Hopper," *LAT*, 10/31/52, HH Clippings; Eells, *Hedda and Louella*, 264–265.

130. "GOP Group Confers with Hedda Hopper," [10/16/56], clipping in Motorcade for Ike folder, HHP; HH to L. D. Hotchkiss, 10/15/56, L. D. Hotchkiss folder, HHP.

131. Edward T. Ingle, Director of Radio Division and Speakers Division RNC, to HH, 10/23/50, and Bertha S. Adkins, Executive Director Women's Division, RNC, Washington, D.C., to HH, 10/19/50, Motorcade for Ike folder, HHP.

132. HH to Francis Sill Wickware, 6/16/44, Life-Time folder; Rymph, *Republican Women*, 100; Mary C. Brennan, *Turning Right in the Sixties: The Conservative Capture of the GOP* (Chapel Hill: University of North Carolina Press, 1995), 9; HH column, *LAT*, 8/3/53, B8.

133. Hopper letters to Eisenhower and McCarthy quoted in Anthony Slide, "Hedda Hopper's Hollywood," *Reader*, 4/4/86, HH Clippings; Eells, *Hedda and Louella*, 265–266; HH column, *LAT*, 5/18/47, 16.

134. HH column, *LAT*, 3/25/47, A2; Hopper quoted in interview with Louis B. Mayer, 2/15/54, Mayer folder.

135. HH to Francis Sill Wickware, 6/16/44, Life-Time folder.

136. Hopper quoted in Greg Mitchell, *Tricky Dick and the Pink Lady: Richard Nixon vs. Helen Gahagan Douglas—Sexual Politics and the Red Scare, 1950* (New York: Random House, 1998), 215; HH, script, box 1, folder "Scripts—The Hedda Hopper Show, #13, January 7, 1951," David Victor Papers, 1938–1964, State Historical Society of Wisconsin, Madison, Wisconsin (hereafter Victor Papers).

137. Gail Collins, *Scorpion Tongues: Gossip, Celebrity, and American Politics* (New York: William Morrow, 1998).

138. Dema Harshbarger to HH, 7/2/52, Republican Convention, 1944 and 1952 folders, HHP; McGirr, *Suburban Warriors*, 167.

139. Benjamin Ginsberg and Martin Shefter quoted in Theodore J. Lowi, "Power and Corruption: Political Competition and the Scandal Market," in Apostolidis and Williams, eds., *Public Affairs*, 76; M. J. Heale, *American Anticommunism: Combating the Enemy Within, 1830–1970* (Baltimore: Johns Hopkins University Press, 1990), 99, 146.

CHAPTER 2

1. As Regina Kunzel emphasized in a pathbreaking study of historical reader response, such letters from readers are representations and constructions of experience, not "unmediated evidence" of experience. Kunzel, "Pulp Fictions and Problem Girls: Reading and Rewriting Single Pregnancy in the Postwar United States," *American Historical Review* 100 (December 1995), 1469.

2. LJG, Oklahoma City, to HH, 9/10/58, Elizabeth Taylor, Letters About, #4 folder, HHP (hereafter Taylor #4 folder).

3. Barbas, *First Lady of Hollywood*, 115; Irving Wallace, "They Snoop to Conquer," *Modern Screen* (November 1941), 26–27, 84.

4. John Fiske, "The Cultural Economy of Fandom," in Lisa A. Lewis, ed., *The Adoring Audience: Fan Culture and Popular Media* (London: Routledge, 1992), 46.

5. HH column, *LAT*, 10/5/41, C3; Rosenstein, *Hollywood Leg Man*, 60.

6. WM to HH, 7/26/47, Life-Time folder; EW, Georgia, to HH, 4/23/47, Frank Sinatra, #1 folder, HHP (hereafter Sinatra #1 folder).

7. For a current examination of the relationship between fandom, politics, and the news that addresses these issues, see Jonathan Gray, "The News: You Gotta Have It," in Jonathan Gray, Cornel Sandvoss, and C. Lee Harrington, eds., *Fandom: Identities and Communities in a Mediated World* (New York: New York University Press, 2007), 75–87.

8. John Morreall considers gossip delivered through the mass media to be "noninteractive, impersonal forms of communication" and, thus, not truly "gossip." Morreall, "Gossip and Humor," in Goodman and Ben-Ze'ev, eds., *Good Gossip*, 58.

9. HH to Leonard Riblett, Assistant Managing Editor, *Los Angeles Times*, 12/5/63, *Los Angeles Times* folder, HHP; Eells, *Hedda and Louella*, 277; Catherine Jurca, "What the Public Wanted: Hollywood, 1937–1942," *Cinema Journal* 47 (Winter 2008), 4–5.

10. Doherty, *Projections of War*, 153; Eells, *Hedda and Louella*, 207; Small, "Gossip Is Her Business," 15.

11. HH column, *LAT*, 12/18/39, A15, and 9/7/48, A7; Thomas Schatz, "World War II and the Hollywood 'War Film,'" in Nick Browne, ed., *Refiguring American Film Genres: Theory and History* (Berkeley and Los Angeles: University of California Press, 1998), 90; Thomas Doherty, *Hollywood's Censor: Joseph I. Breen and the Production Code Administration* (New York: Columbia University Press, 2007), 153.

12. "Louella's Rival," *Time*, 12/16/40; Joan Crawford quoted in Kobal, *People Will Talk*, 286.

13. Peter H. Brown and Jim Pinkston, *Oscar Dearest: Six Decades of Scandal, Politics, and Greed Behind Hollywood's Academy Awards, 1927–1986* (New York: Harper and Row, 1987), 94, 125; Hopper quoted in advertisement, *New York Times*, 7/19/43, 13.

14. Unnamed studio executive quoted in "Hedda's Slam at Studios' 'Abuse' of Stars Rebounds," *Daily Variety*, 11/28/50, HH Clippings.

15. HH to Darryl F. Zanuck, 12/18/46, Darryl Zanuck folder, HHP (hereafter Zanuck folder).

16. HH column, *LAT*, 10/15/63, D6, 2/15/44, 11, and 5/6/39, A7; Hopper, *The Whole Truth*, 131; HH column, *LAT*, 7/8/38, A17, and 12/13/40, A11.

17. HH column, *LAT*, 1/26/45, A2; Small, "Gossip Is Her Business," 15; Hopper quoted by Ann Richards in Doug McClelland, *Forties Film Talk: Oral Histories of Hollywood with 120 Lobby Posters* (Jefferson, N.C.: McFarland, 1992), 156.

18. Doherty, *Hollywood's Censor*, 339; HH column, *LAT*, 8/3/39, 10, and 2/27/40, 12.

19. HH column, *LAT*, 3/10/48, 18, and 2/2/41, C3; Lemon, "Warrior Queens of Gossip," 133; Dore Schary, *Heyday: An Autobiography* (Boston: Little, Brown, 1979), 223.

20. Rosenstein, *Hollywood Leg Man*, 41.

21. "Hedda Makes Hay" *Time*, 5/25/42, 52.

22. Gaile quoted in Eells, *Hedda and Louella*, 194; Small, "Gossip Is Her Business," 15.

23. Ponce de Leon, *Self-Exposure*, 59, 84; HH column, *LAT*, 4/13/54, A6, and 4/13/39, A16.

24. HH column, *LAT*, 4/9/47, A3, 12/13/55, B10, 5/24/55, B6, and 12/17/55, A6; HH, draft article, 5/28/53, James Mason folder, HHP.

25. Hopper, *From Under My Hat*, 271; "Hedda Hopper, Columnist Dies," *New York Times*, 2/2/66, 32.

26. Gabler, *Winchell*, 80.

27. HH column, *LAT*, 5/20/47, A3.

28. Script, box 1, folder "Scripts—*The Hedda Hopper Show*, #1, October 14, 1950," Victor Papers; HH to Robert McCormick, 1/31/52, McCormick folder.

29. Gamson, *Claims to Fame*, 68.

30. For just one example, see Susan Ware, *It's One O'clock and Here Is Mary Margaret McBride: A Radio Biography* (New York: New York University Press, 2004), 34.

31. HH column, *LAT*, 1/13/39 and 9/6/39, collected in "Scrapbook #2—1939 Daily Columns," HHP.

32. HH column, *LAT*, 2/18/39, A9, 10/30/63, E11, and 3/31/47, A2; "Hedda Hopper, Columnist Dies," *New York Times*, 2/2/66, 32.

33. Eells, *Hedda and Louella*, 225.

34. Ponce de Leon, *Self-Exposure*, 58–59.

35. HH column, *LAT*, 4/29/42, 13, and 6/21/39, 13; HH column, 10/8/46, collected in "Scrapbook #7—1946 Daily Columns," HHP; HH column, *LAT*, 4/13/54, A6, and 9/6/39, A18.

36. Gamson, *Claims to Fame*, 29; Patricia Meyer Spacks, *Gossip* (New York: Knopf, 1985), 5–6.

37. HH column, *LAT*, 6/3/40, C3, 9/7/48, A7, 1/21/54, A8, 9/28/39, A14, and 5/26/40, C3.

38. HH, script, box 1, folder "Scripts—*The Hedda Hopper Show*, #9, December 10, 1950," Victor Papers; HH column, *LAT*, 9/1/40, C3, and 10/6/40, C3.

39. HH column, *LAT*, 1/16/39, 10; Studlar, "Perils of Pleasure?" 8; Susan Ohmer, "Female Spectatorship and Women's Magazines: Hollywood, *Good Housekeeping*, and World War II," *Velvet Light Trap*, 25 (Spring 1990), 61.

40. Morreall, "Gossip and Humor," 58; Robert Post, "The Legal Regulation of Gossip: Backyard Chatter and the Mass Media," in Goodman and Ben-Ze'ev, eds., *Good Gossip*, 70.

41. HH column, *LAT*, 3/2/47, collected in "Scrapbook #13—1947 Daily Columns," HHP.

42. LS, NYC, to HH, 12/14/61, Rex Harrison folder, HHP; JW, Venice, Calif., to HH, 9/23/58, Elizabeth Taylor, Letters About #3 folder, HHP (hereafter Taylor #3 folder); Mrs. NR, Long Beach, Calif., to HH, 9/12/53, Lucille Ball folder, HHP (hereafter Ball folder); CLW, North Hollywood, to HH, 9/23/58, Taylor #3 folder; AP, Los Angeles, to HH, 9/13/53, Ball folder.

43. Rosenstein, *Hollywood Leg Man*, 43; David Susskind to Les Blumenthal, William H. Weintraub and Co., 12/13/54, Hedda Hopper folder, box 23, David Susskind Papers, 1935–1987, State Historical Society of Wisconsin, Madison, Wisconsin.

44. EEO, Beverly Hills, to HH, 10/1/58, Elizabeth Taylor, Letters About, #2 folder, HHP (hereafter Taylor #2 folder); Collins, *Scorpion Tongues*, 6.

45. HH column, *LAT*, 5/23/38, A14; Mrs. SH, Racine, Wis., to HH, 8/12/51, Sinatra #1 folder.

46. "One of Your Readers," NYC, to HH, 2/25/48, Humphrey Bogart folder, HHP (hereafter Bogart folder); RF, NYC, to HH, 10/16/46, Sinatra #1 folder. On the significance of reading practices, see Janice Radway, *Reading the Romance* (Chapel Hill: University of North Carolina Press, 1984), 210.

47. TBS, San Diego, to HH, 6/22/64, John Wayne folder, HHP; Corporal Vernon Bilke to HH, n.d., copy in The Papers of the NAACP (microfilm), Group II, Series A, General Office Files: Films—General, 1942 (hereafter NAACP Films, 1942), Box A-275, Reel 15.

48. FS, Long Beach, Calif., to HH, 9/22/58, Taylor #3 folder; MC, San Francisco, to HH, Elizabeth Taylor, 1957–1963 folder, HHP; AMD, Long Island, N.Y., to HH, 9/21/52, Charles Chaplin folder, HHP (hereafter Chaplin folder); HH column, *LAT*, 3/14/42, 9.

49. LV, Chicago, to HH, 12/12/47, McDaniel folder; AMD, Long Island, N.Y., to HH, 9/21/52, Chaplin folder.

50. Máire Cross and Caroline Bland, "Gender Politics: Breathing New Life into Old Letters," in Caroline Bland and Máire Cross, eds., *Gender and Politics in the Age of Letter Writing, 1750-2000* (Aldershot, UK: Ashgate, 2004), 5; Spacks, *Gossip*, 5.

51. Mrs. HCT, NYC, to HH, 12/7/49, Shirley Temple folder, HHP (hereafter Temple folder); EEO, Beverly Hills, to HH, 10/1/58, Taylor #2 folder; RF, NYC, to HH, 10/16/46, Sinatra #1 folder.

52. LJS, Burbank, Calif., to HH, 12/14/47, McDaniel folder.

53. JB, Toledo, Ohio, to HH, 11/8/49, Temple folder; BF, Altadena, Calif., to HH, 9/10/58, Elizabeth Taylor, Letters About, #1 folder (hereafter Taylor #1 folder).

54. Mrs. P, Chicago, to HH, 2/16/65, Ball folder; TBS, San Diego, to HH, 6/22/64, John Wayne folder, HHP.

55. Lisa M. Gring-Pemble, "Writing Themselves into Consciousness: Creating a Rhetorical Bridge Between the Public and Private Spheres," *Quarterly Journal of Speech* 84 (1998), 42.

56. ED, Glastonbury, Conn., to HH, 9/30/58, Taylor #1 folder; REM, Bel Air, Md., to HH, 10/3/58, Taylor #2 folder.

57. Mrs. C. M. Perry, Newport News, Va., to HH, 6/22/50, Temple folder; MDS, Los Angeles, to HH, 10/1/58, Taylor #2 folder.

58. MJ, Chicago, to HH, 9/12/58, Taylor #4 folder.

59. Spacks, *Gossip*, 5.

60. EK, El Cajon, Calif., to HH, 9/26/58, Taylor #3 folder; RA, NYC, to HH, 9/23/52, Chaplin folder; EM, National City, Calif., to HH, 11/15/58, Taylor #1 folder.

61. Gertrude Smith quoted in HH column, *LAT*, 10/29/47, A9; Mrs. NR, Long Beach, Calif., 9/12/53, Ball folder; Gamson, *Claims to Fame*, 172.

62. ID, Scarsdale, N.Y., to HH, 2/28/48, Bogart folder.

63. Mrs. P, Chicago, to HH, 2/16/65, Ball folder; Mr. and Mrs. WNM, Houston, to Judy Garland, 11/6/47, copy sent to HH, Judy Garland #2 folder, HHP (hereafter Garland #2 folder).

64. HH to Kathy Griffith, 11/22/63, James Mason folder, HHP.

65. Ohmer, "Female Spectatorship," 61.

66. JK, NYC, to HH, 8/14/65, Mia Farrow folder, HHP.

67. DS, San Francisco, to HH, 7/28/65, Bette Davis folder, HHP.

68. Louis Sordillo, New York, to HH, 12/14/61, Rex Harrison folder, HHP.

69. Christine Gledhill, "Introduction," in Gledhill, ed., *Stardom: Industry of Desire* (London: Routledge, 1991), xiv–xv; Klinger, *Melodrama and Meaning*, 97–98.

70. Janet Staiger, *Perverse Spectators: The Practices of Film Reception* (New York: New York University Press, 2000), 30–31.

71. Corporal Vernon Bilke to Hedda Hopper, n.d., copy in NAACP Films, 1942, Box A-275, Reel 15.

72. Staiger, *Perverse Spectators*, 1.

73. Mrs. NR, Long Beach, Calif., 9/12/53, Ball folder; BB, New Orleans, to HH, 9/22/58, Taylor #3 folder; Jackie Stacey, "Feminine Fascinations: Forms of Identification in Star-Audience Relations," in Gledhill, *Stardom*, 141–163.

74. MRG, Indianapolis, to HH, 6/16/50, Temple folder.

75. Julie A. Wilson, "Star Testing: The Emerging Politics of Celebrity Gossip," *The Velvet Light Trap* 5 (Spring 2010), 28; LVS, Los Angeles, to HH, 9/22/52, Chaplin folder.

76. ED, Glastonbury, Conn., to HH, 9/30/58, Taylor #1 folder; Mrs. NR, Long Beach, Calif., 9/12/53, Ball folder.

77. Mrs. SH, Racine, Wis., to HH, 8/12/51, Sinatra #1 folder; MDS, Los Angeles, to HH, 10/1/58, Taylor #2 folder.

78. Studlar, "Perils of Pleasure?" 10.

79. Sarah Pedersen, "What's in a Name? The Revealing Use of Noms de Plume in Women's Correspondence to Daily Newspapers in Edwardian Scotland," *Media History* 10 (December 2004), 175; Cross and Bland, "Gender Politics," 6.

80. Steven J. Ross, "Introduction: Why Movies Matter," in Ross, ed., *Movies and American Society* (Malden, Mass.: Blackwell, 2002), 9.

81. Gring-Pemble, "Writing Themselves into Consciousness," 42–43.

82. Rosa A. Eberly, *Citizen Critics: Literary Public Spheres* (Urbana: University of Illinois Press, 2000), 23.

83. HH, script, box 2, folder "Scripts—*The Hedda Hopper Show*, #16, January 28, 1951," Victor Papers; OMM, Hesperia, Calif., to HH, 11/20/63, *Los Angeles Times* folder.

84. No signature—regretfully, to HH, 8/6/51, Frank Sinatra #1 folder.

85. HH column, *LAT*, 3/12/60, C2, and 8/19/55, B5; Bernice E. Jenkins, letter to editor, *LAT*, 8/25/55 A4.

86. Mrs. HCT, NYC, to HH, 12/7/49, Temple folder.

87. MG, Hollywood, to HH, 10/1/58, Taylor #2 folder; IEA, Long Beach, Calif., to HH, 9/18/58, Taylor #4 folder; Mrs. AJ, Chicago, to HH, 7/24/62, Russia—General Information folder (hereafter Russia folder).

88. MAJ, Evanston, Ill., to HH, 9/21/58, Taylor #4 folder; "One Voice," Los Angeles, to HH, 9/13/53, Ball folder.

89. Maryann Ayim, "Knowledge Through the Grapevine: Gossip as Inquiry," in Goodman and Ben-Ze'ev, eds., *Good Gossip*, 86–87; Jack Lule, *Daily News, Eternal Stories: The Mythological Role of Journalism* (New York: Guilford Press, 2001), 21, 35.

90. HH to Niles Trammell, 10/27/50, NBC folder, HHP.

91. MJ, Chicago, to HH, 9/12/58, Taylor #4 folder; Jules Levine quoted in HH column, *LAT*, 11/7/47, 10.

92. "One Voice," Los Angeles, to HH, 9/13/53, Ball folder.

93. Corporal Vernon Bilke to Hedda Hopper, n.d., copy in NAACP Films, 1942, Box A-275, Reel 15; JB, Toledo, Ohio, to HH, 11/8/49, Temple folder.

94. Hedda Hopper, "Republican Women Speak Up," Motorcade for Ike folder, HHP; HH column, *LAT*, 4/13/40, 14.

95. BF, Altadena, Calif., to HH, 9/10/58, Taylor #1 folder; RB, Los Angeles, to HH, 9/13/53, Ball folder; Mrs. JJF, New York, to HH, 9/12/53, Ball folder.

96. The phrase comes from Charles M. Payne, *I've Got the Light of Freedom: The Organizing Tradition and the Mississippi Freedom Struggle* (Berkeley and Los Angeles: University of California Press, 1995).

97. Stacey, *Star Gazing*, 46–47.

98. Sandra F. VanBurkleo, *"Belonging to the World": Women's Rights and American Constitutional Culture* (New York: Oxford University Press, 2001).

CHAPTER 3

1. Rymph, *Republican Women*, 84; HH column, *LAT*, 10/19/39, A11; Michael S. Sherry, *In the Shadow of War: The United States since the 1930s* (New Haven: Yale University Press, 1995), 26–27.

2. Glen Jeansonne, *Women of the Far Right: The Mother's Movement and World War II* (Chicago: University of Chicago Press, 1996), 45; June Melby Benowitz, *Days of Discontent: American Women and Right-Wing Politics, 1933–1945* (Dekalb: Northern Illinois University Press, 2002), 108.

3. Clayton R. Koppes and Gregory D. Black, *Hollywood Goes to War: How Politics, Profits, and Propaganda Shaped World War II Movies* (New York: Free Press, 1987), vii. For

more on Hopper and World War II, please see my "Dissent and Consent in the 'Good War': Hedda Hopper, Hollywood Gossip, and World War II Isolationism," *Film History: An International Journal* 22, no. 2 (2010), 170–181.

4. Doherty, *Projections of War*, 5–6; David Farber, "War Stories," *Reviews in American History* 23 (June 1995), 320.

5. Sherry, *In the Shadow of War*, 486; Doenecke, *Not to the Swift*, 165; Leo P. Ribuffo, *The Old Christian Right: The Protestant Far Right from the Great Depression to the Cold War* (Philadelphia: Temple University Press, 1983), 185.

6. HH column, *LAT*, 9/21/39, A8; Doenecke, *Not to the Swift*, 12; John E. Moser, *Twisting the Lion's Tail: American Anglophobia between the World Wars* (New York: New York University Press, 1999), 2.

7. HH column, *LAT*, 9/21/39, A8, 5/16/40, A10, and 10/19/39, A11; Sherry, *In the Shadow of War*, 26.

8. HH quoted in Friedrich, *City of Nets*, 93; HH column, *LAT*, 10/10/41, A14.

9. Rachel Waltner Goossen, *Women against the Good War: Conscientious Objection and Gender on the American Home Front, 1941–1947* (Chapel Hill: University of North Carolina Press, 1997), 13; Eells, *Hedda and Louella*, 196; "Urge Bill to Admit Refugee Children," *New York Times*, 4/21/39, 6; Benowitz, *Days of Discontent*, 95; HH column, *LAT*, 4/27/39, 12.

10. HH column, *LAT*, 12/9/38, 11.

11. HH column, *LAT*, 4/27/39, 12; Moser, *Twisting the Lion's Tail*, 4, 65; Doenecke, *Not to the Swift*, 27.

12. HH column, *LAT*, 1/1/39, 10.

13. HH column, *LAT*, 1/16/39, 10.

14. David O. Selznick to Ed Sullivan, 1/7/39, in *"Gone With the Wind*: The Search for Scarlett," online exhibition, Harry Ransom Humanities Research Center, University of Texas at Austin, http://www.hrc.utexas.edu/exhibitions/online/gwtw/scarlett/; LMG to HH, n.d., Charles Lindbergh folder, HHP (hereafter Lindbergh folder).

15. Michael R. Beschloss, *Kennedy and Roosevelt: The Uneasy Alliance* (New York: Norton, 1980), 16; CML, NYC, to HH, 5/21/40, Lindbergh folder.

16. HH column, *LAT*, 5/27/39, A7, and 12/18/39, A15.

17. Eells, *Hedda and Louella*, 196; HH column, *LAT*, 9/21/39, A8.

18. EMB, Los Angeles, to HH, 10/3/39, and FV, Cedar Rapids, Iowa, to HH, n.d., Lindbergh folder.

19. Jeansonne, *Women of the Far Right*, 1, 45; Laura McEnaney, "He-Men and Christian Mothers: The American First Movement and the Gendered Meanings of Patriotism and Isolationism," *Diplomatic History* 18 (Winter 1994), 47–57.

20. HH column, *LAT*, 9/21/39, A8. This title was used in a clipping of Hopper's 9/22/39 column, Lindbergh folder, but did not appear in the version that appeared in the *LAT*. It is a variation on the title of Eleanor Roosevelt's 1933 book *It's Up to the Women* and a monthly column in *Ladies Home Journal*. See Benowitz, *Days of Discontent*, 81, 83.

21. HH column, *LAT*, 9/28/39, A14, and 12/6/39, 13; LA, Beverly Hills, to HH, 9/23/39, and Mrs. JRM, South Pasadena, Calif., to HH, n.d., Lindbergh folder.

22. HH column, *LAT*, 9/28/39, A14, and 10/19/39, A11.

23. Mrs. JRM, South Pasadena, Calif., to HH, n.d., HB, Los Angeles, to HH, 10/9/39, and AB, Huntington Park, Calif., to HH, 9/27/39, Lindbergh folder.

24. HH column, *LAT*, 9/21/39, A8; EMB, Los Angeles, to HH, 10/3/39, and FV, Cedar Rapids, Iowa, to HH, n.d., Lindbergh folder.

25. HH column, *LAT*, 9/26/39, A16.

26. Goossen, *Women against the Good War*, 16; Benowitz, *Days of Discontent*, 106–107; HH column, 1/13/39, collected in "Scrapbook #2—1939 Daily Columns," HHP; Ribuffo, *Old Christian Right*, 185.

27. Hedda Hopper to respondents, draft letter, 6/3/40, CML, NYC, to HH, 5/21/40, and CDB, Minneapolis, to HH, n.d., Lindbergh folder.

28. Ribuffo, *Old Christian Right*, 185; Hopper, *From Under My Hat*, 183.

29. Beschloss, *Kennedy and Roosevelt*, 63, 206; HH column, *LAT*, 5/2/40, 12.

30. Beschloss, *Kennedy and Roosevelt*, 226, 229; Eells, *Hedda and Louella*, 223.

31. HH column, *LAT*, 12/3/39, C3.

32. HH column, *LAT*, 3/30/40, 12, and 2/18/40, C3; Larry Ceplair and Steven Englund, *The Inquisition in Hollywood: Politics in the Film Community, 1930–60*, pbk. ed. (Urbana: University of Illinois Press, 2003), 60.

33. Schatz, *Boom and Bust*, 13.

34. D. Worth Clark and Gerald P. Nye quoted in Steven Mintz and Randy Roberts, eds., *Hollywood's America: United States History through Its Films* (St. James, N.Y.: Brandywine Press, 1993), 189, 187.

35. Henry McLemore, "The Lighter Side," *LAT*, 9/30/41, 3; HH column, *LAT*, 9/10/41, 12, and 2/18/40, C3; Barbas, *First Lady of Hollywood*, 233.

36. Gabler, *An Empire of Their Own*, 346; HH column, *LAT*, 2/18/40, C3; Schatz, *Boom and Bust*, 27.

37. FBI quoted in Sbardellati and Shaw, "Booting a Tramp," 500, n. 16.

38. HH column, *LAT*, 5/23/40, A11, and 10/16/40, 17; Dan Kamin, "'Who Is This Man (Who Looks Like Charlie Chaplin),'" in Frank Scheide, Hooman Mehran, and Dan Kamin, eds., *Chaplin: The Dictator and the Tramp* (London: British Film Institute, 2004), 9.

39. Maland, *Chaplin and American Culture*, 197; Ribuffo, *Old Christian Right*, 185; HH column, *LAT*, 1/11/39, A17.

40. HH column, *LAT*, 11/16/39, 16.

41. Judith E. Smith, *Visions of Belonging: Family Stories, Popular Culture, and Postwar Democracy, 1940–1960* (New York: Columbia University Press, 2004), 21; Doenecke, *Not to the Swift*, 9.

42. Hedda Hopper to Maryland and Robert McCormick, 9/25/47, McCormick folder.

43. Lewis L. Gould, *Grand Old Party: A History of the Republicans* (New York: Random House, 2003), 311–312.

44. John Fousek, *To Lead the Free World: American Nationalism and the Cultural Roots of the Cold War* (Chapel Hill: University of North Carolina Press, 2000), 2.

45. Robert B. Westbrook, "Fighting for the American Family: Private Interests and Political Obligation in World War II," in Richard Wightman Fox and T. J. Jackson Lears, eds., *The Power of Culture: Critical Essays in American History* (Chicago: University of Chicago Press, 1993), 218.

46. "Lew Ayres Is a Conscientious Objector," *New York Times*, 3/31/42, 23; "People," *Time*, 4/6/42, 54; Colin Shindler, *Hollywood Goes to War: Films and American Society, 1939–1952* (London: Routledge and Kegan Paul, 1979), 53; Mulford Q. Sibley and Philip E. Jacob,

Conscription of Conscience: The American State and the Conscientious Objector, 1940–1947 (Ithaca, N.Y.: Cornell University Press, 1952), 94, 316; "Objector Ayres," *Newsweek*, 4/13/42, 30.

47. "Boston Awaits Mayor Tobin's Okay on Nixing Licenses of Any Theatres Dating Ayres Pix; Hundreds Cancel," *Variety*, 4/8/42, 7; "Studio Will Remake Lew Ayres Film Play—'Born to Be Bad,'" *New York Times*, 4/17/42, 19.

48. Hopper, *From Under My Hat*, 284; Timothy Stewart-Winter, "Not a Soldier, Not a Slacker: Conscientious Objection and Male Citizenship in the United States during the Second World War," *Gender and History* 19 (November 2007), 528.

49. Hopper, *From Under My Hat*, 284.

50. Lew Ayres, "My Stand for Conscientious Objection" [1942], in author's possession. I am indebted to Jeffrey Kovac, author of *Refusing War, Affirming Peace: A History of Civilian Public Service Camp #21 at Cascade Locks* (Portland: Oregon State University Press, 2009), for providing me with Ayres's statement.

51. Sibley and Jacob, *Conscription of Conscience*, v–vi, 15, 42–43, 52, 83–85; Gretchen Lemke-Santangelo, "The Radical Conscientious Objectors of World War II: Wartime Experience and Postwar Activism," *Radical History Review* 45 (Fall 1989), 6–8; Stewart-Winter, "Not a Soldier," 520.

52. DGF, San Diego, to HH, 3/31/42, MH, Ross, Calif., to HH, n.d., JWH to HH, n.d., "Hedda Hopper's Hollywood," radio transcript, aired 12/25/44, and LH, New York, to HH, 4/21/42, Lew Ayres folder, HHP (hereafter Ayres folder).

53. Mrs. EW, South Bend, Ind., to HH, 4/13/42, and LH, New York, to HH, 4/21/42, Ayres folder.

54. Lew Ayres quoted in M. Richard Applegate, "Lew Ayres Sent to Camp as War Objector," *Detroit News*, 3/31/42, 1.

55. HH, typescript, n.d., and "Hedda Hopper's Hollywood," radio transcript, aired 12/25/44, Ayres folder.

56. "Objector Ayres," *Newsweek* , 4/13/42, 30; HH, typescript, n.d., and "Hedda Hopper's Hollywood," radio transcript, aired 12/25/44, Ayres folder.

57. Lewis Jacobs, *The Rise of the American Film: A Critical History*, reprint (New York: Teachers College, 1939; Columbia University Press, 1969), 528; Judith Crist, "Introduction," in Joe Morella, Edward Z. Epstein, and John Griggs, *The Films of World War II* (Secaucus, N.J. Citadel Press, 1973), 5.

58. John Whiteclay Chambers II, "'All Quiet on the Western Front' (1930): The Antiwar Film and the Image of the First World War," *Historical Journal of Film, Radio, and Television* 14 (October 1994), 397; Remarque quoted in "Ayres 'Conchie Camp' Decision Stuns Hollywood," *LAT*, 4/1/42, A1.

59. Sibley and Jacob, *Conscription of Conscience*.

60. EC, New York, to HH, 4/1/42, PJL, San Francisco, to HH, 4/4/42, HH, typescript, n.d., EA, New York, to HH, 4/7/42, GS, Evansville, Ind., to HH, 4/13/42, Ayres folder.

61. Private RPR, San Francisco, to HH, 4/12/42, Captain JSJ, Fort Devens, Mass., n.d., HH, typescript, n.d., and CC, San Jose, to HH, 4/6/42, Ayres folder; Westbrook, "Fighting for the American Family," 198.

62. DGF, San Diego, to HH, 3/31/42, and PJL, San Francisco, to HH, letter, 4/4/42, Ayres folder; Robert B. Westbrook, "'I Want a Girl, Just Like the Girl That Married Harry

James': American Women and the Problem of Political Obligation in World War II," *American Quarterly* 42 (December 1990), 592.

63. LHH, Seattle, to HH, 4/2/42, BDD, Somerville, Mass., to HH, 4/2/42, HH, typescript, n.d., and Mrs. CS, Dora, Pa., to HH, 4/9/42, Ayres folder.

64. Hopper, *From Under My Hat*, 284; Heather T. Frazer and John O'Sullivan, *"We Have Just Begun to Not Fight": An Oral History of Conscientious Objection in Civilian Public Service during World War II* (New York: Twayne, 1996), 32.

65. "Lew Ayres Granted Request to Serve Medical Corps," *LAT*, 5/17/42, 13; CA, Evansville, Ind., to HH, 4/6/42, and "Hedda Hopper's Hollywood," transcript of radio broadcast, 12/25/44, Ayres folder.

66. "Not Enough B.O. Experience," *Variety*, 4/15/42, 7; Hopper, *From Under My Hat*, 285.

67. Hopper, *From Under My Hat*, 284; HH, typescript, n.d., Ayres folder.

68. "Not Enough B.O. Experience," *Variety*, 4/15/42, 23; Sibley and Jacob, *Conscription of Conscience*, 318; Thomas F. Brady, "A Few Hollywood Aches and Pains," *New York Times*, 4/5/42, X3; "Boston Awaits Mayor Tobin's Okay," *Variety*, 4/8/42, 7.

69. Shindler, *Hollywood Goes to War*, 53; Hopper, *From Under My Hat*, 285.

70. "One of Your Audience" to HH, 4/9/42, and James Thurber, New York, to HH, [April 1942], Ayres folder.

71. Hopper, *From Under My Hat*, 284; HH, typescript, n.d., Ayres folder; John Huston, George Cukor, Mary Astor, Franchot Tone, Olivia de Havilland, George Oppenheimer, Walter Huston, Charles Lederer, and Humphrey Bogart, letter, *Time*, 4/20/42, 6.

72. Richard Slotkin, "Unit Pride: Ethnic Platoons and the Myths of American Nationality," *American Literary History* 13 (Fall 2001), 470, 486; Stephen Vaughn, "Ronald Reagan and the Struggle for Black Dignity in Cinema, 1937–1953," *Journal of Negro History* 77 (Winter 1992), 1–16.

73. HH on *Small World* telecast, 12/6/59.

74. Hopper, *From Under My Hat*, 153; Maland, *Chaplin and American Culture*, 208.

75. Eells, *Hedda and Louella*, 228; publicist quoted on p. 231.

76. Sbardellati and Shaw, "Booting a Tramp," 506; Ponce de Leon, *Self-Exposure*, 236.

77. Eells, *Hedda and Louella*, 230.

78. Hopper, *From Under My Hat*, 148–150; Maland, *Chaplin and American Culture*, 210; HH column, *LAT*, 10/6/43, 14, and 6/3/43, 17.

79. Maland, *Chaplin and American Culture*, 197.

80. Hopper, *From Under My Hat*, 149; Sbardellati and Shaw, "Booting a Tramp," 507.

81. Eells, *Hedda and Louella*, 229; Maland, *Chaplin and American Culture*, 201; Hopper, *From Under My Hat*, 151.

82. Chaplin and Los Angeles attorney quoted in David Robinson, *Chaplin: His Life and Art*, rev. ed. (London: Grafton, 1992), 520; Maland, *Chaplin and American Culture*, 206, 215.

83. Maland, *Chaplin and American Culture*, 202; Robinson, *Chaplin*, 523.

84. HH column, *LAT*, 3/28/44, A10, and 6/17/43, 157; EK, Chicago, to HH, 2/10/44, Chaplin folder.

85. CL, "A Plain Citizen," to HH, 2/12/44, Chaplin folder.

86. Maland, *Chaplin and American Culture*, 205, 212.

87. HH column, *Pittsburgh Press*, 6/22/43, quoted in Maland, *Chaplin and American Culture*, 209 (this content was cut from the version of her column that ran in the *LAT*); Langer quoted in Sbardellati and Shaw, "Booting a Tramp," 506.

88. "Indignant Reader of the *Daily News*," New York, to HH, [1944], Chaplin folder.

89. Sbardellati and Shaw, "Booting a Tramp," 506.

90. Mitchell, *Tricky Dick and the Pink Lady*, 58.

91. HH column, *LAT*, 6/3/43, 17; D. William Davis, "A Tale of Two Movies: Charlie Chaplin, United Artists, and the Red Scare," *Cinema Journal* 27 (Autumn 1987), 48; Maland, *Chaplin and American Culture*, 221, 255–257.

92. HH column, *Chicago Tribune*, 12/27/43, quoted in Maland, *Chaplin and American Culture*, 210 (this content was cut from the version of her column that ran in the *LAT*); Friedrich, *City of Nets*, 393; HH column, *LAT*, 3/22/47, A5.

93. Maland, *Chaplin and American Culture*, 226.

94. HH column, *LAT*, 3/18/47, A2, and 4/18/47, A3.

95. Davis, "A Tale of Two Movies," 52, Tino Balio quoted on p. 54; Russell Birdwell to HH, 9/17/47 and 9/28/47, telegrams, Chaplin folder; Sbardellati and Shaw, "Booting a Tramp," 504.

96. HH column, *LAT*, 10/24/47, A2, and 4/17/47, A3; Maland, *Chaplin and American Culture*, 268; Sbardellati and Shaw, "Booting a Tramp," 505.

97. HH column, *LAT*, 5/13/50, 12; Maland, *Chaplin and American Culture*, 275.

98. Friedrich, *City of Nets*, 395–396.

99. HH column, *LAT*, 8/30/52, 10, and 9/22/52, B8.

100. Robinson, *Chaplin*, 572–575; HH column, *LAT*, 9/22/52, B8.

101. Maland, *Chaplin and American Culture*, 301, 305; HH column, *LAT*, 9/24/52, B8.

102. TS, Long Beach, Calif., to HH, n.d., and MM, Willimantic, Conn., to HH, 10/3/52, Chaplin folder; Davis, "A Tale of Two Movies," 55.

103. Chaplin quoted in Sbardellati and Shaw, "Booting a Tramp," 521.

104. Maland, *Chaplin and American Culture*, 273.

105. Sbardellati and Shaw, "Booting a Tramp," 520–521.

106. McGranery's statement appears differently in various sources; I have quoted from Sbardellati and Shaw, "Booting a Tramp," 509.

107. Motion Picture Alliance Statement of Principles quoted in Steven Watts, *The Magic Kingdom: Walt Disney and the American Way of Life* (Boston: Houghton Mifflin, 1997), 240.

108. Senator Robert R. Reynolds quoted in Edward Dmytryk, *Odd Man Out: A Memoir of the Hollywood Ten* (Carbondale: Southern Illinois University Press, 1996), 34; Elmer Rice quoted in Neal Gabler, *Walt Disney: The Triumph of the American Imagination* (New York: Knopf, 2007), 451.

CHAPTER 4

1. AP, Los Angeles, to HH, 9/13/53, Ball folder.

2. Ribuffo, *Old Christian Right*, xiv; HH to Robert McCormick, 1/31/52, McCormick folder.

3. Michael Kazin, *The Populist Persuasion: An American History* (New York: Basic Books, 1995).

4. Fousek, *To Lead the Free World*, 2.

5. Michael Kazin and Joseph A. McCartin, eds., *Americanism: New Perspectives on the History of an Ideal* (Chapel Hill: University of North Carolina Press, 2006); Gary Gerstle, *Working-Class Americanism: The Politics of Labor in a Textile City, 1914–1960* (Cambridge: Cambridge University Press, 1989), 8; Alan Brinkley, "AHR Forum: The Problem of American Conservatism," *American Historical Review* 99 (April 1994), 414.

6. Stephen J. Whitfield, *The Culture of the Cold War*, 2nd ed. (Baltimore: Johns Hopkins University Press, 1996), 323.

7. Gerstle, *Working-Class Americanism*, 6, 12.

8. "The Gossipist," *Time*, 7/28/47, 60–62, 64.

9. E. K. Gaylort, Oklahoma Publishing Company, to HH, 7/28/47, and Arthur H. Motley, Parade Publications, to HH, 7/28/47, Life-Time folder; Gabler, *Winchell*, 382; Barbas, *First Lady of Hollywood*, 227.

10. James T. Patterson, *Grand Expectations: The United States, 1945–1974* (New York: Oxford University Press, 1996).

11. HH column, *LAT*, 3/22/47, A5.

12. John Elsom, *Cold War Theatre* (London: Routledge, 1992), 8. On Kennan's perspective, see Todd Bennett, "Culture, Power, and *Mission to Moscow*: Film and Soviet-American Relations during World War II," *Journal of American History* 88 (September 2001), 517; on Johnston's view, see Stephen Vaughn, "Political Censorship during the Cold War," in Francis G. Couvares, ed., *Movie Censorship and American Culture* (Washington, D.C.: Smithsonian Institution Press, 1996), 238.

13. Sara Beth Levavy, "*Land of Liberty* in the World of Tomorrow," *Film History: An International Journal*, vol. 18, no. 4 (2006), 440–458; HH column, *LAT*, 6/19/39, A15.

14. "Film Alliance Plans Meeting," *LAT*, 2/15/51, 20; HH to Charlotte W. Dowman, Randolph AFB, Tex., 9/11/61, Myron C. Fagan folder, HHP; RA, NYC, to HH, 9/23/52, Chaplin folder; Mrs. T, Los Angeles, to HH, 9/15/53, Ball folder.

15. Robert H. Haddow, *Pavilions of Plenty: Exhibiting American Culture abroad in the 1950s* (Washington, D.C.: Smithsonian Institution Press, 1997), 14; government report quoted in Kenneth Osgood, *Total Cold War: Eisenhower's Secret Propaganda Battle at Home and Abroad* (Lawrence: University Press of Kansas, 2006), 2, 270.

16. Richard M. Fried, "Selling the Cold War at Home and Abroad," *Diplomatic History* 30 (November 2006), 932; Fousek, *To Lead the Free World*, 2; Kazin and McCartin, *Americanism*, 6.

17. Ellen Schrecker, *Many Are the Crimes: McCarthyism in America* (New York: Little, Brown, 1998), 62.

18. Erle Cocke, script, box 1, folder "Scripts—*The Hedda Hopper Show*, #1, October 14, 1950," Victor Papers; "Hedda Hopper Receives Legion Award at Ball," *LAT*, 11/13/55, HH Clippings.

19. HH to Robert B. Pitkin, Managing Editor, *American Legion Magazine*, 12/9/55, and George Chapman, Jr., Past Commander, John Gantus Post 792, Los Angeles, to HH, 11/23/55, American Legion folder, HHP (hereafter American Legion folder); HH column, *LAT*, 5/29/50, A6.

20. HH column, *LAT*, 6/24/54, A10; David Caute, *The Great Fear: The Anti-Communist Purge under Truman and Eisenhower* (New York: Simon and Schuster, 1978), 350.

21. HH column, *LAT*, 4/21/51, 10.

22. Elaine Tyler May, *Homeward Bound: American Families in the Cold War Era* (New York: Basic Books, 1986), 22.

23. Americans for Constitutional Action, Washington, D.C., 1960, Americanism folder, HHP (hereafter Americanism folder); Ruth M. (Mrs. J. A.) Noble to Jack Warner, 2/28/48, copy to HH, Bogart folder.

24. HH, script, box 1, folder "Scripts—*The Hedda Hopper Show*, #14, January 14, 1951," Victor Papers.

25. HH, script, box 1, folder "Scripts—*The Hedda Hopper Show*, #1, October 14, 1950," Victor Papers.

26. Gerstle, *Working-Class Americanism*, 9.

27. AP, Los Angeles, to HH, 9/13/53, Ball folder.

28. HH, radio show script, box 2, folder "Scripts—*The Hedda Hopper Show*, #22, March 11, 1951," Victor Papers.

29. Watts, *Magic Kingdom*, 289; Michael Kammen, *Mystic Chords of Memory: The Transformation of Tradition in American Culture* (New York: Knopf, 1991), 657.

30. Caute, *Great Fear*, 351.

31. HH, script, box 1, folder "Scripts—*The Hedda Hopper Show*, #1, October 14, 1950," and box 2, folder "Scripts—*The Hedda Hopper Show*, #19, February 18, 1951," Victor Papers.

32. Zelizer, "Uneasy Relationship," 284.

33. HH, script, box 1, folder "Scripts—*The Hedda Hopper Show*, #1, October 14, 1950," and box 1, folder "Scripts—*The Hedda Hopper Show*, #4, November 4, 1950," Victor Papers.

34. LCB, Chicago, to HH, 2/8/51, Bing Crosby folder, HHP; Alonzo L. Hamby, *Beyond the New Deal: Harry S. Truman and American Liberalism* (New York: Columbia University Press, 1973), 379.

35. HH, script, box 2, folder "Scripts—*The Hedda Hopper Show*, #31, May 13, 1951," and box 1, folder "Scripts—*The Hedda Hopper Show*, #9, December 10, 1950," Victor Papers.

36. John Bodnar, "The Attractions of Patriotism," in Bodnar, ed., *Bonds of Affection: Americans Define Their Patriotism* (Princeton, N.J.: Princeton University Press, 1996), 4–5, 11, 15.

37. HH column, *LAT*, 4/9/47, A3.

38. Sara M. Evans, *Born for Liberty: A History of Women in America* (New York: Free Press, 1989), 243.

39. HH column, *LAT*, 4/9/47, A3.

40. "Hedda Hopper Denounces Long Skirts in Ad Club Talk," clipping [9/9/47], HH Clippings; see, for example, HH column, *LAT*, 6/13/58, B8, and 7/31/58, B6.

41. HH column, *LAT*, 5/29/50, A6, and 11/14/46, A3; Darryl F. Zanuck to HH, 11/14/46, Zanuck folder.

42. HH column, *LAT*, 4/12/47, A5, and 5/8/48, 9; Darryl F. Zanuck to HH, 5/10/48, Zanuck folder; Daniel J. Leab, "'The Iron Curtain' (1948): Hollywood's First Cold War Movie," *Historical Journal of Film, Radio, and Television* 8 (June 1988), 156.

43. Fred Landesman, *The John Wayne Filmography* (Jefferson, N.C.: McFarland, 2004), 33; HH column, *LAT*, 9/25/52, B8.

44. Frances Stoner Saunders, *The Cultural Cold War: The CIA and the World of Arts and Letters* (New York: New Press, 1999), 284; Tony Shaw, *Hollywood's Cold War* (Amherst: University of Massachusetts Press, 2007), 203.

45. On "super-" or "hyperpatriotism," see Whitfield, *Culture of the Cold War*, 56.

46. Jerold Simmons, "Violent Youth: The Censoring and Public Reception of *The Wild One* and *The Blackboard Jungle*," *Film History: An International Journal*, vol. 20, no. 3 (2008), 387; Peter Lev, *The Fifties: Transforming the Screen, 1950–1959*, vol. 7, *History of the American Cinema*, ed. Charles Harpole (New York: Scribner's, 2003), 245; James Gilbert, *A Cycle of Outrage: America's Reaction to the Juvenile Delinquent in the 1950s* (New York: Oxford University Press, 1986).

47. Schary, *Heyday*, 286; "Movie Leaders Defend Industry at L.A. Hearing: Kefauver Told Films Try to Stay in Good Taste," [6/17/55], clipping in Hollywood in General folder, HHP; see also folder 2, box 33, Schary Papers.

48. Margot A. Henriksen, *Dr. Strangelove's America: Society and Culture in the Atomic Age* (Berkeley and Los Angeles: University of California Press, 1997), 168; Kashner and MacNair, *The Bad and the Beautiful*, 81; HH column, *LAT*, 8/29/55, B6.

49. HH to Robert B. Pitkin, Managing Editor, *American Legion Magazine*, 12/9/55, American Legion folder; Osgood, *Total Cold War*, 225; HH on *Small World* telecast, 12/6/59.

50. AD to Dore Schary, 8/28/55, folder 2, box 33, Schary Papers.

51. Clare Boothe Luce to Mrs. Ralph Merriam, Pasadena, Calif., 10/24/55, copy included in Clare Boothe Luce to HH, 11/21/55, American Legion folder; HH, quoted in interview transcript "Dore Schary," n.d., Dore Schary folder, HHP; Patsy Gaile quoted in Eells, *Hedda and Louella*, 264.

52. The famous phrase was coined by Joseph S. Nye, but see Matthew Fraser, *Weapons of Mass Distraction: Soft Power and American Empire* (New York: Thomas Dunne Books, 2005).

53. HH column, *LAT*, 10/26/63, B7; Nickerson, "Women, Domesticity, and Postwar Conservatism," 18; HH column, *LAT*, 9/24/53, A10; Moser, "Principles Without Program," 188–189.

54. HH, script, box 2, folder "Scripts—*The Hedda Hopper Show*, #16, January 28, 1951," Victor Papers.

55. Gar Alperovitz and Kai Bird, "A Theory of Cold War Dynamics: U.S. Policy, Germany, and the Bomb," *History Teacher* 29 (May 1996), 293.

56. HH column, *LAT*, 1/3/51, 16, 2/22/51, B8, and 5/3/51, A8. On these new holidays, see Richard M. Fried, *The Russians Are Coming! The Russians Are Coming! Pageantry and Patriotism in Cold-War America* (New York: Oxford University Press, 1998), 51–56, 88–95.

57. See Certificate of Esteem folder, HHP; HH, radio show script, box 2, folder "Scripts—*The Hedda Hopper Show*, #16, January 28, 1951," Victor Papers.

58. HH, script, box 2, folder "Scripts—*The Hedda Hopper Show*, #22, March 11, 1951," Victor Papers.

59. Gould, *Grand Old Party*, 334–335.

60. HH to Harry von Zell, Americanism Education League, 8/15/62, Americanism folder.

61. Walter L. Hixson, *Parting the Curtain: Propaganda, Culture, and the Cold War, 1945–1961* (New York: St. Martin's, 1997), xiii.

62. Critchlow, *Phyllis Schlafly*, 87; HH column, *LAT*, 5/28/58, 24.

63. LR, Hollywood, to HH, 10/5/59, and ER, Tulare, Calif., to HH, 9/18/59, Russia folder; Fried, *The Russians Are Coming!* 143.

64. LAH, Pasadena, Calif., to HH, 9/21/59, MAF to HH, 9/19/59, DCC, Burbank, Calif., to HH, 9/21/59, and Mrs. GM, Pasadena, Calif., to HH, 9/21/59, Russia folder; Fried, *The Russians Are Coming!* 142.

65. AP, Los Angeles, to HH, 9/13/53, Ball folder; Nickerson, "Women, Domesticity, and Postwar Conservatism," 19; Kazin and McCartin, *Americanism*, 9; Kashner and MacNair, *The Bad and the Beautiful*, 126–127.

66. Heale, *American Anticommunism*, 189; HH, script, box 1, folder "Scripts—*The Hedda Hopper Show*, #15, January 21, 1951," Victor Papers; Saunders, *Cultural Cold War*, 279.

67. Fried, *The Russians Are Coming!* 96; Critchlow, *Phyllis Schlafly*, 67; Eells, *Hedda and Louella*, 325; ED, NYC, to HH, 12/11/61, Americanism folder.

68. Eells, *Hedda and Louella*, 269; Caute, *Great Fear*, 422–424; HH, script, box 1, folder "Scripts—*The Hedda Hopper Show*, #6, November 19, 1950," Victor Papers.

69. Caute, *Great Fear*, 224; HH, script, box 1, folder "Scripts—*The Hedda Hopper Show*, #13, January 7, 1951," Victor Papers.

70. McCarthy quoted in Caute, *Great Fear*, 46.

71. David H. Bennett, *The Party of Fear: The American Far Right from Nativism to the Militia Movement*, 2nd ed. (New York: Vintage Books, 1995), 300, 291.

72. HH, script, box 1, folder "Scripts—*The Hedda Hopper Show*, #1, October 14, 1950," Victor Papers; Heale, *American Anticommunism*, 155, xiv; Bennett, *Party of Fear*, 290.

73. Heale, *American Anticommunism*, 149.

74. HH column, *LAT*, 6/19/47, A2.

75. Eric Foner, *Give Me Liberty: An American History* (New York: Norton, 2005), 922.

76. Heale, *American Anticommunism*, 99, 146; Mitchell, *Tricky Dick and the Pink Lady*, 128.

77. "Nixon Radio Broadcast," n.d., Richard Nixon folder, HHP. See also Mitchell, *Tricky Dick and the Pink Lady*, 156.

78. HH, *LAT*, 1/20/53, B6.

79. Caute, *Great Fear*, 21; Bennett, *Party of Fear*, xv; Richard W. Steele, "The War on Intolerance: The Reformulation of American Nationalism, 1939–1941," *Journal of American Ethnic History* 9 (Fall 1989), 10.

80. HH column, *LAT*, 4/9/51, B10.

81. Jonathan Bell, *The Liberal State on Trial: The Cold War and American Politics in the Truman Years* (New York: Columbia University Press, 2004), 249.

82. John A. Noakes, "Racializing Subversion: The FBI and the Depiction of Race in Early Cold War Movies," *Ethnic and Racial Studies* 26 (July 2003), 728.

83. Martin Bauml Duberman, *Paul Robeson* (London: Bodley Head, 1989), 317; HH column, *LAT*, 6/19/39, A15.

84. Dyer, *Heavenly Bodies*, 105–107; HH on *Small World* telecast, 12/6/59.

85. Mary L. Dudziak, "Josephine Baker, Racial Protest, and the Cold War," *Journal of American History* 81 (September 1994), 554.

86. HH column, *LAT*, 3/20/47, A3; Miriam Ransier Higgins, "Letters to 'The Times,'" *LAT*, 4/1/47, A4.

87. Mary L. Dudziak, *Cold War Civil Rights: Race and the Image of American Democracy* (Princeton, N.J.: Princeton University Press, 2000), 62.

88. Barbara J. Beeching, "Paul Robeson and the Black Press: The 1950 Passport Controversy," *Journal of African American History* 87 (Summer 2002), 339–355; HH, script, box 1, folder "Scripts—*The Hedda Hopper Show*, #2, October 21, 1950," Victor Papers.

89. Bogle, *Dorothy Dandridge*, 152.

90. HH column, *LAT*, 9/13/48, B6.

91. Caute, *Great Fear*, 77; Bogle, *Dorothy Dandridge*, 154.

92. Charles Frank Robinson II, *Dangerous Liaisons: Sex and Love in the Segregated South* (Fayetteville: University of Arkansas Press, 2003).

93. Stacy Braukman, "'Nothing Else Matters But Sex': Cold War Narratives of Deviance and the Search for Lesbian Teachers in Florida, 1959–1963," *Feminist Studies* 27 (Fall 2001): 553–575.

94. David K. Johnson, *The Lavender Scare: The Cold War Persecution of Gays and Lesbians in the Federal Government* (Chicago: University of Chicago Press, 2004), 9–10.

95. Nan Levinson, "When the Tough Got Going," *Women's Review of Books* 19 (June 2002), 10; HH to Maryland and Robert McCormick, [November 1950], McCormick folder.

96. Hopper quoted in Dilys Powell, *Sunday Times*, London, to HH, 12/15/60, *Los Angeles Times* folder, HHP; Frank Costigliola, "'Unceasing Pressure for Penetration': Gender, Pathology, and Emotion in George Kennan's Formation of the Cold War," *Journal of American History* 83 (March 1997), 1328; K. A. Cuordileone, *Manhood and American Political Culture in the Cold War* (New York: Routledge, 2005), 88–94.

97. HH to Mary Patterson, 7/11/60, Syndicate 1960 folder; Collins, *Scorpion Tongues*, 171; Johnson, *Lavender Scare*, 141.

98. Pola Negri and HH, radio show script, box 1, folder "Scripts—*The Hedda Hopper Show*, #15, January 21, 1951," Victor Papers.

99. Tom Englehardt, *The End of Victory Culture: Cold War America and the Disillusioning of a Generation* (New York: Basic Books, 1995), 119.

100. Don Debats, "Reflecting on Newly Available Insights into Senator Joseph McCarthy's Times and Methods: Remembering Institutions as Well as Individuals," *Australasian Journal of American Studies* 22 (December 2003), 96.

101. Mitchell, *Tricky Dick and the Pink Lady*, 217–219.

102. HH column, *LAT*, 10/27/50, B10.

103. HH column, *LAT*, 9/30/46, A3.

104. Ibid.; Gerald Horne, *Class Struggle in Hollywood, 1930–1950: Moguls, Mobsters, Stars, Reds, and Trade Unionists* (Austin: University of Texas Press, 2001).

105. Horne, *Class Struggle in Hollywood*, 201; HH column, *LAT*, 10/5/46, A5; Gorham Kindem, "SAG, HUAC, and Postwar Hollywood," in Schatz, *Boom and Bust*, 316.

106. Horne, *Class Struggle in Hollywood*, 213, 15–18; HH column, *LAT*, 9/30/46, A3.

107. Horne, *Class Struggle in Hollywood*, 15.

108. Steve Babson, *The Unfinished Struggle: Turning Points in American Labor, 1877–Present* (Lanham, Md.: Rowman and Littlefield, 1999), 128; Ceplair and Englund, *Inquisition in Hollywood*, 212.

109. Ceplair and Englund, *Inquisition in Hollywood*, 203.

CHAPTER 5

1. Ceplair and Englund, *Inquisition in Hollywood*.

2. "'Town Meeting' Meets Hollywood Dilemma," newsclipping, n.d., HEDDA HOPPER, FBI 94-37177-4. I obtained this file and others to follow directly from the FBI, and my citations include classification, file number, and serial number.

3. HH to J. Edgar Hoover, 8/7/47, HEDDA HOPPER, FBI 94–37177–4; J. Edgar Hoover to HH, 8/25/47, HEDDA HOPPER, FBI 94-37177-3.

4. Gabler, *Winchell*, xiv.

5. Eells, *Hedda and Louella*, 242, 225. For an excellent discussion of this topic, see Feeley, "Louella Parsons and Hedda Hopper's Hollywood," chap. 4.

6. HH column, *LAT*, 9/3/47, A3; Peter Roffman and Jim Purdy, "The Red Scare in Hollywood: HUAC and the End of an Era," in Mintz and Roberts, *Hollywood's America*, 196.

7. Kazin, *Populist Persuasion*, 180–181; Gabler, *An Empire of Their Own*, 364; Dmytryk, *Odd Man Out*, 34; Noakes, "Racializing Subversion," 732.

8. HH column, *LAT*, 9/3/47, A3.

9. Although this line was included in the column collected in "Scrapbook #13—1947 Daily Columns," it was cut from the version of the column that ran in the *LAT*, likely due to doubts about the accuracy of Hopper's attribution and quotation. Clayton R. Koppes and Gregory D. Black, however, quote Lenin saying film was "the most important art." See *Hollywood Goes to War*, 49.

10. HH column, *LAT*, 9/3/47, A3.

11. Schatz, *Boom and Bust*, 276; HH column, *LAT*, 7/3/42, A9; Terry Christensen, *Reel Politics: American Political Movies from Birth of a Nation to Platoon* (New York: Blackwell, 1987), 67–68.

12. John A. Noakes, "Official Frames in Social Movement Theory: The FBI, HUAC, and the Communist Threat in Hollywood," *Sociological Quarterly* 41 (Autumn 2000), 663–664.

13. HH column, *LAT*, 9/3/47, A3; Robert Taylor paraphrased in Graham, *My Hollywood*, 132.

14. Thomas Doherty, *Cold War, Cool Medium: Television, McCarthyism, and American Culture* (New York: Columbia University Press, 2003), 21.

15. Howard Strickling, MGM publicist, to HH, n.d., Mayer folder; HH column, *LAT*, 7/3/42, A9; Eells, *Hedda and Louella*, 224.

16. HH column, *LAT*, 9/3/47, A3; Noakes, "Official Frames," 663–664; John A. Noakes, "Bankers and Common Men in Bedford Falls: How the FBI Determined That *It's a Wonderful Life* Was a Subversive Movie," *Film History: An International Journal*, vol. 10, no. 3 (1998), 314.

17. HH column, *LAT*, 10/30/47, 16.

18. HH column, *LAT*, 5/21/51, B8. On this fundamental difference, see Critchlow, *Phyllis Schlafly*, 74.

19. Englehardt, *End of Victory Culture*, 124.

20. Paul Buhle and Dave Wagner, *Radical Hollywood: The Untold Story behind America's Favorite Movies* (New York: New Press, 2002), 86.

21. Sarah Kozloff, "Wyler's Wars," *Film History: An International Journal*, vol. 20, no. (2008), 456–473; Vaughn, "Political Censorship during the Cold War," 246; Ceplair and Englund, *Inquisition in Hollywood*, 312.

22. John Huston, "Moral Rot," excerpt from *An Open Book* (1980), reprinted in Christopher Silvester, *Penguin Book of Hollywood*, 395. For an excellent discussion of these issues, see John Sbardellati, "Brassbound G-Men and Celluloid Reds: The FBI's Search for Communist Propaganda in Wartime Hollywood," *Film History: An International Journal*, vol. 20, no. 4 (2008), 412–436.

23. HH column, *LAT*, 3/31/47, A2.

24. Schatz, *Boom and Bust*, 308; HH column, *LAT*, 5/14/58, B6.

25. Ceplair and Englund, *Inquisition in Hollywood*, 438; Henriksen, *Dr. Strangelove's America*, 47; Englehardt, *End of Victory Culture*, 124–125.

26. HH column, *LAT*, 10/23/47, A9; Ceplair and Englund, *Inquisition in Hollywood*, 258–260.

27. HH column, *LAT*, 10/23/47, A9; Kindem, "SAG, HUAC, and Postwar Hollywood," 316; Horne, *Class Struggle in Hollywood*, 218.

28. HH column, *LAT*, 9/5/47, A2. How Hopper got this information is difficult to ascertain, but one source may have been "deliberate leaks to the newspapers and trade papers" from the May HUAC hearings in Los Angeles. Ceplair and Englund, *Inquisition in Hollywood*, 259, 449–450.

29. HH column, *LAT*, 3/30/40, 12.

30. Hopper quoted in Eells, *Hedda and Louella*, 225; HH column, *LAT*, 7/4/51, A2; Ceplair and Englund, *Inquisition in Hollywood*, xxiii; Vaughn, "Political Censorship during the Cold War," 245.

31. Eells, *Hedda and Louella*, 225.

32. Horne, *Class Struggle in Hollywood*, 27; Vaughn, "Political Censorship during the Cold War," 246; Walter White, summary of telegram to J. Parnell Thomas, HUAC Chairman, n.d., and Leslie S. Perry to Walter White, 9/11/47, NAACP Films, 1942, Box A-274, Reel 15. But this support did not last long. See Horne, *Class Struggle in Hollywood*, 227.

33. Jon Lewis, "'We Do Not Ask You to Condone This': How the Blacklist Saved Hollywood," *Cinema Journal* 39 (Winter 2000), 9–10; HH column, *LAT*, 6/27/47, A2.

34. Dmytryk, *Odd Man Out*, 8; HH column, *LAT*, 10/30/47, 16. Bosley Crowther disagreed. See Crowther, "Sounding Alarm: A Note on a Brand of Thinking About 'Subversive' Stuff in Films," *New York Times*, 11/9/47, X1.

35. Leab, "The Iron Curtain," 153; Eells, *Hedda and Louella*, 268.

36. HH column, *LAT*, 1/2/50, B6; HH, letter, Albert Dekker folder, HHP.

37. Des Moines and Chicago area readers quoted in HH column, *LAT*, 11/7/47, 10; "One Voice," Los Angeles, to HH, 9/13/53, and Mrs. NR, Long Beach, Calif., 9/12/53, Ball folder.

38. Graham, *My Hollywood*, 131; Caute, *Great Fear*, 614, n. 15.

39. Dunne quoted in Ceplair and Englund, *Inquisition in Hollywood*, 276; Sylvia Kaye quoted in Larry Ceplair, "The Film Industry's Battle against Left-Wing Influences, from the Russian Revolution to the Blacklist," *Film History: An International Journal*, vol. 20, no. 4 (2008), 407.

40. Advertisement cited in Feeley, "Louella Parsons and Hedda Hopper's Hollywood," 197; Ceplair and Englund, *Inquisition in Hollywood*, 275–276, 281–282.

41. Advertisement cited in Kazin, *Populist Persuasion*, 170.

42. Ceplair and Englund, *Inquisition in Hollywood*, 289, 291; Paul Henreid with Julius Fast, excerpt from *Ladies' Man: An Autobiography* (1984), reprinted in Silvester, *Penguin Book of Hollywood*, 371.

43. Graham, *My Hollywood*, 131; HH to Judy Garland, phone conversation transcript, 11/12/47, Judy Garland #1 folder, HHP; Brownstein, *The Power and the Glitter*, 114; HH column, *LAT*, 12/18/47, A10.

44. HH column, *LAT*, 10/29/47, A9.

45. HH to Robert McCormick, 7/11/47, and HH to Maryland and Robert McCormick, 8/7/47, draft letter, McCormick folder; Eells, *Hedda and Louella*, 266.

46. Hackensack reader quoted in HH column, *LAT*, 11/7/47, 10; Los Angeles reader quoted in HH column, *LAT*, 11/1/47, collected in "Scrapbook #13—1947 Daily Columns," HHP. This letter was cut from the version of the column that ran in the *LAT*.

47. Iowa City reader quoted in HH column, *LAT*, 11/1/47, A5; Minneapolis reader quoted in HH column, *LAT*, 11/7/47, 10.

48. Seattle reader quoted in HH column, *LAT*, 11/7/47, 10.

49. Fostoria reader quoted in HH column, *LAT*, 11/1/47, A5.

50. Fort Leavenworth, Long Island, and Inglewood readers quoted HH column, *LAT*, 11/7/47, 1, 10.

51. McGirr, *Suburban Warriors*, 6; Nickerson, "Women, Domesticity, and Postwar Conservatism," 17–21.

52. RMN to Jack Warner, 2/28/48, copy to HH, Bogart folder.

53. Colorado Springs reader quoted in HH column, *LAT*, 11/7/47, 10.

54. HH column, *LAT*, 11/7/47, 10, and 3/19/47, A2.

55. Albert Fried, *McCarthyism: The Great American Red Scare: A Documentary History* (New York: Oxford University Press, 1997), 24; Babson, *Unfinished Struggle*, 130.

56. Schatz, *Boom and Bust*, 312; HH column, *LAT*, 3/7/47, 7.

57. HH column, *LAT*, 11/7/47, 10.

58. HH column, *LAT*, 11/18/47, 8; Gabler, *An Empire of Their Own*, 386.

59. Ceplair and Englund, *Inquisition in Hollywood*, 329; FBI informant quoted in Steven J. Ross, "Little Caesar and the HUAC Mob: Edward G. Robinson and the Decline of Hollywood Liberalism," paper presented at the 2001 Annual Meeting of the Organization of American Historians, Los Angeles, California, April 2001,18.

60. The Waldorf Statement, reprinted in Ceplair and Englund, *Inquisition in Hollywood*, 455.

61. Gabler, *An Empire of Their Own*, 311.

62. Ceplair and Englund, *Inquisition in Hollywood*, 330; Lewis, "We Do Not Ask You to Condone This."

63. Lewis, "We Do Not Ask You to Condone This," 8; Schatz, *Boom and Bust*, 313, 511, n. 94; Catherine Jurca, "Hollywood, the Dream House Factory," *Cinema Journal* 37 (Summer 1998), 20.

64. HH to McCormick, 12/17/47, McCormick folder.

65. Brian Neve, "HUAC, the Blacklist, and the Decline of Social Cinema," in Lev, *The Fifties*, 70; Kindem, "SAG, HUAC, and Postwar Hollywood," 316.

66. RMN to Jack Warner, 2/28/48, copy to HH, Bogart folder.

67. Clippings from Julia Johnson, "The Machine Age on Film," excerpted from *Magill's Survey of Cinema*; Bosley Crowther, "In a Glass House," *New York Times*, 7/17/49; and "The Current Cinema," *New Yorker*, 7/16/49, "The Fountainhead" Clipping File, Herrick Library; Peter Biskind, *Seeing Is Believing: How Hollywood Taught Us to Stop Worrying and Love the Fifties* (New York: Pantheon, 1983), 316.

68. Ceplair and Englund, *Inquisition in Hollywood*, 213, 261; Watts, *Magic Kingdom*, 241.

69. HH column, *LAT*, 6/13/47, A7.

70. HH column, *LAT*, 10/17/47, 12; Axel Madsen, *The Sewing Circle: Sappho's Leading Ladies* (New York: Kensington Books, 1995, 2002), 188.

71. HH column, *LAT*, 2/23/48, 14.

72. "One of Your Readers," New York, to HH, 2/25/48, BT, Los Angeles, to HH, 2/26/48, and IW, Chicago, to HH, 2/26/48, Bogart folder.

73. Ceplair and Englund, *Inquisition in Hollywood*, 325.

74. Gabler, *An Empire of Their Own*, 383; Mitchell, *Tricky Dick and the Pink Lady*, 60, 63.

75. HH column, *LAT*, 3/21/51, B10.

76. Victor S. Navasky, *Naming Names* (New York: Viking, 1980), 89.

77. Friedrich, *City of Nets*, 379.

78. Motion Picture Alliance Meeting Agenda, 3/15/51, American Legion folder.

79. Lillian Hellman, *Scoundrel Time* (Boston: Little, Brown, 1976).

80. Ceplair and Englund, *Inquisition in Hollywood*, 371–372, 361.

81. Mitchell, *Tricky Dick and the Pink Lady*, 112.

82. HH to Charlotte W. Dowman, Randolph AFB, Tex., 9/11/61 and 9/21/61, Myron C. Fagan folder, HHP.

83. Doherty, *Cold War, Cool Medium*, 24–25.

84. See Helen Gahagan Douglas and Jose Ferrer folders, HHP; Caute, *Great Fear*, 522.

85. See Americanism and Adolphe Menjou folders, HHP.

86. Slide, "Hedda Hopper's Hollywood," HH Clippings; "Navair Minde" [Never Mind] to HH, 5/22/50, Zanuck folder.

87. EAA, Pasadena, Calif., to HH, 5/17/51, John Garfield folder, HHP.

88. RD, Colorado Springs, to *Chicago Tribune*, 4/9/51, copy forwarded to HH, Howard Duff folder, HHP.

89. MN, San Gabriel, Calif., to HH, 3/17/50, and to Henry Ginsberg, Paramount, 3/17/50, Howard Da Sylva [sic] folder, HHP; Ceplair and Englund, *Inquisition in Hollywood*, 367.

90. Neve, "HUAC, the Blacklist, and the Decline of Social Cinema," 70.

91. Ceplair and Englund, *Inquisition in Hollywood*, 363; HH column, *LAT*, 4/13/53, B8; Stanley Coben, "J. Edgar Hoover," *Journal of Social History* 34 (Spring 2001), 705.

92. Operative 888 Reporting to Hedda Hopper, n.d., Edward Dmytryk folder, HHP (hereafter Dmytryk folder).

93. HH to J. Edgar Hoover, 4/7/47, HEDDA HOPPER, FBI 94-37177-2.

94. Coben, "J. Edgar Hoover," 705; Memo, Special Agent in Charge, Los Angeles, to Director, FBI, 8/5/54, COMPIC (Communist Infiltration of the Motion Picture Industry), FBI 100-15732, in Daniel J. Leab, ed., *Communist Activity in the Entertainment Industry: FBI Surveillance Files in Hollywood, 1942–1958* (Bethesda, Md.: University Publications of America, 1991), microfilm reel #7.

95. HH column, *LAT*, 7/19/48, 14; Memo, R. B. Hood, Special Agent in Charge, Los Angeles, to Director, FBI, 8/23/44, CHARLES CHAPLIN, FBI 31-68496-266; Memo, Special Agent in Charge, Los Angeles, to Director, FBI, 10/4/51, JOHN GARFIELD, FBI 100-335707-133; Friedrich, *City of Nets*, 393.

96. Memo, Special Agent in Charge, Los Angeles, to Director, FBI, 11/8/51, JOHN GARFIELD, FBI 100-335707-167.

97. "A Citizen Who Wants Fairness" to HH, 3/19/54, and HH, draft letter, Albert Dekker folder, HHP.

98. A. M. Kennedy, *Chicago Tribune*, to HH, 4/13/51, Howard Duff folder, HHP.

99. HH column, *LAT*, 12/16/55, B7; HH to Robert B. Pitkin, Managing Editor, *American Legion Magazine*, 12/9/55, American Legion folder; Bettina Drew, *Nelson Algren: A Life on the Wild Side* (New York: G. P. Putnam, 1989), 104, 237, 95.

100. Neve, "HUAC, the Blacklist, and the Decline of Social Cinema," 70.

101. Zanuck quoted in George F. Custen, *Twentieth Century's Fox: Darryl F. Zanuck and the Culture of Hollywood* (New York: Basic Books, 1997), 303.

102. Editor quoted in Eells, *Hedda and Louella*, 16.

103. Friedrich, *City of Nets*, 377.

104. Spigelgass quoted in Eells, *Hedda and Louella*, 16.

105. BW to HH, 7/9/51, Jose Ferrer folder.

106. HH, radio show script, box 2, folder "Scripts—*The Hedda Hopper Show*, #26, April 8, 1951," Victor Papers.

107. Friedrich, *City of Nets*, 377; HH column, *LAT*, 9/10/49, 8; Eells, *Hedda and Louella*, 272.

108. HH column, *LAT*, 7/19/48, 14, and 7/27/52, D1.

109. Dore Schary to Virginia Durr, 12/14/65, folder 1 "Hollywood Ten," box 100, Schary Papers; HH column, *LAT*, 12/17/56, C10, and 12/1/56, B2; Schary, *Heyday*, 224.

110. Buhle and Wagner, *Radical Hollywood*, 421.

111. "Carl Foreman, Clearing Self with Red Probers, to Produce 4 Col Pix," *Variety*, 3/1/57, Carl Foreman Clipping File, Herrick Library; Foreman quoted in Jeremy Byman, *Showdown at High Noon: Witch-Hunts, Critics, and the End of the Western* (Lanham, Md.: Scarecrow Press, 2004), 83; HH column, *LAT*, 5/23/53, A12; Hopper quoted in Brown and Pinkston, *Oscar Dearest*, 243.

112. Hopper quoted in Brown and Pinkston, *Oscar Dearest*, 245; Zelda Cini, *Hollywood, Land, and Legend* (Los Angeles: Rosebud Books, 1980), 172; Rogers and Wayne quoted in Byman, *Showdown at High Noon*, 87.

113. Hopper and Holden quoted in Bob Thomas, *Golden Boy: The Untold Story of William Holden* (New York: St. Martin's Press, 1983), 113–114.

114. Adolphe Menjou to HH, 12/21/52, Adolphe Menjou folder, HHP; HH column, *LAT*, 4/21/51, 10; Hopper quoted in Eells, *Hedda and Louella*, 274.

115. Whitfield, *Culture of the Cold War*, 107; HH column, *LAT*, 8/9/52, 8; Eells, *Hedda and Louella*, 273.

116. HH column, *LAT*, 4/15/50, 8; Eddie Mannix to HH, 4/25/50, Eddie Mannix folder, HHP.

117. Hopper quoted in Brown and Pinkston, *Oscar Dearest*, 227.

118. J. Hoberman, *The Dream Life: Movies, Media and the Mythology of the Sixties* (New York: New Press, 2003), 27, 36; Hopper quoted in Slide, "Hedda Hopper's Hollywood," HH Clippings; Hopper quoted in Hoberman, *Dream Life*, 27.

119. Parks quoted in Schrecker, *Many Are the Crimes*, 329.

120. Brown and Pinkston, *Oscar Dearest*, 236.

121. HH column, *LAT*, 3/26/51, collected in "Scrapbook #19—1951 Daily Columns," HHP; Eells, *Hedda and Louella*, 274–275.

122. Wayne quoted in Emanuel Levy, *John Wayne: Prophet of the American Way of Life* (Metuchen, N.J.: Scarecrow Press, 1988), 287. See also Garry Wills, *John Wayne's America: The Politics of Celebrity* (New York: Simon and Schuster, 1997).

123. "A Valiant Fighter," *Hollywood Citizen-News*, 4/26/51, HH Clippings; Eells, *Hedda and Louella*, 275; "Hedda Won't Testify at Commie Hearings," *Variety*, 9/24/51, HH Clippings.

124. Eells, *Hedda and Louella*, 276; clippings from *Hollywood Reporter* , 5/14/51; and "Hedda Hissed at ANTA Antics; Top Talent Brings 26G SRO Take," *Variety*, 5/9/51, HH Clippings; Nunnally Johnson to Humphrey Bogart and Lauren Bacall, 5/26/52, reprinted in Silvester, *Penguin Book of Hollywood*, 425.

125. Schrecker, *Many Are the Crimes*, 216; "N.Y. Daily News Exec Editor Reveals Hedda Hopper Frequently 'Warned,'" *Variety*, 11/18/53, HH Clippings.

126. Whitfield, *Culture of the Cold War*, 15; Doherty, *Cold War, Cool Medium*, 210.

127. Hopper, letter, n.d., Joseph McCarthy folder, HHP; *Small World* telecast, 12/6/59; McGirr, *Suburban Warriors*, 143, 113.

128. Heale, *American Anticommunism*, 159.

129. Schrecker, *Many Are the Crimes*, 319.

130. This was observed at the time. See Carey McWilliams, "Hollywood Gray List," *The Nation*, 11/19/49, reprinted in Carl Bromley, ed., *Cinema Nation: The Best Writing on Film from* The Nation, *1913–2000* (New York: Thunder's Mouth Press/Nation Books, 2000), 169–170.

CHAPTER 6

1. Hattie McDaniel to HH, 9/13/50, McDaniel folder; Donald Bogle, *Brown Sugar: Eighty Years of America's Black Female Superstars* (New York: Harmony Books, 1980), 73.

2. Mitchell, *Tricky Dick and the Pink Lady*, 156–157; "Nixon Radio Broadcast," n.d., Nixon folder.

3. Donald Bogle, *Primetime Blues: African Americans on Network Television* (New York: Farrar, Straus and Giroux, 2001), 34.

4. Jill Watts, *Hattie McDaniel: Black Ambition, White Hollywood* (New York: Harper-Collins, 2005), 25.

5. Rymph, *Republican Women*, 78; "Nixon Radio Broadcast," n.d., Nixon folder; Defender Staff, "Convention Round-Up," *Chicago Defender*, 7/19/52, 4.

6. Eells, *Hedda and Louella*, 242; Herman Gray, *Watching Race: Television and the Struggle for "Blackness"* (Minneapolis: University of Minnesota, 1996), 75.

7. Eells, *Hedda and Louella*, 242.

8. Vaughn, "Ronald Reagan"; Lola Young, *Fear of the Dark: "Race," Gender, and Sexuality in the Cinema* (New York: Routledge, 1996).

9. Mary L. Dudziak is one among many; see her *Cold War Civil Rights*, 12.

10. Cripps, "Walter's Thing," 120.

11. Disney quoted in Thomas Cripps, *Making Movies Black: The Hollywood Message Movie from World War II to the Civil Rights Era* (New York: Oxford University Press, 1993), 189.

12. Patricia A. Turner, *Ceramic Uncles and Celluloid Mammies: Black Images and Their Influence on Culture* (New York: Anchor Books, 1994), 107; editorial in *Ebony* quoted in Daniel J. Leab, *From Sambo to Superspade: The Black Experience in Motion Pictures* (Boston: Houghton Mifflin, 1975), 137.

13. Donald Bogle, *Toms, Coons, Mulattos, Mammies, and Bucks: An Interpretative History of Blacks in American Film* (New York: Viking, 1973), 5–8.

14. Kevin K. Gaines, *Uplifting the Race: Black Leadership, Politics, and Culture in the Twentieth Century* (Chapel Hill: University of North Carolina Press, 1996), 67.

15. Michael Rogin, *Blackface, White Noise: Jewish Immigrants in the Hollywood Melting Pot* (Berkeley and Los Angeles: University of California Press, 1996), 37.

16. Michael H. Epp, "Raising Minstrelsy: Humour, Satire, and the Stereotype in *The Birth of a Nation* and *Bamboozled*," *Canadian Review of American Studies*, vol. 33, no. 1 (2003), 25; Langston Hughes and Milton Meltzer quoted in Darlene Clark Hine and Kathleen Thompson, *A Shining Thread of Hope: The History of Black Women in America*, pbk. ed. (New York: Broadway Books, 1999), 254.

17. Walter M. Brasch, *Brer Rabbit, Uncle Remus, and the "Cornfield Journalist": The Tale of Joel Chandler Harris* (Macon, Ga.: Mercer University Press, 2000); Catherine Gunther Kodat, "Disney's *Song of the South* and the Birth of the White Negro," in Douglas Field, ed., *American Cold War Culture* (Edinburgh: Edinburgh University Press, 2005), 115.

18. Peggy A. Russo, "Uncle Walt's Uncle Remus: Disney's Distortion of Harris's Hero," *Southern Literary Quarterly* 25 (Fall 1992), 24–25.

19. Alice Walker, *Living by the Word: Selected Writings, 1973–1987* (New York: Harcourt Brace Jovanovich, 1988), 195.

20. HH column, *LAT*, 2/27/45, A2.

21. Clipping of Hopper column, 7/7/44; Walter F. White to Walt Disney, 7/20/44, Walt Disney to Walter F. White, 7/25/44, The Papers of the NAACP (microfilm), Group II, Series A, General Office Files: Films—*Song of the South*, 1944–1947, Box A-280, Reel 21.

22. Cripps, "Walter's Thing," 120.

23. Clarence Muse and Rex Ingram quoted in Leab, *From Sambo to Superspade*, 137.

24. Watts, *Magic Kingdom*, 278.

25. Anna Everett, *Returning the Gaze: A Genealogy of Black Film Criticism, 1909–1949* (Durham: Duke University Press, 2001), 201.

26. Herman Hill quoted in Leonard Maltin, *The Disney Films*, 4th ed. (New York: Disney Editions, 2000), 78.

27. Wendell Green quoted in Thomas Cripps, *Slow Fade to Black: The Negro in American Film, 1900–1942* (New York: Oxford University Press, 1977), 385; Hope Spingarn and Gloster Current quoted in Cripps, *Making Movies Black*, 193.

28. Maltin, *Disney Films*, 78; Edward D. C. Campbell, Jr., *The Celluloid South: Hollywood and the Southern Myth* (Knoxville: University of Tennessee Press, 1981), 152; Bogle, *Toms, Coons, Mulattos*, 136; Dier quoted in Watts, *Magic Kingdom*, 276; Bernstein quoted in Kodat, "Disney's *Song of the South* and the Birth of the White Negro," 112.

29. Gabler, *Walt Disney*, 435.

30. Hopper, *From Under My Hat*, 286.

31. Noakes, "Racializing Subversion," 731.

32. HH column, *LAT*, 9/27/46, A2; MWD, St. Petersburg, Fla., to HH, 2/20/48, James Baskett folder, HHP (hereafter Baskett folder).

33. LJE, Chicago, to HH, 2/20/48, Baskett folder; Maltin, *Disney Films*, 78.

34. Bogle, *Primetime Blues*, 27.

35. James Oliver Horton, "Humor and the American Racial Imagination," *American Quarterly* 45 (March 1993), 167–168.

36. Horton, "Humor and the American Racial Imagination," 168; LJE, Chicago, to HH, 2/20/48, Baskett folder.

37. Watts, *Magic Kingdom*, 486, n. 33; Campbell, *Celluloid South*, 151; Kodat, "Disney's *Song of the South* and the Birth of the White Negro," 112.

38. Maltin, *Disney Films*, 74.

39. Crowther quoted in Russo, "Uncle Walt's Uncle Remus," 26; Hopper, *From Under My Hat*, 286; LJE, Chicago, to HH, 2/20/48, Baskett folder.

40. Walter F. White quoted in Russo, "Uncle Walt's Uncle Remus," 26.

41. Bogle, *Toms, Coons, Mulattos*, 8.

42. Disney letter quoted in Watts, *Magic Kingdom*, 279.

43. Baskett quoted in Watts, *Magic Kingdom*, 277; HH column, *LAT*, 2/20/48, 18.

44. HH column, *LAT*, 3/1/48, 10; LS, Detroit, to HH, 3/8/48, Baskett folder.

45. TM, Hollywood, to HH, 2/20/48, and MWD, St. Petersburg, Fla., to HH, 2/20/48, Baskett folder.

46. See seventeen letters from schoolchildren in Baskett folder; and HH column, *LAT*, 3/16/48, 16.

47. Edward Mapp, *African Americans and the Oscar: Seven Decades of Struggle and Achievement* (Lanham, Md.: Scarecrow, 2003), 13.

48. Mark A. Reid, *Redefining Black Film* (Berkeley and Los Angeles: University of California Press, 1993), 21; Bogle, *Primetime Blues*, 38; Melvin Patrick Ely, *The Adventures of Amos 'n' Andy: A Social History of an American Phenomenon* (New York: Free Press, 1991).

49. Gloster Current and unnamed critic quoted in Cripps, *Making Movies Black*, 192–193; Etta James quoted in Bogle, *Primetime Blues*, 57.

50. Charles E. Butler, Los Angeles, to HH, 2/20/48, Baskett folder.

51. C. W. Hill, Hollywood, to HH, 3/26/48, Baskett folder; Homi Bhabha quoted in Tania Modleski, *Feminism Without Women: Culture and Criticism in a "Postfeminist" Age* (New York: Routledge, 1991), 119. I am using this concept in a different context than do Bhabha and Modleski, as they were concerned with whites in blackface.

52. Cripps, *Making Movies Black*, 192.

53. Brasch, *Brer Rabbit, Uncle Remus, and the "Cornfield Journalist,"* 281; dedication quoted in Emanuel Levy, *All About Oscar: The History and Politics of the Academy Awards* (New York: Continuum, 2003), 132.

54. James Baskett to HH, telegram, 3/21/48, Baskett folder, and quoted in HH column, *LAT*, 3/25/48, A20; Hopper, *From Under My Hat*, 285–286; Hopper, *The Whole Truth*, 146.

55. Gabler, *Walt Disney*, 435; Campbell, *Celluloid South*, 149.

56. There is debate about the number of films McDaniel appeared in, ranging from 40 to 300. Most filmographies, however, list around 100 films.

57. HH column, *LAT*, 4/7/47, A3; HH column, *Chicago Tribune*, 12/14/47, clipping in McDaniel folder. The article also appeared in briefer form as HH column, *LAT*, 12/14/47, H3.

58. HH column, *Chicago Tribune*, 12/14/47, clipping in McDaniel folder; HH column, *LAT*, 2/16/40, A15; Hine and Thompson, *Shining Thread of Hope*, 254.

59. Bogle, *Toms, Coons, Mulattos*, 83; Jennifer Bailey Woodard and Teresa Mastin, "Black Womanhood: *Essence* and Its Treatment of Stereotypical Images of Black Women," *Journal of Black Studies* 36 (November 2005), 271; Bogle, *Toms, Coons, Mulattos*, 9; Victoria Sturtevant, "'But things is changin' nowadays an' Mammy's gettin' bored': Hattie McDaniel and the Culture of Dissemblance," *Velvet Light Trap* 44 (Fall 1999), 69.

60. Jo-Ann Morgan, "Mammy as Huckster: Selling the Old South for the New Century," *American Art* 9 (Spring 1995), 89, 91, 88; Turner, *Ceramic Uncles and Celluloid Mammies*, 44; Joan Marie Johnson, "'Ye Gave Them a Stone': African American Women's Clubs, the Frederick Douglass Home, and the Black Mammy Monument," *Journal of Women's History* 17 (Spring 2005), 71; Bogle, *Brown Sugar*, 73; Bogle, *Toms, Coons, Mulattos*, 9.

61. HH column, *Chicago Tribune*, 12/14/47, clipping in McDaniel folder.

62. HH column, *LAT*, 12/18/39, A15. In response, McDaniel wrote to thank Hopper for her "very generous criticism." Hattie McDaniel to HH, 1/9/40, McDaniel folder.

63. Critic quoted in Watts, *Hattie McDaniel*, 176.

64. "4 Leading Negro Papers," clipping, and M. Beaunorus Tolson, "Caviar and Cabbage," clipping, The Papers of the NAACP (microfilm), Group II, Series A, General Office Files: Films—*Gone With the Wind*, 1940, Box A-277, Reel 17. See also Everett, *Returning the Gaze*, 291–296; Carlton Jackson, *Hattie: The Life of Hattie McDaniel* (Lanham, Md.: Madison Books, 1990), 99.

65. Tolson, "Caviar and Cabbage"; Jackson, *Hattie*, 98–99.

66. HH column, *Chicago Tribune*, 12/14/47, clipping in McDaniel folder.

67. Woodard and Mastin, "Black Womanhood," 271; Johnson, "Ye Gave Them a Stone," 62, 72.

68. Carlton Moss quoted in Watts, *Hattie McDaniel*, 176.

69. HH column, *Chicago Tribune*, 12/14/47, clipping in McDaniel folder; Jackson, *Hattie*, 95–96; Walter White quoted in Vaughn, "Ronald Reagan," 2.

70. Sturtevant, "But things is changin' nowadays," 70; HH column, 4/13/40, 14; Mapp, *African Americans and the Oscar*, 10.

71. Sturtevant, "But things is changin' nowadays," 69.

72. Ibid., 73, 78. At various times, McDaniel commented on the class and caste/color status of White and his activist colleagues. Jackson, *Hattie*, 99–100, 108; Cripps, "Walter's Thing," 116.

73. Vaughn, "Ronald Reagan," 6.

74. Thomas Cripps, *Making Movies Black*, 291; Vaughn, "Ronald Reagan," 7; Noakes, "Racializing Subversion," 735; Doherty, *Hollywood's Censor*, 242.

75. HH column, *Chicago Tribune*, 12/14/47, clipping in McDaniel folder.

76. Jones quoted in Everett, *Returning the Gaze*, 304.

77. Charles E. Butler, Los Angeles to HH, 12/14/47, McDaniel folder; Sturtevant, "But things is changin' nowadays," 70, 75.

78. EMG, Riverside, Calif., to HH, n.d., McDaniel folder.

79. LJS, Burbank, Calif., to HH, 12/14/47, McDaniel folder.

80. Everett, *Returning the Gaze*, 21; SS, Los Angeles, to HH, 12/14/47, and LS, Chicago, to HH, 12/12/47 and 12/15/47, McDaniel folder.

81. SS, Los Angeles, to HH, 12/14/47, McDaniel folder.

82. LS, Chicago, to HH, 12/15/47, McDaniel folder.

83. McDaniel to HH, 3/29/47, McDaniel folder, reprinted with some editing in HH column, *LAT*, 4/7/47, A3; ATK to HH, 12/16/47, McDaniel folder; Everett, *Returning the Gaze*, 309.

84. HH column, *Chicago Tribune*, 12/14/47, clipping in McDaniel folder; LJS, Burbank, Calif., to HH, 12/14/47, McDaniel folder.

85. Patricia Hill Collins, *Black Feminist Thought: Knowledge, Consciousness, and the Politics of Empowerment*, 2nd ed. (New York: Routledge, 2000), 72–73.

86. Morgan, "Mammy as Huckster," 109, n. 27.

87. HH column, *Chicago Tribune*, 12/14/47, clipping in McDaniel folder; LJS, Burbank, Calif., to HH, 12/14/47, McDaniel folder.

88. Watts, *Hattie McDaniel*, 83.

89. HH column, *Chicago Tribune*, 12/14/47, clipping in McDaniel folder; LJS, Burbank, Calif., to HH, 12/14/47, McDaniel folder.

90. ATK to HH, 12/16/47, and LS, Chicago, to HH, 12/15/47, McDaniel folder.

91. SS, Los Angeles, to HH, 12/14/47, and ATK to HH, 12/16/47, McDaniel folder.

92. LJS, Burbank, Calif., to HH, 12/14/47, McDaniel folder; Reddick quoted in Everett, *Returning the Gaze*, 313.

93. LS, Chicago, to HH, 12/15/47, McDaniel folder.

94. Cripps, "Walter's Thing," 121.

95. ATK to HH, 12/16/47, McDaniel folder.

96. McDaniel quoted in Mapp, *African Americans and the Oscar*, 10; Hattie McDaniel to HH, 3/29/47, McDaniel folder; Earl Morris of the *Pittsburgh Courier* quoted in Watts, *Hattie McDaniel*, 133.

97. McDaniel quoted in Mapp, *African Americans and the Oscar*, 9; Bogle, *Bright Boulevards, Bold Dreams*, 266, 261; Jackson, *Hattie*, 100.

98. Cited in Watts, *Hattie McDaniel*, 86.

99. McDaniel quoted in Dana Stevens, "Caricature Acting," *New York Times Book Review*, 11/27/05, 24; Sturtevant, "But things is changin' nowadays," 70. Different versions of this quote exist, indicating that McDaniel repeated it often, but these discrepancies do not take away from her basic point.

100. LJS, Burbank, Calif., to HH, 12/14/47, and LS, Chicago, to HH, 12/15/47, McDaniel folder.

101. Bogle, *Toms, Coons, Mulattos*, 9; Bogle, *Primetime Blues*, 182, 212; Watts, *Hattie McDaniel*, 91–92.

102. Hilton Als, "Mammy for the Masses," *New Yorker*, 9/26/05, 149.

103. Watts, *Hattie McDaniel*, 196; Hattie McDaniel to HH, 12/26/47, McDaniel folder.

104. Watts, *Hattie McDaniel*, 252–253; McDaniel quoted in HH column, *Chicago Tribune*, 12/14/47, clipping in McDaniel folder.

105. HH column, *Chicago Tribune*, 12/14/47, clipping in McDaniel folder; Arthur Knight, "Star Dances: African-American Constructions of Stardom, 1925–1960," in Daniel Bernardi, ed., *Classic Hollywood, Classic Whiteness* (Minneapolis: University of Minnesota Press, 2001), 404.

106. LJS, Burbank, Calif., to HH, 12/14/47, and ATK to HH, 12/16/47, McDaniel folder.

107. LJS, Burbank, Calif., to HH, 12/14/47, McDaniel folder; Walter White, summary of telegram to J. Parnell Thomas, HUAC Chairman, n.d., The Papers of the NAACP (microfilm), Group II, Series A, General Office Files: Films—Communists in the Motion Picture Industry, 1947, Box A-274, Reel 15; Manfred Berg, "Black Civil Rights and Liberal Anticommunism: The NAACP in the Early Cold War," *Journal of American History* 94 (June 2007), 88.

108. McDaniel quoted in HH column, *Chicago Tribune*, 12/14/47, clipping in McDaniel folder.

109. ATK to HH, 12/16/47, and LS, Chicago, to HH, 12/12/47, McDaniel folder; Jacqueline Najuma Stewart, *Migrating to the Movies: Cinema and Black Urban Modernity* (Berkeley and Los Angeles: University of California, 2005); Balio, *Grand Design*, 344.

110. Charles E. Butler, Los Angeles, to HH, 12/14/47, McDaniel folder.

111. *Chicago Defender*, 2/23/46, quoted in Cripps, "Walter's Thing," 122; Knight, "Star Dances," 389.

112. Francis G. Couvares, "The Good Censor: Race, Sex, and Censorship in Early Cinema," *Yale Journal of Criticism*, vol. 7, no. 2 (1994), 233–251; LS, Chicago, to HH, 12/15/47, and LJS, Burbank, Calif., to HH, 12/14/47, McDaniel folder.

113. Hattie McDaniel to HH, 12/26/47, McDaniel folder.

114. Bogle, *Primetime Blues*, 20; Hattie McDaniel to HH, 9/13/50, McDaniel folder; Watts, *Hattie McDaniel*, 257.

115. Sturtevant, "But things is changin' nowadays," 75; Savage, *Broadcasting Freedom*, 17.

116. Bogle, *Primetime Blues*, 19–20.

117. Cripps, *Making Movies Black*, 291, 284; Reid, *Redefining Black Film*, 2, 78; Smith, *Visions of Belonging*, 111; Aram Goudsouzian, *Sidney Poitier: Man, Actor, Icon* (Chapel Hill: University of North Carolina Press, 2004), 3; Michael Rogin, "'Democracy and Burnt Cork': The End of Blackface, the Beginning of Civil Rights," *Representations* 46 (Spring 1994), 26–28.

118. William R. Grant, IV, *Post-Soul Black Cinema: Discontinuities, Innovations, and Breakpoints, 1970–1995* (New York: Routledge, 2004), 32.

119. HH column, *LAT*, 5/8/54, A6.

120. Andrea Slane, "Pressure Points: Political Psychology, Screen Adaptation, and the Management of Racism in the Case-History Genre," *Camera Obscura* 45 (2000), 77; Reid, *Redefining Black Film*, 58.

121. Goudsouzian, *Sidney Poitier*, 3; Bogle, *Toms, Coons, Mulattos*, 176.

122. Poitier quoted in Turner, *Ceramic Uncles and Celluloid Mammies*, 206; Nora Sayre, "The Man Who Came to Dinner," *New York Times Book Review*, 5/28/00; Donald Bogle quoted in Gladstone L. Yearwood, "The Hero in Black Film: An Analysis of the Film Industry and Problems in Black Cinema," *Wide Angle*, vol. 5, no. 2 (1982), 46.

123. Hopper and Poitier quoted in interview transcript "Sidney Poitier," 5/23/58, Sidney Poitier folder, HHP (hereafter Poitier folder).

124. James Naremore, "Uptown Folk: Blackness and Entertainment in Cabin in the Sky," *Arizona Quarterly* 48 (Winter 1992), 100; Arthur Knight, *Disintegrating the Musical: Black Performance and the American Musical Film* (Durham: Duke University Press, 2002), 2.

125. S. G. F. Spackman, "Passing for Colored: Meanings for Minstrelsy and Ragtime," *Reviews in American History* 23 (June 1995), 238.

126. Bogle, *Toms, Coons, Mulattos*, 183; Hopper and Poitier quoted in interview transcript "Sidney Poitier," 5/23/58, Poitier folder; HH column, *LAT*, 4/31/58, D1.

127. Luce quoted in Mary L. Dudziak, "*Brown* as a Cold War Case," *Journal American History* 91 (June 2004), 36; Hopper and Poitier quoted in interview transcript "Sidney Poitier," 5/23/58, Poitier folder; Dudziak, *Cold War Civil Rights*.

128. Berg, "Black Civil Rights," 75.

CHAPTER 7

1. Hopper, *From Under My Hat*, 294–295; Hopper's column quoted in Leamer, *As Time Goes By*, 192; HH column, *LAT*, 12/13/49, B6.

2. HH column, *LAT*, 12//16/49, A12, and 2/6/50, B8.

3. Friedrich, *City of Nets*, 406, 408, 410; Edwin C. Johnson quoted in "Cinema: The Purity Test," *Time*, 3/27/50, 99; Adrienne L. McLean, "The Cinderella Princess and the Instrument of Evil: Surveying the Limits of Female Transgression in Two Postwar Hollywood Scandals," *Cinema Journal* 34 (Spring 1995), 36–56.

4. Hopper, *From Under My Hat*, 294; Donald Spoto, *Notorious: The Life of Ingrid Bergman*, pbk. ed. (New York: HarperCollins, 1998), 149; David Selznick to HH, 10/2/39, David Selznick folder, HHP.

5. "A Sincere 13 year old, Phill[s]rurg, N.J.," to HH, 6/27/50, Shirley Temple folder, HHP.

6. Spoto, *Notorious*, 285.

7. Smith, *Visions of Belonging*, 2.

8. May, *Homeward Bound*.

9. Jane F. Levey, "Imagining the Family in Postwar Popular Culture: The Case of *The Egg and I* and *Cheaper by the Dozen*," *Journal of Women's History* 13 (Autumn 2001), 125–126.

10. May, *Homeward Bound*.

11. HH column, *LAT*, 10/21/47, A9; Ponce de Leon, *Self-Exposure*, 107; Deborah Nelson, *Pursuing Privacy in Cold War America* (New York: Columbia University Press, 2002), xii–xiii.

12. Wilson, "Star Testing," 35; Jonathan M. Metzl, "Author Exchange," *Gender and History* 15 (August 2003), 260–262, 261.

13. Gerd Horten, *Radio Goes to War: The Cultural Politics of Propaganda during World War II* (Berkeley and Los Angeles: University of California Press, 2002), 182.

14. May, "Movie Star Politics," 146.

15. Doherty, *Projections of War*, 5–6; Elaine Tyler May, "Commentary: Ideology and Foreign Policy: Culture and Gender in Diplomatic History," *Diplomatic History* 18 (Winter 1994), 72.

16. Hopper, "Hopper Gives Some Pointers to Youngsters," [1946], HH Clippings; Hopper quoted in Eells, *Hedda and Louella*, 207.

17. HH column, *LAT*, 7/18/48, C1, and 2/5/50, D1; McLean, "Cinderella Princess," 40.

18. Hopper, "The Riddle of Betty Grable," November 1952, Betty Grable folder, HHP (hereafter Grable folder); Jessica Weiss, *To Have and to Hold: Marriage, the Baby Boom, and Social Change* (Chicago: University of Chicago, 2000), 119.

19. John D'Emilio and Estelle B. Freedman, *Intimate Matters: A History of Sexuality in America* (New York: Harper and Row, 1988), 282.

20. Ibid., 282, 286; Eells, *Hedda and Louella*, 301; HH column, *LAT*, 9/15/53, B6; Cuordileone, *Manhood and American Political Culture*, 83.

21. Susan McLeland, "Elizabeth Taylor: Hollywood's Last Glamour Girl," in Hilary Radner and Moya Luckett, eds., *Swinging Single: Representing Sexuality in the 1960s* (Minneapolis: University of Minnesota Press, 1999), 235.

22. HH column, *LAT*, 7/18/48, C1, and 2/5/50, D1; Hopper, "The Riddle of Betty Grable," November 1952, Grable folder.

23. May, *Homeward Bound*.

24. Weiss, *To Have and to Hold*, 54–57; Joanne Meyerowitz, "Beyond the Feminine Mystique: A Reassessment of Postwar Mass Culture, 1946–1958," in Meyerowitz, ed., *Not June Cleaver: Women and Gender in Postwar America, 1945–1960* (Philadelphia: Temple University Press, 1994), 232.

25. Susan M. Hartmann, "Women's Employment and the Domestic Ideal in the Early Cold War Years," in Meyerowitz, ed., *Not June Cleaver*, 86.

26. HH column, *LAT*, 9/15/47, A3.

27. Meyerowitz, "Beyond the Feminine Mystique," 247; Weiss, *To Have and to Hold*, 59.

28. HH column, *LAT*, 9/20/58, B2; May, *Homeward Bound*, 16–18.

29. HH column, *LAT*, 2/5/50, D1, and 9/18/48, C1; Hopper, "The Riddle of Betty Grable," November 1952, Grable folder.

30. Emily S. Rosenberg, "'Foreign Affairs' after World War II: Connecting Sexual and International Politics," *Diplomatic History* 18 (Winter 1994), 67; HH, radio show script, box 1, folder "Scripts—*The Hedda Hopper Show*, #2, October 21, 1950," Victor Papers.

31. HH column, *LAT*, 8/30/52, 10.

32. Andrea Friedman, "Sadists and Sissies: Anti-pornography Campaigns in Cold War America," *Gender and History* 15 (August 2003), 201.

33. HH column, *LAT*, 4/16/47, A3.

34. Alexander Doty, "The Cabinet of Lucy Ricardo: Lucille Ball's Star Image," *Cinema Journal* 29 (Summer 1990), 12.

35. Lucille Ball quoted in Lori Landay, "Millions 'Love Lucy': Commodification and the Lucy Phenomenon," *NWSA Journal* 11 (Summer 1999), 42.

36. Buhle and Wagner, *Radical Hollywood*, 54, n. 69; Ceplair and Englund, *Inquisition in Hollywood*, 373.

37. Susan M. Carini, "Love's Labors Almost Lost: Managing Crisis during the Reign of *I Love Lucy*," *Cinema Journal* 43 (Fall 2003), 47, 56.

38. Hedda Hopper, "Happy Rumors Cleared, Lucy Tells Columnist," *LAT*, 9/12/53, 1; Mrs. T, Los Angeles, to HH, 9/15/53, Ball folder.

39. Landay, "Millions 'Love Lucy,'" 27; MAR, Hollis, New York, to HH, 9/12/53, Ball folder.

40. Hopper quoted in Kanfer, *Ball of Fire*, 103; WC, Santa Ana, Calif., to HH, 4/26/53, Ball folder.

41. HH column, *LAT*, 1/10/45, 9.

42. Levey, "Imagining the Family," 126; Rosenberg, "'Foreign Affairs' after World War II," 68; Roland L. Hill, President, Motion Picture Research Society, to California Governor Earl Warren, copy to HH, 10/1/47, and Phil Chain, General Chairman, American Legion, Cinema-T.V. Post 561, Burbank, Calif., to HH, 12/27/52, Divorce in Hollywood folder, HHP.

43. Elaine Tyler May, *Great Expectations: Marriage and Divorce in Post-Victorian America* (Chicago: University of Chicago, 1980); Stanley Cavell, *Pursuits of Happiness: The Hollywood Comedy of Remarriage* (Cambridge, Mass.: Harvard University Press, 1981), 103, 132; Weiss, *To Have and to Hold*, 179–180.

44. "Marriage and Divorce—Hollywood Style," *McCall's* (March 1959); Weiss, *To Have and to Hold*, 181.

45. HH column, *LAT*, 9/23/58, 22; Hopper, *The Whole Truth*, 253.

46. Hopper, "Hopper Gives Some Pointers to Youngsters," [1946], HH Clippings; Ponce de Leon, *Self-Exposure*, 129.

47. Hopper, *From Under My Hat*, 63, 115.

48. Hopper quoted in Friedrich, *City of Nets*, 327.

49. HH column, *LAT*, 12/15/47, 15; Wyman quoted in Leonard J. Leff, "What in the World Interests Women? Hollywood, Postwar America, and *Johnny Belinda*," *Journal of American Studies* 31 (December 1997), 401.

50. Hopper and Reagan quoted in Friedrich, *City of Nets*, 327.

51. HH column, *LAT*, 10/7/46, A1.

52. Friend quoted in Hopper, "Why Nancy Sinatra Agreed to Divorce Frank," [1951], Sinatra #1 folder.

53. Hopper, *The Whole Truth*, 50; friend quoted in Hopper, "Why Nancy Sinatra Agreed to Divorce Frank," [1951], Sinatra #1 folder.

54. RJF, NYC, to HH, 10/16/46, Mrs. SH, Racine, Wis., to HH, 8/12/51, and Hopper, "Why Nancy Sinatra Agreed to Divorce Frank," [1951], Sinatra #1 folder.

55. Hopper, "Why Nancy Sinatra Agreed to Divorce Frank," [1951], and "A Reader of the *Times*" to HH, 10/25/46, Sinatra #1 folder.

56. Mrs. SH, Racine, Wis., to HH, 8/12/51, Sinatra #1 folder.

57. HH column, *LAT*, 10/9/46, A2.

58. Jason Loviglio elucidates the various ways in which radio combines intimacy and publicity and crosses the public/private divide in *Radio's Intimate Public: Network Broadcasting and Mass-Mediated Democracy* (Minneapolis: University of Minnesota Press, 2005).

59. RF, NYC, to HH, 10/16/46, and "Ten of his fans in Chicago" to HH, 8/11/50, Sinatra #1 folder.

60. Mrs. JM, NYC, to HH, 10/17/46, and Mrs. SH, Racine, Wis., to HH, 8/12/51, Sinatra #1 folder.

61. David R. Roediger, *Working Toward Whiteness: How America's Immigrants Became White—The Strange Journey from Ellis Island to the Suburbs* (New York: Basic Books, 2005), 239–240.

62. HH column, *LAT*, 10/17/46, A3; "A Reader of the *Times*" to HH, 10/25/46, Sinatra #1 folder.

63. SGF, Pasadena, Calif., to HH, 10/13/46, and Mrs. JM, NYC, to HH, 10/17/46, Sinatra #1 folder.

64. Hopper, *The Whole Truth*, 51.

65. Mayer quoted in Jane Ellen Wayne, *Ava's Men: The Private Life of Ava Gardner* (New York: St. Martin's Press, 1990), 111.

66. GS, North Hollywood, to HH, 2/15/50, and MM, Chicago, to HH, 8/7/51, Sinatra #1 folder.

67. HH column, *LAT*, 2/15/50, 6, and 8/18/51, A6; Hopper paraphrased in Wayne, *Ava's Men*, 133.

68. Anderson, *Mammies No More*, 91; Mrs. SH, Racine, Wis., to HH, 8/12/51, Sinatra #1 folder.

69. HH column, *LAT*, 9/18/53, 21.

70. Mrs. SH, Racine, Wis., to HH, 8/12/51, Sinatra #1 folder.

71. AL, Hoboken, N.J., to HH, 8/19/51, Sinatra #1 folder.

72. Mrs. CC, Southgate, Calif., to HH, 2/10/50, Sinatra #1 folder.

73. "No signature—regretfully" to HH, 8/6/51, MH to HH, 8/9/51, and RF, NYC, to HH, 10/16/46, Sinatra #1 folder.

74. JEH, [Tujungo], Calif., to HH, 10/17/46, and RF, NYC, to HH, 10/16/46, Sinatra #1 folder.

75. AJ, Brooklyn, to HH, 8/9/51, and Mrs. SH, Racine, Wis., to HH, 8/12/51, Sinatra #1 folder.

76. Alison M. Parker, *Purifying America: Women, Cultural Reform, and Pro-censorship Activism, 1873–1933* (Urbana: University of Illinois Press, 1997), 134.

77. MH to HH, 8/9/51, and Mrs. SH, Racine, Wis., to HH, 8/12/51, Sinatra #1 folder.

78. MM, Chicago, to HH, 8/7/51, Sinatra #1 folder.

79. HH column, *LAT*, 9/11/58, 1, 26.

80. McLeland, "Elizabeth Taylor," 231; "Hollywood: The Life of the Senses," *Time*, 4/13/59, 65; Richard Gehman, "Debbie Reynolds: Her Story," *McCall's* (March 1959), 48–49; "Nightclubs: Eddie's Comeback," *Time*, 11/30/59, 72. Even the ostensibly "hard news" *New York Times* devoted twelve articles to the incident from February to December 1959.

81. HH column, *LAT*, 9/18/58, B8; May, *Homeward Bound*, 16.

82. HH column, *LAT*, 9/11/58, 1, 26.

83. Hopper, *The Whole Truth*, 19–23.

84. Fisher quoted in "Tale of Debbie, Eddie, and the Widow Todd," *Life*, 9/22/58, 39–40.

85. Fisher and Reynolds quoted in ibid., 39; "People," *Time*, 12/15/58, 36; "Fast Divorce OK by Debbie," *Life*, 4/13/59, 41.

86. MAW, Los Angeles, to HH, 9/11/58, and Mrs. ED, Glastonbury, Conn., to HH, 9/30/58, Taylor # 1 folder.

87. Reynolds, quoted in interview transcript, 9/11/58, Debbie Reynolds folder, HHP (hereafter Reynolds folder); "Interested," Chicago, to HH, 9/12/58, Taylor #1 folder; TMB, Phoenix, to HH, 9/20/58, Taylor #3 folder; EB, Evanston, Ill., to HH, 9/13/58, and Mrs. G. L. H., Lompoc, Calif., to HH, 9/11/58, Taylor #1 folder.

88. "People," *Time*, 12/15/58, 36; "Fast Divorce OK by Debbie," *Life*, 4/13/59, 41.

89. FRD, San Diego, to HH, 9/21/58, LH, Beverly Hills, to HH, 9/19/58, and Mrs. HB, Redwood City, Calif., to HH, 9/13/58, Taylor #3 folder; KO, Chicago, to HH, 9/12/58, Taylor #1 folder; GTF, Los Angeles, to HH, 9/25/58, Taylor #3 folder.

90. LH, Los Angeles, to HH, 9/16/58, and "Your Admirer," Denver, to HH, 9/12/58, Taylor #1 folder; TMB, Phoenix, to HH, 9/20/58, Taylor #3 folder; CD, Coronado, Calif., to HH, 9/11/58, Taylor #4 folder.

91. GDC, Glendale, Calif., to HH, 9/15/58, Taylor #1 folder; KH, Omaha, to HH, 10/1/58, Taylor #4 folder.

92. Lev, *The Fifties*, 306.

93. McLeland, "Elizabeth Taylor," 228–240; Hopper, interview and draft column, 5/17/52, Reynolds folder.

94. Haskell, *From Reverence to Rape*, 261.

95. LH, Los Angeles, to HH, 9/16/58, Taylor #1 folder; CQ, San Gabriel, Calif., to HH, 10/9/58, Taylor #3 folder.

96. Lois Banner, *American Beauty*, reprint (New York: Knopf, 1983; Chicago: University of Chicago Press, 1984), 283; Glenna Matthews, *"Just a Housewife": The Rise and Fall of Domesticity in America* (New York: Oxford University Press, 1987), 210; MK, Chicago, to HH, 9/18/58, Taylor #4 folder.

97. Banner, *American Beauty*, 283–284; Brandon French, *On the Verge of Revolt: Women in American Films of the Fifties* (New York: Frederick Ungar Publishing, 1978), 79, 81.

98. JP, Berkeley, to HH, 9/19/58, Taylor #4 folder; JS, North Hollywood, to HH, 9/19/58, Taylor #3 folder.

99. Mrs. ERG, State College, Miss., to HH, 10/14/58, Taylor #1 folder; Haskell, *From Reverence to Rape*, 253.

100. "Debbie Comes Up Dancing," *Life*, 3/30/59, 68, 2; "Tale of Debbie, Eddie, and the Widow Todd," *Life*, 9/22/58, 39–40; Richard Gehman, "Debbie Reynolds: Her Story," *McCall's* (March 1959), 48–49.

101. KO, Chicago, to HH, 9/12/58, and "Your Admirer," Denver, to HH, 9/12/58, Taylor #1 folder.

102. Oscar Levant quoted in Kashner and MacNair, *The Bad and the Beautiful*, 167; IMT, Inglewood, Calif., to HH, 9/13/58, and PR, Chicago, to HH, 9/11/58, Taylor #4 folder.

103. Marjo Buitelaar, "Widows' Worlds: Representations and Realities," in Jan Bremmer and Lourens van den Bosch, eds., *Between Poverty and the Pyre: Moments in the History of Widowhood* (London: Routledge, 1995), 7; HH column, *LAT*, 5/7/58, B12.

104. "Tale of Debbie, Eddie, and the Widow Todd," *Life*, 9/22/58, 39; Gehman, "Debbie Reynolds," 137; Hopper, *The Whole Truth*, 19.

105. HH column, *LAT*, 9/11/58, 1, 26; Donald Spoto, *Elizabeth Taylor*, pbk. ed. (New York: Warner, 1996), 210; Eells, *Hedda and Louella*, 330.

106. Mrs. HB, Redwood City, Calif., to HH, 9/19/58, and Mrs. PBH, Baltimore, to HH, 9/17/48, Taylor #3 folder; JP, Berkeley, to HH, 9/19/58, Taylor #4 folder.

107. Mrs. CGC, Los Angeles, to HH, 9/11/58, Taylor #4 folder; JS, North Hollywood, to HH, 9/19/58, Taylor #3 folder.

108. BB, New Orleans, to HH, 9/22/58, Taylor #3 folder; JJS to HH, 9/15/58, Taylor #4 folder.

109. BR, Beverly Hills, to HH, 10/7/58, Taylor #1 folder.

110. Eugenia Kaledin, *Mothers and More: American Women in the 1950s* (Boston: Twayne Publishers, 1984), preface; Barbara Ehrenreich, *The Hearts of Men: American Dreams and the Flight from Commitment* (Garden City, N.Y.: Anchor Press, 1983); Friedman, "Sadists and Sissies," 223.

111. E, Pasadena, Calif., to HH, 9/12/58, and GDC, Glendale, Calif., to HH, 9/15/58, Taylor #1 folder; LH, Beverly Hills, to HH, 9/19/58, Taylor #3 folder; Mrs. JLP, Affton, Mo., to HH, 9/30/58, Taylor #2 folder.

112. MDS, Los Angeles, to HH, 10/1/58, Taylor #2 folder.

113. GES, San Francisco, to HH, 11/1658, Taylor #1 folder.

114. HH column, *LAT*, 9/25/58, C10; Mrs. LM, Lynwood, Calif., 9/25/58, Taylor #4 folder.

115. Mrs. LMW, Sierra Madre, Calif., to HH, 9/16/58, and TT, Calif., Pasadena, 10/14/58, Taylor #1 folder.

116. Mrs. RAL, Omaha, to HH, 10/1/58, and Mrs. TCH, El Cajon, Calif., to HH, 9/25/58, Taylor #2 folder.

117. ML, Chicago, to HH, 9/21/58, Taylor #2 folder.

118. Nickerson, "Women, Domesticity, and Postwar Conservatism," 17; "Just a Viewer," Oklahoma City, to HH, 9/19/58, Taylor #3 folder; "Eight mothers," Los Angeles, to HH, 9/13/58, Taylor #1 folder.

119. Mrs. HSR, Hollywood, to HH, 9/19/58, Taylor #3 folder; MG, Hollywood, to HH, 10/1/58, Taylor #2 folder; Mrs. L. Moreland, Lynwood, Calif., 9/25/58, Taylor #4 folder; Parker, *Purifying America*, 134; Spoto, *Elizabeth Taylor*, 212.

120. HEW, Los Angeles, to HH, 9/11/58, Taylor #1 folder; MG, Hollywood, to HH, 10/1/58, Taylor #2 folder; "A Reader," Berkeley, to HH, 9/13/58, Taylor #4 folder.

121. MM, New York, to HH, 9/15/58, Taylor #4 folder; "A disgusted Eddie Fisher fan," Rockwood, Mich., to HH, 9/23/58, Taylor #3 folder; anonymous, Chicago to HH, 9/18/58, Taylor #4 folder.

122. Reynolds quoted in Brown and Pinkston, *Oscar Dearest*, 94.

123. Mrs. JLP, Affton, Mo., to HH, 9/30/58, Taylor #2 folder.

CHAPTER 8

1. McLeland, "Elizabeth Taylor," 239; HH column, *LAT*, 3/26/62, C11.

2. HH column, 3/31/62, 18; EH, Binghamton, N.Y., to HH, 7/8/63, Elizabeth Taylor, 1957–1963 folder, HHP (hereafter Taylor folder).

3. HH column, *LAT*, 4/4/62, C12; HH to FA, 10/31/63, Taylor folder; Eleanor Packard, "Vatican Press: Liz Near 'Vagrancy,'" *Daily News*, 4/13/62, clipping in Liz and Eddie's Wedding folder, HHP (hereafter Wedding folder).

4. "Study Urged to Bar U.S. to Liz Taylor—Burton, Too," [5/23/62], clipping in Wedding folder.

5. RMM, San Francisco, to HH, 5/6/63, Taylor folder.

6. Clipping, [5/12/62], in Taylor folder; Peter Levathes quoted in HH column, *LAT*, 8/26/62, A7.

7. HH column, *LAT*, 8/26/62, A7, and 3/31/62, 18; Hopper, *The Whole Truth*, 24.

8. RMM, San Francisco, to HH, 5/6/63, Taylor folder.

9. Hopper, *The Whole Truth*, 25; Paul Monaco, *The Sixties: 1960–1969*, vol. 8, *History of the American Cinema*, ed. Charles Harpole (Berkeley and Los Angeles: University of California Press, 2001), 127.

10. HH column, *LAT*, 11/2/63, B7; HH to FA, 10/31/63, and RMM, San Francisco, to HH, 5/6/63, Taylor folder.

11. Monaco, *The Sixties*, 11, 3.

12. This term comes from Kenneth Anger's famous book series on the underside of Hollywood, *Hollywood Babylon* (San Francisco: Straight Arrow Books, 1975); and *Hollywood Babylon II* (New York: Dutton, 1984).

13. "Through a Keyhole Darkly," *Time*, 2/15/63, 52; Maurice T. Reilly, Executive VP Syndicate, to HH, 2/2/62, Syndicate 1962 folder.

14. Syndicate advertisement for Women's Features, Syndicate 1962 folder, syndicate advertisement for "Looking at Hollywood," and Louis Wolf to HH, 12/12/63, Chicago Tribune–New York News Syndicate, 1963 folder, HHP (hereafter Syndicate 1963 folder); Eells, *Hedda and Louella*, 335.

15. RMM, San Francisco, to HH, 5/6/63, Taylor folder.

16. HH to Mary Patterson, 10/30/62, Syndicate 1962 folder; see Woman of the Year folder, HHP; Eells, *Hedda and Louella*, 326.

17. Ronald L. Davis, *The Glamour Factory: Inside Hollywood's Big Studio System* (Dallas: Southern Methodist University Press, 1993), 370–371; Gabler, *Winchell*, 449, 448; Barbas, *First Lady of Hollywood*, 333.

18. See Hedda Hopper folder, box 23, David Susskind Papers, 1935–1987, State Historical Society of Wisconsin, Madison, Wisconsin.

19. Landay, "Millions 'Love Lucy,'" 45, n. 2.

20. Vincent Brook, "The Americanization of Molly: How Mid-Fifties TV Homogenized *The Goldbergs* (and Got 'Berg-larized' in the Process)," *Cinema Journal* 38 (Summer 1999), 45; Christopher Anderson, "Television and Hollywood in the 1940s," in Schatz, *Boom and Bust*, 442.

21. HH column, *LAT*, 4/14/40, C3, and 12/30/47, A2; William Boddy, "The Studios Move into Prime Time: Hollywood and the Television Industry in the 1950s," *Cinema Journal* 24 (Summer 1985), 23.

22. Hilmes, *Hollywood and Broadcasting*, 1; Anderson, "Television and Hollywood in the 1940s," 436.

23. HH column, *LAT*, 5/31/50, 26; Harold J. Bock, NBC, Hollywood, to HH, 6/1/50, NBC folder, HHP.

24. Dennis Bingham, "'Before She Was a Virgin . . .': Doris Day and the Decline of Female Film Comedy in the 1950s and 1960s," *Cinema Journal* 45 (Spring 2006), 27; Janet Wasko, "Hollywood and Television in the 1950s: The Roots of Diversification," in Lev, *The Fifties*, 135.

25. Hedda Hopper, "Under Hedda's Hat," *Photoplay* (January 1966), 18; Neil Postman quoted in Brownstein, *The Power and the Glitter*, 9.

26. Hank Raduta, Promotion for Syndicate, to HH, 4/25/63, Syndicate 1963 folder; Lloyd Wendt to HH, 1/24/61, *Chicago Tribune* Sunday Stories, Correspondence, 1959–1960 folder, HHP (hereafter Sunday Stories folder); Louis Wolf to HH, 8/24/65, Chicago Tribune–New York News Syndicate, 1965 folder, HHP (hereafter Syndicate 1965 folder).

27. Hopper quoted in Eells, *Hedda and Louella*, 309–310.

28. Hopper, *The Whole Truth*, 60; Eells, *Hedda and Louella*, 328–329.

29. Sullivan quoted in "Moses and the Money Changers," *Time* (January 11, 1960), 38; Mary Desjardins, "'Marion Never Looked Lovelier': *Hedda Hopper's Hollywood* and the Negotiation of Glamour in Post-war Hollywood," *Quarterly Review of Film and Video* 16 (Summer 1999), 423–424.

30. Eells, *Hedda and Louella*, 310; HH to Roy E. Larsen, President of *Time*, 1/6/60, Life-Time folder.

31. Promotional materials quoted in Eells, *Hedda and Louella*, 329.

32. Mann, *How to Be a Movie Star*, 326–329; Eells, *Hedda and Louella*, 330–333; Suzy Traynor quoted in Eells, *Hedda and Louella*, 331. For my discussion, I am indebted to Mann's thorough research on the Wilding libel case.

33. HH to Walter Simmons, Sunday Editor, *Chicago Tribune*, 9/25/62, and HH to Don Maxwell, 12/6/62, Syndicate 1962 folder.

34. "Fan Magazines Not Striking Out," *Variety*, 12/29/54, 7, 14; Gamson, *Claims to Fame*, 42, 89.

35. Mrs. EH, Binghamton, N.Y., to HH, 7/8/63, Taylor folder; HH column, *LAT*, 10/24/63, A9; "The Nation's Placebo," newsclipping, Taylor folder.

36. Mary Desjardins, "Systematizing Scandal: *Confidential* Magazine, Stardom, and the State of California," in Adrienne L. McLean and David A. Cook, eds., *Headline Hollywood: A Century of Film Scandal* (New Brunswick, N.J.: Rutgers University Press, 2001), 208.

37. HH to Gardner Cowles, Editor of *Look*, 9/11/57, *Look* Magazine folder, HHP (hereafter *Look* folder); HH column, *LAT*, 5/7/55, 14; Eells, *Hedda and Louella*, 301.

38. "Liz Squeezed Out," *New Haven Journal-Courier* (April 14, 1962), clipping in Wedding folder.

39. HH to Jack Podell, 3/17/58 and 7/3/58, *Motion Picture Magazine* folder, HHP.

40. Sunday Stories folder.

41. HH column, *LAT*, 4/5/62, A10.

42. Eells, *Hedda and Louella*, 309; Sumner Locke Elliott, "The Cracked Lens: Notes on Hedda, Hollywood, TV, and Me," *Harper's* (December 1960), HH Clippings.

43. Clipping of HH article, *Look* (January 1951), *Look* folder; HH column, *LAT*, 4/5/50, B8.

44. HH to Mollie Slott, 9/15/64, Syndicate 1964 folder; HH to Lenore Hershey, *McCall's* Magazine, 12/9/65, *McCall's* Magazine folder, HHP (hereafter *McCall's* folder); Hopper, *The Whole Truth*, 132.

45. JD, San Francisco, to HH, 8/10/62, Marilyn Monroe, Letters folder, HHP (hereafter Monroe folder); Eells, *Hedda and Louella*, 290.

46. Hopper, *The Whole Truth*, 131; HH column, *LAT*, 12/1/56, B2; Davis, *The Glamour Factory*, 363.

47. HH to Herbert Mayes, President, McCall's Corporation, 7/23/65, *McCall's* folder; HH to Lloyd Wendt, 2/3/61, Sunday Stories folder; HH column, *LAT*, 8/24/58, E3, and 5/21/58, A8.

48. HH column, *LAT*, 12/15/55, B14; Hopper, *The Whole Truth*, 319–320.

49. Hopper, special feature story [1/20/66], Syndicate 1965 folder; HH column, *LAT*, 5/30/64, B6.

50. Stephen Vaughn, *Freedom and Entertainment: Rating the Movies in an Age of New Media* (Cambridge: Cambridge University Press, 2006), 1.

51. Marion quoted in HH column, *LAT*, 10/15/63, D6, 6/1/58, E1, and 6/30/47, A3.

52. Haskell, *From Reverence to Rape*, 323; Monaco, *The Sixties*, 120; Thomas Doherty, *Teenagers and Teenpics: The Juvenilization of American Movies in the 1950s*, rev. ed. (Philadelphia: Temple University Press, 2002), 2.

53. HH column, *LAT*, 5/10/58, B2; Poitier quoted in interview transcript "Sidney Poitier," 5/23/58, Poitier folder.

54. HH column, *LAT*, 4/23/64, C8, and 5/4/55, B8; Lev, *The Fifties*, 62; Gregory D. Black, *The Catholic Crusade against the Movies, 1940–1975* (Cambridge: Cambridge University Press, 1998).

55. Tennessee Williams, "Tennessee Williams Presents His POV," *New York Times*, 3/12/60, 253; Hopper quoted in Eells, *Hedda and Louella*, 333.

56. "Study Urged to Bar U.S. to Liz Taylor—Burton, Too," [5/23/62], clipping in Wedding folder.

57. FW, Los Angeles, to HH, 9/22/58, Taylor #3 folder; HH column, *LAT*, 5/3/64, B6; EFR, Encino, Calif., to HH, 6/4/62, Otto Preminger folder, HHP.

58. HH column, *LAT*, 6/1/50, A8, and 11/2/63, B7.

59. HH column, *LAT*, 5/3/64, B6; Hopper, special feature story [1/20/66], Syndicate 1965 folder; Doherty, *Hollywood's Censor*, 314.

60. Johnston and producer quoted in HH column, *LAT*, 5/24/55, B6; Y. Frank Freeman quoted in HH column, *LAT*, 1/4/54, B8.

61. Vaughn, *Freedom and Entertainment*, 5; Doherty, *Hollywood's Censor*, 318, 324; "Hollywood: Decoded," *Time*, 11/3/58, 78.

62. HH to Edward F. Reed, 5/22/62, Otto Preminger folder, HHP.

63. Parker, *Purifying America*, 140, 150; HH column, *LAT*, 4/18/64, 17.

64. HH column, *LAT*, 1/9/65, A11.

65. MT, Fort Smith, Ark., to HH, 9/27/62, and SM, Fairhaven, Mass., to HH, [9/27/62], *McCall's* folder; Hal Humphrey, "Hedda's Hollywood Ain't What It Used to Be," *Mirror News*, 1/7/60, HH Clippings.

66. HH to William R. Fritzinger, *The News*, 7/21/64, Syndicate 1964 folder.

67. Hopper, *The Whole Truth*, 98; Eells, *Hedda and Louella*, 314.

68. Gamson, *Claims to Fame*, 41, 85.

69. HH column, *LAT*, 3/23/47, B1 and B4; Gamson, *Claims to Fame*, 49.

70. "Liz Says She Doesn't Mind Nasty Opinions," [4/23/63], clipping in Wedding folder; HH column, *LAT*, 3/30/52, D1.

71. SD, Evansville, Ind., to HH, 9/16/48, Robert Mitchum folder, HHP; Jean Viel, Cincinnati, Ohio, to HH, 9/14/48, Robert Mitchum #1 folder, HHP; "The Riddle of Betty Grable," November 1952, typescript article, Grable folder.

72. HH to Mr. Barrett, 3/30/64, copy, Poitier folder; HH column, *LAT*, 7/5/63, D10.

73. Yearwood, "The Hero in Black Film," 46, 44; Judith Mayne's comment on James Baldwin's critique of Poitier's film roles in Mayne, *Cinema and Spectatorship* (New York: Routledge, 1993), 155; HH, quoted in Sidney Poitier interview transcripts, 3/16/64 and 5/23/58, Poitier folder; HH to Lloyd Wendt, 5/16/58, Sunday Stories folder; MLS to HH, 5/23/64, Poitier folder.

74. Cripps, *Making Movies Black*, 291; Grant, *Post-Soul Black Cinema*, 33.

75. Monaco, *The Sixties*, 122; HH column, *LAT*, 4/21/56, 12.

76. HH column, *LAT*, 9/22/64, C8, 4/23/64, C8, 6/18/58, B6, and 9/18/58, B8; Lev, *The Fifties*, 306, 205, 211.

77. Joanne Meyerowitz, "Women, Cheesecake, and Borderline Material: Responses to Girlie Pictures in the Mid-Twentieth-Century U.S.," *Journal of Women's History* 8 (Fall 1996), 23–26.

78. No name, North Hollywood, to HH, 9/23/58, Taylor #3 folder; HH column, *LAT*, 2/2/50, B10.

79. HH column, *LAT*, 6/22/50, B6, and 8/7/62, C8. On Monroe's politics, see Lois W. Banner, "The Creature from the Black Lagoon: Marilyn Monroe and Whiteness," *Cinema Journal* 47 (Summer 2008), 16.

80. Adrienne L. McLean, "Introduction," in McLean and Cook, eds., *Headline Hollywood*, 24, n. 33; David Shipman, *Judy Garland: The Secret Life of an American Legend* (New York: Hyperion, 1993), 257.

81. Hopper, "Hollywood Takes Its Medicine," *Modern Screen* (May 1950), 101; Barbas, *First Lady of Hollywood*, 316.

82. HH column, *LAT*, 6/22/50, B6, and 8/7/62, C8; Klinger, *Melodrama and Meaning*, 104–106.

83. Garland #2 folder.

84. Mrs. RD to HH, 7/12/50, Mrs. CC, Los Angeles, to HH, 6/19/50, MS, New York, 6/23/50, and anonymous letter to HH, Judy Garland #2 folder.

85. VTS to HH, 6/22/50, Garland #2 folder; Nancy Schnog, "On Inventing the Psychological," in Joel Pfister and Nancy Schnog, eds., *Inventing the Psychological: Toward a Cultural History of Emotional Life in America* (New Haven, Conn.: Yale University Press, 1997), 4; Nikolas Rose, *Governing the Soul: The Shaping of the Private Self,* 2nd ed. (London: Free Association Books, 1999), xxv.

86. Mrs. CH, Fremont, Neb., to HH, 8/19/62, and JT, Vestal, N.Y., to HH, 8/5/62, Monroe folder; Schnog, "On Inventing the Psychological," 4.

87. Shipman, *Judy Garland,* 257.

88. McLean, "Introduction," 24, n. 33.

89. HH column, *LAT,* 6/22/50, B6.

90. Schatz, *Boom and Bust,* 208.

91. OB, Newburgh, N.Y., to HH, 6/24/50, MB, New York, to HH, 6/22/50, and DS, Annapolis, Md., to HH, 6/21/50, Garland #2 folder.

92. JD, San Francisco, to HH, 8/10/62, Monroe folder.

93. Monaco, *The Sixties,* 123; HH column, *LAT,* 8/7/62, C8.

94. Mrs. JK, Brookhaven, Mass., to HH, n.d., Monroe folder.

95. Dyer, *Heavenly Bodies,* 50; Haskell, *From Reverence to Rape,* 254; MR, Dell Rapids, S.Dak., to HH, 8/18/62, and WC, San Francisco, to HH, 8/13/62, Monroe folder.

96. MR, Dell Rapids, S.Dak., to HH, 8/18/62, Monroe folder; HH to Gardner Cowles, Editor of *Look,* 9/11/57, *Look* folder; Hopper, *The Whole Truth,* 329.

97. Brennan, *Turning Right in the Sixties,* 10–11.

98. Kurt Schuparra, *Triumph of the Right: The Rise of the California Conservative Movement, 1945–1966* (Armonk, N.Y.: M. E. Sharpe, 1998), 144.

99. Noakes, "Bankers and Common Men," 313; Hopper, *Small World* telecast; HH column, *LAT,* 6/12/65, clipping in box 99, folder 12 "Hedda Hopper," Schary Papers.

100. Richard Clarke, Editor, *The News,* to HH, 1/2/62, and HH to Richard Clarke, 1/8/62, Syndicate 1962 folder; Caute, *Great Fear,* 471–473.

101. Thomas Cripps, *Hollywood's High Noon: Moviemaking and Society before Television* (Baltimore: Johns Hopkins University Press, 1997), 144; Adams interview with Hopper, 6/13/65, quoted in Slide, "Hedda Hopper's Hollywood," HH Clippings.

102. HH to Lloyd Wendt, 5/16/58, Sunday Stories folder; Hopper and Poitier quoted in interview transcript "Sidney Poitier," 3/16/64, Poitier folder. This content appeared in print in HH column, *LAT,* 5/24/64, C1.

103. GG, Falls Church, Va., to HH, 5/20/64, Poitier folder.

104. Hopper quoted in Slide, "Hedda Hopper's Hollywood," HH Clippings.

105. David F. Prindle, *The Politics of Glamour: Ideology and Democracy in the Screen Actors Guild* (Madison: University of Wisconsin Press, 1988), 82–85; HH column, *LAT,* 3/9/60, A8, and 3/12/60, B2; Rudy Unger to Mr. Kennedy, 3/10/60, Sunday Stories folder.

106. Hopper quoted in Ron Silverman, "225 Dissident SAG Members Protest Strike," *Daily Variety,* 3/4/60, and "150 Actors Turn Out For Anti-Strike Meet," clippings in SAG folder, HHP.

107. Bennett, *Party of Fear,* 332.

108. TIM, Los Angeles, to HH, 5/11/60, Marlon Brando folder, HHP.

109. HH column, *LAT*, 3/28/64, B6; Hopper quoted in interview transcript "Sidney Poitier," 3/16/64, Poitier folder.

110. HH column, *LAT*, 10/24/63, A9.

111. HH column, 4/17/60, clipping in Yves Montand folder, HHP (hereafter Montand folder). This content did not appear in the version of her column that ran in the *LAT*.

112. DAP, Los Angeles, to HH, 4/22/60, Montand folder; HH column, *LAT*, 4/21/60, B10; Signoret, *Nostalgia Isn't What It Used to Be*, 281.

113. HH column, *LAT*, 12/19/61, 19, and 10/14/61, A8; HW and AW, West New York, N.J., to HH, 10/15/61, KH, Los Angeles, to HH, 10/14/61, and MH, Los Angeles, to HH, 10/14/61, Montand folder.

114. Schuparra, *Triumph of the Right*, 26.

115. HH to Richard Clarke, 7/19/60, Syndicate 1960 folder; HH to Clare Boothe Luce, 10/23/62, Life-Time folder.

116. HH to Mary Patterson, *New York News*, 11/6/62, Syndicate 1962 folder; Hopper quoted in Eells, *Hedda and Louella*, 329.

117. HH column, *LAT*, 7/15/64, D8; HH to Don Maxwell, Managing Editor, *Chicago Tribune*, 10/16/63, Syndicate 1963 folder.

118. Mary C. Brennan, "Winning the War/Losing the Battle: The Goldwater Presidential Campaign and Its Effects on the Evolution of Modern Conservatism," in David Farber and Jeff Roche, eds., *The Conservative Sixties* (New York: Peter Lang, 2003), 69; Richard Clarke to HH, 6/27/64, Syndicate 1964 folder.

119. Handwritten note on bottom of letter to Hopper, 6/15/64, Life-Time folder; Hedda Hopper to Mollie Slott, VP of Syndicate, 7/2/64, Syndicate 1964 folder.

120. Hedda Hopper to Richard and Joy Clarke, 7/16/64, Syndicate 1964 folder; Brennan, "Winning the War/Losing the Battle," 77; HH to Mrs. Robert E. Hoffman, 8/1/64, Republican Convention 1964 folder, HHP; Phyllis Schlafly, "A Choice, Not an Echo," in Gregory L. Schneider, ed., *Conservatism in America since 1930* (New York: New York University Press, 2003), 231–237.

121. HH to George Dixon, 10/28/64, Mothers for Moral America folder, HHP (hereafter MMA folder); HH to Ben Gross, *New York News*, 10/28/64, Syndicate 1964 folder; HH to Richard Clarke, 11/30/61, Syndicate 1962 folder.

122. Michelle Nickerson, "Moral Mothers and Goldwater Girls," in Farber and Roche, *The Conservative Sixties*, 58; Rymph, *Republican Women*, 171; HH to George Dixon, 10/28/64, MMA folder.

123. Hoberman, *Dream Life*, 117–119; HH to George Dixon, 10/28/64, MMA folder.

124. Brennan, "Winning the War/Losing the Battle," 63.

125. ECM, St. Louis, to HH, 1/20/65, Lyndon B. Johnson folder, HHP; JN, Los Angeles, to HH, 11/20/64, Americanism folder; Nickerson, "Moral Mothers and Goldwater Girls," 52.

126. Column draft, 1/5/65, Syndicate 1964 folder; HH to John Fink, *Chicago Tribune*, 5/17/65, Syndicate 1965 folder.

127. Hopper quoted in Slide, "Hedda Hopper's Hollywood," HH Clippings; Brownstein, *The Power and the Glitter*, 177; Peter Bart, "Liberals vs. Their Movies," *New York Times*, 8/29/65, X9.

128. WHM, Northridge, Calif., to HH, 10/14/61, Montand folder.

129. HH to Valentine Davies, President of the Academy of Motion Picture Arts and Sciences, 4/19/61, and Davies to HH, 5/29/61, Academy of Motion Picture Arts and Sciences folder, HHP.

1. Hedda Hopper lines in Billy Wilder, *Sunset Boulevard*, screenplay by Charles Brackett, Billy Wilder, and D. M. Marshman, Jr., with an introduction by Jeffrey Meyers (Berkeley and Los Angeles: University of California Press, 1999), 113; Lev, *The Fifties*, 60.

2. Barbas, *First Lady of Hollywood*, 313.

3. *The Daily Worker* quoted in HH column, *LAT*, 2/24/51, 10; Sam Staggs, *Close-Up on Sunset Boulevard: Billy Wilder, Norma Desmond, and the Dark Hollywood Dream* (New York: St. Martin's Press, 2002), 229.

4. Jeffrey Meyers, "Introduction" in Wilder, *Sunset Boulevard*, xv.

5. Linda M. Austin, *Nostalgia in Transition, 1780–1917* (Charlottesville: University of Virginia Press, 2007), 201; HH column, *LAT*, 4/16/50, C1.

6. Ben Furnish, *Nostalgia in Jewish-American Theatre and Film, 1979–2004* (New York: Peter Lang, 2005), 15.

7. Thomas Doherty, "Documenting the 1940s," in Schatz, *Boom and Bust*, 421; Lev, *The Fifties*, 60.

8. Joe Gillis lines in Wilder, *Sunset Boulevard*, 39; HH column, *LAT*, 5/26/64, C6.

9. Hedda Hopper, "Unmasking Hollywood Society," *Picture Play* (June 1939), HH Clippings.

10. Eells, *Hedda and Louella*, 194–195; Jon Meacham, "Bill and God's Excellent Adventure," *New York Times Book Review*, 10/17/04, 29.

11. Ross, "Introduction," *Movies and American Society*, 9.

12. Stacey, *Star Gazing*, 66.

13. John Howard, "Coming to Terms with the Right," *Radical History Review* 84 (Fall 2002), 167.

14. James Donald and Stephanie Hemelryk Donald, "The Publicness of Cinema," in Christine Gledhill and Linda Williams, eds., *Reinventing Film Studies* (London: Arnold, 2000), 126–127; Apostolidis and Williams, "Introduction," in Apostolidis and Williams, eds., *Public Affairs*, 14.

15. HH to Richard Clarke, 7/28/64, Syndicate 1964 folder; Hopper and Bill Hopper quoted in Eells, *Hedda and Louella*, 61, 328, 25.

16. Merrick quoted in Eells, *Hedda and Louella*, 338; Pamela Mason, "Who Knows What Goes on in the Heart of Hollywood? Pamela Mason Knows," *Photoplay* (June 1966), 27.

17. Bob Thomas, AP Movie-Television Writer, untitled clipping, 2/4/66, HH Clippings; Champlin quoted in "Hedda," *Newsweek*, 2/14/66, 91.

18. Hopper quoted in Eells, *Hedda and Louella*, 233.

Index

Academy of Motion Picture Arts and Sciences, 37, 217
Actors Laboratory Theater, 107–8
Adams, Nick, 211
Alert, 130
Alexander, Jane, 223
Algren, Nelson, 132
Alice Adams (1935), 13, 150
All Quiet on the Western Front (1930), 68, 77–79
Altoona, Pennsylvania, 7–9, 12, 14–15, 23, 52, 194, 221
America First Committee, 68, 73, 75, 76
American Legion, 36, 51, 66, 77, 81, 87, 94, 96, 99, 111, 115, 122, 124–25, 129, 132, 135, 174
American Legion Magazine, 94, 115, 132
Americanism, 89, 91–94, 96, 102–4, 106, 110–11, 123, 171
Amos 'n' Andy (radio program), 145–48
Anderson, Marian, 39
anti-Communism, 6, 35–36, 62, 67, 74, 76, 79, 81, 94, 96, 98, 100–106, 109, 111, 114, 117, 120, 123–25, 129, 136–37, 141, 145, 163, 188, 201, 210, 213, 216; Red-baiting, 86, 89, 105, 111, 114, 119, 127, 130, 139, 141, 150, 158
anti-Semitism, 36, 69, 73, 75, 89, 109–10, 183
Arbuckle, Roscoe "Fatty," 40
Arnaz, Desi, 31–32, 172–73, 195
Ayres, Lew, 68, 77–82, 175

Baby Doll (1956), 202, 206
Bacall, Lauren, 121, 126–27
Baker, Carroll, 206
Balio, Tino, 86

Ball, Juliette, 108
Ball, Lucille, 31–32, 58–59, 172–73, 177–78, 195
Barbas, Samantha, 19, 35, 219
Bardot, Brigitte, 206
Barry, Joan, 83–84, 88, 181, 223
Barry, Sarah, 33
Barrymore, Ethel, 8
Baskett, James, 140, 142–49, 154, 159, 160, 162, 163
Battle of Hearts (1916), 11
Beauchamp, Cari, 15
Beavers, Louise, 138, 139, 152
Bells of St. Mary's, The (1945), 49
Bennett, Joan, 30
Bergman, Ingrid, 29–30, 32, 48–49, 165–67, 180, 182, 187
Berkeley, Martin, 134–35
Bernstein, Matthew, 144
Beulah (radio show), 159–60
Big Jim McLain (1952), 98
Binford, Lloyd T., 153
Birdwell, Russell, 86
Blackboard Jungle (1955), 98–99, 133, 201–2
Blitch, Iris F., 191
block booking, 35–36
Bogart, Humphrey, 51, 81, 121
Bogle, Donald, 142, 146, 150, 157–58, 160, 162
Bond, Ward, 98, 134
Boorstin, Daniel J., 25
Boyd, Stephen, 213
Brackett, Charles, 9
Brando, Marlon, 200, 204–5
Brave One, The (1956), 135
Breen, Joseph, 203

Brewer, Roy, 111, 119
Bridge on the River Kwai, The (1957), 134
Brown Derby restaurant, 28
Bundle of Joy (1956), 184
Burton, Richard, 189, 191–93, 198–99, 205
Burton, Sybil, 191
Butler, Charles E., 148, 154, 159
Butterfield 8 (1960), 188

Cabin in the Sky (1943), 25
Calhoun, Rory, 198
California, 12, 34, 42, 54, 64, 74, 84–85,
    102–3, 105, 107–8, 125, 152, 194, 211, 214,
    216, 222
Capra, Frank, 116–17
Cat on a Hot Tin Roof (1958), 184–85, 188, 202
Catholic Legion of Decency, 159, 166, 202
Catholic War Veterans, 87
Caute, David, 104
celebrity journalism, 5, 7–11, 13, 17–18,
    20–22, 31, 50, 114, 167, 197–99, 204–5,
    209–10, 221
censorship, 99, 117, 153, 159, 180, 202,
    204. *See also* Production Code
    Administration
Ceplair, Larry, and Steven Englund, 74, 111
Champlin, Charles, 223
Chaplin, Charlie, 38–39, 68, 75–76, 82–88,
    109, 119, 130–31, 181, 223
Chicago Tribune, 34, 76, 132, 198–99
Choice (Goldwater campaign film), 215
cinema spectatorship, 4, 27, 46, 54, 57–60,
    64, 117–18, 123, 154, 221
Citizen Kane (1941), 49–50
Civil Rights Movement, 82, 139–41, 143–46,
    148–53, 158–59, 160–63, 206, 211–12;
    politics of representation, 59, 82, 120,
    137, 140–41, 143–45, 150–56, 159–62, 206
Clark, D. Worth, 75
Cleopatra (1963), 191–93, 199, 204
Cold War, 37, 67, 76, 93–94, 97–104, 127,
    131, 187, 202; American families, 166–73,
    179, 186–87; civil rights, 140–41, 163;
    containment policy v. "rollback," 101;
    cultural exchanges, 101–2; Hungarian
    Revolution, 101–2

Collins, Gail, 42, 54
Collins, Patricia Hill, 155
Columbia Broadcasting System (CBS), 100
Committee for the First Amendment
    (CFA), 121–23, 125–26, 172
Communists/Communist Party USA
    (CPUSA), 36–37, 41–42, 62–63, 74, 85,
    88–89, 99, 104–8, 111, 113–37, 144–45,
    163, 166, 169, 172, 201, 211–13, 219; *Daily
    Worker*, 118, 129, 132, 219
Conceit (1921), 14
Conference of Studio Unions (CSU),
    110–11, 119
Confessions of a Nazi Spy (1939), 75
Confidential magazine, 198–99
conscientious objection/objector (CO), 68,
    77–82
conservatives/conservatism, 2–3, 5–6,
    11–12, 34–35, 41, 75–76, 92–93, 100–102,
    114, 117, 123, 126, 137, 147, 168–70, 188,
    210–11, 214–16, 222; California and, 12,
    54; "fusionism," 42; gender and, 123, 188;
    libertarian and traditionalist, 6, 42, 215;
    "New Right" and "Old Right," 3, 6, 34,
    42, 193, 210–11, 216, 222; populism and,
    91. *See also* Republican Party
Cotton, Joseph, 30
Couvares, Francis, 159
Crawford, Joan 25, 29, 31–33, 48, 197
Cripps, Thomas, 156, 160
Crist, Judith, 79
Critchlow, Donald T., 6, 102
Crosby, Bing, 96, 133
Crosby, John, 199
Crossfire (1947), 120, 133
Crowther, Bosley, 98, 126, 146
Current, Gloster, 144

Da Silva, Howard, 130
David and Bathsheba (1951), 103
Davies, Joseph E., 116
Davies, Marion, 13–14, 30
Davis, Bette, 19, 51, 58, 197
Day, Doris, 206
Defiant Ones, The (1958), 161–62
De Havilland, Olivia, 81

Dekker, Albert and Esther, 131
DeMille, Agnes, 21
DeMille, Cecil B., 21, 24, 37, 88, 93, 109–10, 200, 219
Democratic Party, 15, 17, 30, 33–34, 41–43, 82, 86, 100, 103, 105, 108, 121, 139, 177, 214, 216, 223
Dier, Richard B., 144
Dies, Martin, P., 36
"Dilemma of the Negro Actor, The" (Muse), 157
Dior, Christian, 97
Disney, Walt, 50, 74, 88, 96, 118, 140–47
Dmytryk, Edward, 119–20, 126, 130–31, 133. *See also* Hollywood Ten
Doherty, Thomas, 48, 68, 116, 129
Douglas, Helen Gahagan, 42, 105, 125, 127, 129
Douglas, Melvyn, 42, 121
Dr. Strangelove (1964), 202
Duberman, Martin, 106
Duff, Howard, 130, 132
Dulles, John Foster, 101
Dunbar, Robin, 3
Dunne, Irene, 33, *138*
Dunne, Philip, 121
Dyer, Richard, 33

Eells, George, 10–11, 22, 25, 35, 82, 103, 205
Eisenhower, Dwight David, 33–34, 41, 97, 101–2, 105–6; "Modern Republicanism" of, 214
Eisler, Gerhardt, 107
Elsom, John, 93
Evans, Sara, 97
Everett, Anna, 154

Fagan, Myron, 129
Fair Play Committee, 157
fans and fan letters, 2–4, 64, 159, 178, 198, 225n7, 235n1, 235n7; of Hedda Hopper, *44, 45*, 196; of motion pictures, 45–47, 52–65
Farnham, Marynia, and Ferdinand Lundberg, 170
Federal Bureau of Investigation (FBI), 36, 75, 84–88, 105–6, 113–17, 120, 125, 128, 130–32, 136, 145, 211

Federal Communications Commission, 195–96
Ferrer, Jose, 129
Fidler, Jimmie, 18, 46
Fisher, Carrie, 32
Fisher, Eddie, 32, 167, 180–88, 191, 199
Fiske, John, 46
Foreman, Carl, 133–35
Fort Apache (1948), 49
For Whom the Bell Tolls (1943), 48
Fountainhead, The (1949), 126–27
Friedan, Betty, 169
Furry, Elda. *See* Hopper, Hedda

Gable, Clark, 28, 151
Gabler, Neal, 3, 35, 114, 145
Gaile, Patsy, 50, 221
Gamson, Joshua, 52, 205
Garbo, Greta, 29
Gardner, Ava, 167, 175, 178–80, 182
Garfield, John, 130–31
Garland, Judy, 58, 121, 207–10
General Federation of Women's Clubs, 206
Gerstle, Gary, 92
Goldwater, Barry, 40, 210–12, 214–16
Gone with the Wind (1939), 69–71, 139–40, 149–55, 157–58
gossip, 2–4, 6, 47, 52, 54, 56, 57, 88, 114, 221; as private talk, 3–5, 7, 17, 55, 88, 113, 207–8; as public sphere, 6–7, 46–47, 60–65, 222; gender and, 3, 54; mass media, 2–4, 22, 47, 222, 236n8; privacy and, 3, 5, 20–21, 55, 113; traditional, 3–4, 57
Goudsouzian, Aram, 161
Gould, Lewis L., 101
Grable, Betty, 133, 168–69, 171
Graham, Sheilah, 18, 30
Great Dictator, The (1940), 75–76, 82, 85
Green Pastures (1936), 59, 142
Gwynne, Edith, 18

Habermas, Jürgen, 6–7, 61, 222
Hammett, Dashiell, 130
Hansen, Miriam, 7
"hard" news. *See* newspaper journalism
Harris, Joel Chandler, 143

Harshbarger, Dema, 23, 50
Haskell, Molly, 184, 201
Hayward, Susan, 29
Hayworth, Rita, 165–66, 168–71, 180
Heale, M. J., 104, 137
Hearst, William Randolph, 13, 35, 67; press
 syndicate of, 18, 136
Hellman, Lillian, 116–17, 129
Henreid, Paul, 119, 121
Hepburn, Katharine, 13, 121–22, 125
Hersholt, Jean, 147, 149
High Noon (1952), 133–34
Hill, Charles W., 148
Hill, Herman, 144
Holden, William, 134, 220
Hollywood motion picture industry, 1–4,
 12, 23, 27–28, 34, 67–68, 124, 168, 192–93,
 200–1, 207–8; Academy Awards/Oscars,
 48, 98, 135, 142, 147–49, 152, 159, 161, 188,
 213; blacklist/graylist, 86, 113–15, 124–29,
 134–37, 172, 178, 211, 212; changing film
 content, 200–203; contractual "morals
 clause," 40, 125, 165; golden age, 1, 3–4,
 27, 196, 200; labor conflict, 92, 110–11,
 212; "New Hollywood," 4, 193–94, 200,
 205, 210, 216; production process, 117;
 racial representations, 39, 59, 82, 120,
 137, 140–45, 148, 150–56, 159–63, 178–79,
 206; star system, 4, 11, 53, 204–5; typecasting, 11, 32, 152–53. *See also* censorship; television.
Hollywood Ten, 113, 119–23, 125–26, 128, 133,
 135, 177
Hoover, Herbert, 14–15, 40
Hoover, J. Edgar, 36, 105, 113–14, 129–31, 145
Hope, Bob, 28, 100, 133
Hopper, De Wolf, 9–10, 20, 83
Hopper, Hedda: Academy Awards/Oscars
 and, 48, 135, 147–49, 213, 216–17; acting
 career of, 9–15, 22–25, 27; Americanism of, 8, 89, 91–111, 136, 163, 171, 216;
 Anglophobia of, 69–70, 213; anti-civil
 rights efforts of, 6, 39, 106–8, 139–63,
 210–12; anti-Communism of, 6, 36, 53,
 62, 67, 74, 76, 95, 98, 101–2, 104–7, 109,
 111, 113–37, 141, 145, 163, 201, 210–13;

anti-intervention in World War II of, 6,
 37, 67–76, 79, 82, 93, 100, 119; anti-Semitism of, 38–39, 69, 109–10; antistatism
 of, 6, 35–36, 67, 82, 96, 210–12, 214; antiunion attitudes of, 37, 62, 110–11, 210,
 212; appearance, 9, 22, 52, 97, 199; birth,
 8; celebrity journalism/mass media
 gossip, approach to, 5, 14, 20–22, 27, 49,
 50–51, 120, 132, 199, 221; charity efforts,
 26; civil liberties and, 77, 81–82, 103, 113,
 120–21, 133; Cold War interventionism
 of, 37, 67, 76, 93, 99–101, 210–11; column,
 1, 13, 24, 27, 47–54, 122–23, 197–99;
 conservatism (moral and political) of,
 1–2, 5–8, 11–12, 14–15, 17, 31, 33–43, 49,
 60, 62, 64, 67, 69, 76, 88, 91, 97, 101, 105,
 117, 137, 139–40, 163, 168–69, 193, 204,
 206–7, 210–17, 221–22; death, 222–23;
 employment, 11–13, 18–19, 26–27, 34,
 69, 194; family, 8–9, 26, 39, 52, 222–23;
 "family togetherness" and, 168–75; fan
 magazines, 21, 24, 199; fashion, 8, 14, 24,
 97; feminism and, 40, 49, 65, 170, 201;
 film content and, 4, 40, 200–204, 206–7;
 friends, 13–15, 22–23, 29–30, 38, 40, 129,
 172, 197, 201; gays and lesbians, attitude
 towards, 32, 40, 108, 197, 199; gossip
 columnist function of, 1, 4, 12, 27–28,
 30–33, 35–36, 39–40, 47–50, 58, 193, 197,
 200–201, 204–5, 207, 221, 232n77 (*see
 also* star personas); gossip columnist
 persona of, 12, 18, 22–25; hats and, 1,
 8, 23–24, 52, 194, 200, 222; Hollywood
 blacklist/graylist and, 86, 111, 113–37,
 211, 212; Hollywood stars/filmmakers,
 relationships with, 29–33, 77, 81–82,
 133, 149, 160, 165, 172, 181, 200, 204–10;
 home, 26, 32; honors, 194; income, 11,
 13, 24–25, 92; marriage, 9–10, 20, 83;
 maternalism, 72, 188, 204, 215; memoirs,
 8–14, 92, 196–97, 214; nativism of, 38–39,
 69, 109, 212–13; nostalgia of, 7, 12, 28,
 96, 193, 200, 210, 215, 220–22; office, *16*,
 50, *112*; Louella Parsons, relationship/
 rivalry with, 1, 13–14, 17, 19–20, 29–30,
 55–56, 81, 92, 165, 194, 196, 219; personal

life, 8–15, 24, 199–200, 222–23; racism of, 39, 107–8, 139–40, 146, 160, 162, 206, 212; radio appearances, 13, 24–25, 41, 51, 63, 67, 92, 94–95, 105, 136, 139, 196; readership, 1, 18, 92, 194; religion, 8, 15, 37, 39, 77, 102–3; reporting techniques, 17, 28–33; Republican Party, activism/membership in, 6, 8, 14–15, 33–34, 40–43, 61, 86–87, 105, 108, 139–40, 193, 210–11, 214–16; reputation, 1, 22–26, 197, 204; respondents, 2–4, 7, 45–47, 52–65, 72–73, 102, 122–23, 127, 159, 173, 177, 180, 187–89, 203–4, 210, 216; staff, 28, 50; television appearances, 92, 194–97; Wilding libel suit, 197

Hopper, William (Bill), 10, 20, 71, 195, 222–23

Horne, Gerald, 111

Horne, Lena, 25, 156

Horton, James Oliver, 146

Hotchkiss, L. D., 95

House Committee on Un-American Activities (HUAC), 36, 107, 113, 115–25, 127–30, 133–37, 145, 149, 172

House I Live In, The (1945), 120, 177

Howard, Leslie, 69–70

Hudson, Rock, 32, 199

Hughes, Langston and Milton Meltzer, 143

Hunter, Tab, 31

Hurrell, George, 29

Huston, John, 81, 118, 121

Ickes, Harold L., 75–76

I Love Lucy, 172–73, 194–95

Imitation of Life (1934), 139

Immigration and Naturalization Service (INS), 87–88

income tax, 36, 96, 211

Ingram, Rex, 144

Intermezzo (1939), 30

International Alliance of Theatrical Stage Employees (IATSE), 110–11, 119, 126

I Remember Mama (1948), 20

Iron Curtain, The (1948), 98

Jackie Robinson Story, The (1950), 39

James, Etta, 148

Joan of Arc (1948), 166

John Birch Society, 216

Johnny Belinda (1948), 175

Johnny Got His Gun (1939 novel), 74

Johnson, David K., 108

Johnson, Edwin C., 166, 180

Johnson, Lyndon B., 211

Johnson, Nunnally, 136

Johnston, Eric A., 93, 125, 203

Jones, Robert, 153

Kahn, Gordon, 79

Kammen, Michael, 96

Kaye, Sylvia, 121

Kefauver, Estes, 99

Kennan, George F., 93

Kennedy, A. M., 132

Kennedy, John F., 103, 135, 214

Kennedy, Joseph P., 73–74

Kennedy, King, 28

Khrushchev, Nikita S., 101–2, 171, 214; Hollywood visit, 102

Kinsey reports (1948 and 1953), 169

Korean War, 95, 97, 99–101, 104, 127, 136

Koverman, Ida, 13–14

Kramer, Stanley, 161

Land of Liberty (1939), 93

Langer, William, 85

Lardner, Ring, Jr., 119, 126. *See also* Hollywood Ten

"Lavender Scare," 108

Lawson, John Howard, 74, 119–20. *See also* Hollywood Ten

Leigh, Vivien, 69–71, 151, 155

Levathes, Peter, 192

Lewis, Jon, 120

liberalism, 34, 97, 108, 111, 117–18, 137, 160–61, 215, 221

Lilies of the Field (1963), 205–6, 213

Limelight (1952), 82, 87

Lindbergh, Anne Morrow, 73

Lindbergh, Charles A., 73–74

Locke, Alain, 144

Los Angeles Times, 1, 13, 17–19, 21–22, 34, 80, 130, 180, 182, 194

loyalty oaths, 103, 109–10, 124
Luce, Clare Boothe, 25, 99, 163
Luce, Henry, 92

Maland, Charles J., 87–88
"Malice in Wonderland," 1, 223
Maltz, Albert, 119–20, 177. *See also* Hollywood Ten
mammy stereotype, 150–52, 155, 160
Mankiewicz, Joseph L., 109–10
Mann, William J., 40, 197, 267n32
Mannix, Eddie, 135
Marion, Frances, 9, 13, 15, 22–23, 39, 201
Mason, Pamela, 223
May, Elaine Tyler, 166, 169–70
Mayer, Louis B., 11, 13–15, 29, 38, 116, 133, 178, 200, 209
McCall's, 167, 181, 196
McCarthy, Joseph R., 41, 104–5, 127, 137
"McCarthyism," 137
McClure, Spec, 26
McCormick, Colonel Robert R., 34–35, 38, 69, 76
McDaniel, Hattie, 31, 138–40, 149–60, 162–63, 206, 257n56
McGranery, James, 86–88
McGuire, Dorothy, 168–71
McLean, Adrienne, 208
McWilliams, Carey, 12
Meet John Doe (1941), 116–17
Menjou, Adolph, 118, 129–30, 134
Merrick, Molly, 223
Metro-Goldwyn-Mayer (MGM), 11–15, 25, 27, 77, 81, 98–99, 116, 126, 133, 135, 175, 178, 184, 200, 207, 209
Meyerowitz, Joanne, 170
Meyers, Jeffrey, 220
Milestone, Lewis, 79
Miller, Arthur, 1
minstrelsy, 142–43, 145–46, 148, 162
Misfits, The (1961), 209
Mission to Moscow (1943), 115–16, 118
Mitchell, Margaret, 70–71
Mitchum, Robert, 205
Modern Woman: The Lost Sex (Farnham and Lundberg), 170

Monroe, Marilyn, 207–10
Monsieur Verdoux (1947), 82, 85–86
Montand, Yves, 213
Moorehead, Agnes, 19
Moser, John, E., 69
Moss, Carleton, 152
Mothers for a Moral America, 215
Motion Picture Alliance for the Preservation of American Ideals (MPA), 88–89, 92–93, 98, 111, 115–16, 118–19, 134, 136, 171
Motion Picture Association of America (MPAA), 93, 118, 125–29, 203, 211
Mr. Smith Goes to Washington (1939), 116–17
Muir, Florabel, 23, 83, 223
Murphy, George, 210–11
Muse, Clarence, 144, 153, 157

National Association for the Advancement of Colored People (NAACP), 120, 141, 143–44, 148, 150–54, 158–59
National Broadcasting Company (NBC), 94, 188, 195–96
National Legion of Mothers of America, 71
National Negro Congress, 144
National Review, 221
National Urban League, 141, 144
nativism, 69, 212–13
Nazi-Soviet Pact (1939), 74, 115
Negri, Pola, 109
"New Hollywood." *See* Hollywood motion picture industry
"New Right." *See* conservatives/conservatism
New York Daily News, 18, 108, 215
newspaper journalism, 2–3, 5, 21–22, 26, 51, 194, "civic," 63; "hard" and "soft" news, 3, 5, 21–22, 33, 198–99; syndication services, 18; women and, 5, 22
Night World (1932), 77
Niven, David, 28–29
Nixon, Richard M., 41–42, 62, 86, 105–6, 125, 127, 139–40, 171, 214
North Star (1943), 116–17
No Way Out (1950), 161
Nye, Gerald P., 75

Oberon, Merle, 1
"Old Right." *See* conservatives/
 conservatism
O'Neill, Oona, 83

Paramount case, 35, 92, 153, 193, 195, 200
Parks, Larry, 135–36
Parsons, Harriet, 19–20, 25, 33
Parsons, Louella, 1–3, 5, 18, 25, 27–28, 31–32,
 35, 46–47, 50, 70, 75, 114, 140, 166, 207, 223
patriotism, 97
Patterson, Eleanor (Cissy), 13
Pauling, Linus C., 211
Pearl Harbor, 76
Pepper, Claude, 108, 121
Perry, Lincoln/Stepin Fetchit, 140, 142, 150
Poitier, Sidney, 98, 140–41, 160–63, 202,
 205–6, 211–13
Ponce de Leon, Charles L., 5, 31
Porgy and Bess (1959), 162
Production Code Administration (PCA),
 49, 144, 203–4
psychology, popular, 207–8
public sphere, 6–7

Rand, Ayn, 126–27
Reagan, Nancy, 215
Reagan, Ronald, 12, 32, 41–42, 110–11, 119,
 126, 174–75, 196, 210–12, 216, 222
"Reagan Revolution," 222
Red Scare, 88. *See also* anti-Communism
Red-baiting. *See* anti-Communism
Reddick, Lawrence, 156
Reid, Mark A., 148
Remarque, Erich Maria, 79
Republican Party, 6, 14–15, 40–43, 67, 86,
 101, 105, 118, 139–40, 193, 210–12, 214–16
Republican Women's Clubs, 40, 215
Reynolds, Debbie, 24, 32, 167, 180–88
Reynolds, Robert R., 88–89
Rice, Elmer, 89
Riefenstahl, Leni, 69
RKO, 27, 120, 126, 130, 133, 165–66, 193
Robeson, Paul, 106–7, 156
Robinson, Jackie, 39
Rogers, Ginger, 36, 134

Rogers, Henry, 134
Rogers, Walter, 202
Rogin, Michael, 12
Room at the Top (1959), 213
Roosevelt, Eleanor, 121
Roosevelt, Franklin, 15, 17, 34–35, 40, 42,
 73–76, 79, 81, 116, 118, 214
Roosevelt, James, 17, 29
Rosenstein, Jaik, 28, 50, 54
Ross, Steven J., 11
Rossellini, Roberto, 165
Rowe, Billy, 25
Russell, Rosalind, 25, 201
Russo, Peggy A., 143

Sahara (1943), 120
Saunders, Frances Stoner, 103
scandal, 14–15, 21, 33, 40, 43, 60, 62, 64, 125,
 167, 188, 198–99, 214; star suicide and,
 207–8. *See also* Ball, Lucille; Bergman,
 Ingrid; Chaplin, Charlie; Garland, Judy;
 Mitchum, Robert; Monroe, Marilyn;
 Roosevelt, James; Sinatra, Frank; Taylor,
 Elizabeth
Schary, Dore, 30, 50, 98–99, 120, 133, 200
Schatz, Thomas, 27, 124
Schlafly, Phyllis, 215
Schuyler, George S., 151
Scott, Adrian, 119–20, 126, 133. *See also* Hol-
 lywood Ten
Screen Actors Guild (SAG), 37, 110, 118–19,
 126, 168, 175, 212
Screen Directors Guild (SDG), 109–10
Screen Guide for Americans, 126–27
Screen Writers Guild, 110, 119
Selznick, David O., 30, 69–71
Sherry, Michael, S., 67
Shindler, Colin, 81
Show Boat (1936 and 1951), 106, 178
Signoret, Simone, 29, 213, 217
Sinatra, Frank, 167, 171–72, 175–80, 181–82,
 186–88
Sinatra, Nancy, 167, 175–80
Sinclair, Upton, 34
Skolsky, Sidney, 18
So Well Remembered (1947), 120

social problem and "conscience liberal" films, 98, 117, 119–20, 133, 153, 160–61, 206
"soft" news. *See* newspaper journalism
"soft power," 99
Sokolsky, George E., 136
Song of Russia (1943), 116
Song of the South (1946), 140–49
Sorrell, Herbert, 111
Soviet Union, 37, 74, 85, 101–2, 104, 107, 115–16, 118, 127, 163, 166, 187, 213
Spartacus (1960), 135
Spigelgass, Leonard, 132
Spingarn, Hope, 144
Stacey, Jackie, 221, 225n6
Staggs, Sam, 219
Stanwyck, Barbara, 127
star personas, 4, 32–33, 58, 172, 205; on- and off-screen/"reel" and "real" lives, 4, 12, 14, 33, 58, 70, 78, 80, 127, 148, 157, 166, 184, 191–92, 205, 207, 223, 226n17
Stevenson, Adlai, 108
Stromboli (1950), 165–66
Sturtevant, Victoria, 154
Sullivan, Ed, 18, 26, 35, 70, 114, 121, 129, 196–97
Sunset Boulevard (1950), 219–20
Supreme Court, 64, 128, 153, 203, 211; *Brown v. Board of Education*, 163; *Shelley v. Kraemer*, 157. *See also* Paramount case
Susskind, David, 194
Swanson, Gloria, 219–20

Taft, Robert A., 37–38, 41, 76, 100, 111, 214
Taft-Hartley Act (Labor-Management Relations Act of 1947), 111, 124
Tammy and the Bachelor (1957), 184
Taylor, Elizabeth, 167, 180–89, 191–93, 197, 198–99, 204–5, 210, 223
Taylor, Robert, 88, 116, 118, 127
television, 195–97, 203, 211
Temple, Shirley, 62, 64
Ten Commandments, The (1956), 103
Tenney, Jack B., 85
Thurber, James, 81
Tierney, Gene, 29
Time, 17, 22, 24, 27, 87, 90, 92, 135, 197, 203
Todd, Mike, 181, 185

Tolson, Melvin B., 151
Triumph of the Will (1935), 69
Truman, Harry S., 42, 86–87, 101, 108, 124
Trumbo, Dalton, 74, 119, 126, 135. *See also* Hollywood Ten

Uncle Remus stereotype, 142–43, 146, 160
United Nations (UN), 42, 97, 100
United States Department of Defense, 100
United States Department of Justice, 84, 87–88
United States Department of State, 104, 163
United States Information Agency, 99

Vandenberg, Arthur, 76
Vietnam War, 211
Virtuous Wives (1918), 11–12

Waldorf Statement, 125. *See also* Hollywood motion picture industry
Walker, Alice, 143
Warner Brothers, 27, 58, 75, 115, 118–19, 127, 195
Waters, Ethel, 152, 156
Watts, Jill, 155, 158
Wayne, John, 88, 98, 133–36, 171
We Were Strangers (1949), 118
Wheeler, Burton, K., 74–75
White, Josh, 107
White, Walter F., 143–44, 146, 151–53, 158–59
Whitfield, Stephen, 92
Wilder, Billy, 219
Wilding, Michael, 181, 197, 199
Williams, Tennessee, 202, 206
Wills, Garry, 32
Winchell, Walter 2–3, 5, 18, 20, 23, 25–26, 35, 50–51, 92, 114, *190*, 194
Woman's Christian Temperance Union, 180
Women, The (1939), 25
Wood, John, 136
World War I, 69, 79, 106
World War II, 28, 37, 67–82, 84, 85, 88, 140–41, 166–67, 168, 175, 209
Wyler, William, 110, 117, 121
Wyman, Jane, 32, 174–75

Zanuck, Darryl, 98, 130, 132

About the Author

JENNIFER FROST teaches U.S. history at the University of Auckland, New Zealand. She received her PhD in United States women's history at the University of Wisconsin–Madison and is the author of *"An Interracial Movement of the Poor": Community Organizing and the New Left in the 1960s,* also published by NYU Press.